The
Priority
of Christ

The
Priority
of Christ

Toward a Postliberal
Catholicism

ROBERT BARRON

BrazosPress
Grand Rapids, Michigan

Published by Brazos Press
a division of Baker Publishing Group
P.O. Box 6287, Grand Rapids, MI 49516-6287
www.brazospress.com

Printed in the United States of America

Scripture quotations, unless otherwise noted, are from the New Revised Standard Version of the Bible, copyright 1989 by the Division of Christian Education of the National Council of the Churches of Christ in the USA. Used by permission. All rights reserved.

Library of Congress Cataloging-in-Publication Data
Barron, Robert E., 1959–
        The Priority of Christ : toward a postliberal Catholicism / Robert Barron.
            p.   cm.
        Includes bibliographical references and index.
        ISBN 10: 1-58743-198-X (pbk.)
        ISBN 978-1-58743-198-2 (pbk.)
        1. Catholic Church—Doctrines—History—20th century. 2. Postmodernism—Religious aspects—Christianity. 3. Jesus Christ. I. Title.
    BX1751.3.B37 2007
    230'.2—dc22   2006031658

Contents

Foreword

Faith and reason, wrote Pope John Paul II, are the two wings the human spirit uses to reach truth. The dialogue between faith and reason is a constant in human conversation, with faith using reason to understand more adequately faith's own truths, and reason using faith to understand better reason's own nature and that of its findings.

This centuries-old conversation, characterized in Patristic literature as a dialogue between Jerusalem and Athens, finds new expression in Fr. Robert Barron's highly significant work. The dialogue takes on new importance today because some believers reject any rational critique of their faith, and some rationalists imagine the possibility of a purely secular reason. The danger in such positions is that faith without critique has too often legitimated violence, and reason divorced from faith has constructed utopian or "scientific" experiments that kill the human spirit along with millions of human beings.

Father Barron's work is theological, for his own reflection is shaped by the task the Church has given him to teach theology at Mundelein Seminary in the Archdiocese of Chicago. He situates the dialogue between faith and reason in the conversation between those who begin theologizing with the data of revelation, shaping human experience by its demands, and those who begin theologizing from a philosophical or anthropological base, fitting revelation into the contours of reason and human experience.

The Priority of Christ puts this ancient and contemporary dialogue to new music. Fr. Barron creates a "postliberal" theology that is neither a return to Scholasticism nor even to the Fathers, although he draws upon the resources of earlier theologians. His is a theology that reaches back for its sources and forward for its concerns. Precisely to move forward, Fr. Barron must disempower modernity's critique of faith and modify the exaggerated claims advanced by historicity. The priority of Christ is ontological, epistemic and ethical; but the new melodies chanting who Christ is can't be heard without first muting the tired songs derived from Cartesian subjectivism. The original sin of liberal Christianity is to reduce divine self-revelation to personal religious experience.

When I was a seminarian over four decades ago, an experienced spiritual director used to take my many concerns about the spiritual life and the life of faith and bring them to the light of Christ. He suggested to me a practice I've maintained over these many years. Each year, he advised, I should not just read theology or philosophy, but take and make my own at least one book on the life of Christ. He was concerned neither with the quest for the historical Jesus nor with having me answer naively what Jesus might do with my questions. He was insistent only that constantly living with the Lord creates a curiosity about him that cannot be satisfied by purely intellectual investigations. Jesus is not an idea but a person. In encountering him and surrendering to him, faith is born and reason challenged creatively.

This book gives analogous advice and insight to theologians today. Fr. Barron presents Jesus as an icon, beyond concept but not beyond rationality, a "super-saturated" phenomenon that is the central character in narratives that are always unique and never generic. Idols are manipulative expressions of our making; icons, by contrast, destroy special interests because they draw us into their world and prevent ours from becoming absolute. God is like a noisy shutter insistently banging in the night. We resist listening because we fear moving out of beds of our own making. Jesus, the revelation of God, tells us we have nothing to fear because God is not in competition with us. He is not a threat; he sets us free to think truthfully and to act rightly. God's self-revelation is a natural complement to human reason, not its competitor; and God himself is "neither one being among many nor the sum total of creatures understood collectively."

Fr. Barron explores the relations among metaphysics, epistemology, and ethics when each of these rational disciplines is enlightened by faith in Christ. A metaphysics of gift that elucidates creation as a unity of order traces the ontological relationships that enable creatures to participate in being and acting. An epistemology of co-inherence that studies the relation of subject and object in the act of knowing explains how love enters into knowing. An ethics elaborated in reference to iconic disciples of Christ respects individual distinctiveness while uniting every moral agent in the quest for holiness. None of Fr. Barron's solutions will be the last word, but each resituates the conversation to get us talking among ourselves and with the Lord.

Will this book get a hearing? It enters the conversation today, but its arguments are of more than topical importance. For some, it may sound a discordant note; for others it will be like a shutter banging in the wind of grace, a call to intellectual and moral conversion. It is a hopeful work, designed to help the Church today work through many sterile debates and express the truths of the apostolic faith clearly and persuasively. Hope in Christ is consistent with a certain pessimism about a sinful world that rejects him and refuses to understand its own need for divine grace to set things right. Hope in Christ, nevertheless, knows that, in the end, all will be well because all is grace. Fr. Barron's book is a gift, a grace, for us today.

Francis Cardinal George, OMI
Archbishop of Chicago

Introduction

The Grandmother, the Misfit, and the One Who Throws Everything Off

Flannery O'Connor's short-story masterpiece "A Good Man Is Hard to Find" centers on a deadly duel between a superficially pious and self-regarding grandmother and the Misfit, a brutal killer and escaped convict. The grandmother's fear of the Misfit is made clear in the first paragraph of the story. As her family prepares to set out on an automobile journey to Florida, she reminds them of the danger lurking on their route: "Here this fellow that calls himself The Misfit is aloose from the Federal Pen and headed toward Florida. . . . I wouldn't take my children in any direction with a criminal like that aloose in it."[1] This statement signals the woman's fear, but it also reveals her character. It is confirmed in the course of the story that she is rather bossy and self-righteous, typically chagrined that people around her don't come up to her high moral expectations. Through a strange set of circumstances—narrated with O'Connor's customary blend of irony and black humor—the Grandmother and her family do indeed come face to face with the Misfit. When the old lady blurts out, "You're The Misfit! I recognized you at once!"[2] the criminal becomes as frightened of her as she is of him, and the story moves quickly to a climax.

As his men lead the grandmother's family one by one into the woods for execution, the Misfit and the old lady fall into a troubled theological

1. Flannery O'Connor, "A Good Man Is Hard to Find," in *Collected Works* (New York: Library Classics, 1988), 137.
2. Ibid., 147.

conversation. "If you would pray," said the grandmother, "Jesus would help you . . . why don't you pray?"

The Misfit responds, "I don't want no hep, I'm doing all right by myself."[3] What we learn through this simple exchange is that the Misfit and the woman are, despite their enormous superficial differences, in basically the same spiritual space, for each is convinced of his own self-sufficiency. As the shots coming from the woods confirm that her family is being killed, the grandmother begins to mutter, "Jesus, Jesus." The Misfit takes the cue: "Yes'm. . . . Jesus thrown everything off balance. . . . If he did what he said, then it's nothing for you to do but throw away everything and follow him, and if he didn't, then it's nothing for you to do but enjoy the few minutes you got left the best way you can—by killing somebody or burning down his house or doing some other meanness to him. No pleasure but meanness."[4]

Though the old lady has invoked him in an act of desperate piety, it is clear that the Misfit possesses a more searching and theologically profound understanding of Jesus. Jesus, he knows, compels a choice, posing by his words and actions a Kierkegaardian either-or: either Jesus is everything or he is nothing; either you hand your entire life to him or you sink back into the vilest sort of selfishness. When in a sort of daze the grandmother says, "Maybe he didn't raise the dead," the Misfit frantically responds, "Listen lady, if I had of been there I would of known and I wouldn't be like I am now."[5]

O'Connor commented that her stories center on "the offer of grace, usually refused"; this is one of those moments. Under the influence of the terrible acts that he is performing and his own powerful understanding of Jesus, something in the Misfit breaks open. The one who had, just moments before, declared his spiritual self-sufficiency now declares his need of grace. And in that same instant, something shifts in the grandmother: "She saw the man's face twisted close to her own . . . and she murmured, 'Why you're one of my babies. You're one of my own children!'"[6] Having long feared the Misfit and having seen her very worst fears confirmed, she now declares that they are connected to each other by the closest bonds, that they are in the same spiritual family. Both, despite their terror of each other, are sinners in need of grace.

Inspired by this intimacy, the old woman reaches out and touches the Misfit, who responds by jumping back as though bit by a snake and shooting her three times through the chest. As the grandmother lies dead in the

3. Ibid., 150.
4. Ibid., 151.
5. Ibid., 152.
6. Ibid.

ditch, her face smiling up to heaven, the killer wipes off his glasses. Back from the woods and excited by what he has done, the Misfit's associate cries out, "Some fun!" The Misfit retorts, "Shut up, Bobby Lee, ain't no pleasure in life." On that seemingly despairing note, the story staggers to an unlikely end.[7]

O'Connor said that her stories were comedies, but could such a description possibly be applied to "A Good Man Is Hard to Find"? We recall that the Misfit had said that the stark choice is between giving one's life utterly to Jesus and finding the only pleasure one can through acts of violence. Yet after an orgy of violence—thrilling to Bobby Lee—the Misfit finds no joy in his soul. Does this denial of one side of the either-or signal at least an openness to conversion, and does the wiping of his glasses indicate that he is beginning to see in a new way? Certainly, there are no clear answers to these questions, but as the story ends, grace does seem, once more, to be on offer.[8] The discussion of Jesus had led the grandmother from prissy self-righteousness to something like real compassion, and it has, perhaps, brought the Misfit to the compunction necessary for *metanoia*.

This troubling and strange story is a particularly apt metaphor for the relationship between modernity and the late-medieval form of Christianity that gave rise to it. Though they have long viewed one another with deep suspicion, modern liberalism and late-medieval Christianity are in fact close relatives, the latter in many ways the mother of the former ("You're one of my own babies!"). And both stand in need of salvation from the person to whom they both, to varying degrees of accuracy, refer: Jesus Christ, the one who throws everything off.

What I propose to develop in this book is neither a modern form of Christianity nor a Christian attack on modernity, but rather a postmodern or postliberal Catholicism, a view of God and the world that flows from the still surprising event of Jesus Christ and that pushes beyond the convictions of both modernity and conventionally construed Christianity.

A Decadent Christianity and One of Its Own Children

There have in recent years been numerous accounts of the etiology of modernity. Jürgen Habermas, Hans Urs von Balthasar, John Milbank, Colin Gunton, and Louis Dupré, among many others, have offered explanations of the transition from the premodern to the modern.[9] I subscribe to the

7. Ibid., 153.

8. See Robert Barron, *And Now I See: A Theology of Transformation* (New York: Crossroad, 1998), esp. 165–67.

9. See Colin E. Gunton, *The One, the Three, and the Many: God, Creation, and the Culture of Modernity* (Cambridge: Cambridge Univ. Press, 2000), esp. 56–61. Also see Louis Dupré, *Passage*

proposal that liberal modernity can best be seen as an energetic reaction to a particular and problematic version of nominalist Christianity. Early modernity saw itself as a salutary response to oppressive and obscurantist strains in Christian culture, but since it was reacting to a corruption of true Christianity, it itself became similarly distorted and exaggerated. As a result, the two systems settled into a centuries-long and terribly unproductive warfare. Even when the two attempted a reconciliation (as in all forms of liberal Christianity in the past two centuries), the results were less than satisfactory, precisely because each party was itself a sort of caricature.

The trouble began with Duns Scotus's option for a univocal conception of being in contradistinction to Thomas Aquinas's analogical understanding.[10] For Thomas, God, as the sheer act of to-be itself (*ipsum esse subsistens*), is that through which all creatures exist. What follows epistemologically from this metaphysical claim is that the meaning of "to-be," in reference to God and creatures, must be analogical, with God as primary analogue and created things as secondary.[11] In accord with this intuition, Aquinas maintained consistently throughout his career that God is inescapably mysterious to the human intellect, since our frame of reference remains the creaturely mode of existence, which bears only an analogical resemblance to the divine mode of being. We may say that God exists, but we're not quite sure what we mean when we say it; the "cash value" of the claim that God exists is that there is a finally mysterious source of the to-be of finite things.

In an effort to make the to-be of God more immediately intelligible, Duns Scotus proposed a univocal conception of existence, according to which God and creatures belong to the same basic metaphysical category, the genus of being. Though God is infinite and therefore quantitatively superior to any creature or collectivity of creatures, there is nevertheless no qualitative difference, in the metaphysical sense, between the supreme being, God, and finite beings. Whereas Aquinas insisted that God is categorizable in no genus whatsoever, Scotus held that God and creatures do belong together to a logical category that, in a real sense, transcends and includes them. The implications of this shift are enormous and, to my mind, almost entirely negative. If the analogical conception of being is rejected, creatures are no longer seen as participating in the divine to-

---

to Modernity: An Essay in the Hermeneutics of Nature and Culture (New Haven, CT: Yale Univ. Press, 1993), esp. 39–45.

10. See John Milbank, *Theology and Social Theory* (Oxford: Blackwell, 1990), 302–3. Also *Passage to Modernity*, 170, 189. Also John Milbank, *The Word Made Strange: Theology, Language, and Culture* (Oxford: Blackwell, 1997), 16.

11. See David Burrell, *Aquinas: God and Action* (Notre Dame, IN: Univ. of Notre Dame Press, 1979), 137.

be; instead, God and creatures are appreciated as existing side by side, as beings of varying types and degrees of intensity. Furthermore, unanchored from their shared participation in God, no longer grounded in a common source, creatures lose their essential connectedness to one another. Isolated and self-contained individuals (God the supreme being and the many creatures) are now what is most basically real.

Scotus's intuition was confirmed a generation later by his Franciscan successor William of Occam. Congruent with his nominalism, which denied ontological density to the unifying features of being, Occam held that there is nothing real outside of disconnected individual things (*praeter illas partes absolutas nulla res est*).[12] As for Scotus so for Occam, God and creatures are set side by side, joined only through a convention of logic that assigns them to the category of "beings." A consequence of this conception is that God and finite things have to be rivals, since their individualities are contrastive and mutually exclusive. Just as a chair is itself precisely in the measure that it is no other creaturely thing, so God is himself only inasmuch as he stands over and against the world he has made, and vice versa. Whereas in Aquinas's participation metaphysics the created universe is constituted *by its rapport with God*, on Occam's reading it must realize itself through disassociation from a competitive supreme being. A further concomitant of this individualistic ontology is voluntarism. Since the metaphysically dense and natural link between God and creatures has been attenuated, any connection between the divine and the nondivine has to be through will. God's relation with his rational creatures is therefore primarily legalistic and arbitrary.[13] This understanding of divine power influenced Occam's conception of the human will as well. Finite freedom is, for him, absolute spontaneity, an action prompted by nothing either interior or exterior to the subject. Accordingly, human power is a distant mirror of divine power: both are self-contained, capricious, absolute, and finally irrational. The most obvious practical consequence of this nominalist and voluntarist metaphysics is that divine and human freedom find themselves pitted against one another, God imposing himself arbitrarily on a necessarily reluctant and resentful humanity.

Both Martin Luther and John Calvin were formed according to the principles of late-medieval nominalism, and one does not have to look far to see evidence of that formation in their writings.[14] A distant and majestic God who chooses, apparently in complete arbitrariness, that some be saved and others be damned is on clear display in Calvin's *Institutes*, and

12. Quoted in Umberto Eco, *Art and Beauty in the Middle Ages* (New Haven, CT: Yale Univ. Press, 1986), 88.

13. See Gunton, *The One, the Three, and the Many*, 57–58.

14. See Alister McGrath, *Reformation Thought: An Introduction* (Oxford: Blackwell, 1999), 70–76.

a God whose power effectively trumps the freedom and integrity of the human will is readily apparent in Luther's *On the Bondage of the Will*.[15] Was the Reformation, at least to some degree, a radical ratification of the breakdown of an analogical conception of being?

From at least the time of Étienne Gilson, a number of scholars have acknowledged the important relationship between early modernity and medieval culture. I follow Colin Gunton and John Milbank's suggestion that the modern can be viewed as a sharp reaction to precisely the elements in late-medieval Christianity that I have been highlighting. Many of the early modern philosophers called for a Heraclitean revolt of the many individuals against the Parmenidean imposition of divine demands, especially as those were made concrete in the church and in traditional culture. Martha Nussbaum, one of the most articulate contemporary defenders of the liberal/modern perspective, says that liberalism is essentially the valorization of the prerogatives of the individual subject, more precisely, an affirmation of that subject's right to choose, even the meaning of his or her own life.[16] What is the enemy of this freedom? For many of the fathers of modernity, it is nothing other than those traditional institutions (supported by the voluntarist conception of God) that bind the will and quash individual initiative and imagination.

We can see this paradigmatically in Descartes's affirmation of the epistemological primordiality and meaning-creating capacity of the *cogito*. Dupré has remarked that subjectivism as such is not a distinctive quality of the modern, for no one was more subjective than Plato, Plotinus, or Augustine. Rather, it is the claim that the subject is itself the ground and measure of meaning and value.[17] This is what we find in René Descartes's insistence that all sense experience, all received ideas and traditions, and the very existence of God be brought before the bar of subjectivity for adjudication and evaluation. And we can see it, too, in Immanuel Kant's claim that the moral life is grounded neither in the objectivity of nature nor in any hetereonomous law, but rather in the self-legislation of the categorical imperative.[18] It is furthermore apparent in Jean-Jacques Rousseau's conviction that the only legitimate form of government is a democracy so pure that obedience to law is coincident with obedience

15. See especially the discussions of double predestination in John Calvin, *Institutes of the Christian Religion*, Bk. III, ch. 21 (Grand Rapids: Eerdmans, 1998), 202–211, 239–276. Also Martin Luther, *On the Bondage of the Will* in *Martin Luther: Selections from his Writings*, ed. John Dillenberger (New York: Doubleday, 1962), 166–203.

16. See Martha Nussbaum, *Upheavals of Thought: The Intelligence of Emotions* (Cambridge: Cambridge Univ. Press, 2001), 414–25.

17. Dupré, *Passage to Modernity*, 89.

18. See Immanuel Kant, *Foundations of the Metaphysics of Morals* (Indianapolis: Bobbs-Merrill, 1978), 22–32.

to self.[19] It comes to perhaps clearest expression in Friedrich Nietzsche's uncompromising elevation of the prerogatives of the will (a perfect mirror of the voluntarist divine will in Occam) and the concomitant need of that heroic will to put the competitive God to death.[20]

Lest all of this seem too abstractly philosophical, the modern preference for the freedom of the individual is no more baldly and forcibly defended than in the U.S. Supreme Court's judgment in the case of *Casey v. Planned Parenthood*: "At the heart of liberty is the right to define one's own concept of existence, of meaning, of the universe, of the mystery of human life."[21] This judicial formulation is an almost perfect exemplification of Jean-Paul Sartre's archetypically modern dictum that existence (concrete freedom) precedes essence (meaning and value).[22]

In all of this modern assertiveness, we see the reaction of the many against the one, of individuals against the tyranny of institutions and of that threatening Other lurking, acknowledged explicitly or not, behind them. In my judgment, this tension is the finally unproductive warfare between the grandmother and the Misfit, between a not very convincing form of Christianity and the opponent to whom it naturally gave rise. Modernity and decadent Christianity are enemies in one sense, but in another sense, they are deeply connected to one another and mirror one another. In most of the disputes between Christianity and modernity, we have advocates of the prerogatives of the voluntarist God facing down advocates of the voluntarist self. A central argument of this book amounts to "a plague on both your houses," for I am convinced that both need to be saved, precisely by that person who throws everything off, including and especially the competitive understanding of God and the world that produced the conflict between them in the first place.

Authentic Christianity and the Claims of Modernity

The Misfit and the grandmother are enemies because each is deathly afraid of the other. The moment of grace comes when the old woman notices their shared need for redemption. So modernity and nominalist Christianity—enemies with much in common—stand in need of salvation. This redemption will come not through the clarification of ideas and certainly not through a successful *Aufhebung* of the two systems;

19. Jean-Jacques Rousseau, *The Social Contract* (New York: Hafner, 1947), 34–35.
20. See Friedrich Nietzsche, *Thus Spoke Zarathustra*, in *The Portable Nietzsche*, edited by Walter Kaufmann (New York: Penguin, 1976), 124–30.
21. *Casey v. Planned Parenthood of Southeastern Pennsylvania*, 112 Sup. Ct. 2791 at 2807.
22. Jean-Paul Sartre, *L'existentialisme est un humanisme* (Paris: Editions de Nagel, 1970), 17–18.

rather, it will come through the still surprising power of a person, the God-human Jesus Christ. The central affirmation of classical Christianity is that in Jesus of Nazareth God and humanity met in a noncompetitive and nonviolent way. According to the formulary of the Council of Chalcedon, the human nature of Jesus is not compromised, truncated, or undermined in the process of becoming united to a divine nature. Rather, the two come together "without mixing, mingling, or confusion" in a hypostatic union, producing one who is perfect in divinity and perfect in humanity.[23] This implies that the human mind, will, passion, and freedom of Jesus are brought to fullest pitch precisely through their union with the incarnating God. And this in turn says something of great importance about the divine. If the incarnation is an accomplished fact, then the presence of the true God is not invasive or interruptive but rather noncompetitive. In light of this coming together, we must say that there is a rapport of coinherence between divinity and humanity, each abiding in the other in such a way that humanity is elevated by the proximity of the divine.[24] St. Irenaeus summed up this radical idea in the pithy formula *Gloria Dei homo vivens* (the glory of God is a human being fully alive). God does not have to assert his prerogatives in an aggressive way over and against the claims of the created will, and hence voluntarism obtains on neither side of the Creator-creature divide. And this is precisely why Jesus throws everything off. He upsets a worldview predicated upon the primordiality of competition and ontological violence, replacing it with a vision predicated upon the primordiality of relationship and mutual indwelling.

Something very similar is on display in the surprise of the Paschal Mystery. The crucified Jesus returned alive to those who had abused, abandoned, denied, and fled from him, but he confronted them not with threats and vengeance but with the nonviolence of compassion and forgiveness. The moral disorder produced by the crucifixion of the Son of God was restored not through a violent imposition of divine retributive justice but through restorative divine forgiveness, not through a suppression of will by Will but by an insinuating invitation to love. On the basis of this luminous revelation, Christians concluded the nonviolent and relational character of God's own being.[25] God is not so much a monolith of power and ontological perfection as a play of love and relationality. The author of the first letter of John stated this revolutionary insight with admirable

23. Norman P. Tanner, ed., *Decrees of the Ecumenical Councils* (Washington, DC: Georgetown Univ. Press, 1990), 1:86.

24. See Robert Sokolowski, *The God of Faith and Reason* (Washington, DC: Catholic Univ. of America Press, 1995), 39.

25. See James Alison, *The Joy of Being Wrong: Original Sin through Easter Eyes* (New York: Crossroad, 1998), 202.

laconicism: "God is love." In the course of the tradition, the perception was formalized in the doctrine of the Trinity, the claim that God is a family of coinherent yet subsistent relations, each marked by the capacity for self-emptying. This trinitarian dynamic is neither the crushing weight of the one nor the fissaparous plurality of the many, but rather the one in the many and the many in the one, that mutual indwelling which is the characteristic of love. If for Aristotle relationality is accidental, for Christian metaphysics it is elemental and irreducible in itself.

From the noncompetitiveness of the incarnation and the Trinity, classical Christian theology concluded the noninvasiveness of creation. In many of the ancient myths of creation, cosmic order comes as the result of a primeval battle between the gods or through a divine victory over some recalcitrant force. And these cosmogonic myths were perpetuated in more rational form in the philosophical cosmologies of the ancient world. So for both Plato and Aristotle, worldly order comes through an intelligent shaping of some primal stuff existing alongside of divine intelligence. In both tellings of the story—mythic and philosophical—the cosmos emerges through violence, the pressing of some other into obedience through an exercise of external force. But there is none of this in the classical Christian accounts of creation. From the patristic period up until the emergence of modern deism, Christian thinkers held the doctrine of *creatio ex nihilo,* God's bringing of the whole of finitude into being from nothing.[26] This construal of the act of creation calls into question the entire tradition that I have just described, for it teaches that the order and existence of the world come not through any sort of invasion, manipulation, or external interference but through a sheerly generous and nonviolent act of selfless love. Herbert McCabe caught this truth beautifully when he said that the world is sustained in being by God much as a song is sustained in being by a singer. What follows from the nonviolence of *creatio ex nihilo* is the worldview that I hinted at earlier—the analogical conception of being and the participative connection of all creatures in a coinherent nexus.

This book will be an exploration and elaboration of this distinctively Christian metaphysics, and as such it will be not antimodern but postmodern. For it will take with great seriousness the modern valorization of the prerogatives of the individual and her freedom, but will show how both are preserved not over and against a competitive god but precisely in relation to the God of coinherent love. And it will be unabashedly Catholic, for it will state the radical ontology that flows from the revelation contained in Jesus Christ and that was brought to rich expression in the greatest doctors of the church, including and especially Thomas Aquinas.

26. Milbank, *Theology and Social Theory,* 423–30.

The Structure of the Book

The argument of this book begins, in line with postliberal instincts, not with general religious experience, nor with the supposed universal truths of reason, but with Jesus Christ in all his specificity. Whereas most of the major liberal theologies of the past two hundred years—Friedrich Schleiermacher's, Ernst Troeltsch's, Rudolf Otto's, Paul Tillich's, Karl Rahner's—commenced with some grounding experience deemed to be transcultural, this postliberal theology will commence with what Hans Urs von Balthasar referred to as the *concretissimus*, the stubbornly particular Christ.[27] And the presentation of Jesus will not be determined by foundationalist assumptions. Unlike most modern Christologists, I will neither search for the religious experience of which Jesus supposedly gives privileged expression nor seek to uncover the "historical" Jesus underneath the Gospel portraits. Rather, I shall present an "iconic" Christology, one that takes seriously the dense particularity and spiritual complexity of the picture of Jesus as it emerges in the New Testament narratives. I shall share Balthasar's intuition that one must approach Jesus in a Goethean spirit, which is to say, in an attitude of contemplative love, allowing the object of one's contemplation to control the gaze of the mind. Accordingly, I will explore nine "icons" or sacred scenes from the Gospels, organizing them under the headings of Jesus as Gatherer, Jesus as Warrior, and Jesus as Lord.

Next, in light of this presentation, I will develop a christocentric epistemology. I will argue that Christians know and seek knowledge in a distinctive way, precisely because they take the narratives concerning Jesus Christ as epistemically basic. If, as the author of Colossians argues, all things hold together in Christ, then the deepest truth of things must become fully intelligible only through Christ. I will set this understanding against both great forms of modern epistemological foundationalism: John Locke's brand of empiricism and René Descartes's subjectivism.

In the fourth major section of the book, I will develop the themes that I've already adumbrated: God's trinitarian nature and the unique mode of divine existence vis-à-vis what is other than God. I will place special focus on the issue of primary causality and secondary causality in relation to both nature and the will, arguing for the noninterruptive coinherence of God and the world. Making constant reference to Christology, I will also examine the metaphysics of the gift as it applies to God's rapport with creation. Precisely because God does not need the world, God is capable of an utterly selfless gift on behalf of the other, breaking the rhythm of

27. Hans Urs von Balthasar, *Explorations in Theology*, vol. 1, *The Word Made Flesh* (San Francisco: Ignatius, 1989), 162.

economic exchange that effectively undermines ordinary gift giving. The sheer graciousness of God's presence to the world becomes, in turn, the ground for our participation through love in the divine life. Throughout this section, my concern will be to demonstrate the uniquely noncontrastive transcendence of the God disclosed in Jesus Christ.

In the final section of the book, I shall attempt to show the ethical implications of this christocentric metaphysics. Departing from both Kantian deontologism and a too abstract and rationalistic construal of the natural law, I will develop a densely christological ethic, one that flows from the biblical portrayal of the way of being characteristic of Jesus. But I will not focus directly on narratives concerning Jesus. Instead, I will paint icons of four saints who, in various ways, participated in the new life made available in Christ: Thérèse of Lisieux, Katharine Drexel, Edith Stein, and Mother Teresa of Calcutta. I will show how each of these women exemplifies the peculiar transformation that occurs when a natural virtue is elevated by contact with grace. In the process, I shall endeavor to present a christological, iconic, and narrative ethic.

Just as Flannery O'Connor saw the struggle between the Misfit and the grandmother as both tragic and an occasion of grace, so I see the battle between liberal modernity and nominalist Christianity as, at the same time, frustrating and hopeful—frustrating because both combatants are exhausted, worn out, and wounded from the struggle, and hopeful because in the very fruitlessness of the fight, both sides have come to appreciate their common need for a savior. What I propose to do in this book is to present this savior, the God-human Jesus Christ, and to explore the ramifications of his coming for both the grandmother and the Misfit, for both a decadent Christianity and a reactive modernity. This is the project of my postliberal Catholicism.

PART I

Iconic Christology

1

Jesus as Symbol

One of the most significant trends in the Christology of the modern era was the tendency to render Jesus a symbol for, or exemplification of, a universal religious sensibility. Accordingly, many modern theologians and philosophers separated the figure of Jesus (construed in either a relatively historical or a relatively literary way) from the sacred reality, holiness, religious consciousness, or divinity that he bore. This specifically christological move was in line with the general modern distinction between a "rational" religion—available in principle to all—and the specificities of the various positive revelations, about which there was, it seemed, endless and finally unresolvable disagreement. And it was congruent with one of the deepest and most abiding strains in modern consciousness: Descartes's privileging of the interior and abstract over the exterior and specific. Descartes builds his philosophy on the foundation of the cogito, and when he addresses the world outside of his mind, he does so in a mathematicizing way, reducing objects and things to their most abstract form (*res extensae*).

The modern presentation of Jesus as symbol or cipher has, I will argue, emptied Christology of its content and robbed it of its evangelical bite. By focusing attention on a more abstract principle above Jesus, it has muted the strange, countercultural, and surprising novelty of what God has accomplished in Christ. Showing an alternative to this relatively abstract Christology will be the central task of this chapter.

23

Though this favoring of the abstract over the particular can be seen in the religious philosophies of many of the greatest modern thinkers—G. W. F. Hegel, Baruch Spinoza, G. W. Leibniz—it is nowhere more remarkably apparent than in the thought of Immanuel Kant. It therefore behooves us to examine Kant's Christology in some detail. Having in the *Critique of Pure Reason* precluded the possibility of properly theoretical knowledge of God, Kant showed in the *Critique of Practical Reason* that God's existence must be posited—along with freedom and immortality—as a condition for the possibility of an authentic moral life. The following of the categorical imperative—act in such a way that the maxim of your will could become a universal law—entails a sharp demarcation between duty and inclination, but the *summum bonum* (the highest happiness possible) involves the coincidence of those two tendencies. In order to live the moral life realistically, we must therefore postulate the existence of a being powerful enough to reconcile the stringent demand of duty with the pleasant pull of inclination, and this can only be the God who is Lord not only of earth but of heaven as well.

And this is why, though it does not, strictly speaking, require anything outside of itself for justification, the moral life "leads ineluctably to religion, through which it extends itself to the idea of a powerful moral Lawgiver outside of mankind."[1] In other words, religious belief is the generalized phenomenon that proceeds from the demand of the categorical imperative that can be found at the ground of every human will. Though it is wildly diverse in its particular manifestations, religion is one in its basic ethical structure and grounding. Importantly for Kant, it is philosophy, and not biblically based theology, that appreciates this universal and rational dimension of religion. As a consequence, if biblical theology finds itself at odds with rational religion, the former must cede to the latter.[2] In this typically modern move, Kant reverses the logic of faith and reason that had held sway from the patristic period through the late Middle Ages. Religion is then finally and fundamentally about not metaphysics or cosmology but morality, the disciplined response to the demand of the categorical imperative.

Now as one examines the ethical life more precisely, one finds that the press of the moral imperative is countered by a powerful and finally anomalous attraction toward evil. When he poses the question as to the origin of this evil tendency, Kant famously and surprisingly answers, "The rational origin of this perversion of our will whereby it makes lower incentives supreme among its maxims, that is, of the propensity toward

1. Immanuel Kant, *Religion within the Limits of Reason Alone*, translated by Theodore M. Greene and Hoyt H. Hudson (New York: Harper and Row, 1960), 5–6.
2. Ibid., 9.

evil, remains inscrutable to us."[3] The tendency of the will away from the categorical imperative, and hence away from its own nature, can be characterized only as an irrational perversion; yet it is undeniably real. The drama of the moral life is the struggle between duty and inclination, between the rational and irrational conditioning of desire.

In the great narratives of the Bible, we have, according to Kant, a sort of pictorial representation of this inner tension. The good and evil principles—these dynamics of the moral life—are vividly pictured in the characters and dramas of the Scriptures. Thus in the book of Genesis we read of the struggle between the first human being and a figure who is the emobodiment of evil, and we see throughout the Old Testament how this original battle plays itself out over and again. For instance, the good principle is symbolized in the establishment of the Jewish theocracy, but the insinuating influence of the evil principle is given expression in the corruption and worldliness of that purportedly godly kingdom.[4] In the measure that it promoted the moral virtues, the Jewish religious establishment—kings, prophets, the temple, judges, etc.—was upright, but in the measure that it fostered fussy ceremonial practcices and wallowed in wealth and worldly power, it undermined itself. So the riven soul, caught between duty and self-interest.

Just as the Jews were feeling the full weight of their corrupt religious system, the biblical story takes a decisive turn. There appeared among the Jewish people a person whose wisdom was so pure that it surpassed that of the greatest philosophers, so pristine in fact that it could be described only as having descended from heaven. This man was obviously human, but he was also appreciated as an envoy from a higher world, precisely because the purity of his moral will, his incomparable innocence, indicated that he was in no way involved in the compromise with the evil principle. As his public career began, he came into conflict with the devil, who promised him total command of the earthly order if only he would bow down and worship. When this overture was turned down, the evil power took from him any worldly wealth, status, or power and sent against him "all the persecutions by means of which evil men can embitter life, causing him such sorrows as only the well-disposed can feel deeply."[5] When even these sufferings did not turn the godly man from his mission of preaching and exemplifying the moral life, the devil stirred up such hatred among his opponents that he was arrested, unjustly condemned, and put to death. But even *in extremis*—mocked, rejected, a failure, in agony—this good man did not sway from his mission and did not sully the purity of his will. In

3. Ibid., 38.
4. Ibid., 74.
5. Ibid., 75.

this, he effectively rendered impotent the evil principle, since he showed that a thoroughly upright moral life is possible, even in the face of the direst opposition. "So the moral outcome of the combat, as regards the hero of this story, is really not the conquering of the evil principle . . . but merely the breaking of its power to hold, against their will, those who have so long been its subjects, because another dominion, a moral dominion, is now offered them as an asylum."[6] Evil perdures, both personally and institutionally, after the death of this moral exemplar, but it no longer holds sway and is no longer feared as inevitable.

Now what gives this story—obviously that of Jesus—its greatest power is that it corresponds to an ideal that Kant maintains is present at the ground of the will, that is, the archetype of the person perfectly pleasing to God, a sort of imaginative representation of the categorical imperative. Like the idea of an infinite being in Descartes's epistemology, this image, for Kant, is not something that the ego creates; rather it is given to consciousness. So "exterior" and unbidden is this archetype that it is most accurately described as having "come down from heaven and assumed our humanity."[7] Its role is to serve as a sort of asymptotically approached ideal of the moral life; as such, it is both efficient and final cause of ethical attainment.

What precisely are its contours? Who is the person perfectly pleasing to God? First, he is someone "who would be willing not merely to discharge all human duties himself but to spread about him goodness as widely as possible by precept and example."[8] Second, he would be confronted with the most powerful temptations and beset with the most dreadful persecution, even confronting the fear of death itself, and remain through it all true to himself and to the demand of the categorical imperative. This notion or archetype (and here we come to the heart of it) need not correspond to any real historical figure. For Kant, the image of the person perfectly pleasing to God is "from the practical point of view . . . completely real in its own right, for it resides in the morally-legislative reason."[9] So what do we make of the rather remarkable correspondence between this supposedly a priori archetype and the life of Jesus as presented in the Gospel narratives? The Gospel story of Jesus, says Kant, should be construed as an especially powerful and accurate exemplification of the moral ideal and hence as a particularly effective spur to moral excellence. Even if we were to assume that a real historical figure stood behind the narrative concerning Jesus, that figure would contribute nothing beyond the power

6. Ibid., 77.
7. Ibid., 54.
8. Ibid., 55.
9. Ibid.

of the idea itself. Might a real person have inspired the narrative of Jesus? Perhaps, but one's theological attention ought to be focused not on him but rather on the story to which he gave rise, or even more properly to the archetype that the story stirs to life.

This radical Kantian disjunction between the actual historical Jesus and the archetype of the person perfectly pleasing to God is, as we have seen, the result of a generally modern tendency to separate the inner and the outer, but it flows, more specifically, from the problem that Gotthold Lessing raised just before Kant commenced the critical stage of his philosophy. In 1777, four years before the *Critique of Pure Reason* appeared, Lessing published a short essay entitled "On the Proof of the Spirit and Power," in which he made the distinction between "the accidental truths of history" and "the necessary truths of reason."[10] Reason is hungry for apodictic truth, for a certainty beyond the vagaries of time, space, and particularity, but the contingent events of history are known in a far less than apodictic way, for they come to us only through questionable sources and often less than reliable witnesses. Thus it appears that conditional historical knowledge can never ground unconditional certitude, that there yawns, in Lessing's phrase, a great gulf or ditch between these two ways of knowing. Now this distinction becomes especially illuminating and problematic when it is applied to the relentlessly historical religion of Christianity. On the one hand, Christian faith seems to demand certitude at both the epistemological and practical levels, but on the other hand, that faith is grounded in a particular first-century figure mediated to us by witnesses whose credibility could be questioned and texts whose interpretation is, to say the least, open ended. Lessing, to his chagrin, saw no way to get from the shaky evidence of history to the firm conviction of faith.

Kant, and most of the theologians who followed him in the nineteenth and twentieth centuries, felt the knottiness of this problem in his bones. Hence negotiating, bridging, leaping, denying, or weeping over Lessing's gulf become defining moves of much modern Christology. Kant himself set the tone by performing the operation we have just followed—the minimizing, almost to the point of irrelevancy, of the Jesus of history. In the categorical imperative and the archetype of the person perfectly pleasing to God, Kant found certain truths of reason—clear, unambiguous, universal, and accessible through immediate experience—and he effectively denied the necessity of grounding those truths in the conditioned figure of the historical Jesus. In a way, Kant solved the Lessing problem by reversing the movement: instead of proceeding from the particular to the

---

10. Cf. G. E. Lessing, "On the Proof of the Spirit and Power," in *Lessings Werke*, vol. 3, *Schriften 2*, edited by K. Wolfel (Frankfurt: Insel, 1967), esp. 307–12.

universal, he went the opposite way, allowing the truth of the archetype to condition the telling of the story.

Toward the end of Kant's life, in 1799, Friedrich Schleiermacher published his groundbreaking reflections *On Religion: Speeches to Its Cultured Despisers*, in which he endeavored to root religious truth in the universal experience of "sensing and tasting the infinite."[11] In the later and more systematic *Glaubenslehre*, he specified the sense of the infinite as the feeling of absolute dependency, and he identified this intuition, deeper than either thought or emotion, as the ground of religious dogma and practice. The spiritual person, he argued, is someone who, amidst all of the proximate dependencies of his life, "feels" an all-embracing and all-conditioning dependency of his being upon the power of Being itself. The source of that feeling is what religious people designate with the word *God*.

But what has enabled people to have this intuition? Unlike Kant's categorical imperative, which is simply given in the structure of the will, Schleiermacher's feeling of absolute dependency breaks into awareness through a particular historical event: the "perfect God-consciousness" of Jesus of Nazareth. Jesus is the one who, throughout his life and despite enormous opposition and strife, maintained a sense of God and, more to the point, allowed himself to be determined by God in every move, decision, and action. The steadiness and perfection of Jesus's consciousness of God constituted, for Schleiermacher, "a real presence of God in him" and in turn made possible the pure feeling of dependency in his followers, who in their turn bequeathed it to the Christian church, thus enabling people today to participate in its power.[12] One of the clearest and most beautiful presentations of Schleiermacher's Christology is his little dialogue *Christmas Eve*, in which he speculates that the feeling of real joy that people experience at Christmas is made possible by the breakthrough of divinity in the perfect God-consciousness of Jesus.[13]

Thus Schleiermacher negotiates Lessing's gulf, not through reason but through intuition. Because we have the feeling of absolute dependency now—a feeling that is not automatically given to human consciousness—it must have been grounded in a real historical person/event and carried through time and space. Therefore, for him, Jesus is much more than a literary character or the exemplification of an a priori archetype; he is, as a concrete historical person, the condition for the possibility of our present Christian religious experience. Thus Jesus takes on, in Schleiermacher's

11. Friedrich Scheiermacher, *On Religion: Speeches to Its Cultured Despisers*, in *Friedrich Schleiermacher: Pioneer of Modern Theology* (Minneapolis: Fortress, 1991), 85.

12. Friedrich Scheiermacher, *Glaubenslehre—First Doctrine: The Person of Christ*, in *Friedrich Schleiermacher: Pioneer of Modern Theology*, 218.

13. Friedrich Schleiermacher, *Christmas Eve: Dialogue on the Incarnation* in *Friedrich Schleiermacher: Pioneer of Modern Theology*, 195–203.

Christology, a density and particularity that is missing from Kant's account. At the same time, we remain in a clearly modern framework. The focus of Schleiermacher's theological attention is, as we've come to expect, on a general sensibility rather than on a specific revelation. Though Jesus was its trigger, the feeling of absolute dependency can and does exist apart from him; though we "learned" it through him, we can experience it without him. He is the cause of it in us, and he remains its greatest exemplification, but it transcends him and finally leaves him behind. Balthasar has commented that just as Luther urges us to look away from Christ in accord with the logic of the *sub contrario*, so Schleiermacher compels us to look away from him in accord with the emphasis on the primacy of experience: finally it is not Jesus that matters but the feeling that he makes possible in us.[14]

Something very similar can be found in Schleiermacher's most faithful twentieth-century disciple, the Lutheran theologian Paul Tillich. Adapting Schleiermacher's feeling of absolute dependency in a Heideggerian mode, Tillich identifies the ground of religion in the sense of being unconditionally concerned. In the German of his *Marburg Dogmatics*, this is specified as a state of being affected by *was uns unbedingt angeht* (what in an unconditioned way presses on us).[15] Amidst all of the proximate interests, goals, fears, and hopes that press upon us in a less than ultimate way, there is, Tillich wagers, a concern that preoccupies us in an unceasing and absolute manner. This *Unbedingte* (unconditioned) can be named variously as justice itself, the good itself, the true itself, but Tillich's preferred appellation—following both Schleiermacher and Heidegger—is *Sein Selbst* (Being itself). All religious feeling, thought, and action are rooted, finally, in the sense of being seized by the revealing power of this reality, both radically immanent and radically transcendent.

As a post-Kierkegaardian and post-Freudian, Tillich is more conscious than Schleiermacher of what goes wrong with our religiosity, how this ultimate concern becomes twisted and misconstrued. The basic problem, as he reads it, is the all-too-human tendency to substitute the less than unconditioned for the unconditioned—in biblical terms, to fashion idols. Thus a political party, a nation-state, a charismatic leader, money, sex, or power is deemed unsurpassably important, and the result is a skewing of the soul's order, an estrangement of the person and God. Tillich's Lutheranism becomes especially apparent in his identification of the religious traditions themselves as key culprits in this process of alienation. Precisely because

14. Hans Urs von Balthasar, *The Glory of the Lord: A Theological Aesthetics*, vol. 1, *Seeing the Form* (San Francisco: Ignatius, 1982), 45–47.

15. Paul Tillich, *Dogmatik: Marburger Vorlesung von 1925*, edited by Werner Schussler (Dusseldorf: Patmos Verlag, 1986), 41.

they bear the most sacred reality, religions have a particular proclivity toward inflation, that is to say, toward a self-idolatry, an identification of their own laws, practices, and beliefs with the unconditioned God.

Now where precisely does Jesus fit into this schema? The fact that I am posing the question in this way shows, of course, that we are dealing with a modern Christology, one that situates Jesus within an overarching and preexisting general frame of reference. For Tillich, Jesus is the bearer of the unconditioned who, in the most radical and complete sense, points beyond himself to that which he bears and thereby allows God in his fullness to appear. Every other religious figure or tradition collapses in on itself, hence blocking the breakthrough of the unconditioned, but Jesus remains utterly transparent. This is clear not only in his ministry and teaching but above all in his cross. In that culminating moment, Jesus permits himself to be cast aside, disregarded, forgotten, so that the divinity he bears might remain the focus of attention. In this, paradoxically enough, he embodies the perfection of revelation.[16] Through the cross, Jesus becomes the mediator of a perfect revelation, because in that awful moment he, as the bearer of the unconditioned, is "shaken" and questioned, and therefore any tendency he might have to block the light of God is precluded. In his later *Systematic Theology*, Tillich makes much the same point when he says that Jesus is the breakthrough of the New Being under the conditions of estrangement. Into a sinful world came someone who, despite every temptation to idolatry and self-inflation, remained connected to the unconditioned. When this purity of being was recognized by Peter ("You are the Christ"), Christianity came into existence.

Does the historical Jesus matter for Tillich? Yes, for he construes the christological project in a fundamentally Schleiermacherian way: our capacity to be seized by the unconditioned now depends upon the real breakthrough of that power in time, mediated by a real historical figure. But, as with Schleiermacher, this Jesus matters only "thinly," which is to say, as a symbol of or cipher for a more general existential condition. Consequently, Tillich remained essentially uninterested in the details of historical-critical research into the life of Jesus, once quipping, "I do not wish the telephone in my office to ring and to hear from some New Testament colleague: 'Paulus, our research has now finally removed the object of your ultimate concern; we cannot find your Jesus anywhere.'"[17] His point was not that Jesus's existence doesn't matter but that our knowledge of it is not dependent primarily upon an analysis of the past.

So far we have examined this strain of modern Christology as it manifested itself in three Protestant thinkers. It is also apparent in a

16. Ibid., 67.
17. Quoted in Langdon Gilkey, *Gilkey on Tillich* (New York: Crossroad, 1990), 151.

Catholic framework. The best known and most influential Catholic who worked in the Kant/Schleiermacher tradition was Karl Rahner. Though he was a professor of systematic theology, Rahner's starting point for theological analysis was almost invariably *Religionsphilosophie*—more precisely, a Kantian/Heideggerian philosophical anthropology. In every concrete act of knowing, the human being, says Rahner, is oriented to the horizon of all that can possibly be known, toward the fullness of being. And in every particular act of the will, he is lured toward the horizon of all that can possibly be desired, toward the good in itself. This orientation toward what Rahner calls *das heilige Geheimnis* (the Holy Mystery) constitutes the transcendentally religious structure of the human spirit; it is the human being's capacity to be a "hearer of the Word."[18] Like the feeling of absolute dependency, the categorical imperative, and ultimate concern, this standing in the presence of absolute mystery is the subjective existential ground for religion. It amounts, in Rahner's famous phrase, to a "supernatural existential," a basic orientation toward the supernatural present in the natural structure of the human spirit.

The opening section of *The Foundations of Christian Faith*, the closest that Rahner ever came to writing a complete systematics, is a detailed development of the anthropology that I have just sketched. Only in the second section does Rahner address the person of Jesus, placing him in the context of the general philosophical view. This approach—so structurally similar to Kant's, Schleiermacher's, and Tillich's—identifies Rahner as a modern. Jesus is presented as the fullest exemplification and realization of transcendental anthropology, as that human being who responded most completely and consistently to God's offer of grace. Rahner states this in a memorable adage: "Christology is fully developed anthropology; anthropology is incomplete Christology." Once more, Jesus is looked at not directly but obliquely as the prime exemplar of a general religious sensibility. In Tillich's *Systematic Theology*, the doctrine of God as the source of ultimate concern is extremely well developed, while the doctrine of Jesus is remarkably sketchy. So in Rahner, theological anthropology is articulated at great length, while Christology is quite thin. These imbalances are the result of the basic decision that both these theologians took to mute the specificity and strangeness of Jesus in favor of the relative accessibility of religious experience.

How do we assess this modern christological style that places emphasis on Jesus as symbol or cipher? In one sense, it grows up out of the classical concern to show the continuities between the Logos that appears in Jesus of Nazareth and the religiosity that is a natural dimension of the human

18. Karl Rahner, *Hearers of the Word* (New York: Herder and Herder, 1969), esp. 53–68.

spirit. From the time of Justin Martyr and Origen, Christian theologians have been keen to demonstrate this relationship, lest Jesus be construed as simply anomalous. Even Tertullian, who posed the famous rhetorical question "What does Athens have to do with Jerusalem?" nevertheless could speak of an *anima naturaliter Christiana*. Therefore that Christ should be placed in relationship to the moral clarity of the categorical imperative or to the intuitive sense of absolute dependency or ultimate concern is not only possible but theologically desirable.

A problem arises, however, when we consider the hermeneutical assumptions that govern this juxtaposition. In the modern thinkers that we have been analyzing, interpretive primacy is consistently given to the generic over the specific, so that Jesus is "positioned" by something beyond him. In Kant, for instance, it is not Jesus in his uniqueness who determines the content of the categorical imperative; rather, it is the imperative that renders Jesus intelligible as a religious symbol. And in Rahner, it is not the concrete Christ that specifies the nature of absolute mystery but rather the experience of the absolute mystery that renders Christ credible. But does this mode of interpretation adequately account for the sense of novelty and evangelical excitement that can be found on practically ever page of the New Testament and that animated the first proclaimers of the faith to preach Christ even at the risk of their lives? If Jesus is simply a symbol for or bearer of a general religious consciousness, why would his life and death matter so much, and why would people have to witness precisely to him? Even if we say, with Schleiermacher and Tillich, that the unsurpassable religious insight broke through with Jesus, why would we have to dwell on his story in all of its peculiarity once we had experienced absolute dependency or ultimate concern? Wouldn't he be much like the ladder that, having gotten us to the level we desire, could simply be kicked away? Would he not devolve—as in Roger Haight's very typically modern christological project—into one bearer of divinity among many?[19]

Another aspect of the Gospel witness that this strain of modern Christology tends to overlook is the summons to action. One could argue that the Gospels organize themselves around two poles: the call to conversion ("repent and believe the good news") and the call to mission ("go out to all the nations and preach the good news"). Though it has from the beginning included a contemplative dimension, Christianity is not essentially a contemplative form of life, as are, for example, Buddhism and Platonism. It is rather a mission and a way. In *The Grammar of Assent*, John Henry Newman distinguishes between what he calls "notional assent" and "real assent," the intellectual acquiescence that we give, respectively, to abstrac-

19. Roger Haight, *Jesus: Symbol of God* (Maryknoll, NY: Orbis, 1999), esp. 12–15.

tions and to particulars.[20] Thus, one assents notionally to the formulas and arguments in Aquinas's *Summa contra gentiles*, but one assents really to the north rose window at Notre Dame. When one wants, says Newman, to move others to action, one ought to appeal not to the notional but to the real, since abstractions engage the mind but particulars impel a person to act. So when Winston Churchill wanted to summon his compatriots to the defense of their homeland, he offered them not arguments but "blood, toil, tears, and sweat." Thus, what must stand at the center of the activity that is Christianity cannot be an abstraction, a principle, a sensibility, or a conviction, but rather Christ himself, the one from whom real assent can be elicited.

When the particularity of Jesus is read through the interpretive lens of abstract religion, conversion and mission are compromised. No one will give her life for the feeling of absolute dependency or for the sustenance of ultimate concern; but she might be willing to give her whole self to *this* Christ, *this* crucified and risen Lord.

Though he was reluctant to embrace Karl Barth's image of Christ's purely perpendicular relationship with the world, Balthasar was pleased to compare Jesus to a mountain flood that overwhelms the turbines pathetically poised to master it. Whatever receptive capacity there is in us (and Balthasar certainly affirmed this *capax Dei*), it is filled to the point of overflowing, finally overwhelmed, by the novelty and fullness of Jesus. This is furthermore why Balthasar claimed that Christian theology becomes truly compelling precisely at the point where Rahner's theological anthropology ends: it is not the human being in the presence of absolute mystery that finally matters but rather the Jesus who shows in an utterly surprising way the true nature of that mystery. It also explains why Balthasar kept focusing his (and our) theological attention on the concrete form that is Jesus (*Schau der Gestalt*): you have to look here, at him, and not at the hazy background that surrounds him.

The most elemental difficulty with the liberal Christology we've been examining—a difficulty that gives focus to the two problems already discussed—is that it compromises the proclamation of Jesus's divinity. In its refutation of Nestorianism, the Council of Ephesus in 431 maintained that Jesus cannot be construed simply as a "God-bearing man," someone who, like an ordinary saint, would point to God or be in close relationship with God.[21] Nestorius had referred to Jesus as divine, but he meant this only

---

20. John Henry Newman, *An Essay in Aid of a Grammar of Assent* (Notre Dame, IN: Univ. of Notre Dame Press, 1979), 49–52.

21. "If anyone dares to say that Christ was a God-bearing man and not rather God in truth, being by nature one Son, even as 'The Word became flesh,' and is made partaker of flesh and blood precisely like us, let him be anathema." *Decretals of the Council of Ephesus* in *Decrees of the Ecumenical Councils*, edited by Norman Tanner (London: Sheed and Ward, 1990), 60.

in the highly analogical sense that Jesus was transparent to God through the perfection of his moral and spiritual life. But the council insisted that this extrinsicist and relational reading failed to honor the radicality of the New Testament witness that in dealing with Jesus one is dealing with God, and hence it opted, in line with Nicaea and anticipating Chalcedon, for an ontological presentation. Are the modern Christologies of Kant, Schleiermacher, Tillich, and Rahner not susceptible to the charge of neo-Nestorianism? Can they account adequately for the distinction between Jesus and the great saints? Is the difference between the God-consciousness of Jesus and that of, say, Francis of Assisi only quantitative and not qualitative? Or more precisely, is the posing of the question around an issue such as God-consciousness or the feeling of ultimate concern not to be prejudiced necessarily in favor of a merely quantitative demarcation?

One of Balthasar's most trenchant critiques of Rahner's Christology is that Rahner cannot finally distinguish between the radical openness to God found in his Jesus and that found in Mary, the one who, in the depth of her being, said yes to the invitation of the Holy Spirit. The Council of Ephesus is helpful on just this point, because while it famously referred to Mary as *Theotokos* (God-bearer), it assiduously denied, as we saw, that Jesus could be similarly named. Jesus is not simply greater than Mary; he is somehow else. Are the largely symbolic interpretations that we have been considering capable of articulating this strangeness?

2

The Jesus of History

We turn now to a second major trend within modern Christology: the examination of Jesus through the use of historical-critical methods. If the symbolic approach was derived from Descartes's radical disjunction between interior and exterior, the historical style was derived from Descartes's interest in clear and distinct starting points and his accompanying distrust of distorting traditions. Just as the *cogito* (and its logical accompaniments) became the ground for certitude and the criterion for distinguishing what is valid from what is invalid in the philosophical tradition, so the Jesus of history, recouped through scientific examination, became for many modern theologians the ground and measure of what is adequate in the christological tradition. It would be a mistake, however, to see Descartes as the only principal source for this method, for Luther, with his deep concern to find the fundaments of the faith behind the obfuscations of the ecclesial heritage, is also a major inspiration. The fact that until the 1950s practically all of the practitioners of the historical-critical method were Protestant confirms this interpretation.

For our purposes, I will briefly analyze the work of two Catholics—Hans Küng and Edward Schillebeeckx—who in the mid-1970's made the historically recovered Jesus basic to their christological projects. As a young man, Hans Küng fell under the influence of Karl Barth, writing his doctoral dissertation on Barth's doctrine of justification and joining the circle of Hans Urs von Balthasar, one of the most important Catholic proponents of the Barthian method. The radical and uncompromising

Christocentrism of Barth is on clear display in Küng's treatise *On Being a Christian*. He insists that Christianity is not an ideology, a philosophy, a point of view, or a set of convictions but rather a movement that centers on the "dangerous memory" of the very particular figure Jesus of Nazareth.[1] But the question then arises: which Christ, which Jesus? It cannot, says Küng, be the Christ of "piety," for there are many conflicting images of Jesus that rise up from the religious practice and devotion of Christians: the Sacred Heart, the child in the Christmas crèche, the beardless shepherd of early Christian art, the Man of Sorrows so beloved of medieval artists, the Savior proclaimed by Billy Graham. How could one possibly decide which of these is normative? It cannot be the Christ of dogma, for the language of the doctrinal formulations of the first councils—nature, person, essence, etc.—is almost incomprehensible to modern people and, in fact, unfaithful to the biblical witness.[2] It cannot be the Christ of the "enthusiasts," ranging from Marxist revolutionaries to charismatics, rock singers to social activists, all of whom invoke Jesus but in a superficial and fragmentary way. Nor can it be the Christ of the novelists and poets, from Dante and Fyodor Dostoyevsky to Rainer Maria Rilke and Nikos Kazantzakis, for any author will fit Jesus into the framework of his literary project and his own aesthetic purpose. There is no guarantee, therefore, that he will reveal the authentic Jesus, even if he paints a deeply moving and theologically rich portrait.[3]

It must, Küng concludes, be the "real" Christ, and this turns out to be the Jesus described by the practitioners of the various types of modern biblical analysis categorized as "the historical-critical method." These include source criticism, literary criticism, and form and redaction criticism as well as the more straightforward "historical" criticism whose purpose is to ferret out the nuggets of verifiable facts buried in the biblical narratives. Do these intellectual practices produce faith? No, but "with the historical-critical method in this comprehensive sense, theology is provided with an instrument enabling the question about the true, real, historical Christ to be asked in a way that was simply not possible in former centuries."[4] Now, in other words, modern people have a tool that enables them to dig through the rubble of both the tradition and the New Testament itself in order to find the firm and indisputable starting point for an authentic Christology.

Unlike Küng, Edward Schillebeeckx did his earliest theological work in a more classically Catholic vein, commenting on ecclesiological and

---

1. Hans Küng, *On Being a Christian* (New York: Doubleday, 1976), 125–26.
2. Ibid., 131–32.
3. Ibid., 143–44.
4. Ibid., 156.

sacramental issues in light of Aquinas and contemporary philosophy. But starting in the 1960s he began to listen to the numerous criticisms of standard dogmatics that were coming from the camp of the biblical ex-egetes. Much systematic theological reflection, they charged, was done in dialogue with philosophy, both ancient and modern, but often with little or no connection to the Scriptures. And this indifference, they continued, was especially puzzling in light of the remarkable strides made in biblical analysis through the development of modern critical methods. With his books *Jesus: An Experiment in Christology* and *Christ: The Experience of Jesus as Lord*, Schillebeeckx responded to these challenges with a vengeance. Over the course of nearly two thousand pages, Schillebeeckx constructed a Christology that relied massively on the research of contemporary biblical exegetes.

In the methodological opening section of *Jesus: An Experiment in Christology*, Schillebeeckx makes his case for the use of historical-critical exegesis. He first remarks in the New Testament itself a disconcerting plurality of images, symbols, and theologies purporting to describe Jesus of Nazareth. Then, like Küng, he wonders whether there might be a central idea that could serve as a "constant unitive factor" amid all of this diversity, some pole around which the myriad perceptions of Jesus might reasonably be organized. He first eliminates several possibilities. It cannot be the Gospels themselves, taken either individually or as a whole, for within each Gospel and among the four, there remains an irreducible diversity of theological perception. Nor can it be a sort of canon within the canon, some "best of the best" of the Gospel witness, for such determinations remain hopelessly subjective (for instance, is Luther right in seeing the Pauline justification by faith alone as normative, or is Augustine right in seeing the command to love God and neighbor as determinative?). Nor can it be the most primitive picture of Jesus (supposing we could recover it), for even at the earliest stages of the tradition there is pluralism. Insisting that the Gospels are not psychological biographies, Schillebeeckx furthermore rules out that favorite criterion of the romantic searchers for Jesus, the self-consciousnes of the Lord. Finally, he questions the centrality of the doctrinal claims and *kerygmata* that can be found in the New Testament, for these too are plural, ambiguous, often at odds with one another.[5] What remains, he concludes, is not so much the "historical Jesus" as the Christian movement itself, a form of life that, despite its diversity, finds unity in the act of pointing to and speaking of the one Jesus of Nazareth. In other words, it is the Jesus as experienced and witnessed to by the first Christian communities that emerges as the unifying factor of a

5. Edward Schillebeeckx, *Jesus: An Experiment in Christology* (New York: Seabury, 1979), 53–55.

coherent Christology. Now how precisely is this experience accessed by contemporary researchers? Like Küng, Schillebeeckx here enthusiastically embraces historical-critical method: form criticism, redaction criticism, literary analysis, historical analysis with its criteria of coherence, discontinuity, and the rejection of Jesus's message.[6]

What picture of Jesus emerges from the application of the methodologies outlined by Küng and Schillebeeckx? In the case of Küng, Jesus was the preacher of the inbreaking kingdom of God, the primary meaning of which is that God's cause is humanity's cause, that God fosters human flourishing.[7] Jesus's table fellowship with the poor and destitute, his embrace of the sick and the sinful, his critiques of the Pharisees and temple authorities were all challenges to the religious and cultural status quo, which stands opposed to God's order.[8] Jesus's message to the people was to surrender totally to the will and purposes of God and to embody that surrender in acts of love and forgiveness of enemies. In connection with his preaching, Jesus performed some miracles, though many of the accounts of these signs are inventions or theologically motivated literary constructs.[9] The radicality of Jesus's preaching and lifestyle led to his rejection by the religious and political authorities and finally by every major group in his society: Essenes, Pharisees, Saducees, Romans, temple priests, Zealots.[10] The thoroughness of this opposition conduced almost inevitably to Jesus's arrest, trial, and crucifixion for blasphemy and sedition. After his death, Jesus presented himself alive again to his disciples. Though the resurrection cannot in the strict sense be categorized as an historical event, it was nonetheless more than a subjective experience or a literary expression of a theological conviction.[11] This great event must be interpreted as God's definitive affirmation of the life and teaching of Jesus, and it is only through the power of this event that the emergence of the Christian church can be adequately explained.

What does one make of the accounts of Jesus's birth and infancy as found in the Gospels of Matthew and Luke? They are, concludes Küng, almost totally legendary—theologically rich indeed but historically groundless. And what of the interpretation of Jesus's death as sacrificial? Though it has some scriptural basis (especially in the letter to the Hebrews), it is not central to the biblical witness and is certainly out of step with contemporary notions.[12] Most important, how, on the basis of historical-critical

6. Ibid., 91–95.
7. Küng, *On Being a Christian*, 251.
8. Ibid., 252–53.
9. Ibid., 231–35.
10. Ibid., 177–210.
11. Ibid., 349–30.
12. Ibid., 424–26.

analysis, do we answer the central christological question of the identity of Jesus? Küng takes seriously the traditional claim that Jesus is "truly God and truly man," but he attempts, on the basis of his research, a modern interpretation of that claim. Since from a strictly historical standpoint, the true humanity of Jesus is not really controversial, the real focus of Küng's reinterpretation is on the meaning of Christ's divinity. "The whole point of what happened in and with Jesus depends on the fact that, for believers, God himself as man's friend was present, at work, speaking, acting and definitively revealing himself in this Jesus who came among men as God's advocate and deputy, representative and delegate."[13] We notice something here that I remarked in the Christologies of Schleiermacher and his successors: the predilection for relational rather than strictly ontological language. A deputy or representative is someone who stands in for another, speaking for him and bearing his intention, but he is not to be identified with the one whom he represents, except in the most attenuated sense of the term. In speaking of Jesus as God's human delegate, Küng seems not far from the position that the Council of Ephesus rather explicitly condemned, that Jesus is the God-bearing man. As we saw above, Küng felt that the classical dogmatic language of person and nature was simply unintelligible to modern people, and here we see, in this language of representation and deputization, the substitution he proposes.

What is the portrait of Jesus that Schillebeeckx paints, using the brushes of historical-critical method and the colors of the earliest church's experience? Like Küng, Schillebeeckx puts great stress on Jesus's proclamation of the reign of God, and again like Küng, he tends to interpret that kingdom as God's advocacy of the *humanum*.[14] The nature of God's order was revealed in the parables and eschatological preaching of Jesus, but it was especially embodied in his acts of inclusion and love. Nowhere was this kingdom style of life more vividly on display than in Jesus's praxis of open and gracious table fellowship.[15] Jesus probably performed certain acts that awakened a sense of wonder in those around him and led to conflicting readings as to their provenance: from God or from Satan? In the context of the New Testament narratives, these stories were meant, above all, to communicate theological truths about "Jesus's freedom to do good" and the nature of the Kingdom. In his rather detailed analysis of the Gospel miracles, Schillebeeckx downplays their objectivity and historicity even more than Küng does.[16] As for Küng, so for Schillebeeckx it was

13. Ibid., 449.

14. Schillebeeckx, *Jesus*, 140–42.

15. Ibid., 200–2. John Dominic Crossan will develop this idea under the heading of Jesus's "open-commensality." See John Dominic Crossan, *The Historical Jesus: The Life of a Mediterranean Jewish Peasant* (San Francisco: HarperSanFrancisco, 1991), 261–64.

16. Schillebeeckx, *Jesus*, 183–94.

the countercultural quality of Jesus's message and lifestyle that excited enormous opposition from the religious and political leadership. Because his way of life challenged the patriarchal, domineering, and exclusivist practices of his time, he was hunted down and put to death by tenders of the status quo.

At this point, something remarkable clearly happened. Those who had misunderstood, betrayed, and abandoned Jesus came together to announce with great enthusiasm and purpose that the crucified one was alive. What was that something? In the course of nearly one hundred pages of dense argumentation, Schillebeeckx endeavors to show that it was, in its most basic form, an event of conversion experienced by the disciples of Jesus. The story of the empty tomb was most likely a later addition, and even if it were historically grounded, it would never be enough, in itself, to establish belief in the resurrection. Furthermore, the "appearances" of the risen Jesus cannot themselves be the source of resurrection faith, since they are not even present in the earliest strands of the Gospel tradition (they are absent from Mark and ambiguous in Matthew).[17] So what happened? When the appearance narratives are analyzed critically and theologically, three essential elements emerge: first, the initiative for the encounter with Jesus came not from the disciples but from Jesus himself; second, the disciples recognized and acknowledged the risen Lord; and third, they felt themselves, on the basis of the experience, commissioned, sent to proclaim.[18] The critic who probes behind these theologically colored accounts, seeking the real historical ground, comes up with something like the following. After the terrible death of Jesus, the disciples were profoundly discouraged and guilt ridden. But when they reflected, prob- ably at the prompting of Peter, on the teaching and ministry of Jesus, they realized that a God of radical forgiveness was at the heart of Jesus's life and proclamation. As this realization sank in, they felt forgiven by Jesus himself, the one who had mediated to them this new vision of God. Since only someone who is alive can offer forgiveness, they experienced and then announced Jesus as the risen Lord. Enlightened by the Lord, they began to speak of "seeing" him, as having encountered him after his death, and it was this basic experience that was given stylized expression in the Gospel accounts of the appearances of the risen Jesus.[19]

Schillebeeckx's reading of the encounter between Mary Magdalene and the risen Christ is especially illuminating. The tender exchange of names—Mary and *rabboni* (John 20:16)—indicates that "death has not shattered living communication with Jesus: that is, he continues after his

17. Ibid., 352.
18. Ibid., 353.
19. Ibid., 384.

death to offer those who are his a fellowship belonging to and constituting life."[20] In fact, on the basis of this story, Schillebeeckx goes so far as to suggest that Mary Magdalene may have had a role in the regathering of the disciples and the propagation of resurrection faith that was as basic as Peter's.

Now, having presented what historical-critical analysis yields regarding the experience of Jesus in the early Christian communities, Schillebeeckx endeavors to answer *the* christological question concerning the identity of this Jesus. Like Küng, he brackets the explicitly dogmatic language of the conciliar tradition, seeking to reinterpret it on the basis of something more elemental, in his case, the *Abba* experience of Jesus. Everything in Jesus's preaching and style of life—his open table fellowship, his praxis of forgiveness, his outreach to the marginalized—flowed from this intimate sense that he was the son of *Abba* God, the tender "daddy" who made and guides the universe. His entire ministry—up to and including his death—was an attempt to draw others into the power of that relationship.

What precisely constituted this intimate rapport that Jesus had with his heavenly Father? Schillebeeckx's answer is that it was a particularly intense and clearly felt intuition of creatureliness. Basic to the experience of being human is that one's existence, while remaining one's own, is rooted in and comes from the "other" who is God. A curious decentering of the ego occurs when one seeks out the deepest roots of one's own being. Even as we possess our identity, we know that we don't belong to ourselves. To borrow from the language of the early Christological disputes, we could say that every human personality is *enhypostatic*, which is to say, embedded in the personhood of God. In this sense, every creature is a "hypostatic union," and humans are those creatures who are fully conscious of their true ontological status. What is Jesus's *Abba* experience but the intensest and deepest mode of this general creaturely and human sense of rootedness in the being of God? "The human being aware of his creatureliness apprehends himself to be pure gift of God. Because of the totally unprecedented depth of Jesus's experience (of himself as gift of God, the Father) the faith of the Church . . . proceeded to call Jesus 'the Son.'"[21] If for Schleiermacher the uniqueness of Jesus was a matter of the unsurpassable intensity of his God-consciousness, for Schillebeeckx the special quality of Jesus is the particular "depth" of his sense of being a creature. In both cases, the differentiation between Jesus and other human beings is quantitative and not qualitative. And once more, as we saw in regard to Küng, the clear option is for relational rather than ontological language, or rather, the collapse of the latter into the former.

20. Ibid., 345.
21. Ibid., 655.

How do we assess these Christologies that take as their point of departure Jesus as recovered through historical-critical analysis? An adequate response would obviously require the writing of an entire book, but I can make at least some clarifying remarks. Like the "Jesus as symbol" approach, the "historical Jesus" Christology is rooted in elements and intuitions of the classical tradition. Küng and Schillebeeckx are quite right in insisting that Christianity must never devolve into a generic philosophy of life or symbolic system, that it must, on the contrary, maintain its clear and unambiguous connection to the very particular first-century Jew, Jesus of Nazareth. The Gospels, the Epistles of Paul, the first kerygmatic proclamations, the sermons of the earliest missionaries, the creeds and dogmatic statements of the patristic church all depend upon and circle around this Jesus. Therefore, in brushing away certain encrustations and obfuscations in the christological tradition and focusing our attention on the irreplaceable character of Jesus, Küng and Schillebeeckx and their historical-critical colleagues have done the church a great service. Furthermore, in insisting that the high dogmatic claims of Christology should be consistently informed by a biblical sensibility, the historical critics have compelled Christology to abandon mere flights of speculation and to remain, thereby, truer to its proper origins and ground. The "Jesus of history" can indeed function as a sort of check on unwarranted theological exploration.

That said, there remain, in my judgment, serious problems with the historical-critical method itself and therefore even more serious questions regarding the placing of that method at the heart of the christological enterprise. Given the long and powerful opposition, in Catholic circles, to critical study of the Bible, it is understandable that the first openings to such an undertaking would be met with enormous enthusiasm. The issuance of Pius XII's encyclical *Divino Afflante Spiritu* in 1943 opened the floodgates of modern Catholic biblical scholarship, and the conciliar document *Dei Verbum* served strongly to encourage that work. Furthermore, the early writings of Joseph Fitzmyer, Raymond E. Brown, Roland Murphy, John Kselman, and many others convinced Catholics that historical-critical analysis did not pose a threat to the faith or to the integrity of the Scripture as a revealed text.

But I wonder whether this initial enthusiasm allowed for the emergence of a certain uncritical spirit with regard to the new criticism. As has already been hinted above, the historical-critical spirit is deeply Protestant in the measure that it seeks to uncover the "real" and authentic Jesus who lies beneath a veil of theological and ecclesial distortions. If Luther and his colleagues were primarily concerned with such accretions as they appeared in the course of the Christian tradition, historical critics were only too willing to deal with them in the scriptural text itself. The Jesus recovered and presented by historical criticism thus became a canon within the canon, a core by which the rest of the Scripture (and tradition) could be judged. Whatever was coherent with the Jesus of history was valid; whatever was incongruent with that reconstruction—from New Testament descriptions and narratives to doctrinal formulations—was problematized, rejected, or radically reinterpreted. But this sort of one-sided privileging of the origins and the beginnings is out of step with a Catholic sense of organic development. John Henry Newman felt that the fully grown plant is far more revealing of the nature of the organism than is its seed, and that the mouth of a river is far more interesting and deep than its source. In a similar way, the literarily, spiritually, and theologically evolved portrait of Jesus is more instructive than any historical core, however carefully recovered. The Catholic instinct is not so much to assess the development by the origin as to appreciate the development as the full flowering of the origin.

One of the most faithful and careful practitioners of the historical-critical method today is John Meier, but Meier's famous thought experiment, proposed at the commencement of his multivolume quest for the historical Jesus, is indicative of the problem I have been discussing. Meier playfully suggests that we gather "a Jew, a Catholic, a Protestant, and an agnostic" in the basement of Harvard Divinity School and then compel them to come to agreement on the truth of the historical Jesus.[22] His books are meant to reflect that hypothetical consensus. There are two problems with this proposal. First, it assumes (in a typically modern way) that later developments, doctrinal convictions, and literary elaborations are necessarily distorting of the foundational historical truth and thus that all players in the conversation must set those assumptions aside if they want to come to clarity about the real Jesus. But perhaps those elements are not distorting overlay but rather indispensable illuminations of the Jesus of history, the Jesus who really existed. To be sure, those who cling to these convictions must be ready for a fight, but it is not the least bit clear to me that this would not be a fight worth having. Second, such a gathering will produce a picture of Jesus but one that is void of the very features that make Jesus so compelling (in different ways) to Catholics and Protestants and so problematic (for different reasons) to Jews and agnostics. And this blandly agreeable portrait—a Jesus stripped down to bare essentials—corresponds precisely to the modern fantasy of a rational and therefore presumably universal and nonviolent religion. But is this a Jesus worth honoring or arguing about—or for that matter, even a Jesus who resembles the feisty, prickly figure in the Gospels?

22. John P. Meier, *A Marginal Jew: Rethinking the Historical Jesus* (New York: Doubleday, 1991), 1–2.

Now when such a Jesus, reconstructed on historical-critical grounds, becomes, as in Küng and Schillebeeckx, the center of the christological undertaking and the criterion by which both the biblical and theological traditions are judged, it is obvious that we face the problem of reductionistic distortion. In place of a vibrant and interdependent *circumincessio* of biblical theology, image, doctrine, and practice, we have a univocal and unidirectional reduction of the many to the one, the artificially constructed Jesus of history becoming norm and measure of everything else. In light of this methodological move, it is not therefore the least surprising that both Küng and Schillebeeckx present flattened-out and rationalized readings of christological dogmas.

If Protestantism is one of the principal inspirations for historical-criticism, then philosophical modernity is another. David Dungan and others have reminded us that the roots of the critical method of biblical scholarship stretch back well beyond the nineteenth century, as far as the seventeenth century and the early modern period, especially the writings of the philosopher Baruch Spinoza.[23] Like many of the moderns, Spinoza was keenly interested in finding a universal form of religion that would appeal to people beyond their petty debates about particular revelations and doctrines. There were two moves central to Spinoza's religious program. First, he had to develop a purely rational, indeed geometric, understanding of God, the world, and human flourishing (this he did in the *Ethics*), and second, he had to debunk traditional readings of the Bible and reinterpret the Scripture along the lines of his rationalistic philosophy (and this he did in the *Tractatus Theologico-Politicus*). Central to Spinoza's metaphysical project was the identification of God and nature, or the sum total of all that exists. *God* did not designate, for him, a distinctive being or a supernatural subject, but rather the universe considered as a whole: *Deus sive natura*, in his well-known formula. Spinoza adapted and radicalized the Cartesian definition of substance—that which exists totally through itself—seeing that that description can apply only to the act of being itself, only to God.[24] The world in all its evolving complexity is but the showing forth of the primal substance, the collectivity of the "modifications" of God's being. Hence there is only *natura naturans* (God as ground) and *natura naturata* (God in his *modi*). The ethical life consists in a loving surrender to the finally unchangeable and unavoidable "purposes" of God, which is to say, the unfolding of *Deus sive natura*. The Spinozan ethic is hence a fascinating blend of ancient Stoicism and modern mechanistic science: since the universe is fixed, it is best simply to adjust oneself to it.

23. David Laird Dungan, *A History of the Synoptic Problem* (New York: Doubleday, 1999), esp. 198–260.
24. Baruch Spinoza, *The Ethics* (New York: Dover, 1955), 48–52, propositions 8–10.

Does the Bible speak these metaphysical and ethical truths? Yes, but in an extremely problematic and confusing way, since it does so through symbol, metaphor, anthropomorphizing imagery, and narrative. The contribution of the philosopher (and here Spinoza calls to mind Averröes) is to translate the jumbled and misleading language of Scripture into rational discourse. Dungan presents the Spinozan method of deconstruction/reconstruction in terms of four steps: first, "the negation of the traditional interpretation of all major biblical concepts," second, the "redefinition of these same concepts so that the Bible would be in accord with the worldview of mechanistic science," third, "prescription of a new method of historical biblical interpretation that would forever block people from finding the traditional concept of God," fourth, "the repetition of a few simple moral principles for people to cling to as 'the teaching of the Bible.'"[25] Thus in accord with the first and second of these hermeneutical prescriptions, an immanentism and thoroughgoing antisupernaturalism is elemental for a correct interpretation of the Bible. And in accord with the third and fourth, the careful Scripture reader must distract himself from the woolly metaphysics implied in the narratives with which he deals. In the course of the *Tractatus*, Spinoza throws up a jumble of "historical" questions concerning the text of the Bible itself and not its theological meaning: "Where did the books of Scripture originate? Who wrote them? How did they come into the collection? Were those who collected them also inspired? What do the words mean? What do the miracle stories mean? Did they actually happen?"[26] All of this constitutes, according to Dungan, a smokescreen or an elaborate changing of the subject, so that the attention of the biblical reader is now permanently on the opaque surface of the text and not on its spiritual and theological significance. The Spinozan critic places the biblical text itself so radically into question that one is no longer even tempted to seek its meaning on its own terms. The fourth prescription is another means to undermine the metaphysical integrity of the biblical witness, for it compels us to focus not on the primitive cosmology and theology of the scriptural authors but rather on the simple ethical message that they, almost despite themselves, manage to communicate: love God and love neighbor. Here, of course, we notice a link between Spinoza's rationalistic ethical interpretation of the Bible and Kant's reduction of Jesus to an archetype of the moral imperative.

To be sure, as it has developed from the seventeenth to the twenty-first century, the historical-critical method has undergone enormous changes, but one may wonder to what degree it is still marked by the antidogmatism, antisupernaturalism, immanentism, and moralism of its Spinozan begin-

25. Dungan, *History of the Synoptic Problem*, 212.
26. Ibid., 172.

nings. In both Küng and Schillebeeckx we notice, for instance, a bracketing
of the dogmatic claims of the church, followed by a reinterpretation of
those claims in light of a rationalist historical reconstruction. In Schillebeeckx (and to a lesser degree Küng), we find a skeptical rereading of
most of the miracle stories and a largely subjectivistic interpretation of the
resurrection of Jesus. Finally, and perhaps most strikingly, we see in both
theologians a tendency to express the essence of Christianity in basically
moral terms, not so much the private morality characteristic of Kant but
the postmodern political ethic of inclusiveness, equality, and collective
human flourishing. All of these Spinozan assumptions and prejudices can
be seen even more clearly in many of the recent participants in the "third
quest" for the historical Jesus: Marcus Borg, Burton Mack, and especially
John Dominic Crossan.[27]

I do not feel that all of those who practice some form of historical criticism are burdened with the weight of the entire Spinozan program, but I
do think that Christians ought to be, at the very least, wary of an approach
with such a questionable provenance. And I certainly contend that the
placing of this method at the very heart of the theological program is, at
best, problematic and at worst disastrous for Christian theology. If the
attitude toward the world opened up by the scriptural narratives—in all
of its metaphysical and supernatural density, in all of its strangeness—is
one of skeptical rationalism, then the uniqueness and power of the biblical
worldview are fatally compromised. Once more, I am convinced that some
version of historical criticism can be employed in the theological project,
but provided that it is placed in a critical *circumincessio* with dogmatic
and liturgical perceptions.

This leads to a third consideration. Balthasar has frequently complained
about the aggressive rationalism of historical criticism, by which he means
its tendency to dissect the biblical forms, analyzing them into their com-
ponent parts rather than seeing them as wholes. Since "dissection can take
place only on a dead body," this process presumes that biblical stories,
characters, and patterns are no longer living spiritual realities, integrated
totalities. Like the Newtonian scientist criticized by Johann van Goethe,
the historical critic thus assembles data but misses organic life. What, for
Balthasar, is the proper approach? It is one that reads the biblical texts
"in the Spirit," for it was in the Holy Spirit and for his purposes that they
were written. When the historical critic places a strictly analytical grid
over the biblical text, he will almost necessarily distort what he seeks to
interpret, for that text was not composed in accordance with rationalist presuppositions. It is the great form (*Gestalt*) of Jesus that lies at the

27. See Ben Witherington III, *The Jesus Quest: The Third Search for the Jew of Nazareth*
(Downers Grove, IL: InterVarsity Press, 1997), 58–125.

heart of the New Testament—whether presented in narrative style in the Gospels, as apocalyptic in the book of Revelation, or as the object of doctrinal and pastoral meditation in the Pauline epistles—and this form is fully accessible only to those who approach it in the Spirit. Balthasar once commented that the windows of a Gothic cathedral are unimpressive, drab, unintelligible when seen from the outside. Only when one enters the church and sees the light streaming through them do the windows reveal their beauty and narrative density. So the Bible, when viewed from the "outside," from an analytical distance, necessarily appears flat and uninspired, but that same Scripture, when surveyed from inside the life of the church, through the light of doctrine, practice, and prayer, takes on depth, color, and spiritual power. Again, this is not to encourage naiveté or credulousness in biblical interpretation; but it is to summon the reader of the Bible to respect the distinctively spiritual and ecclesial nature of the documents that she approaches.

These observations lead to a final concern. At the conclusion of chapter 1, I remarked that the "Jesus as symbol" approach conduces toward a severely attenuated expression of the divinity of Christ. Jesus was, at best, the paradigmatic human being who pointed beyond himself to the Mystery or the moral ideal. We confront a similar problem with the historical Jesus Christology. When the historically reconstructed Jesus is construed as the criterion for determining the meaning of Christian faith, we find, with Küng, that Jesus is but the "deputy" or "representative" of God and, with Schillebeeckx, that he is but the human with a particularly rich experience of childlike dependence upon God. But again we face the problem of explaining what I have referred to as the excitement that percolates throughout the New Testament. Why precisely would first-century Jews like Peter, Paul, Barnabas, and John have made the proclamation of one more prophet, one more human spokesperson, the very center of their lives, even to the point of courting death that others might know of him? Why would the table-fellowship-practicing and counterculturally inclusive Jesus be of *such* significance that one could, in the words of Paul, "count all as loss" in comparison to him? And why, for that matter, would the first proclaimers of Jesus have shown almost no interest in his life and teaching—as rich and important as they undoubtedly are—in their enthusiasm to speak of his resurrection from the dead? In a word, a reductively historical-critical assessment of Jesus just does not make sense of the *difference* of the one whom the New Testament authors called the Christ.

3

Doctrine and Narrativity

Both of the approaches presented so far look away from the same thing. The Kant-Schleiermacher-Tillich school looks away from the specificity of the narratives concerning Jesus in order to find the religious sensibility that they indicate, and the Küng-Schillebeeckx school looks away from those same narratives in order to find the historical core that they, at the same time, contain and mask. The practitioners of the liberal approach look, in a sense, to something bigger than the narratives (religion), and the practitioners of the historical-critical approach to something smaller (the real Jesus), but both rather pointedly miss the narratives themselves. A sign of this is a curious separation discernible in both camps. The liberals tend to put Jesus aside in order to concentrate on the "Christ" that he bears (Tillich's reading of the cross as the putting to death of Jesus in order for the unconditioned to be seen is the best example of this tendency), while the historians tend to set Christ aside in order to get at Jesus (both Küng's and Schillebeeckx's relative impatience with classical christological dogma is a sign of this tendency).

But the first of the Gospels commences with this simple declaration: "The beginning of the good news of Jesus Christ, the Son of God" (Mark 1:1). The first telling of the *euangelion* is a presentation in narrative form of Jesus as the Christ, the anointed of God. In the course of the story, we will learn how and why those two names fit together; we will see how the meaning of Jesus is illumined by the title "Christ" and how the meaning of that title is illumined by the narratives concerning Jesus. In a word, the good news is told in the measure that "Jesus" and "Christ" enter into a relationship of mutual interpretation, each existing in the hermeneutical light of the other. Any separating of the two will result in the undermining of the gospel. More to the point, the fact that this story is *news* indicates that we are not to look under, around, or over it in order to get the point. Rather, the story itself, the narrative of Jesus as the Christ, in all of its peculiarity, surprise, and novelty *is the point*. Ludwig von Beethoven once played one of his piano concertos to a small audience. After the performance, one of the listeners said, "But what does it mean?" Indignant, Beethoven sat down and played it through again. It meant precisely what it was, nothing more or less.

When another Ludwig, Wittgenstein, was a student of Bertrand Russell in the years just prior to World War I, he sought the universal logical form that, he supposed, undergirded all languages. His hope, so typically modern, was that in finding the overarching and unifying form of communication, he could dissolve many of the pseudoproblems of philosophy produced by linguistic oddities and anomalies.[1] But in his later writings, Wittgenstein rather vigorously turned away from this project of his youth. He became convinced that there is no basic or unifying linguistic form but rather that each language has its own integrity, style, set of rules, and peculiar genius. Languages are in fact, he famously concluded, like games, and the only way to learn them is by playing them.

The Gospels—for which Wittgenstein himself had an interesting feel— are not primarily religious texts, repositories of spiritual wisdom, or archaeological sites; they are more like a language that we learn by speaking or a game that we are compelled to enter into. And just as a language can never really be learned through translation, so the Gospels cannot be known through transposition into more familiar "religious" or "historical" frameworks. Or to use a more Barthian metaphor, they constitute a densely textured world that cannot be facilely compared to any other world, that must instead be explored on its own terms. One doesn't teach an adept to play baseball by showing her how the game is a particular expression of the generic category of "sports," though that logical relationship might hold; nor does one do so by indicating at every turn how the moves and rules of baseball are like and unlike those of football or hockey, though those analogies and comparisons might be interesting. Rather, one would invite the prospective player onto the field, teaching her how to handle the instruments of the game, showing her the requisite moves of sliding, throwing, hitting, and fielding, compelling her arms and legs and head to

1. How appropriate that, at the prompting of G. E. Moore, Wittgenstein entitled his first great philosophical effort *Tractatus Logico-Philosophicus* in conscious imitation of Spinoza, another modern seeking an Urform of language.

move in perhaps unexpected ways, instructing her in the rules precisely as her play brings her up against the limits of the game. Drawing her into the world of baseball, one would show her how to move, think, gesture, and strategize like a baseball player. So we draw others into the biblical frame of reference—its assumptions, characters, perspectives, typical questions, modes of behavior, theology—and thereby instruct them in a new way of thinking, moving, and deciding.

When, at the beginning of John's Gospel, two of John the Baptist's disciples approach Jesus, the Lord turns round on them and asks, "What are you looking for?" They do not respond as we might expect, requesting wisdom or direction or insight. Instead, they answer the question with another question: "Where are you staying?" (John 1:38). The term *stay* (*menein*) is replete with spiritual overtones in the fourth Gospel. It indicates where someone roots himself, where he derives his spiritual power. Hence "the Father and I will stay with you," and "I remain in the Father and the Father in me" (see John 14:18–23). So the disciples, in inquiring where he stays, are asking Jesus *about himself*, to show them the source of his life. Obviously pleased with their question, Jesus says, "Come and see" (John 1:39). They will find what they seek, not simply by listening to his speech but by watching him at close quarters, moving in with him, participating in his world. So the one who today seeks to understand Jesus cannot be content with either religious abstraction or historical archaeology; rather, she must stay with him. She must enter into his distinctive way of being, as this has been made available through the dense tangle of the biblical narratives.

Now at this point we face an obvious difficulty. Doesn't all this talk of the uniqueness and irreducibility of the biblical text lead to the embrace of the Protestant *sola scriptura* principle, and does it not entail at least the bracketing of doctrinal language and liturgical practice—all of which would be rather dramatically at odds with a postliberal Catholicism? How does high and relatively abstract doctrine relate to the very particular "world" that I've been describing? Newman contended that ideas don't exist on the printed page but rather in the play of lively minds, which is to say, in the give-and-take of question, analysis, judgment, and debate.[2] The same must undoubtedly be said of narrative worlds. While retaining their basic form, they unfold and develop as they are read, discussed, lived in, and fought over by those who participate in them. This process of theological appropriation of the story of Jesus commences within the biblical world itself, as is evident in the magnificent meditations on the significance of Jesus in John's Gospel and in the sometimes overwrought wrestling with

2. John Henry Newman, *An Essay on the Development of Christian Doctrine* (Westminster, MD: Christian Classics, 1968), 33–36.

the meaning of the cross and resurrection in the letters of Paul. And it continues unceasingly throughout the tradition—indeed that process *is* the tradition itself. Therefore, in the strict sense, we couldn't bracket doctrinal development even if we wanted to; willy-nilly, we enter the densely textured world of the Bible with the help of various interpretive guides.

To get a clearer sense of precisely what it is that doctrines do, I suggest we stay with this last image. To find one's way in an unfamiliar world, one requires an experienced guide, someone who has become so at home in the place that he knows its highlights, its dangers, its history, its denizens, and the various paths that lead through it. In William Faulkner's great story *The Bear*, young Ike McCaslin learns to hunt and navigate in the deep woods through the ministrations of Sam Fathers, his half-black, half–Native American mystagogue.[3] So the journeyer through the thickets of the biblical world requires a sort of mystagogic initiation. Doctrines perform this function in a number of ways. First, they have a heuristic function, indicating to the biblical seeker what she ought to be looking for and how to find it. When one enters a strange world, she can suffer from disorientation brought on by sensory and cognitive overload; what she needs is someone to show where her attention ought to be focused so that the entirety of the scene can eventually be taken in. Doctrines similarly indicate, in an orienting way, the key elements and features in the landscape of the biblical world. For instance, the two-natures doctrine of Chalcedon (which I will discuss shortly) shows that as the story of Jesus unfolds, both a divine and a human narrative are simultaneously on display. Thus, in the complex story of this first-century Jewish prophet, we should be attentive not only to human psychology, political dynamics, and religious struggles typical of the time but also and especially to the features of God.

Second, doctrines serve to resolve certain puzzlements that threaten to block further investigation. When exploring unknown terrain, a person might come to an unfordable stream. Until he is shown a way over or around or through, he cannot continue his exploration. Similarly, when working through the dense biblical narratives, anomalies, difficulties, and aporias arise: How, for example, can Jesus be the forgiver of sins and calmer of storms *and* be limited in knowledge and power? Or how could the especially beloved Son of God be allowed to suffer and die on a cross? If these and similar difficulties remain unaddressed, they can simply lock up the mind and shut down the investigation. Christological doctrines can function here as bridges over the stream, resolutions sufficient for the furtherance of progress. Thus, the various doctrinal interpretations

3. Robert Barron, *And Now I See: A Theology of Transformation* (New York: Crossroad, 1998), 93–101.

of the death of Jesus as victory (as in many of the fathers) or satisfaction (as in Anselm) or love engendering love (as in Abelard) allow the mind to overcome its hesitancies with regard to the cross.

Third, doctrines serve a negative or delimiting purpose, indicating the modes of interpretation that are counterproductive to the proper understanding of the story. As a guide might urge one to stay on a marked path or as guardrails direct a car on the highway, so doctrines keep one's mind on relatively correct or productive hermeneutical avenues. Thus, the anti-Arian doctrine of the Council of Nicaea indicates how one oughtn't to read the story of Jesus, that is, as a mythologically inspired account of a demigod; and the anti-Nestorian doctrine of the Council of Ephesus turns one against an interpretation of Jesus as merely a human spiritual hero.

Fourth, doctrines can function as pithy and evocative encapsulations of the meaning of the story. Two of the earliest "doctrines" of Christianity are the kerygmatic formula "Jesus is Lord!" and Paul's shorthand *Christos Iesous*. Both are ecstatic summaries of the core meaning of the career, preaching, miracles, death, and resurrection of Jesus. They reflect the *Eureka!* moment, the grasping of the heart of the matter in regard to Jesus and his story. More developed forms of this mode of doctrinal expression include "in Christ God was reconciling the world to himself" (2 Cor. 5:19), "it is no longer I who live, but it is Christ who lives in me" (Gal. 2:20), and "the Word became flesh and lived among us" (John 1:14). As the process of sifting, weighing, and meditating unfolds, these become even more refined and give rise to the abstract doctrines of Chalcedon and the sustained analyses of Augustine's *De Trinitate* and Aquinas's treatment of the incarnation in the fourth book of the *Summa contra gentiles*. Even these more abstruse expressions can be seen as organic developments of the original kerygmatic exclamations. Balthasar spoke of the *Ganze im Fragment* (the whole in the fragment) quality of each pericope in the Gospels, implying that each particular scene could be interpreted as the totality of the story in miniature.[4] Doctrines, in this final mode I have been describing, have a similar quality. In the two-natures teaching of Chalcedon, for example, the whole of the story is on display in iconic form.

Now in all of their modalities—heuristic, clarifying, protective, and encapsulating—doctrines circle around and return to the originating narratives. At their best (and it is only fair to admit that sometimes speculative developments are in fact distorting), they comment upon and illumine the narratives from which they sprang. So important is this commentary and illumination that, in certain cases, doctrines and theological formulations, though clearly derivative, are indispensable to the interpretation of the

4. Hans Urs von Balthasar, *The Glory of the Lord: A Theological Aesthetics*, vol. 1, *Seeing the Form* (San Francisco: Ignatius, 1982), 512–13.

core stories. As the tradition has evolved, certain moments of insight and perception have occurred that are so powerful that they cannot be ignored in subsequent readings of the stories. Therefore, though the grounding narratives have a clear chronological and substantive primacy over the doctrines, both narratives and doctrines exist in a sort of inseparable *circumincessio*. The Vatican II document *Dei Verbum* expressed this complex relationship well. It taught that Scripture and tradition are not separate sources of revelation, precisely because tradition refers and points to Scripture, but it held, nevertheless, to the unavoidable (and finally welcome) *Ineinander* of the two.[5]

Granted the inseparable relationship between narrative and doctrine, can we make a methodological decision with regard to starting points in theological investigation? As I will argue at some length in the following chapter, starting point is a particularly modern preoccupation. In fact, it is the most salient feature of the foundationalism flowing from Descartes and his intellectual successors. I think it is counterproductive to look for a unambiguous *point de départ* for the christological project. Whether we like it or not, we are born in the stream, and there is no way of ever extricating ourselves from it to get the view from the bank. That is to say, we are immersed from the beginning in the flow of narrative and doctrine, appreciating one necessarily in light of the other. Therefore, just as it is altogether possible (and for certain purposes, preferable) to commence with the biblical narratives, it is also possible (and for other purposes, preferable) to commence with the doctrinal guides.

I have decided to look at the narratives of the New Testament through the lens of certain central christological doctrines and speculative frameworks. I do so for two basic reasons. In both of the major approaches considered above, the classical doctrinal statements concerning Jesus get fairly short shrift. The Schleiermacher-Tillich-Rahner tradition tends to interpret them in light of present religious experience, and the Küng-Schillebeeckx tradition tends to approach them with an extreme suspicion, convinced that they will distort the picture of the real Jesus. A sign of the first tendency is Schleiermacher's famous treatment of the doctrine of the Trinity in an appendix to the *Glaubenslehre*: he placed this central doctrine in a subordinate position in his dogmatics, since it didn't find any correspondence in the experience of absolute dependency. And a sign of the second is Küng's rather cavalier dismissal of the language of the early

---

5. "Further, Holy Scripture requires to be read and interpreted in the light of the same Spirit through whom it was written. . . . All that concerns the way to interpret Scripture is ultimately subject to the judgment of the church, to which God has entrusted the commission and ministry of preserving and interpreting the word of God." *Decretals of the Second Vatican Council: Dei Verbum*, para. 12, in *Decrees of the Ecumenical Councils*, edited by Norman Tanner (London: Sheed and Ward, 1990), 977.

councils as simply unintelligible to modern readers. Perhaps it is my slightly playful desire to redress the imbalance that leads me to commence with the doctrinal heritage. But second, and more seriously, I wish to affirm the unapologetically ecclesial nature of this project. I don't think scholars should even attempt to situate themselves outside of the guiding and defining hermeneutical principles of the great Christian tradition. Our hermeneutic of suspicion with regard to doctrine has, in recent years, been overworked; it is time to supplement it with a grateful acknowledgment that the Holy Spirit has had at least something to do with the unfolding of the tradition, especially in the key moments when it the tradition has, as it were, gathered and defined itself. With this ecclesial confidence, I will attempt to read the narratives concerning Jesus as the Christ through the imposition of certain doctrinal and theological grids.

Four Doctrinal Guides

The first hermeutical guide I wish to consider—the "two-natures" doctrine of the Council of Chalcedon—is in some ways the most important dogmatic claim ever made by the Christian church. In defining precisely who Jesus is, it implicitly sets out the Christian view of both God and the world and shows the modalities of the divine-nondivine relationship. It is thus a view of the whole, a lens through which all that is can be viewed. It would be far beyond the purview of this book to examine in detail the historical setting of the council and the various factors—political, ecclesial, philosophical—that contributed to the christological formula that it produced. Suffice it to say that after oscillations between a hyper-emphasis on the divinity of Jesus (various forms of monophysitism), a hyper-emphasis on his humanity (Nestorianism), and odd compromises between the two (forms of Arianism), Chalcedon settled on a thoroughly paradoxical both/ and statement of the full divinity and full humanity of Christ. In this the council fathers did far more than cobble together a relatively adequate formulation of the doctrine of the incarnation; they effectively preserved the strangeness and uniqueness of Christian faith itself.

In line with the letter of Pope Leo the Great, which had a profound impact on the council's deliberations, the statement rocks back and forth between powerful statements of unity and diversity.[6] In the central sec-

6. "So following the saintly fathers, we all with one voice teach the confession of one and the same Son, our Lord Jesus Christ: the same perfect in divinity and perfect in humanity, the same truly God and truly man, of a rational soul and a body; consubstantial with the Father as regards his divinity, and the same consubstantial with us as regards his humanity . . . acknowledged in two natures which undergo no confusion, no change, no division, no separation; at no point was the difference between the natures taken away through the union, but rather the property

tion of the formula—lines 14 through 45—there are six variations of the word *autos* (he, one, and the same). The authors never want us to forget that we are dealing with one reality, Jesus the Son of God. But this one Lord is perfect in humanity and perfect in deity (*teleion en anthropoteti kai teleion en theoteti*), a hybrid of two distinct natures (*en duo phusesin*), which are so clearly demarcated that they are described, even in their unity, as "unconfused, unchanged, undivided, and inseparable" (*asugchutos, atreptos, adiairetos, achoristos*). What does this coming together of two radically distinct natures into a real ontological unity entail? As we have seen, it implies that the natures in question—divine and human—must, despite their obvious differences, be essentially noncompetitive. But we know from direct experience that human nature is indeed competitive with other worldly natures. To be itself, it stands over and against the whole panoply of other finite things. It can *become* another nature only by being absorbed into it (if it were, say, devoured by another creature) or by devolving into it (if it were, for instance, burned to ashes). We could never speak (except in the most playful and poetic way) of a horse-human or a man-tree. To be sure, we could imagine some fanciful hybrid of worldly natures, such as a centaur, but this would not be, in the strict sense, a horse-human but rather a mixture of elements characteristic of each species. The point is this: there is a mutual exclusivity in regard to finite natures, so that any one is quite properly named in contrast to all others.

Therefore, if in Jesus a divine and human nature come together noncompetitively in ontological unity, there must be something altogether different about the divine nature. The divine way of being must not be a worldly nature, one type of creaturely being among many; rather, it must be *somehow else*. The difference between divinity and creatureliness (unambiguously affirmed by the Chalcedon formula) must be a noncontrastive difference, unlike that which obtains between finite things. God is indeed other than any worldly nature, but he is, if I can put it this way, *otherly other*. Nicholaus of Cusa expressed this paradox neatly when he said that God is both *totaliter aliter* (totally other) and the *Non-Aliud* (the nonother). And it is precisely this qualitatively different kind of otherness that allows for the union described by the Chalcedonian fathers. If God were a being in or alongside of the world, he could become something else only through aggression or compromise. But God becomes a creature without ceasing to be God (Jesus is *theon alethos)* and without overwhelming the creature he becomes (Jesus is also *anthropon alethos*). Were God

---

of both natures is preserved and comes together into a single person." *Decretals of the Council of Chalcedon*, in *Decrees of the Ecumenical Councils*, edited by Norman Tanner (London: Sheed and Ward, 1990), 86.

only relatively other than the world, and not absolutely other, this sort of nonaggressive unity would be impossible.

This means that the proximity of God is not a threat to a creature but, on the contrary, that which allows the creature to be most fully itself. If a fellow creature were to enter into the very constitution of my being, I would be the victim of an aggression, and my freedom and integrity would be undermined. But the true God can enter into the most intimate ontological unity with a creature, and the result is not diminution but enhancement of creaturely being. God and the worldly are therefore capable of an ontological coinherence, a being-in-the-other, so that each can let the other be even as they enter into the closest contact. This has nothing to do with distantiation or indifference; rather it is the letting-be that is characteristic of nonviolence and love, willing the good of the other as other. God can give the gift of his own existence without being diminished himself and without aggressing the one who receives the gift. In our greatest acts of love, we barely approach this kind of love of which the noncontrastively transcendent God is capable. Irenaeus's counterintuitive claim *Gloria Dei homo vivens* (the glory of God is a human being fully alive) finds its metaphysical ground in the two-natures doctrine.

We have seen that the Chalcedonian fathers affirm the duality of natures within a fundamental unity of being. In the later section of the formula, they give a more precise metaphysical account of this unity. The two natures in their integrity are united in one person (*prosopon*) or subsistence (*hypostasin*), which is identified as "one and the same only-begotten Son, God, Word, Lord Jesus Christ" (*ton auton huion monogene theon logon kurion Iesoun Christon*). Greek metaphysics dictates that a nature, which is in itself an abstraction, becomes real in the measure that it is borne or instantiated in a principle of subsistence. When the nature is a rational one, the instantiation is referred to as a person. The novelty in the case of the Chalcedonian doctrine, of course, is that the person in question instantiates not one but two natures, viz., those oddly compatible divine and human essences. That the bearer is identified as the second person of the Trinity, the divine Son of God, is of great moment, for by such a move the Chalcedonian fathers explicitly state what is implied in the two-natures claim: that the coming together of divinity and humanity is possible only through the power of God. No worldly subsistence could bear the weight or tolerate the juxtaposition of the divine and human natures.

And this has the further implication that the union being described can never be interpreted adequately from the humanward side, but only from the Godward side. Stated more spiritually, this means that the coming together of divinity and humanity is not possible through any kind of human striving or creaturely aspiration upward. The grasping attempted by Adam and Eve, the building of the Tower of Babel, justification through works—all are metaphysically ruled out by the doctrine of the divine hypostatization of the two natures. It is only through a divine Gift, through grace, that divine-human unity can be affected.

Here we notice the essential asymmetricality of the divine-nondivine rapport. Though the two natures come together without mixing, mingling, and confusion, though they are equally maintained in their integrity and independence, a greater weight is given to the divine.

In the course of a conference on religion and postmodernity, Jacques Derrida asked John Milbank to comment on the play between immanence and transcendence in the incarnation. Milbank responded that though the incarnation involves both immanence and transcendence (both humanity and divinity), it is predicated upon and made possible by transcendence.[7] This catches well the unique balance and rhythm of the Chalcedonian statement. It is never right to interpret Chalcedon as implying that there is simply a coequality of divinity and humanity in Jesus, an equilibrium of the two, *tout court*. Rather, the two natures—divine and human—are able to be juxtaposed and concurrently instantiated only because of the metaphysical primacy and power of God. In much contemporary Christology there is a tendency to emphasize the humanity of Jesus because there has been, allegedly, an overstress on his divinity. In the measure that the integrity of the human nature of Jesus has been compromised in some older, implicitly monophysite, theologies, this instinct is a good one. But inasmuch as older Christologies were reverencing the legitimate asymmetry to which I have been pointing, the intuition is problematic and deeply misleading.

What therefore is this subtle metaphysical statement telling us about the New Testament narratives concerning Jesus of Nazareth? It is telling us that when we read the stories of Jesus, we will be seeing simultaneously a paradigmatic display of divinity and humanity. A human nature—mind, will, imagination, personality, aspirations, in all of their cultural determinations and limitations—will be shown in the tightest connection with, and subordination to, a noncompetitive divine nature. The very juxtaposition of divinity and humanity will indicate at every turn the hyper-generosity and other-orientation of the true God. If Chalcedon is correct, the God revealed in the New Testament narratives is one who pours himself out fully for the good of the other, the one who is most himself precisely in the act of letting the other be fully alive. Furthermore, the coming together of the natures shows that authentic humanity is disclosed not in autonomy but in a kind of theonomy, a surrender to the will and purposes of God. What we should look for in the New Testament stories, if we take Chalcedon as our guide, is a meeting of two ecstasies, divine and human: the

7. See John D. Caputo, *Questioning God* (Bloomington: Indiana Univ. Press, 2001), 67.

always prior and ever greater self-gift of God confronting a responsive and grateful self-gift on the part of humanity—God in Christ reconciling the world to himself.[8]

This properly ecstatic quality comes to even fuller expression in the second of our theological schemas: Thomas Aquinas's account of the incarnation at the beginning of the third part of the *Summa theologiae*. Aquinas's treatment, which draws on the wealth of the patristic and philosophical traditions available to him, amounts to a densely textured commentary on the laconic Chalcedon formula. The first question that Thomas poses is not so much metaphysical as aesthetic: *utrum fuit conveniens Deum incarnari* (whether it was fitting for God to become incarnate).[9] The objections center on the distastefulness, the aesthetically and morally unpleasant quality, of the coming together of the divine and human. Since the supremely good God is from all eternity without flesh, it would be *inconveniens* if, at a particular time, he would condescend to unite himself with a human nature; things that are infinitely distant are most unfittingly joined; and it would be highly problematic were the very highest reality to be contained in the smallest.[10] Though ostensibly they are defending the primacy and purity of God, all of these objections could also be read to reflect the creaturely distaste for an invasive and overbearing presence of God in the world. Wouldn't it be better, more aesthetically pleasing, if the Creator and creatures stayed in their proper metaphysical places?

Thomas's *Respondeo* is of great interest because, in answer to this absolutely key question in Christian theology, he departs from his customary reliance on the divine name of Being and considers God under the rubric "good." Whether a quality is fitting in regard to a given thing must be determined in the measure that that quality is suited to its nature. Thus, reasoning is fitting to human beings, who are properly called rational animals. But the very nature of God is goodness (*bonitas*), and thus whatever pertains to the essence of the good is most fittingly ascribed to God. At this point Aquinas turns to a favorite source, the *Divine Names* of Dionysius the Areopagite. According to this author, who for Thomas had a quasi-apostolic authority, the good is *diffisivum sui*; it tends by its very nature *se aliis communicare* (to communicate itself to others). "Thus it pertains to the nature of the supreme good to communicate itself in the supreme mode to a creature. And this is accomplished to the highest degree through the joining of a created nature to itself so that from three—the Word, a soul, and flesh—one person is made. . . . Hence it is

8. Robert Barron, *Thomas Aquinas: Spiritual Master* (New York: Crossroad, 1996), 57–59.
9. Thomas Aquinas, *Summa theologiae* (Milan: Marietti, 1952), 3a q. 1, art. 1.
10. Ibid.

evident that it was fitting that God become incarnate."[11] In many ways, the whole radicality of Christian faith is contained in these words. Unlike the gods of pagan mythology, whose greatness consisted in the hoarding of privilege and praise for themselves, the true God manifests his onto-logical perfection and goodness precisely in his capacity for self-gift, for *kenosis*. Since God, by nature, is a being-for-others, his own nature is no more fully revealed than in the act by which he raises a creaturely nature to participate in the divine life.

The aesthetics of the incarnation are further explored in the second article of question 1: "whether it was necessary for the reparation of the human race that the Word of God become incarnate."[12] Thomas wrestles in this article with the theological heritage of Anselm, for whom the incarnation followed with a sort of strict logical necessity from the facts of sin and the justice of God. Thomas seems uneasy with the rigor and quasi-necessitarianism of Anselm's account and opts for a more nuanced reading of the rationale for the divine condescension. In his *Respondeo*, he distinguishes between an absolute necessity and a necessity of "con-venience," illustrating them, as is his wont, with rather homely examples. Food, he tells us, is absolutely necessary for the maintenance of bodily life, whereas a horse is necessary for travel only in the sense that one moves more speedily and conveniently by horse than by foot. In the first and stricter sense of the term, God's incarnation, he says, was not necessary, since "God through his omnipotent power could have repaired human nature in many other ways."[13] Presumably God could simply have declared human beings forgiven or could have contrived another means for the mediation of his salvation. However, in the second and more flexible sense of the word, the incarnation was indeed necessary for the redemption of the human race, for there was no more fitting, "convenient," perfect, aesthetically satisfying way for God to save the world.

In exploring the grounds for this claim, Thomas demonstrates the human ecstasy awakened by God's ecstatic gift of self. For what makes the en-fleshment of God so appropriate is the way it evokes a responsive and surprising self-transcendence in those human beings who see it and take it in. First, faith (the ecstasy of the mind) is stirred to full expression be-cause, in Christ, God himself is speaking through a human mind and voice.

11. "Unde ad rationem summi boni pertinet quod summo modo se creaturae communicet. Quod quidem maxime fit per hoc quod naturam creatam sic sibi coniungit ut una persona fiat ex tribus, Verbo, anima et carne. . . . Unde manifestum est quod conveniens fuit Deum incarnari" (ibid.).

12. "Utrum fuerit necessarium ad reparationem humani generis Verbum Dei incarnari" (ibid., q. 1, art. 2).

13. "Deus enim per suam omnipotentem virtutem poterat humanam naturam multis aliis modis reparare" (ibid.).

Second, hope (a kind of ecstasy of the spirit) is brought to full expression because we appreciate through the incarnation just how thoroughly God has identified himself with us. Third, love (an ecstasy of the will) is "maximally excited" (*maxime excitatur*) by this act of total and unexpectedly generous love on the part of God. All of the preceding is summed up in the claim that through the incarnation, our capacity to participate in the divine life is made fully possible. Quoting from Augustine, who in turn relies on earlier traditions, Aquinas says that "God became human that humans might become God" (*factus est Deus homo, ut homo fieret Deus*). God's becoming flesh was necessary for human salvation therefore in the sense that through it alone human beings were given the capacity to enter into, by their own responsive ecstasy, the ecstasy that God is. God's gift of self awakens a human gift of self, and the two together constitute a coinherence of divinity and humanity. And this is why the incarnation, when read from either "side," is so *conveniens*.

When we use this Thomistic lens to read the Gospel narratives, what comes into focus? In the stories concerning Jesus Christ, if Thomas is right, we will see the goodness of God on display, which is to say, the divine tendency *se communicare aliis* (to communicate itself to others). We will see God giving himself away, being for others. And we will remark the concomitant human response of self-gift and self-transcendence, both in Jesus of Nazareth himself and in the men and women whom he confronts. In short, we will see a manifestation of ecstatic divine and human coinherence, the human-being of God that conduces toward the coming to-be-divine of humans.

A third theological framework is provided by the contemporary phenomenologist Jean-Luc Marion. In a number of his texts, but especially in his book *God without Being*, Marion makes an illuminating contrast between an idol and an icon. It is upon this distinction that his understanding of Jesus as the "icon of the invisible God" will depend. That the two forms of visibly representing the divine are closely linked is obvious, and that one can in practice slide easily from one to the other is a commonplace of the religious traditions. What then precisely constitutes the difference between them? It is not, Marion argues, primarily a question of what they are—pictures, statues, representations, etc.—for the same physical object can function as either an idol or an icon. Instead, "the icon and the idol determine two manners of being for beings, not two classes of beings."[14]

An idol is, as the term itself suggests (*eidolon*, from *eido*, to see), something visible, in fact supremely and uncomplicatedly so. What Marion means is that the idol invites and takes in the gaze of the observer so

14. Jean-Luc Marion, *God without Being* (Chicago: Univ. of Chicago Press, 1991), 8.

thoroughly that it is effectively exhausted in the act of being seen: "the idol fascinates and captivates the gaze precisely because everything in it must expose itself to the gaze, attract, fill, and hold it."[15] The identity of an idol is not derived from its being made (for the same must be said of an icon), but rather from the decision of the viewer to fix his gaze upon it and to find a sort of final visual satisfaction in it: "when the idol appears, the gaze has just stopped: the idol concretizes that stop."[16] In this sense, an idol functions as more of a mirror than a portrait, for it reflects back to the viewer the nature, quality, and purpose of his gaze, even as it dazzles by its beauty and visibility. And this is, of course, precisely why an idol is an inadequate mediator of the divine. When the sacred appears in an idol, it is necessarily "measured by what the scope of particular human eyes can support, by what each aim can require of visibility in order to admit itself fulfilled."[17] So on this reading, biblical prophets, as well as Ludwig Feuerbach and his numerous disciples, legitimately criticized as idolatrous a conception of God that amounts to a projection of one's idealized self-understanding.

So what of the icon? Whereas the idol absorbs and exhausts the gaze, "the icon summons sight in letting the visible . . . be saturated little by little with the invisible."[18] Like an idol, an icon is visible, but its very visibility lures the regard of the looker into and through itself to the finally invisible, which suffuses and transcends it. Whereas in the idol the transcendent becomes and remains visible, in the icon it retains its invisibility even as it comes to a kind of appearance. Therefore, the authentic icon "summons the gaze to surpass itself by never freezing on the visible, since the visible only presents itself here in view of the invisible."[19] The very look of the looker is rendered uneasy and restless in the presence of the icon, whereas it rests in the presence of the idol. In the case of an idol, the gaze of the viewer determines its meaning, but in the case of the icon it is, as it were, the gaze of the icon that determines the viewer. In the spirituality associated with the production and viewing of icons, the looker is drawn into the world of the figure depicted in the icon—Mary, a saint, Christ himself—so that the visibility of the picture is a means employed by the invisible person to change the looker. "The icon alone offers an open face, because it opens in itself the visible onto the invisible, by offering its spectacle to be transgressed—not to be seen but to be venerated."[20] Marion is influenced here not only by the spirituality of icons but also by the ethics

15. Ibid., 10.
16. Ibid., 11.
17. Ibid., 14.
18. Ibid., 17.
19. Ibid., 18.
20. Ibid., 19.

of Emanuel Levinas, especially Levinas's emphasis on the "calling" that
comes from the face of the victim or the person in need. In this sense, the
visage of the suffering other is an icon—a visible manifestation—of the
properly infinite and invisible demand of the moral life itself.[21]

This way of speaking seems, at least *prima facie*, problematic for someone
like Marion, who stands in the tradition of phenomenology, the philosophical method that places particular stress on appearance and visibility.
How can a phenomenologist, qua phenomenologist, not inevitably fall
into what Marion calls idolatry when attempting to speak of the divine?
One way to respond to this objection, of course, is to draw attention to
Edmund Husserl's account of intending an absence. That an absence can
"appear" as the focus of one's conscious attention is one of the most important discoveries of phenomenology. But Marion does not exploit this
dimension of the phenomenological tradition. Instead he speaks, in later
texts, of the "saturated phenomenon," the appearance that is so filled with
givenness and meaning that it overwhelms the one who would attempt
to take it in. Whatever comes to manifestation in any way is given, but
certain appearances are filled to overflowing with givenness, so much so
that they dazzle the gaze and the mind that would perceive them. Both
idol and icon are phenomena, but the latter is super-saturated with the
invisibility of God.

The New Testament account of the transfiguration of Jesus displays
brilliantly the dynamics of the super-saturated phenomenon. The Christ
whom Peter, James, and John had come to know through ordinary perception became, on the mountain of transfiguration, dazzlingly white, and
Moses and Elijah appeared alongside him. The brightness signals a kind
of surplus of visibility, a flooding of the eyes, and the presence of the two
great Old Testament figures hints at the new dimensions and profiles of
meaning opening up. The reaction of Peter and the other disciples is altogether understandable. "Rabbi," says Peter, "it is good for us to be here;
let us make three dwellings, one for you, one for Moses, and one for
Elijah" (Mark 9:5). In the presence of the icon, that which awakens and
lures the gaze beyond what it can see, one feels oneself in the presence of
that which is extraordinarily good. In line with the Dionysian perspective
that we saw above in Aquinas, Marion sees the good as that which gives
itself. When therefore Peter stands before the hyperdonation of the super-
saturated phenomenon of the transfigured Jesus, he properly remarks at
the goodness of what is happening to him.

Then comes the odd comment about the booths, a remark that has
been interpreted in a variety of ways throughout the tradition. The best
reading is, I would maintain, suggested by Mark himself: "He did not

21. See John Caputo, *Against Ethics* (Bloomington: Indiana Univ. Press, 1993), esp. 28–30.

know what to say, for they were terrified" (Mark 9:6). Peter is not so much trying to cling to the moment or to control these sacred figures; he is babbling. When the faculties are flooded, as they are in extraordinary experiences, we often say things that make no sense. The "terror" of which Mark speaks is precisely this fear born of the incapacity to control or take in what is happening.

Then there is the final detail concerning the cloud and the voice. The cloud bespeaks the overshadowing of the perceptive powers associated with the hyperluminosity of the transfiguration. The disciples are thrown into the dark, not for want of light but from surplus of light. (An evocative peculiarity of Matthew's account is the "brightness" of the cloud, the juxtaposition of light and shadow signaling the paradox of hypervisibility leading to blindness [Matt. 17:5]). And the voice—the divine proclamation regarding the identity of Jesus—evokes the sacred nonvisibility that saturates the visibility of the icon. The transfigured Christ is so filled with the givenness of the divine presence that that presence can only be heard and not seen. More to the point, the voice carries an instruction, "Listen to him," suggesting, as we saw, that an icon is never controlled or measured by the gaze of the looker, but rather vice versa. Peter, James, and John are not so much seeing and measuring God as being seen and being measured by God.

Something very similar can be discerned in the opening verses of the first letter of John. The author speaks of something that he has "seen and looked upon," namely the humanity of Jesus, but then he specifies that the content of this vision is "the word of life" (1 John 1:1). As in the transfiguration story, properly iconic seeing ends in a nonseeing and in the hearing of a word of command. Then, in an eloquent reversal, the content of the message (or word) is that "God is light" (1 John 1:5). Once more, this is the luminosity and visibility that flood the receptive powers and make ordinary seeing impossible; this light is so intense that it can be received only as a word. The same rhythm occurs in the prologue to the Johannine Gospel, where it is the Word (the nonvisible) that becomes flesh, this very juxtaposition constituting the light that illumines the world.

So what will we expect to see if we look at the narratives concerning Jesus through the lens of Marion's phenomenology? We will appreciate Christ as the icon and super-saturated phenomenon par excellence. We will "see" him in the ordinary way, but our seeing will not stop at his visibility or be absorbed by it. If that were the case, Jesus would become an idol. Instead, our gaze (in both the physical and intellectual senses) will be drawn into the humanity of the Lord toward the divinity that hyper-radiates through it. Mind you, this has nothing to do with docetism, as though Jesus's humanity were either unreal or uninteresting; rather, it is an incarnational perspective, according to which "the glory of God [shines] in the face of Jesus Christ" (2 Cor. 4:6). Marion's hermeneutic will encourage us to see clearly and critically what appears on the surface of the Gospel narratives, but it will compel us to attend to the ever-greater and ever more compelling invisibility that saturates this surface. Furthermore, it will force a reorientation of our subjectivity, so that even as we read and look at the stories of Jesus, we are more thoroughly read and looked through by the one who appears in them. Finally, like Thomas's treatment of the incarnation, it will help us to see the goodness of God in these accounts. Any phenomenon, as we have seen, is an instance of "givenness." What appears is not the product of subjectivity but the gift of an other that offers itself to subjectivity. In the case of the icon, the givenness of the appearance is flooded by an infinitely greater, finally inexhaustible, givenness, that of the God whose very nature is to be *diffisivum sui*. Therefore, in the narratives concerning Jesus, we should look ever more deeply and fully for evidence of the one who gives. If we follow Marion, Jesus is the human self-donation that draws the heart and the eye toward *the* Self-Donation, the saving God.

Before turning to some of the New Testament texts themselves, let us consider one last interpretive framework, this one coming from the Christology of the contemporary Protestant thinker James William Mc-Clendon. As a propadeutic to the presentation of his own point of view, McClendon discusses what he judges to be an inadequacy in the two-natures doctrine of Chalcedon. Though it accounted for certain essential truths about Jesus—especially the transcendent source of his identity—the two-natures doctrine did not sufficiently emphasize the real humanity of the Lord as expressed in the narratives of the New Testament, and this led, implicitly, to a skewing of its account of Jesus's divinity as well. "The Christ thus affirmed seems remote indeed from the humble savior of the four Gospels—a remoteness borne out in Byzantine art with its *Christos Pantokrator*, a Christ fit to rule empires, but hardly recalling the way of the cross."[22] Though it formally affirmed Jesus's humanity, the conciliar statement, precisely by abstracting that humanity from the narratives in which it was presented, allowed it to be effectively absorbed by a conventional sense of divinity.

Though I hope it is clear from what I argued above that I don't fully subscribe to this analysis of Chalcedon, I do think McClendon is onto something important: the danger of hyperabstraction in regard to the natures. *Nature*, perforce, is an abstract term, representing a distillation of essential elements from particular cases, and the very nonspecificity of such an abstraction permits one to use it with a certain logical fluency.

22. James William McClendon, *Doctrine*, vol. 2 of *Systematic Theology* (Nashville: Abingdon, 1994), 256.

But as Newman knew, this same quality renders an abstraction incapable of representing the necessarily peculiar and atypical features of a given individual. The "nature" of the very particular human being Jesus of Nazareth—the altogether unique quality of his mind, will, imagination, body, and passions—can scarcely be caught by a universal philosophical category. Instead, it must be displayed in the dense texture of the narratives that describe him in action. And the same must be true of the divine "nature" that inheres in Jesus: whatever the church means by ascribing divinity to Christ becomes intelligible only in the specificity of the stories.

Though he does not do so explicitly, McClendon could offer a similar critique of Marion's phenomenology of the icon. Whatever else it might be, an icon is a fixed image, and no static form could ever hope to represent the complex and multidimensional quality of a life story, played out in time as well as space. What we must do, therefore, if we want to get at what the New Testament is telling us about both divinity and humanity in Jesus, is to ground the nature and to set the icon in motion.

Accordingly, McClendon proposes a "two-narratives" Christology to supplement the classical two-natures doctrine.[23] Throughout the great sweep of the biblical narrative, from Genesis to the coming of Christ, we are dealing essentially with the intertwining of two stories: that of God and that of his people Israel. We hear, on the one hand, of God's steady fidelity, his willingness to walk in the cool of the evening with Adam, his deliverance of his suffering people from bondage in Egypt, his gift of the law, his gracious sending of prophet after prophet. And on the other hand, we hear an accompanying narrative of Israel's stumbling, deeply imperfect, sometimes inspiring attempt to respond to the faithful God. We hear of "the trembling of Adam and Eve . . . of prophets, men and women too, who dare not, dare not speak any word but the Lord's own, of priests and people who keep the faith and rebuild the shattered wall of God's Zion."[24] That these interconnected tales are unambiguously two is the result not only of the irreducible distinction between God and creation but also of "the fragmentation that have been a part of the creature's story . . . from Adam and Eve to Cain, from Samson and Delilah to King Ahab and Queen Jezebel, from the Pharaohs to the Caesars."[25] Though they gesture toward one another, the narratives of God and of Israel never run smoothly together. Even the greatest and most faithful figures in Israelite history—Abraham, Moses, Joseph, David, and Solomon—are marked by moral imperfection and spiritual blindness. Hence, though we could say that God's story is "in" theirs, we could never do so in an unqualified way.

23. Ibid., 263–75.
24. Ibid., 275.
25. Ibid.

And then there is the story of the faithful Israelite Jesus from Nazareth. So tight is the correspondence between the narrative concerning this Jew and the story of God that the two become one. In light of the resurrection of Jesus from the dead, we can say God is "in" this story without qualification or hesitation. "The action of Jesus is God's action; what Jesus suffers, God suffers. Here the twoness of the story, however we care to name it, converges completely, and we see a human story that God will without qualification acknowledge as his own."[26] In Jesus, the stories of Israel and Israel's God coincide to the point of identification. Though they can be separated for the sake of analysis (much as the two natures can be), they cannot be divided, so that in fact there is finally only one story to be told, the good news of Jesus Christ, the Son of God.

The obvious advantage of this manner of speaking is, as indicated above, its dynamic quality, its capacity to display the range and meaning of a life with far greater adequacy. At the same time, I realize full well that language such as "God's acknowledgment of Jesus's life as his own" carries at least the overtone of adoptionism. I wonder whether the orthodoxy of McClendon's position might be preserved if, in line with the logic of his proposal, we radicalize the meaning of *acknowledge*. Just as Chalcedon grounded the two natures in one divine person, might we suggest that McClendon's theology grounds the two narratives in one divine story-teller? Who precisely is the "I," the person or subject of responsibility, if we are operating in a narrative framework? It would be the teller of a life story, the one who, amidst myriad vicissitudes and despite obstacles, sets the agenda and establishes the purpose and direction of a life. We might say that a personhood exists in the measure that a narrative coherency emerges from a welter of otherwise random events and happenings.

So, in the case of Jesus, there are really two stories going on—human and divine—but there is one storyteller, God, who acknowledges both stories as his own, who tells himself in both. This "acknowledgment" therefore is far more than an acquiescence from a distance; instead it is God's claiming as his own a human narrative as the instrument of the telling of his own story. Does this compromise the integrity of the human mind and will of Jesus or call into question the reality of his human choices? No more or less than does the two-natures doctrine, which affirms the human nature of Christ but makes it enhypostatic, which is to say, rooted in the divine person. So in this narrative framework, couldn't one say that the fully and richly human story of Jesus is enhypostatically grounded in the intentionality of the divine storyteller? With these clarifications (admittedly not McClendon's own) in mind, we could claim the two-narratives Christology as a more dynamic and still faithful rendering of the Chalcedonian doctrine.

26. Ibid., 276.

If we examine the biblical narratives concerning Jesus through the lens of McClendon's proposal, what will we see? We will remark a fully human story in all of its peculiarity, complexity, limitation, psychological density, and historical specificity. We will uncover the career of neither a superman nor a demigod, but rather a human life concretely lived. But this human life will be, at every turn and in every detail, the grammar, syntax, and vocabulary that God uses to tell his own story. Jesus's human voice, actions, choices, and movements will be construed as the representation of the voice, action, choice, and purpose of God. If I might blend the perspectives of McClendon and Marion, we will see in the narrative of Jesus's life the perfect and undistorted icon of God, but displayed in motion and across time.

I might bring these various perspectives together as such: the human story of Jesus should be interpreted as the unsurpassably clear iconic representation of the noncompetitive and infinitely generous love of God for the human race and for the world. In the narrative concerning this particular Jew from Nazareth, we will come to see the invisibility of the One Who Gives. We will sense, furthermore, the coinherence of divinity and humanity, God living a human life and a human being living the divine life, in such a way that neither divinity nor humanity is compromised. We should expect to discover two stories that come together without mixing, mingling, or confusion and that are narrated by one Storyteller who is telling himself in them.

PART II

The Narratives

Within the confines of a few chapters I can only begin a sketch of this narrative and iconic Christology. There is no way that all of the relevant Gospel stories and scenes can be adequately analyzed and placed in relation to one another. What I shall endeavor to do is to identify three major titles/themes that emerge in the Jesus stories—the Gatherer, the Warrior, and the King—and then consider certain representative narratives under each of those major headings. In an earlier work, I identified three major paths of the Christian spiritual life as finding the center, knowing that you are a sinner, and realizing that your life is not about you.[1] Jesus the Gatherer corresponds to the first path, Jesus the Warrior to the second, and Jesus the King to the third. In the narratives concerning Jesus of Nazareth, we shall perceive God as the power that gathers the disparate tribes of Israel and through them the sundered peoples of the world; we shall perceive God furthermore as the warrior who does battle with the sin that has produced a splintered and shattered world; and finally we shall perceive God as the King who sends missionaries to effect through love the reconstitution of the divine order.

As I hope is clear from the foregoing, I will follow neither of the great liberal paths in this investigation. I will not seek out the undergirding religious sensibility awakened or indicated by the stories of the New Testament, nor will I attempt to dig out the "real" Jesus buried under the

1. Robert Barron, *The Strangest Way: Walking the Christian Path* (Maryknoll, NY: Orbis, 2002).

stories. Rather, I will endeavor to study and analyze the narratives on their own terms, hoping thereby to make their iconic quality more apparent. In the course of his *Church Dogmatics*, Karl Barth took his readers on an elaborate and detailed tour of the dense jungle of the biblical world; I will attempt something similar, on a much smaller scale but, I hope, in the same spirit.

4

The Gatherer

The English word *sin* is derived from the German term *Sünde*, which carries the connotation of sundering or dividing. The Greek word *diabalos*, from which various terms for the evil one derive—*diablo, diable, devil, Teufel*—means basically "scatterer." In the book of Genesis, the original sin—incited by the serpent—amounts to a sundering of the human relationship to God (expulsion from the Garden) and a radical division and scapegoating among creatures. When Adam is challenged by God, he responds, "The woman whom you gave to be with me, she gave me fruit from the tree, and I ate," and when the woman is confronted, she passes the buck to nature: "The serpent tricked me, and I ate" (Gen. 3:12–13). Over-and-againstness, separation, suspicion, mutual hatred, blaming—all are signs that the scattering power of sin is let loose.

In the course of the Old Testament, the twelve tribes of Israel—gathered together as one people through the power of God's covenant—are periodically separated, divided, carried into exile because of their infidelity to that covenant. The hope for a united Israel, for a return of the exiled tribes, is expressed in the Prophets and in Psalms: "Jerusalem—built as a city that is bound firmly together. To it the tribes go up" (Ps. 122:3–4), "the joy of all the earth, Mount Zion, in the far north, the city of the great King" (Ps. 48:2). A large part of the mystique of King David was that he had united the disparate people of Israel and had governed them from the central capital city, Jerusalem. And despite his numerous failings, David's son Solomon enjoyed great renown, first because he had built the temple

71

in Jerusalem, which had become a physical and spiritual focal point for the nation, and second because his reputation had drawn to the capital potentates from around the world, most famously the Queen of the South. In this he had embodied Israel's mission to be a light to the nations, the true pole of the earth, the gathering point of the world.

When a Jewish prophet of the first century announced that the reign of God is at hand, N. T. Wright has argued, he would be taken to mean something very specific: that the scattering of the tribes of Israel (in both a literal and a spiritual sense) was over and that Yahweh was coming to reign in Jerusalem, this reconfiguration inaugurating the illumination and salvation of the entire world.[1] In other words, he would be interpreted as saying that the dream of Israel—realized only fitfully and inadequately throughout its history—was now coming definitively true. So when Jesus of Nazareth said, "The time is fulfilled, and the kingdom of God has come near; repent, and believe in the good news" (Mark 1:15), he was not calling attention to general, timeless spiritual truths, nor was he urging people to make a decision for God; he was telling his hearers that Yahweh was actively gathering the people of Israel and, indirectly, all people into a new salvific order, and he was insisting that his hearers conform themselves to this new state of affairs. In this gathering, he was implying, the forgiveness of sins—the overcoming of sundering and division—would be realized. In a word, the proclamation of the kingdom was tantamount to an announcement that the Gatherer of Israel had arrived and had commenced his work. What is most remarkable about Jesus, according to Wright, is that he not only indicated this fact but embodied it and acted it out, taking, in his words and gestures, the very role of the Gatherer. Origen said substantially the same thing when he described Jesus as *autobasileia*, the kingdom in person.

The Wedding at Cana

The first narrative that I will consider under the rubric of the Gathering is the Johannine account of the wedding feast at Cana. Throughout the Old Testament, the motif of the wedding is used to symbolize the marriage of God and his people as well as the good cheer that obtains when human beings come together in love. It is accordingly a particularly apt expression of the overcoming of the sundering of sin. Thus it is no accident that in the context of John's Gospel, Jesus's first public "sign" takes place at a wedding feast, for he himself is the marriage of divinity and humanity.

1. N. T. Wright, *Jesus and the Victory of God* (Minneapolis: Fortress, 1996), esp. 172–90.

The narrative begins with an elegant Johannine code: "On the third day there was a wedding in Cana of Galilee . . ." (John 2:1). Throughout the Gospel, *te hemera te trite* (on the third day) is the expression for the day of Jesus's resurrection from the dead. More to the point, this marriage feast takes place in Cana *of Galilee*, and Galilee, in the symbolic system of John, is the country of resurrection, that place where Jesus would meet his friends after Easter. Therefore, this story must be read through the lens of the resurrection, which is to say, the act by which God in an unprecedented and unsurpassable way gathered humanity to himself and inaugurated the process of the universal gathering ("Christ has been raised from the dead, the first fruits of those who have died," 1 Cor. 15:20). The wedding feast of Cana and the wedding feast of the resurrection will stand in one another's hermeneutical light.

We hear that the disciples of Jesus—presumably at this point Andrew, Simon Peter, Philip, Nathanael, and the disciple whom Jesus loved—were invited to the wedding along with the Lord himself and his mother. The presence of both the *mathetai* and the mother are key. In calling disciples to himself, Jesus had already inaugurated the gathering of his people (eventually the Twelve will be seen as evocative of the twelve tribes of Israel), and so their presence signals the novelty and future purpose of Jesus's ministry. Mary is a rich and multivalent symbolic figure in all of the Gospels. In Luke's infancy narrative, she emerges as the spokesperson for ancient Israel, speaking, in her Magnificat, in the words and cadences of Hannah; and as the recipient of an angelic announcement of a miraculous birth, she calls to mind not only Hannah but also Sarah and the mother of Samson as well. In Matthew's Christmas account, she is compelled to go into exile in Egypt and is then called back to her home, recapitulating thereby the journey of Israel from slavery to freedom. She is thus the symbolic embodiment of faithful and patient Israel, longing for deliverance. In John's Gospel, she is, above all, mother—the physical mother of Jesus and, through him, the mother of all who would come to new life in him. As mother of the Lord, she is, once again, Israel, that entire series of events and system of ideas from which Jesus emerged and in terms of which he alone becomes intelligible. Hans Urs von Balthasar comments in the same vein that Mary effectively awakened the messianic consciousness of Jesus through her recounting of the story of Israel to her son. So in the Cana narrative, Mary will speak the pain and the hope of the chosen people, scattered and longing for union.

We hear that in the course of the wedding celebration "the wine gave out" (John 2:3). In an era when such parties lasted upward of several days, this was not a minor difficulty. With the wine depleted, the spirit of conviviality would dissipate, the celebration would wind down quickly, and the hosts, as well as the bride and groom, would be profoundly embarrassed. Noticing the difficulty, the mother of Jesus said to him, "They have no wine" (John 2:3).

Let us press ahead with a symbolic reading of this iconic episode. Wine—that which changes, uplifts, and enlivens the consciousness, that which produces good feeling and good fellowship—evokes the Spirit of God, the divine life. When we are linked to that infinite source, when we partake freely of it, we are brought to personal joy and a deep sense of community connection. It is the elixir that makes of human life a communal celebration; it is the condition for the possibility of the gathering. To be in sin is nothing other than to be sundered from that source and hence to fall into a depression of the spirit, a listlessness and loneliness. When Mary quietly suggests to Jesus that the wedding party has run out of wine, she is ancient Israel speaking to its God, reminding him that the people have run out of joy, purpose, and connection to one another, that they have become dry bones with no life. She is taking up the lament of so many of the Hebrew prophets and sages: "How long, O Lord?"

What follows is the most puzzling part of the story, Jesus's seemingly cold distancing of himself from this reasonable request of his mother: "Woman, what concern is that to you and to me? My hour has not yet come" (John 2:4). First, his addressing her as "woman" should not be construed as a mark of disrespect; rather, it should be interpreted as a densely textured symbolic act. Eve, in the Old Testament context, is the woman par excellence; Mary is presented here as the new Eve, the new representative of the human race, with whom God is seeking union. As is fitting in this Cana setting, the theme of human bride and divine bridegroom is being hinted at. But if she is the Woman with whom God seeks union, why the aloof and off-putting words? The best explanation, in my judgment, is that this is a narrative device that serves to highlight the importance of Jesus's "hour" and shows the relation between what he does at Cana and what will transpire in that hour. Like "the third day," "hour" is code for the Paschal Mystery, Jesus's passage through death to life. In that event, God will effect the perfect marriage between himself and the human race, for he will enter into the most intimate union with us, embracing even death itself and leading us into the bridal chamber of the divine life. Thus, the exchange with Mary brings to our attention the ultimate purpose and correct symbolic setting for the action that Jesus will perform for the humble bride and groom of Cana.

Unfazed by her son's response, Mary says to the *diakonoi* (the table servers), "Do whatever he tells you" (John 2:5). Once again, this is Israel who is speaking. The rupture between God and humanity is irreparable from the human side and through human effort. The dysfunction into which men and women have fallen is like an addiction or an obsession: any attempt on their part to overcome the difficulty will only sink them deeper into it. Therefore the proper attitude in the presence of the saving God is obedience and acquiescence, imitating his moves, responding to his commands, doing whatever he tells us.

We come to the heart of the matter as Jesus commences his work of transformation. "Now standing there were six stone water jars for the Jewish rites of purification, each holding twenty or thirty gallons" (John 2:6). These huge containers, used in connection with the religious life of the people, are empty, and this calls to mind the tiredness and uselessness of a religiosity unconnected to the divine Spirit. In this regard, these jars play the same symbolic role as the priest and Levite in the parable of the Good Samaritan. But they are, we might say, eloquently empty, for they represent the potential for life: in relation to God, human religiosity, indeed human being, is a passive receptacle, something waiting to be filled.

Jesus now does two things—one visible and one invisible—and we must attend carefully to both. He first tells the servants to fill the jars with water, and John pointedly tells us that "they filled them up to the brim" (John 2:7). The divine giver is now responding to the request of long-suffering Israel. The first thing he gives is the opportunity for them to contribute to the process of their vivification. Mind you, this is not in conflict with what I just specified concerning the attitude of total acquiescence, since he himself is giving, through his command, their very capacity to coop- erate. So the filling of the jars to the limit is symbolic of all that human agency—through the divine prompting and power—can bring to the task of cultivating human flourishing: art, music, science, technology, politics, spirituality. All of this is obviously good, but it remains provisional and inadequate, for remember that the problem is that they are out of wine, not water. What they (Israel, the human race) require is not just the ordi- nary nourishment that water provides but rather intoxication, elevation, something greater.

Jesus tells them, "Draw some out, and take it to the chief steward" (John 2:8). When the steward tastes the water (now transformed into wine), he remarks on its extraordinary quality and undoubtedly passes on to the bride and groom the good news that they have wine in super- abundance—180 gallons! Jesus has changed the water into wine, taking something relatively insipid and making it tasty and intoxicating. He has received what they gave him and has not negated it, but rather raised it to a new pitch of intensity. Augustine's comment that Jesus simply acceler- ates and concentrates a natural process that occurs all the time—rainwater gives rise to grapes, which give rise to wine—is pertinent here. The water isn't cleared out in order for the divine contribution to be made; instead, the divine contribution is precisely the "perfecting" of the water. This quality of God's giving is congruent, of course, with the Christology of Chalcedon, the noncompetitive coming together of the divine and human natures: when God and a creature meet, the creature is confirmed and made more authentically itself. What is being hinted at in the Cana miracle is the elevation and expansion of human culture under the influence of the divine life. Filled with God's Spirit, architecture, art, science, politics, etc., become more completely themselves and realize their own deepest purposes. God gives our very capacity to give, and then he gives further by transfiguring our gift to our greater benefit. This miracle is hence a particularly apt iconic representation of divine-human coinherence.

Now we mustn't forget that the purpose of this water made wine is to increase and prolong the celebration of a wedding. Because of Jesus's miracle, a large group of celebrants will continue to be gathered around a couple who have chosen to form, themselves, an intimate community for the rest of their lives. Read symbolically, this wine is the divine Spirit which alone grounds authentic human coinherence. When human solidarity is based upon something other than God's love—mutual self-interest, political considerations, shared convictions, etc.—it will inevitably shake apart and dissolve. Aristotle knew that a friendship endures only in the measure that both friends have commonly given themselves to a good that transcends them individually, and Augustine knew that people love each other most appropriately when they do so for the sake of God. What both appreciated was that without a transcendent ground or point of reference, the other orientation of the partners would quickly devolve into self-preoccupation. When God and humanity are married, the connections between human beings intensify and deepen, vertical coinherence giving rise to horizontal coinherence. This fully developed one-in-the-otherness is on iconic display in the story of the wedding at Cana. It is a picture of the divine gatherer at work.

The Parable of the Prodigal Son

One of the greatest showings of the Gathering is Jesus's parable of the prodigal son, or better, of the father and his two sons. In considering this narrative, we are, hermeneutically, on interesting ground, for we are dealing with an icon of the Father told by the one who is himself the Icon of the Father. Thus we have Jesus indirectly crafting a subtle self-portrait. The gathering technique of the father in the story mirrors that of the heavenly Father, which in turn is iconically represented in that of Jesus. In the course of this narrative, we will see who the father/God/Jesus is and how he brings to himself an Israel that had, in a double sense, wandered into exile.

A man, Jesus tells us, had two sons, and "the younger of them said to his father, 'Father, give me the share of the property that will belong to me'"

(Luke 15:11). As many have commented, this demand is presumptuous and highly insulting, for normally a son would not receive his inheritance until after his father has died. Thus, in claiming his money now, the younger son is none too subtly suggesting that he wishes his father would hurry up and die. Especially in Jesus's time and culture, a more stinging remark could scarce be imagined. The parable opens, then, with the declaration of a clear break in the communion and coinherence that one would expect to hold between a father and his son. And if we attend closely to the language of the parable, we will sense further dimensions of this rupture. The boy doesn't ask his father, he tells him: "Give me the share of the property that will come to me." By definition, a gift cannot be demanded; it can only be received graciously and as a sort of surprise. In making his demand, therefore, the younger son is precluding the possibility of a gifted relationship between himself and his father; he is cutting off the flow of grace.

Second, in asking for *property* that is coming to him, he emphatically confirms the gracelessness of the exchange. Property is what is "proper" to a person, what is uniquely his, what he can claim in at least a quasi-legal sense. In common usage, the word indicates what is to be held on to and defended against counter-claimants: we might hear someone say, "Get off my property," or set up a sign that defiantly declares "Private property." Jean-Luc Marion has helpfully drawn attention to the Greek term that undergirds "property" in this story, *ousia*.[2] This is the only time in the New Testament that this famously controversial and theologically charged term is employed. In this context it obviously doesn't have the fully developed metaphysical sense that it has, for instance, in Aristotle, but it does have at least an overtone of the philosophical usage. The more ordinary meaning of *ousia* (displayed here) is money, property, or what is "presently disposable," ready to hand for use. Thus there is a link to the metaphysical "substance," which could be construed as that which a thing possesses as its own, that which it has ready to hand—as opposed to its more fleetingly possessed accidents. In demanding this *ousia*, then, the younger son is asking emphatically for something to have and hold as his own, free of any merely accidental link to either the source or the possible destination of his possession. He expects the gift (in a substantive sense) apart from giving, and this is precisely what he receives when his father "divided his property between them" (Luke 15:12).

Here is a portrait in miniature of God in relation to sin. In the Garden of Eden, Adam and Eve sought to eat of the tree of the knowledge of good and evil, taking God's place and seizing his prerogatives. At the prompting of the tempter, they wanted to take for themselves a life that can only be

---

2. Jean-Luc Marion, *God without Being* (Chicago: Univ. of Chicago Press, 1991), 96.

received as a gift. Prior to the fall, God and Adam had walked together in the cool of the evening as friends, giving and receiving in a circle of grace, and the original sin is nothing but the rupture of this friendship through the desire to possess *ousia*. The true God can be "had" only when one disposes oneself to receive the divine life as a grace and to give that life away in turn as a gift. Grace is "possessed" only in the measure that it is received and offered and never held on to.

A key implication of this analysis is that God is himself not an *ousia*, not a substance, not a supreme being in solemn possession of an infinite range of perfections. Rather, God is a supreme letting-be, a being-for-another, his perfections fluid and generously given. Consequently, in the measure that a human person endeavors to be a supreme being, she falls out of right relation with this God.

As the story unfolds, we hear what happens to "substance," so possessed. We are told that after a few days, the young man "gathered all he had and traveled to a distant country" (Luke 15:13). We notice the frenzy of possessiveness implied in that "gathering" to himself all that was uniquely his, and we remark the thoroughness of the relational rupture with his father in his journey to a far country. The Greek here is instructive: the young man sets out to a *choran makran*, literally a great open space, a place without borders or points of reference. In Plato, the *chora* is the space in between the forms and physical objects, the realm of nonbeing and nonvisibility. The implication of the parable seems to be that this ontological emptiness is the consequence of the younger son's severing of relation to his father. This is made explicit in the next phrase, "and there he squandered his property on dissolute living" (15:13).

He had made bold to seize *ousia* from his father and claim it as his own, and now he sees what inevitably occurs when a gift becomes a possession. It is a basic biblical intuition that as long as one is receiving being as a grace and resolving to pass it on as a grace, one paradoxically keeps it. But if one endeavors to interrupt the flow and seize what is received, then that possession quickly withers away, dissipates. When the young man had spent everything, "a severe famine took place throughout that country, and he began to be in need" (Luke 15:14). Read symbolically, this famine is not merely an unhappy accident that happens to intensify the young man's suffering; rather, it is the natural condition of the *chora makra*. Cut off from relationality and the giving and receiving of gifts, one necessarily experiences famine, a starvation of the soul.

So great became the young man's need that "he went and hired himself out to one of the citizens of that country, who sent him to his fields to feed the pigs" (Luke 15:15). In these few laconic phrases, Jesus describes the spiritual dynamics of the "far country." The only relationship that a citizen of the *chora makra* could envision is a professional one involving hiring and the paying of salaries. There it cannot be a question of giving and gratefully receiving, but only of the paying out and possessing of *ousia*, the hardened detritus of gracious exchange. Second, the feeding of pigs (animals particularly repugnant to pious Jews) indicates the dehumanization that characterizes the far country: grubbing for what is one's own reduces one to the level of competitive and self-absorbed beasts. So pathetic is the younger son's situation that he "would gladly have filled himself with the pods that the pigs were eating," but—and here we come to the heart of it—"no one gave him anything" (Luke 15:16). This is *the* mark of the far country: it is the place where there is no giving. It is the country whose citizens only hire, pay, and receive what is strictly agreed to, and thus it is the polar opposite of the land where the young man's father is lord.

The younger son wandering in a distant land is evocative of the human race—all the descendants of Adam and Eve—who have lost contact with the flow of the divine life. Living in the land of hiring, taking, paying, and possessing, they starve spiritually. They are like the sad guests at the wedding feast of Cana who have run out of wine; they are like Israel in the land of exile, pining for Zion; or they are like the psalmist's deer yearning for flowing streams. How appropriate, by the way, is that last image. The divine life flows because it is a process of giving and receiving; sin is substantive and fixed, "hard" currency. The only solution is a return to a graced mode of being.

And this is precisely what the prodigal realizes in a moment of clarity: "But when he came to himself he said, 'How many of my father's hired hands have bread enough and to spare, but here I am dying of hunger!'" (Luke 15:17). Even those whom his father has hired—even those only professionally related to him—have enough and more than enough, with superabundance indicating that they are in the circle of grace. Were they merely possessing what their employer paid them, they would be psychologically and spiritually in the far country and would soon enough run out. And this is why the younger son resolves, in the carefully rehearsed speech that we overhear, to ask his father to treat him as one of his hired hands: even the least in the country of grace have more than enough. Then, full of contrition, he sets out to return to his father.

While he is still a long way off (still to some degree in the land of exile), his father catches sight of him (he had obviously been looking for him) and is "filled with compassion; he ran and put his arms around him and kissed him" (Luke 15:20). The word used in the Greek here for the feeling of compassion is *esplagnisthe*, meaning literally that the father's guts are moved, the visceral connection to his child stirred up. This same term is applied in the New Testament to the feelings of Jesus himself: "When he saw the crowds, he had compassion for them, because they were harassed and helpless, like sheep without a shepherd" (Matt. 9:36). This powerful feeling leads to an extraordinary gesture. As many have pointed out, in ancient Jewish society, it was considered terribly unseemly for an elderly man to run to meet someone; rather, he was the one to whom others would come in a spirit of respect and obeisance. So the Father's running, throwing caution and respectability to the wind, is an act of almost shocking condescension and other orientation.

When they meet, the father embraces his son and kisses him; then the boy speaks: "Father, I have sinned against heaven and before you; I am no longer worthy to be called your son" (Luke 15:21). The embrace of the father is one of the most powerful biblical symbols of the Gathering: exiled Israel has returned, and the father-God takes him to himself, drawing him back into the circle of light. How evocatively Rembrandt van Rijn depicted this inclusion-enlightenment in his late-career painting of the return of the prodigal: the penitent son is embraced by his father and participates thereby in a light that does not so much come from without as radiate from within the father himself.

The saint, remarked G. K. Chesterton, is someone who knows he is a sinner.[3] Whenever characters in the Bible come close to the divine grace, they experience a heightened sense of their own unworthiness: Isaiah in temple, Jeremiah at the moment of his call, Peter at the miraculous draught of fishes. This is the dynamic at work in the case of the prodigal son. Precisely in the measure that he is reconnected to the graciousness of God and the flow of his mercy, he knows unambiguously his sorry spiritual state. His cruel leavetaking and subsequent sojourn in the *chora makra* had perverted his relationship to his father, and it is in the embrace of his father that he truly senses this.

However, his worthiness to be called son has nothing to do with his own moral achievement or lack thereof. His father ignores his carefully rehearsed speech, and with an eagerness bordering on impatience, he instructs his servants: "Quickly, bring out a robe—the best one—and put it on him; put a ring on his finger and sandals on his feet. And get the fatted calf and kill it, and let us eat and celebrate" (Luke 15:22–23). Our participation in the flow of the divine life is, necessarily, a gift, not so much because God arbitrarily chooses those who should receive it but because it is itself nothing but the giving and receiving of gifts. It cannot, in principle, be earned or merited, but only accepted. We can only be embraced by it.

The father's comment on the reason for the celebration—"For this son of mine was dead and is alive again" (Luke 15:24)—is theologically

3. See Robert Barron, *The Strangest Way: Walking the Christian Path* (Maryknoll, NY: Orbis, 2002), 67.

accurate. When the divine life hardens into a possession, it is, as we've seen, effectively lost; when one wanders away from the living stream of God, one necessarily dries up, and one's "life" is merely biological. Like the Gerasene demoniac—living among the tombs—the prodigal son had been one of the living dead. Authentic spiritual life is had only when one enters into the flow of grace, when one can accept robe, ring, and fatted calf.

With that the narrative of the parable turns to the elder brother, a man superficially quite unlike the prodigal son, but practically identical to him at the spiritual level. The strategy that the father employs to gather him in should be the focus of our attention. While the father was attentively waiting for the return of the younger son, the older brother was "in the field," a somewhat more subtle version of the *chora makra*, obviously indifferent to his brother's fate. Hearing the sounds of celebration, he approaches the house, and when he discovers the reason for the festivities, he is filled with indignation: "then he became angry and refused to go in" (Luke 15:28). In accord with his relentlessly inclusive character, the father comes out to this second exile and pleads with him to join the circle of celebration.

Then we hear the words that reveal the spiritual state of the older son: "Listen! For all these years, I have been working like a slave for you, and I have never disobeyed your command; yet you have never given me even a young goat so that I might celebrate with my friends" (Luke 15:29). Though he has remained physically close to his father, his exile is just as dramatic as his younger brother's, for he too has allowed his relationship to his father to harden into possessiveness. The harshly economic vocabulary gives away the game: working like a slave, obeying commands, getting something of his own, *his* friends. Just like his brother, this man wants to claim the father's love as his own possession and use it as he sees fit. Whereas the younger brother demanded it in a presumptuous way ("give me the share of the property that will belong to me"), the elder brother "slaves" for it, working in a calculating way in order to earn it.

The problem is that, as we have already seen, the divine love—which is a flow of grace—cannot be received in this manner. The economic exchange model just cannot work, so slaving is every bit as ineffectual as hoarding. Rebellion against God and resentful obedience to his "commands" are equally hopeless strategies, since both attempt to transform the flow of grace into *ousia* that can be made one's own.

The gatherer-father then speaks to his older son: "Son, you are always with me, and all that is mine is yours" (Luke 15:31). From the father's perspective, his son is connected to him, *with* him in such an intimate way that the life of the father flows to the son. The economic language of the son is therefore metaphysically and spiritually inappropriate, the result of a basic misperception. The Creator God relates to creation in just this ontologically intimate fashion, giving being every moment to whatever exists in the realm of finitude. Though a creature could imagine itself as existing in an extrinsic relation to God, this would be an incorrect, a distortion. The Redeemer God wants nothing more than to give his own inner life away to the human race—"all that is mine is yours." The problem is that the sinner persists in misperceiving along competitive lines—"I have slaved for you"—and thus fails to receive the gift.

The prophetic motif of the return of the exile applies, according to N. T. Wright, not only to those who are physically distant from Judea and Jerusalem but also to those who are in a kind of internal exile, spiritually alienated from what Zion symbolizes.[4] The prodigal son and his brother are perfect evocations of both types: while the younger son goes literally into a far country, the older son retreats into an interior *chora makra*. They are coequally far from the flow of grace. In Rembrandt's picture, the older brother resembles the father physically, and like him, he wears a sumptuous red cape, but he stands outside the circle of light that envelops his father and brother. The resemblance hints at the superficial similarity to the father that comes from physical proximity and mimicking the father's behavior (obeying his commands), but the darkness points to the spiritual exile that the older son endures.

The father, with equal vehemence and devotion, reaches out to both wanderers and seeks to bring them into the celebration. Here we can see how this parable is an icon of the Icon of God. In his work of gathering the scattered tribes of Israel—in both external and internal exile—Jesus is the living icon of the Father, whose whole purpose is to gather his alienated creation back to himself. The embrace of the father and his words "All that is mine is yours" are representations of Jesus's ministry of gathering Israel into his circle of influence, which in turn is the Icon of the Father's noncompetitive and life-enhancing proximity to his creation.

The Chalcedonian hermeneutic helps us to appreciate the spiritual dynamics of this parable. The fundamental problem for both sons is their deep conviction that their relationship to their father is competitive and promethean. In order for them to be fully alive, they must wrest what is "their own" from him. So it goes when one stands in relation to a god who is only other, and not otherly other. Human beings will always resent a supreme being, because they will be locked, necessarily, in a terrible zero-sum game with him. And their rapport with such a god will devolve, accordingly, into the mercenary and the calculating, as we see clearly in Jesus's story. The spiritual strategy of the father is to convince his sons that they are not in competition with him, that in fact their own being and life will increase inasmuch as they accept the gift of his life. As we saw earlier,

4. Wright, *Jesus and the Victory of God*, 268ff.

this is the "spirituality" of the two-natures doctrine: a divine and a human nature remain utterly themselves, in the moment of deepest connection and mutual participation. What obtains between the creaturely and the Creator is the polar opposite of a zero-sum game, precisely because it is a matter of grace and not *ousia*.

The Woman at the Well

We continue our analysis of the Gathering by looking at one more splendid Johannine icon: the carefully crafted story of the meeting between Jesus and a Samaritan woman alongside a well. Like many of the other narratives in John's Gospel—the woman caught in adultery, the man born blind, the raising of Lazarus—this story is both a literary and a theological masterpiece. And like the wedding feast account, it is, I will argue, a nuptial tale, a presentation of the process by which Jesus gathers to himself a bride.

As the fourth chapter of the Johannine Gospel opens, Jesus is making his way from Jerusalem (where he had cleansed the temple) back home to Galilee. Perforce, he passes through Samaria, that in-between country, taking the term in both a geographical and a spiritual sense. Samaritans stood on the margins of official Judaism, partaking of its Scriptures and most of its practices but barred from full participation in temple worship and community life. Jesus's work during his brief stay in this land will be to draw the marginal to the center.

At noon, he sits down to rest by the side of Jacob's well, a place of powerful symbolic significance. There are numerous encounters at wells in the Old Testament that are associated with engagements and marriages. In the book of Genesis, the servant of Abraham finds a wife for Isaac at a well after uttering this prayer: "I am standing here by the spring of water; let the young woman who comes out to draw . . . let her be the woman whom the LORD has appointed for my master's son" (Gen. 24:43–44). In the book of Exodus, we read of Moses's sojourn by a spring of water: "But Moses fled from Pharaoh. He settled in the land of Midian and sat down by a well."[5] After chasing away shepherds who were interfering with the daughters of the priest of Midian, Moses was welcomed into the priest's home and given his daughter Zipporah in marriage (Exod. 2:15–21). Most important for our purposes, there is the Genesis narrative of Jacob's journey to the land of Laban, his mother's brother. While reclining near a well, Jacob inquires after Laban and is told that Laban's daughter Rachel is

---

5. Bruno Barnhart, *The Good Wine: Reading John from the Center* (New York: Paulist, 1993), 201.

approaching. When he meets her, Jacob kisses her and then weeps for joy; later, of course, after many adventures and misadventures, he marries this girl, whose effect on him was like that of Beatrice on Dante. So as Jesus sits down beside a well (especially because it is identified as Jacob's), we know that an engagement and a wedding are in the offing.

John tells us that Jesus rested at the well because he was "tired out by his journey" (John 4:6). Augustine commented that the fatigue of the Lord was a function of his total identification, through the "journey" of the incarnation, with the condition of sin. Sometimes the Gospel speaks of the Logos *in forma Dei* (in his exalted form as Son of God), and other times it shows him *in forma servi* (in his humble incarnate state). The "tired" Jesus is a prime example of this second form of description, and what it points to is not simply the physical weariness of Christ but his entry into the life-denying and energy-draining state of sin. "I have come that [you] might have life and have it to the full," says Jesus (John 10:10); but he brings that life through solidarity with the lifelessness of those who have wandered from grace. So his sitting by the well is quite similar, theologically, to his standing shoulder to shoulder in the waters of the Jordan with those seeking John's baptism of repentance: both are saving acts of identification with the debilitating condition of the sinner. We also hear that this session took place when it "was about noon" (John 4:6). We are at the high point of the day and hence a natural time to stop to rest and eat, but at the symbolic level we are at the moment of greatest illumination, a time when the light of the world will be on particular display.

"A Samaritan woman came to draw water" (John 4:7). From the standpoint of a Jewish man, we are dealing here with a triple outsider. First, as a woman, she would be considered inferior; second, as a Samaritan, she would be looked down upon as a half-breed and a heretic; and finally, coming as she does at midday (hardly the optimal time for physical labor) and unaccompanied by other women, she would be suspect as a person of probably questionable morals. Barriers religious, ethical, racial, and cultural would naturally separate her from someone like Jesus and make of her an exile par excellence.

As is his wont, Jesus reaches out to establish contact with the outsider: "Give me a drink" (John 4:7). Throughout the Gospels, Jesus identifies himself with food and drink—"I am the bread of life" (John 6:35); "Take, eat, this is my body. . . . Drink from it, all of you; for this is my blood of the covenant" (Matt. 26:26–28)—but here he assumes the stance of one who needs sustenance. In the chapter on God, we will look in some detail at the question of God's relationship vis-à-vis creation, but for now I will simply indicate that this thirst on Jesus's part has nothing to do with divine "neediness," as though God required something from the world that he makes in its entirety. It has everything to do with the establishment of the loop or pattern of grace that I discussed in the analysis of the prodigal son. Jesus asks the woman to give him a gift, but this is only so that he can give her an even greater gift. The point is that he wants to draw her out of her isolation and exile, her tendency to be *curvatus in se*, and his strategy is to tempt her into generosity.

Conditioned by years of prejudice and the violence of marginalization, she naturally draws back: "How is it that you, a Jew, ask a drink of me, a woman of Samaria?" (John 4:9). She has come to get water for herself, and a powerful enemy is asking her to give him the very thing that she seeks. This sounds, in short, like a typical game of antagonism in the realm of *ousia*, and so she turns in on herself in a defensive crouch. John 4:9 signals the lack of grace—the "far country" quality of the Jew-Samaritan relationship—in a wonderfully laconic aside: "(Jews do not share things in common with Samaritans)." Anticoinherence is the rule.

Under the full light of the noonday sun, Jesus then commences the disclosure of his identity: "If you knew the gift of God, and who it is that is saying to you, 'Give me a drink,' you would have asked him, and he would have given you living water" (John 4:10). What better description of the being of Jesus is there than this pithy formula "the gift of God"? Like the father of the two sons who entrusts his entire being to his children—"all that is mine is yours"—Jesus, the Icon of God, presents himself as the giver of gifts, and the purpose of his gift is the gathering of those who have themselves forgotten how to receive and give. He wants to draw the Samaritan woman into that peculiar rhythm of grace through which alone authentic being can be maintained. The loop of grace is the engagement ring that this new Jacob, this new Moses, is proffering to his bride.

In line with John's usual way of advancing a spiritual argument, the woman takes Jesus's words at the literal level: "Sir, you have no bucket, and the well is deep. Where do you get that living water?" (John 4:11). Earthly realities can only hint symbolically at the spiritual truth of the law of the gift, for no matter how superabundant, any material source eventually gives out.

What Jesus is driving at is the divine life that is never exhausted even as it is given, since it is, in its essence, nothing other than giving: "Everyone who drinks of this water will be thirsty again, but those who drink of the water that I will give them will never be thirsty. The water that I will give will become in them a spring of water gushing up to eternal life" (John 4:13–14). When the divine gift is received, it becomes in the recipient that which can be given away infinitely and indefinitely, and that which, even as it is given away, never gives out. This is why it "bubbles up" to inexhaustible life.

On Augustine's reading, the well water, which the woman seeks every day and which leaves her thirsting for more, represents the various objects of concupiscent desire. The deepest thirst in us is for the divine life, and when we seek to slake that thirst with something less than God—money, sex, power, the esteem of others—we necessarily become thirsty again, much as a drug user becomes increasingly addicted to the narcotics that fail to satisfy him. Further, we turn those finite goods, which are meant to be used as instruments in the flow of grace, into "substances," what is ours, what is coming to us. What is being revealed in the exchange between Jesus and the woman at the well is that the fiercest thirst in us is not for possession but for the capacity to give, and this to the ultimate degree; to have this (by not having it) is to experience the spring of eternal life within.

In light of this clarification, Jesus's sitting by the well in his fatigue takes on a new resonance His tiredness is a participation in the weariness that follows from the sinner's repeated journeys to the well, which is to say, the incessant attempt to satisfy the desire that cannot be satisfied through possession.

Finally beginning to see with spiritual eyes, the woman replies, "Sir, give me this water, so that I may never be thirsty again or have to keep coming here to draw water" (John 4:15). Her words reveal that she is well acquainted with the rigors of the life of sin, with the fatigue that comes from concupiscent desire.

With that, the conversation takes a most unexpected turn: "Jesus said to her, 'Go, call your husband, and come back'" (John 4:16). Why would the woman's husband be of such concern? As we have seen, this entire episode is a wedding story, an account of how the Samaritan woman finds her proper spouse. In the context of an admittedly sexist culture, a woman's quest for a husband is her search for governance and direction in her life. Hence, once Jesus sees that she has come to a sufficient spiritual insight to ask for the living water, he explicitly introduces the theme of the husband or "headship," essentially asking this: "Show me who or what governs your life." When she says, "I have no husband," she is witnessing, on the one hand, to her moral drift (she is at the mercy of her conflicting desires) but also to her openness to a new orientation (as spiritually unattached, she is able eventually to take Jesus as her husband). Sometimes it is our very dysfunction that allows for the advent of grace.

Jesus then compliments her for her honesty, but like a good spiritual director, he spies the rest of the truth hidden by her cagey response: "You are right in saying, 'I have no husband'; for you have had five husbands, and the one you have now is not your husband" (John 4:17–18). In accord with the hermeneutic that I have been developing, Jesus discerns that the Samaritan woman's life is currently unfocused (no husband) but that she was formerly under the thrall of five powers from which she has managed to free herself.

Who or what are these five? Augustine suggests that they represent the five senses or the five books of the Torah. In her quest for meaning, she had submitted herself, first, to the tyranny of the senses, orienting her life to the empirically verifiable world of color, sound, taste, and pleasure, embracing the hedonist option. When this failed, as it necessarily would, she turned to a somewhat more refined form of idolatry, seeking satisfaction in the rigors of a moralizing religion. This progression is, of course, a familiar one: the hedonist becoming the puritan, while retaining the same basic spiritual maladjustment of seeking joy in some worldly object or set of values. The fussy moralist is often just the sensualist in a flimsy religious disguise. By reminding her that she comes each day to the well and never finds satisfaction and that she has, in frustration, discarded five husbands in turn, Jesus tells the Samaritan woman's hard truth, compelling her to see her spiritual condition: anyone but the Word made flesh is inadequate food for the soul.

Impressed by his clairvoyance, the woman tells Jesus, "Sir, I see that you are a prophet," but then, with almost comic alacrity, she changes the subject: "Our ancestors worshiped on this mountain, but you say that the place where people must worship is in Jerusalem" (John 4:20). The prophet has revealed her truth, but she is not yet ready to deal with the implications of that revelation, so she redirects the conversation onto the far less threatening plane of abstract religious controversy. The Samaritans based their cult on Mount Gerizim, while the Jews centered their religious practice on the temple in Jerusalem. Perhaps if she can direct the attention of this "too perceptive young rabbi"[6] to this speculative question, she can avoid the issue of her life's direction.

But the prospective bridegroom is not so easily put off the trail. With breathtaking directness and clarity, Jesus dissolves the question that had helped to divide Jews from Samaritans: "Woman, believe me, the hour is coming when you will worship the Father neither on this mountain nor in Jerusalem . . . [but] in spirit and truth" (John 4:21–24). We recall that one of the principal tasks of the Messiah was to gather the tribes of Israel and then, through them, to gather the nations of the world. What the Messiah opposes, therefore, is division (Origen knew this when he said, "Ubi divisio, ibi peccatum"), especially that division which is perversely caused by religion itself. The Samaritan-Jewish battle over the correct place of the cult is a prime example of just this sort of corruption.

What the Father of Jesus desires is not geographically correct worship, but worship in "spirit and truth" (*en pneumati kai aletheia*). Both of these central Johannine symbols speak of the force of unity. The *pneuma* of God is the breath that God breathes into living things, awakening in them the

6. Ibid., 205.

corresponding breathing in of the *psyche* (from which our word *suck* is derived). Thus worship *en pneumati* is praise born of a living relationship with the Spirit of God, a breathing out in prayer of what was breathed in from the divine source. It is to be in the loop of grace, giving what had been received.

And the truth, which God is, is a universal power, transcending time, space, and artificial cultural boundaries. To worship in truth, therefore, is not to be sectarian or cultish but to pray in the power that unites the tribes of the world. We might draw a contrast between the twin mountains of Gerizim and Zion, standing over and against one another in opposition, and the well of Jacob that serves as a point of contact between Jesus and the woman. The mountains embody the great divorce, while the circular well bespeaks the wedding ring.

Beginning to sense that she is speaking to one who is even more than a prophet, the Samaritan woman says, "When he [the Messiah] comes, he will proclaim all things to us" (*anaggelei hemin hapanta*, John 4:25). This is one of the most extraordinary descriptions of the Messiah in the Bible. She is implying that in the Christ, the Icon of the living God, the fullness of truth, will be announced and made clear, not so much in the sense that he will give us every piece of data as that he will be the lens through which the whole of reality is properly viewed. The highest truth about God and ourselves will be made plain iconically in his way of being.

Genesis tells us that Yahweh walked with Adam in the cool of the evening as a friend. This easy relationship was interrupted when Adam sought on his own terms and through his own power to seize the knowledge that belongs naturally to God and that can be received by another only as a gift. In attempting to cling to this knowledge of good and evil (this lens through which the whole of reality can be properly viewed), he put an end to the friendship he had enjoyed with God. The Messiah, the person through whom God wishes to reestablish intimacy with the human race, is thus correctly described as the one "who will tell us everything." But the key is that this divine interpretation must be given and received as grace.

Realizing that his interlocutor is ready for marriage, Jesus discloses his true identity: "I am he, the one who is speaking to you" (John 4:26). The Greek formula behind the first phrase is *ego eimi* (I am), evoking, obviously, the "I AM WHO I AM" of Exodus 3:14, the title by which Yahweh announced himself as the deliverer of his people. So the Samaritan woman, an archetype of the sinful and searching human race, is being rescued from the slavery of concupiscent desire through the taking of the Messiah as her bridegroom. And this Messiah is the one who is speaking personally to the woman (*ho lalon soi*). Sin, the rupture inaugurated in the Garden of Eden, is a breakdown in the easy conversation between divinity and humanity. In the playful, almost teasing repartee between Jesus and the Samaritan woman, we witness the act by which God, through grace, puts himself and humanity back on speaking terms.

After the full manifestation of Jesus's messianic identity, we see the dramatic effects of grace in the sinner: "then the woman left her water jar and went back to the city" (John 4:28). The jug that she had carried on her head day after day, seeking after the water that would never finally quench her thirst, is symbolic of the weight of concupiscence. Fixed to worldly objects, human desire can never adequately enter into the ecstasy associated with the loop of grace and hence remains tied down, burdened. In the *Purgatorio*, the prideful are compelled to carry around huge boulders in order to feel the weight of the ego pressing them down; when Dante is freed from sin, at the end of his purgatorial journey, he is weightless and can therefore fly through the spheres of paradise. The putting aside of the water jar is evocative of this lightness of being which comes from the correct orientation of desire. Gifts are not heavy, for once they are received, they are given away, only to be received and given again.

I suggested at the outset of this analysis that the isolation of the woman probably indicated her social ostracization. How fitting therefore that, having set down her burden, she immediately runs into the town. Whatever had shamed her is now eclipsed, and she is filled with enthusiasm to speak: "Come and see a man who told me everything I have ever done! He cannot be the Messiah, can he?" (John 4:29). Hans Urs von Balthasar has argued that the beautiful calls to the one who perceives it and then sends him on a mission to spread the word. Having seen the young Beatrice, Dante is seized by the compulsion to write a poem more beautiful than any other; having spied his future wife in the surf off the Dublin strand, James Joyce is compelled to become an artist, the reporter of epiphanies. So the woman at the well, having been drawn into a saving conversation with the Son of God, having been freed from concupiscent desire, and having realized that water is bubbling up in her to eternal life, becomes a missionary, indeed the first evangelist in the Gospel of John. The beauty of the coinherence has seized her, and now she must tell of it. We notice that the heart of her message is that the divine hermeneutics has appeared—"[he] told me everything I have ever done." The implication is that this saving insight—this knowledge of good and evil, which was lost through grasping—is now available to everyone through grace.

The effectiveness of her evangelization becomes clear when we hear, a few verses later, that "many Samaritans from that city believed in him because of the woman's testimony" (John 4:39). The prime consequence of the divine gathering is a desire on the part of those gathered to gather others in turn. Like a storm over water, the circle of grace grows as it moves, irresistibly drawing others into its power.

5

The Warrior

In unpublished notes for a retreat that he gave in 1950, John Courtney Murray commented that a major motif of the Gospels is the ever-increasing *agon* (struggle) that characterizes Jesus's life. From the very beginning, he is opposed: Herod trembles in fear at his birth and then tries in the most brutal manner possible to stamp him out, forcing him and his family into exile. And from the first moments of his public ministry, he awakens fierce opposition, from both the cosmic powers and the representatives of the religious establishment. As the narrative unfolds, the warfare only becomes more intense, verbal violence giving way to threats of physical harm and finally to institutional violence that culminates in execution by crucifixion. The theological meaning of this struggle is made clear in Peter's post-Pentecost speech to the crowds gathered in the temple precincts: "But you rejected the Holy and Righteous One and asked to have a murderer given to you, and you killed the Author of life, whom God raised from the dead" (Acts 3:14–15). The opposition to Jesus is divine judgment on the dysfunction of the world. God's own life and truth appeared in the flesh, and human beings did not simply ignore or marginalize him; rather, they killed him, proving as dramatically as possible that there was something structurally wrong with their way of seeing and being.

Jesus is the icon of God the gatherer. As such, he is also necessarily the icon of God the warrior, who struggles against all the powers of dissolution, antagonism, and violence that have marred his creation. Jesus the warrior gives concrete expression to the righteous anger of

90

God that is apparent on practically every page of the Old Testament. The divine anger has nothing to do with trivial and superficial emotionality, as though God were drifting in and out of foul moods; rather, it is the symbolic representation of God's passion to set things right. As the very ground of coinherence, of gifted being-for-the-other, God stands opposed to hatred and division and longs therefore to undermine them. I will now turn to three narratives that display the features of the warrior God.

The Christmas Narrative

Jesus entered the world, notes C. S. Lewis, so anonymously and clandestinely—as a baby born to insignificant parents in an out-of-the-way corner of the Roman Empire—because he was a warrior compelled to slip quietly behind enemy lines. Though there is truth to Teilhard de Chardin's claim that God entered his world like an artist entering his studio, which is to say, with utter confidence and familiarity, there is also something quite importantly right about Lewis's observation. The universe that God entered in Christ was not alien to God, but it was, by the same token, hardly friendly to the Creator; rather, it was "enemy occupied territory," or to adapt Teilhard's metaphor, it was indeed the artist's studio, but it was filled with trashed, broken, and half-finished pieces. Raymond Brown reminds us that the Christmas stories are not charming tales that we tell to children; despite their undoubted charms, they are harsh and terrible, for the shadow of the cross falls over them.

The second chapter of the Gospel of Luke opens with an invocation of two of the weightiest political potentates of the time: "In those days a decree went out from Emperor Augustus that all the world should be registered. This was the first registration and was taken while Quirinius was governor of Syria" (Luke 2:1). Caesar Augustus was the *kyrios* of the civilized world, and Quirinius was his satrap, charged with the task of implementing Augustus's will in the eastern corner of the empire. In mentioning those names, Luke is drawing our attention to the domination system, the power establishment, of the Roman authority. With the help of Quirinius, Caesar is performing an act uniquely characteristic of one who wields political power—the taking of a census. An emperor would count his people in order to tax them more judiciously or to draft them more efficiently into his armies or to enable his underlings in the chain of command to manage them more thoroughly. The manipulative and overbearing quality of census taking becomes clear in the Old Testament, when David's desire to take a census of his people is met with the sternest divine disapproval.

In commencing his story this way, calling to mind the mighty and powerful, Luke was in line with the best traditions of his day. Poems, narratives, and encomia in the ancient world centered almost invariably on the exploits of the best and brightest. If ordinary persons found their way into such literary accounts, they functioned as, at best, comic relief and more typically as foils to the heroic protagonists.[1] But Luke effects a great reversal, because it becomes clear as the narrative unfolds that it this story is not about Augustus and Quirinius at all, but rather about two very ordinary people making their way from one shabby village to another. And in point of fact, Augustus and his aide function in the narrative precisely as a foil to them. Because of the census, "Joseph also went from the town of Nazareth in Galilee to Judea, to the city of David called Bethlehem, because he was descended from the house and family of David" (Luke 2:4). The decree, which Augustus took to be indicative of his lordship of the world, in fact serves the purpose of moving Joseph and his wife to the city of David so that the Messiah may be born in the place that God had declared. Real divine power, we are being told, is above worldly power and uses it for its ends, and hence we oughtn't concentrate on the negligible authority of Augustus. Rather, we must look to this couple.

"While they were there, the time came for her to deliver her child," but she was compelled to give birth in a primitive place, a shelter for animals, because "there was no place for them in the inn" (Luke 2:6-7). We are meant to meditate on the contrast between this unspeakably primitive setting—baser even than the traveler's hostel at tiny Bethlehem—and the palace of Augustus on the Palatine hill in Rome, the site from which the census decree undoubtedly went out. Quite naturally we associate power with luxury and the possession of fine things, but in light of this unsettling narrative, we realize that such an association would be mistaken. The power that animates the cosmos has much more to do with the emptying of self than with the pampering of self. Augustus's home, in the heart of the capital city of a world-spanning empire, would be the safest and most comfortable place imaginable, while a stable or a cave outside Bethlehem would be just about the most vulnerable, least protected space that we could imagine. Real power comes not from the protection of the ego from danger but rather from willingness to expose the ego to danger for the sake of love. *Kyrios* Jesus has begun his battle, in short, with *kyrios* Augustus; a tale of competing kingdoms, competing conceptions of power, is being told.

"She gave birth to her firstborn son and wrapped him in bands of cloth" (Luke 2:7). Augustus was certainly considered the freest man in

1. William Placher, *Narratives of a Vulnerable God* (Louisville, KY: Westminster John Knox, 1994).

the world of the first century. Wielding absolute political power, commanding an unchallenged army, he could do practically whatever he wanted; there were no restrictions placed on the ranginess of his will. But the son born to Joseph and Mary is, from the first moment, wrapped up, tied, confined. Bound by no one, Augustus seems to be utterly free; but real freedom, Luke is telling us, is enjoyed by the child totally bound by his Father's will and hence tied to the good of the world he has come to serve. Once he has decided to create, God cannot remain indifferent to the world and its needs; on the contrary, he is bound by a fiercely parental love to everything that participates in his being. Authentic divine freedom therefore has nothing to do with a capricious voluntarism, whereby God groundlessly and arbitrarily decides how or whether he will act. The Christ child—wrapped up in swaddling clothes—is the icon of this God of bound freedom, a God who faces down the ersatz divinity on the Palatine hill.

Luke then tells us that this humble and bound child is "laid . . . in a manger" (2:7). In his imperial splendor, Caesar Augustus would have been undoubtedly the best-provided-for person in the ancient world. Any material need he had—for food, drink, sex, bodily pleasure—would have been met easily and fully. In common conceptions of the good life, this kind of access to physical satisfaction would play an important role. Once more, the Lukan infancy narrative turns things upside down. The baby king is not fed; rather, laid in the place where the animals eat, he is offered as food for the world. This act anticipates the dynamism of his public life, during which he will be given over and again for the feeding of others. At the climax of his career, Jesus will present himself as bread to be eaten and wine to be drunk, giving himself away rather than drawing fame, protection, honor, sustenance to himself. When he is pierced on the cross, blood and water flow from his side, signaling that, to the very end, life goes out from him for the good of the church. Here again the law of the gift is on iconic display: being increases in the measure that it is given away; life is enhanced in the measure that one participates in the loop of grace.

"In that region there were shepherds living in the fields, keeping watch over their flock by night" (Luke 2:8). We ought not to be romantic about shepherds, imagining them as winsomely bucolic figures. In New Testament times, shepherds were considered rather shady characters, ne'er-do-wells unable to hold down a steady job, unreliable and dishonest. So questionable was their reputation that their testimony was inadmissible in a court of law. They would be the last people with whom Quirinius or Caesar Augustus were likely to have dealings, the most removed from the corridors of power, responsibility, and respectability. Yet it is to them that a messenger from the heavenly court appears: "then an angel of the

Lord stood before them, and the glory of the Lord shone around them, and they were terrified" (Luke 2:9). Jesus commenced his public life standing in the muddy waters of the Jordan shoulder to shoulder with sinners, seeking a baptism of repentance. The deep embarrassment that this association caused can be sensed in the defensiveness of both Matthew and John in their recounting of the incident. He scandalized his coreligionists by consistently eating and drinking with known sinners, in clear violation of well-established purity codes. At the end of his life, he hung on a cross between two criminals, a writ of condemnation over his head. So here, the announcers of the incarnation find their way precisely to the ordinary, the lowly, the unsavory. The divine life is not kept behind a metaphysical *cordon sanitaire* but rather expresses itself in the act by which it goes in love into what is opposed to it. Augustus would meet his enemy through some form of violence, but Christ meets his enemy with engagement and invitation.

Because they are in the presence of the numinous, the shepherds are, naturally, afraid, but the emissary from God's circle is not interested in perpetuating their fear: "Do not be afraid; for see—I am bringing you good news of great joy for all the people: to you is born this day in the city of David a Savior, who is the Messiah, the Lord" (Luke 2:10–11). Worldly powers are deeply concerned with the inculcation of fear. Every system of domination, every political or cultural tyranny, is predicated upon the fear of punishment, ostracization, torture, or death. Because the relatively weak can be cowed by the relatively strong, the latter stay in power and a sort of dysfunctional equilibrium is maintained. But the divine lordship is predicated not on the domination born of terror but rather on the inclusivity born of love. Augustus's empire, as Augustine argued so persuasively in *The City of God*, was held together by violence and the threat of violence, and its order was therefore a pseudojustice, the kind of order that holds sway in a band of thieves. What the angel proposes to the shepherds is another *kyrios*, the Messiah Jesus, whose rule will constitute a true justice because it is conditioned not by fear but by love and forgiveness, and oriented not to maintenance of the tyrant's power but toward the production of "joy for all the people." That this is not simply an idle dream or a vague abstraction becomes clear in the course of the Gospels as Jesus's kingdom is pitted in a desperate struggle against the established order, coming to a climax on the battle of the cross. In the contrast between Augustus and the child king in the second chapter of Luke, this contest is quietly adumbrated.

The political dimension of the angel's message emerges with even greater clarity when Luke tells us, "Suddenly there was with the angel a multitude of the heavenly host, praising God and saying, 'Glory to God in the highest heaven, and on earth peace among those whom he favors!'" (Luke 2:13–14). Again, we shouldn't be overly romantic or sentimental here. As we have seen, the customary reaction to an angel is terror, and now there is a host of these terrifying beings. Moreover, the word employed, *stratias* (host), has a definite military overtone[2]: there emerges on Christmas night, Luke is telling us, an entire army of angels arrayed for battle.

The contrast between Augustus, the *kyrios* of the most impressive fighting force on the earth, and Jesus, the *kyrios* of a heavenly host, couldn't be clearer or more telling. These soldiers—more powerful by far than Caesar's—don't brandish swords and utter battle cries; they sing the praise of God. What gives them harmonic cohesiveness is precisely their common devotion to the divine power that transcends them. What has led to violent divisions on earth—giving rise to the need for armies like Caesar's—is none other than a loss of this common praise of God among human beings. When God is no longer acknowledged as primary, when he is no longer glorified, the ego quickly emerges as the center of the soul's preoccupations, and this in turn leads inevitably to the war of all against all. And this is why the liturgical song of the angels is correlated to peace on earth: when our voices—as the Roman liturgy has it—blend with those of the celestial choir (when we assume the same properly ordered psychological and spiritual stance as they), order follows here below. Once more the conflict is on display: the emperor's *ordo* maintained through fear and violence versus the Christ's *ordo* maintained through the praise of God.

To round out this Christmas icon, I should like to turn from Luke's account and consider, however briefly, one section of Matthew's infancy narrative. In the second chapter of Matthew's Gospel, we read the account of the infant Jesus's struggle with a second king, not Caesar this time but one of his local representatives, Herod the Great. Just after the birth of Jesus, "wise men from the East came to Jerusalem, asking, 'Where is the child who has been born king of the Jews?'" (Matt. 2:1–2). This seemingly innocent question is fraught with tension and implicit challenge, for "king of the Jews" is Herod's own title. That a child, not of his own family, would be so acclaimed obviously produces deep anxiety, especially in someone in love with power: "when King Herod heard this, he was frightened, and all Jerusalem with him" (Matt. 2:3).

In his commentary on the book of Exodus, Origen argues that the Israelites symbolize the positive powers of the soul—mind, will, imagination, creativity—while the Egyptians stand for the tyranny of sin. According to this allegorical schema, holy qualities within us have be-

---

2. In the Greek, *strateia* is a military engagement; *strateuma* is an army; *strategos* is a general, etc.

come the slaves of egotism and fear and are now pressed into service for unspiritual purposes, for the building of an unholy city. Similarly, Jerusalem, in Matthew's account, is the holy city, God's dwelling, which has tragically fallen under the sway of an alien power and hence become corrupt, like the empire presided over by Augustus. And this is why both Herod and the enslaved city tremble in fear at the prospect of a new king. It is of course by no means accidental that the hostility of Jerusalem and its leader is invoked at the beginning of Jesus's story, for this is a foreshadowing of the angry Jerusalem, led by another Herod, that thirty years later would definitively reject Jesus, placing over his head the sign ironically reminding the world that he is indeed their true King. The battles lines are drawn early in the Gospel, and they remain in place until the end.

The intensity of the opposition to the child king becomes eminently clear as Matthew's second chapter unfolds. Knowing the full implications of the appearance of his rival, Herod seeks to kill the child, employing the desperate and terrible means of eradicating all children in Bethlehem under the age of two. This act, of course, links Herod symbolically to the Pharaoh of Exodus, who affected a similar mass infanticide at the time of Moses's birth. Warned in a dream by an angel—a warrior in the heavenly host—"Joseph got up, took the child and his mother by night, and went to Egypt, and remained there until the death of Herod" (Matt. 2:14–15). Like another Joseph the dreamer, the protector of Jesus ventures into Egypt, the land of exile and slavery, and stays with his family until the danger passes. As Yahweh fought for his people in the land of Egypt, entering into close combat with their enslavers, so Yahweh's icon goes into Egypt, symbolically anticipating his later journey into the realm of sin and death and his battle against the keepers of the oppressive order. Matthew's comment makes this connection explicit: "This was to fulfill what had been spoken by the Lord through the prophet, 'Out of Egypt I have called my son'" (Matt. 2:15). Yahweh sends (and will send) his only begotten son into battle against the Egypt of sinful dysfunction and will then call him forth through the victory of the resurrection.

Finally, in a chilling coda to an already frightening story, Matthew tells us that when Joseph, Mary, and the child return to Palestine after hearing of the death of Herod, they avoid Judea, where Herod's son Archelaus now holds sway, and finally settle in out-of-the-way Nazareth. Like the child in the book of Revelation whom the dragon seeks to devour from the moment of its birth, the Christ child is, from the very beginning, relentlessly sought out and hunted down. The *agon* of which John Courtney Murray speaks was present from beginning to end of the warrior's life.

The Temptation in the Wilderness

One of the most puzzling features of the Gospels is Jesus's persistent struggle with demons. Since the Enlightenment, this has proved a bit of an embarrassment, a holdover from a primitive and superstitious time, a distraction from the central themes of the Jesus story. Thomas Jefferson—a paradigmatically modern figure—took a pair of scissors to the Gospels, snipping out passages dealing with the supernatural, the bizarre, the miraculous—anything unrelated to the simple and beautiful ethical teaching of Jesus. He thus made short work of Jesus's exorcisms.

There are two basic problems with this rationalist demythologizing of the demonic. First, were we to take Jefferson's scissors to the Synoptic Gospels, we would be left with drastically altered texts. The accounts of miracles and exorcisms are not peripheral to the Gospel traditions, mere decorative additions to the ethical substance; on the contrary, they are woven throughout, from beginning to end. Second, the struggle with "the Satan" (*ho Satanas*) is a structuring motif of the Gospel story. It is not simply the sheer number of such narratives that is striking but the thematically central role that they play. Though the *agon* with Rome and its various political representatives is key to Jesus's ministry, argues N. T. Wright, far more basic and essential is his *agon* with the spiritual power of the evil one, the force that transcends Roman power and expresses itself through it.[3]

When Jesus enters onto the public stage in the Gospel of Mark, he announces that the reign of God has arrived, and then he confronts and expels a demon (Mark 1:23–28). These two moves are not unrelated. Jesus preaches that in him the new *ordo* of God has broken into human affairs, and then to prove the legitimacy of what he is saying, he demonstrates it in dramatic fashion by expelling one of the representatives of the old *ordo*.

I'm not particularly concerned here with exploring the question of the metaphysical status of New Testament demons. Suffice it to say that they are forces that stand behind the more immediately apparent manifestations of evil in the world—oppression, racism, violence, war. Whether we construe them personally or impersonally is less important than that we understand their influence. Paul referred to them as "powers and principalities" and clearly anticipated the Gospel claim that they have been defeated by Jesus. This ultimately victorious struggle is at the heart of the Gospel narratives.

Now what gave Jesus the confidence to wage war against the demonic and even to claim that the kingdom of Satan has been in principle de-

3. N. T. Wright, *Jesus and the Victory of God* (Minneapolis: Fortress, 1996), 451–67.

feated: "I watched Satan fall from heaven like a flash of lightning" (Luke 10:18)? The Synoptic Gospels are rather unambiguous on this point, agreeing that just before the inauguration of his public ministry, Jesus waged a successful battle against the prince of the powers of darkness. In the wake of that victory, he felt empowered to commence his work of preaching, healing, and exorcism. Again, I don't think that it is necessary to work out the precise metaphysical makeup of this opponent, and I certainly don't advocate a literalistic reading of the Gospel accounts; however, I am convinced that some struggle—whether we interpret it physically, psychologically, or spiritually, interiorly or exteriorly—took place between Jesus and the power that he took to be elemental in the determination of the sinful *ordo*. Because that battle was successful, he was furthermore convinced that war could be fruitfully waged against the remaining minions of the primordial evil.

Therefore, as we explore this icon of Jesus the warrior, it is imperative that we look with careful attention at the story of the temptation in the wilderness, watching for the dynamics of the battle, not this time between Christ and Augustus, the greatest worldly power, but between Christ and *ho poneros*, the evil one, so pervasive and powerful that it uses Augustus and his colleagues as pawns.

Matthew's narrative of the temptation is found at the beginning of the fourth chapter of his Gospel, directly after the story of Jesus's baptism by John in the Jordan. This juxtaposition is, of course, far from accidental. Having discovered that he is the beloved Son of God, Jesus is compelled immediately to explore the practical and spiritual ramifications of that identity. Hardly a quiet, meditative affair, this exploration amounts to a warfare, for we hear that the Spirit of God "led [him] into the wilderness to be tempted by the devil" (Matt. 4:1). In the desert, therefore, the two forces are arrayed: the Holy One, whose icon Jesus is, and *ho diabolos*, the scatterer—the one who wishes to gather the tribes of Israel and the one whose whole nature is to divide. How they engage one another becomes a hermeneutical key to reading the whole of the Gospel.

Matthew tells us that Jesus "fasted forty days and forty nights, and afterwards he was famished" (Matt. 4:2). The desert locale and the mystical number of forty call to mind, of course, the forty-year sojourn of the people Israel in the wilderness after the exodus. Just as the child Jesus was called out of Egypt, so now, on the verge of his public ministry, the mature Christ walks, like the former slaves, through the liminality of the wasteland. Jesus is recapitulating the political liberation of his people in order to signal the more far-reaching liberation from Satan that he will effect for them in his own person.

At the limits of his endurance, Jesus confronts the enemy: "The tempter came and said to him, 'If you are the Son of God, command these stones to become loaves of bread'" (Matt. 4:3). The devil's conditional clause—"if you are the Son of God"—reveals that what is at stake in this struggle is the nature of Jesus's messiahship. Throughout Israelite history, the Messiah's office had been imagined in a variety of ways: liberator, eschatological prophet, suffering servant. In the measure that Jesus realizes true Christ-hood, he will be able to outmaneuver his opponent; in the measure that the scatterer can lure Jesus into a false conception of his mission, he will carry the day.

This first temptation is low level, symbolized by the desert floor strewn with stones. It is the attempt to move Jesus away from the will and pur-poses of God through a crude appeal to his animal instincts. Hunger for food is spiritually equivalent to the desire for sexual pleasure and sensual delight, for the satisfaction of the most immediate needs of the body. Precisely because they are immediate and insistent, these desires can easily dominate the soul, becoming an addictive preoccupation. Thomas Merton commented that they are like noisy and petulant children and that indulging them only intensifies their mastery over the self. In associating messiahship with the satisfaction of personal sensual desire, the tempter is drawing Jesus away from his gathering task, for hedonism is essentially egocentric, an attempt to use the world for self-gratification.

The countermove of Jesus is to quote the Scripture: "It is written, 'One does not live by bread alone, but by every word that comes from the mouth of God'" (Matt. 4:4). How wonderful that he answers a temptation having to do with the mouth (eating) by appealing to a higher Mouth. In accord with a venerable scriptural tradition, Jesus implies that the word of God is a type of food that the human being requires more even more urgently than physical nourishment, but he also orients the devil away from the inevitably self-centered quality of sensual satisfaction to the essentially communitarian quality of feasting on the divine word. God's word can be heard by all and never runs out; further, by its very nature, it is meant to be passed on once it has been taken in. It is an expression of that graced manner of being—what is had precisely as it is given away and shared—that we saw earlier in the account of the prodigal son. What Jesus tells *ho poneros* is that he chooses to live primarily off this food and hence to remain in the loop of grace.

The topography shifts as we move to the second temptation: "Then the devil took him to the holy city and placed him on the pinnacle of the temple" (Matt. 4:5). We have now moved to a higher, more spiritually refined challenge. Having failed to dissuade the warrior through sensual desire, the tempter displays the allurements of the heights, what Aquinas calls *gloria*. The temple plays an extremely important role in the Gospel tradition. Jesus's prophetic cleansing of the temple is mentioned in all four Gospels, and it was undoubtedly this act that precipitated the fierce official reaction—both Jewish and Roman—that conduced eventually to the crucifixion. That particular act of Christ was so charged with tension precisely because the temple was so charged with significance. At the center of the capital city of Jerusalem, the temple was the economic, political, cultural, and religious pole of the nation. Of course this separation of these various dimensions reflects a modernism that would have confused a first-century Jew. Since it was the religious center, and since religion informed and impinged upon every aspect of life, it was naturally the focus of everything else. To grasp the status of the temple in our terms, we would have to imagine some combination of the Capitol, Lincoln Center, Wall Street, and the National Cathedral. Because he made bold to utter prophetic judgment on such a place, and even more disturbingly, to act out that judgment, Jesus was a marked man.

Now all of this is, in a very ironic way, anticipated in the temptation account. The scatterer brings Jesus to the temple and places him at the very pinnacle of it, in a position of prominence and supreme visibility. At the tip-top of the temple, Jesus is symbolically at the very height of the society and culture of his time, master of the realms of economy, politics, and religion, the undisputed center of attention. Moreover, he even has the prospect of being the focus of the divine attention: "If you are the Son of God, throw yourself down; for it is written, 'He will command his angels concerning you,' and 'On their hands they will bear you up, so that you will not dash your foot against a stone'" (Matt. 4:6). What the devil is offering him is, in a word, the inflation of the ego through honor.

Aquinas pointed out the folly of seeking the mere *sign* of achievement as an end in itself; nevertheless, glory and fame are sought by many as passionately as food or sex. Like an inordinate desire for sensual satisfaction, a desire for honor is essentially divisive, since it hinges on the ego's need to draw the outside world into itself, and it is therefore a favorite lure of the *diabolos*. If Jesus had succumbed to this suggestion, he might have become a kind of gatherer of the tribes of Israel—everyone is fascinated by famous and successful people—but the community so formed would have been extremely unstable and dysfunctional. He would properly draw the people together precisely by eschewing their esteem and accepting the will of his Father for them. And this fidelity would lead him to be not the darling of the temple but the cleanser of it.

In response to Satan's temptation, Jesus once more cites the Scriptures: "Again it is written, 'Do not put the Lord your God to the test'" (Matt. 4:7). To be in the grip of the lust for honor is to need the constant attention and appreciation of the other. It is to require the other to "bear me up," inflate me, protect me from harm, no matter what I do. It is to make of another subject, even of God himself, an audience, and hence to reduce that subject to a means. In insisting that God should never be put to the test, Jesus is resisting just that spiritual danger.

For the third temptation, the scatterer raises Jesus to the loftiest possible point of vantage: "Again, the devil took him to a very high mountain and showed him all the kingdoms of the world and their splendor" (Matt. 4:8). If the lure of sensual pleasure is the most elemental temptation, and the lure of glory the intermediate, the seduction of power—the mountain-top experience—is the most sublime and dangerous. Power is obviously a positive value, since God himself is referred to as the Almighty One, and the mountain, the point of contact between God and the world, is in the biblical framework holy ground. The devil has thus brought Jesus into a dizzying, rarefied atmosphere, a heady place where it is not easy to distinguish the real from the apparent good. We notice here the temptation is not to be looked at (as in the last episode) but rather to look. All the kingdoms of the world are displayed from this height, and Jesus is encouraged to look out at them in a mastering way, casting his glance and his will on them simultaneously.

Having prepared his interlocutor, the tempter makes his move: "All these I will give you, if you will fall down and worship me" (Matt. 4:9). What emerges as both most illuminating and most disturbing is that the devil can offer all of the kingdoms of the world precisely because they all belong to him. This connection is made even clearer in Luke's account: "And the devil said to him, 'To you I will give their glory and all this authority; for it has been given over to me, and I give to anyone I please" (Luke 4:6). Here the nature of the power in question here becomes clear. It has nothing to do with the legitimate power by which God governs the cosmos; it has everything to do with the devil's essential task of scattering.

René Girard has identified the scapegoating mechanism as basic to the maintenance of order in most human communities. When tensions arise among people due to mimetic and competitive desire for limited goods, scapegoats—usually outsiders, or those who are different in any way—are automatically identified, and upon them is cast the collective anxiety of the group. This dynamic is at play from the gossiping conversation circle to the academic society, to the nation-state: the establishment of order through blaming and expulsion. In claiming that the kingdoms of the world belong to the scatterer and are based upon worship of him, Matthew's Gospel seems to be in line with the Girardian instinct.

What Girard saw as the greatest contribution of Christianity was just this unveiling of the demonic character of the scapegoating mechanism and the consequent proposal of a new nonviolent model of social order, based not on exclusion but on forgiveness and positive mimesis. One of the clearest demonstrations of both dysfunctional social dynamics and the new form of Christian ordering is the Johannine story of the woman caught in adultery (John 8:1–11). The scribes and Pharisees bring to Jesus a woman to whose adultery they have been eyewitnesses. Where, one wonders, must they have been standing and how long must they have been waiting in order to catch this unfortunate *in flagrante*? Their eagerness to find a victim, their willingness to go to great extremes in the process, is eloquent testimony to the common and insatiable human need for scapegoats.

Having discovered her in her sin, they rush her to a prominent religious spokesperson. Girard shows throughout his writings that the scapegoating move typically finds a religious sanction because it is appreciated as the means whereby a kind of peace is brought to a riven group. God or the gods must smile on such a process. Hence, the woman's accusers confidently quote the scriptural demand: "Now in the law Moses commanded us to stone such women. Now what do you say" (John 8:5)? The novelty of the gospel is revealed in Jesus's refusal to contribute to the energy of the gathering storm: "Jesus bent down and wrote with his finger on the ground" (John 8:6). Because it creates a sense of community, however perverted, scapegoating is practically irresistible, especially to those who feel threatened by already-existing tensions and rivalries within a group. By declining to cooperate with the process, Jesus effectively breaks its momentum.

Obviously frustrated by this unexpected opposition from a representative of religion, the scribes and Pharisees press him, but they are met with one of the most devastating one-liners in the Bible, a remark that is not only rhetorically smart but spiritually revolutionary: "Let anyone among you who is without sin be the first to throw a stone at her" (John 8:7).

Jesus thereby directs the counterproductive energy of scapegoating violence back toward the accusers, compelling them to see their own mimetic desire and to appreciate the ways that it has led to a breakdown in community. In so doing, he effectively unveils the dangerous secret that the unstable order of the society has been predicated upon a violent act of exclusion. The church fathers emphasized this point with a neat interpretive move: they imagined that Jesus was writing in the sand none other than the sins of those who were threatening the woman. The effect of this unveiling was to compel an identification between the accusers and the accused, so that a new community of compassion and forgiveness could be forged. Whether they knew it fully or not, the scribes and Pharisees were connected to the woman by Jesus's words.

And that healthier connection necessarily forced the breakdown of the scapegoating society: "When they heard it, they went away, one by one, beginning with the elders" (John 8:9). Having stopped its momentum by his silence, Jesus dissolves the crowd by his speech.

Then we see, at least in seminal form, the new order: "And Jesus was left alone with the woman standing before him. Jesus straightened up and said to her, 'Woman, where are they? Has no one condemned you?' She said, 'No one sir,' And Jesus said, 'Neither do I condemn you. Go your way, and from now on do not sin again'" (John 8:9–11). Jesus and the woman—in Augustine's magnificent phrase *misericordia et misera*—are the core of a renewed communion, for their connection is not the consequence of condemnation but rather the fruit of forgiveness offered and accepted. As giver and receiver of compassion, Jesus and the woman embody the social form that participates in the loop of grace.

The ending of this episode constitutes a reversal of the opening. The scribes and Pharisees were intensely interested in the woman's behavior, because they needed her as a scapegoat; this is why, as we saw, they had been watching her so closely. At the end of the story, Jesus lets her go. Phony communions are but collectivities of egotists, in which each member of the group is trying to draw every other into his sphere of influence. This is especially true with regard to scapegoats themselves, who are clung to possessively even as they are despised. A *communio* of love, on the other hand, is predicated upon the connection whereby each looks to the good of the other, letting the other be for his own sake. Even were she to wander hundreds of miles away, the woman caught in adultery would be inextricably connected to Jesus and he to her, precisely through an act of love proffered and taken in.

The final admonition of the Lord to sin no more is perfectly congruent with this interpretation. As I have been arguing, sin is always a form of sundering. Even a seemingly "private" or "victimless" sin such as adultery is, in fact, divisive and hence both participates in and contributes to the overall spirit of false *communio*. Jesus is therefore telling the woman not to return to the way of being from which he has just extricated her, much as, in Mark's Gospel, he tells the blind man not to return to the city that had blinded him (Mark 8:26).

Thus, when Jesus resists the temptation to worship the scatterer and to become the lord of the kingdoms of the world, he is turning away from the pseudo-*ordo* that has bedeviled the human race from the beginning. "Away with you, Satan! for it is written, 'Worship the Lord your God, and serve only him'" (Matt. 4:10). Here, at the close of the ordeal, Jesus addresses the devil for the first time by name. In light of the Girardian reading I have just developed, the choice of titles could not be more telling, for *Satan* means "the one who accuses."[4] Jesus sends away the blamer/scapegoater in whose spirit the lords of this world exercise their authority, and he announces that the worship of God alone is the matrix for true power. At the end of his ministry, Jesus is nailed to the cross and is declared, in a supreme irony, to be the King of the Jews, the wielder

4. Ibid., 451.

of authentic authority. He hangs there accused, a scapegoat cast outside the walls of the city, but what comes from his mouth is not a curse but a prayer of forgiveness for those who are killing him. In this he shows what it means to exercise power that comes from the worship of the true God. God is the one who gives, a *communio* of grace, a fountain of forgiveness, and hence the King who worships him wields a power conditioned in every sense by love and inclusion.

After this successful struggle, Jesus, as we saw, began his campaign. After this initial supernatural *agon* against the powers and principalities, the earthly *agon* against their lesser representatives commenced. Both dimensions of the war are intertwined throughout the Gospel narratives—scribes, Pharisees, Sadducees, Romans, and his own disciples the immediate opponents and, lurking behind them, the cosmic scatterer and accuser. The depth and surface enemies come together most clearly at the climax of the war, the *agon* of the cross, where we see the supreme icon of Jesus the warrior.

The Passion

Pope Leo the Great gave voice to a patristic commonplace when he said in reference to Christ, "Nec alia fuit Dei Filio causa nascendi quam ut cruci possit affigi" (the reason for the birth of the Son of God was none other than that he might be fixed to a cross).[5] In some more recent Christologies it has been suggested that the death of Jesus was the result of merely social and political forces: the conservative establishment's resistance to his radical agenda; the Roman authorities' fear that his claim to kingship threatened their hegemony; the religious leaders' unwarranted concern that his language was blasphemous. The classical view that the death of Jesus was, in some sense, part of God's own purposes is, in these Christologies, either passed over in embarrassment or explicitly denied. But if we abandon the conviction that the death of Jesus was not simply an historical accident but an expression of God's intentionality, then we fly in the face of the overwhelming bulk of the tradition *and* of the New Testament itself. An interpreter would make a mockery of the Gospels were she to remove from the texture of the narrative the *dei*, the divinely grounded necessity of Jesus's going to the cross. And were one to propose that the Pauline letters could be read on the supposition that the cross of Christ was merely the consequence of political forces, he would be running consistently against the grain of those texts.

5. Pope Leo the Great, quoted in Hans Urs von Balthasar, *Mysterium Paschale* (Edinburgh: T & T Clark, 1990), 21.

We can begin to make sense of the providential necessity of the cross when we see Jesus's death in terms of the warrior icon. Because he is the incarnation of God's *ordo*, he has come to fight. As we have seen, he fights the most obvious forms of disorder as they appear in the political, cultural, and interpersonal realms, and he fights the powers and principalities—the spiritual forces—that undergird those more immediately apparent dysfunctions. But his fighting will not be complete until he has conquered the final enemy, that which the powers use to do their work: the fear of death. That terror of final extinction is the cloud that broods over the whole of the apparatus of human misery, and so it is that terror that Jesus must face down. That he does so in accordance with his Father's will is thus perfectly consistent with the logic of the incarnation: the bringing of the divine love to the darkest corners. The Passion narratives are the accounts of this ultimate battle, and this explains why they bristle with such enormous spiritual energy. For the purposes of this iconic analysis, I will look at Luke's narrative, which unfolds over the course of the twenty-second and twenty-third chapters of his Gospel.

Chapter 22 opens ominously enough: "The chief priests and the scribes were looking for a way to put Jesus to death, for they were afraid of the people" (Luke 22:2). We see here not only opposition but the particular form of opposition that is scapegoating. The leaders of the nation are seeking to isolate and eliminate Jesus because they are anxious to soothe tensions among the people. The author of John's Gospel stresses this dimension when he puts in the mouth of Caiaphas the words "You do not understand that it is better for you to have one man die for the people than to have the whole nation destroyed" (John 11:50). In Jesus, the true God will undermine this officially sanctioned scapegoating by becoming the scapegoat himself.

"Then came the day of Unleavened Bread, on which the Passover lamb had to be sacrificed" (Luke 22:7). The drama commences on a day of ritual slaughter, symbolically anticipating Jesus's nonviolent struggle against the powers. Just as the Passover lamb was killed in order to protect the nation of Israel, so Jesus will surrender to the executioner in order that his own blood might shield the whole of the human race. The divine warrior never fights in the customary way but rather outmaneuvers and tricks the enemy by refusing to fight with his weapons and according to his suppositions.

That night, Jesus and his disciples gathered in a large furnished room in order to eat the Passover meal, and he expressed his heartfelt affection for his friends: "I have eagerly desired to eat this Passover with you before I suffer" (Luke 22:15). Throughout his ministry, Jesus used festive meals as a sign of the kingdom that he was announcing (indeed, we saw an example of this in the story of the wedding at Cana). In hosting these suppers to which all were invited—the good, the bad, the morally questionable, the ill, the marginalized—Jesus acted out his role as the gatherer of the tribes of Israel: he became the center around which the disparate and unrelated elements of God's creation found their proper place and their connection to one another. So here, at the climax of his life, he once more sits down for a meal, this time with the disciples whom he had carefully chosen to symbolize the twelve tribes of Israel.

In this setting of unity and interconnection, Jesus performs the supreme coinherent act of his life: "Then he took a loaf of bread, and when he had given thanks, he broke it and gave it to them, saying, 'This is my body, which is given for you.' . . . And he did the same with the cup after supper, saying, 'This cup that is poured out for you is the new covenant in my blood'" (Luke 22:19–20). The father of the prodigal son told his elder child, "All that is mine is yours," indicating that his whole being was the offering of grace. Here the icon of the invisible God shows that his very self—his body and blood—is not his to cling to but is a gift given away for the sustenance of others. Jesus is not giving himself as a gift to be admired from a distance but as food that will become the flesh and blood of the other. As the disciples consume this first Eucharist, the coinherence that Jesus had embodied from the beginning of his ministry reaches an unprecedented level of intensity and completeness.

But just as the arrival of Jesus awakened the enmity of Herod and the emergence of the Son of God on the public scene stirred the opposition of demons and humans, so the climactic expression of coinherence, the laying bare of who Jesus is, brings forth the dark powers. Immediately after the cup has been shared, Jesus says, "But see, the one who betrays me is with me, and his hand is on the table" (Luke 22:21). Earlier, Luke told us that "Satan [had] entered into Judas called the Iscariot, who was one of the twelve" (Luke 22:3), and thus we see that the accusing and scattering power that had dogged Jesus from the outset of his work was still operative, even (we might say especially) here where the anti-Satanic act of coinherence was most vividly on display. How telling the detail of the betrayer's "hand on the table," soiling the beauty and interrupting the flow of grace at that sacred spot.

After this startling declaration, there follows a scene that, were it not so tragic, would be high comedy: "A dispute also arose among them as to which one of them was to be regarded as the greatest" (Luke 22:24). In the course of his public ministry, Jesus had, time and again, railed against grasping at power—"the last will be first, and the first will be last" (Matt. 20:16), "unless you change and become like children, you will never enter the kingdom of heaven" (Matt. 18:3)—and now, just after he has signaled in an unmistakable manner that the essence of his own being lies not in grasping but in giving, his most intimate followers prove, once again, that they don't understand. The concern for greatness, which is to say, for recognition and glory, is a standard type of mimetic desire, and it leads inevitably (as we see here) to quarreling and rivalry. The whole point of Jesus's preaching and praxis had been to teach a new form of desire through positive mimesis: the wishing of the good of the other as other, the letting be in love of one's neighbor and one's enemy alike. And so, with infinite patience, as his own death approaches, Jesus once more explains: "The kings of the Gentiles lord it over them; and those in authority over them are called benefactors. But not so with you; rather, the greatest among you must become like the youngest, and the leader like one who serves" (Luke 22:25–26). As his words to the scribes and Pharisees stopped and then reversed the momentum of scapegoating violence, so his words here dissipate the energy of the ambitious frenzy for power, by redirecting desire toward service and away from rivalrous self-inflation.

Once more, we are reminded that the battle here is not simply with flesh and blood and not merely on the psychological or political stage, when Jesus says to the chief of his apostles: "Simon, Simon, listen! Satan has demanded to sift all of you like wheat, but I have prayed for you that your own faith may not fail" (Luke 22:31–32). The accuser will be particularly interested in breaking up and testing (putting through the sieve) the seminal community that Jesus has tried so hard to establish. It is especially when the church lives in accord with the Spirit of Jesus that it should expect spiritual warfare to heat up. Christ's prayer for Peter represents the organic linking of the community with its founder and through him to the mystery of the divine grace, the coinherent nesting of the church in Jesus and Jesus in the Father. The implication is that the community can fend off the scattering and accusing power only when it is so aligned.

That the newborn church will be in for a fight becomes eminently clear in the surprising words of Jesus that follow: "But now, the one who has a purse must take it, and likewise a bag. And the one who has no sword must sell his cloak and buy one" (Luke 22:36). He is setting up a contrast, of course, between these instructions and those that he gave them when he sent them on their missionary way earlier in the Gospel, but the latter should not be seen as contradicting the former. In giving the first set of directives—carry no bag, no traveling staff, no sandals, etc.—he was encouraging in them an attitude of radical dependency upon God; in giving the second—including the recommendation to carry a sword—he is readying them for a struggle. The two are reconcilable when we realize that success will be had in the fight precisely when total dependency upon grace is inculcated. That he means "sword" in a symbolic sense becomes clear when, misunderstanding again, the disciples say "Lord, look, here are two swords," and he quickly replies, "It is enough" (22:38), as though to say, "That's enough of that." There will indeed be a fight, but it will not be with the counterproductive weapons of worldly power.

After the supper, Jesus and his disciples make their way up the Mount of Olives and come to a place (not named in Luke) that was a familiar haunt. Frequently in the Gospels, Jesus is referred to as the son of David, and here the connection to the warrior king is especially clear. During the armed rebellion of his son Absalom, David retreated up the Mount of Olives with his weary and depressed entourage and was verbally abused by Shimei (2 Sam. 15:30–16:12). The Son of David is similarly involved in a terrible struggle, involving the cosmic powers, the political authorities, and perhaps most distressingly, those closest to him, one of whom will betray him and another of whom will deny him—and he similarly trudges up the Mount of Olives.

What will enable him to win the war is what he does in that place: "Then he withdrew from them about a stone's throw, knelt down, and prayed, 'Father, if you are willing, remove this cup from me; yet, not my will but yours be done'" (Luke 22:41). The play of wills is where the coinherence of divinity and humanity is crucially on display. I have been operating throughout this section on the assumption that Jesus is the icon of the invisible God, the *instrumentum* of the divine purposes, and that the narrative concerning him is, in a complete sense, a narrative concerning God. Implicit in these hermeneutical postulates is that what is integral to Jesus in his humanity is not compromised or overwhelmed by the presence of God to that humanity. Thus, in this context, the human will of Jesus is most itself precisely when it enters into a coinherent harmony with the noncompetetive and noncontrastively transcendent divine will. When he resists the temptation to set his human will over and against the divine, Jesus makes a decision that is both spiritually and metaphysically correct. And it is this move that strengthens him for the fight against those powers which operate out of a metaphysical misalignment.

As if to signal the cosmic dimension of Jesus's struggle and resolution, Luke tells us, "Then an angel from heaven appeared to him and gave him strength" (Luke 22:43). This detail should not be dismissed as a bit of pious decoration. At the moment when the coinherence of creature and Creator is realized, that point that links every one creature to every other is simultaneously accessed, and it is therefore not surprising that beings from another dimension of creation are summoned to Jesus's aid precisely here.

After the anguished prayer, a crowd of people led by Jesus's disciple Judas appears. When they see this threatening group, the other disciples ask, "Lord, should we strike with the sword?" (Luke 22:49); then one of them (unnamed) cuts off the ear of the high priest's slave. The most obvious sign of the breakdown of coinherence is violence, and one of the most immediate consequences of violence is a loss of communication. Within the symbolic structure of this account, it is by no means accidental, therefore, that it is the *ear* of the high priest's slave that is severed: when connection is lost, no one listens and no one tries to be heard. In the course of his public ministry, Jesus frequently performed miracles of healing, and almost invariably what he cured were organs of communication: blind eyes, deaf ears, mute tongues, palsied legs. *Communio* entails communication. Indeed, as we shall see in some detail in the next section, the very to-be of God is a play of persons in constant communication with each other, a nonviolent coinherence. And therefore, even as his enemies are closing in, the icon of the invisible God says, "No more of this!" (Luke 22:51), and then performs his last act of healing, curing the man's ear.

Luke's passion narrative opened with an iconic presentation of the properly constituted community: the disciples gathered around Jesus, eating his body and drinking his blood. But as we saw, this beautiful community rather quickly devolved into bickering and rivalry. As the story moves to its climax, we see the iconic display of a variety of false *communiones*, predicated upon scapegoating and issuing in violence. The supreme irony is that the very one whose life was a battle against scapegoating becomes, directly or indirectly, the scapegoat.

The mob seizes Jesus and leads him away to the high priest's residence, while Peter follows warily behind. In the courtyard, Peter joins an unfocused and disparate group, gathered, it seems, only by their common need for warmth. But soon enough, they seek a deeper bond: "Then a servant-girl, seeing him in the firelight, stared at him and said, 'This man also was with him'" (Luke 22:56). Jesus had already been identified as a failed Messiah and had been accordingly scapegoated; this established a vortex into which Peter is now being drawn. Excited by the singling out of a victim, "someone else, on seeing him, said, 'You are also one of them'" (22:58). Like the mob that surrounded the woman caught in adultery, this society grows in number and intensity of fellow feeling, the scapegoating impulse spreading like a contagion: "Then about an hour later still another kept insisting, 'Surely this man was also with him; for he is a Galilean'" (22:59).

A giveaway here is the identification of Peter as an outsider; indeed, in Matthew's account, the bystanders comment that his Galilean *accent* betrays him. Girard teaches that the victim chosen by the scapegoating mob is usually an "other," someone whom they are predisposed to dislike due to a difference in appearance, speech, or style of life.

Knowing full well what is happening, Peter defends himself vigorously: "Woman, I do not know him. . . . Man, I am not! . . . Man, I do not know what you are talking about!" Peter's vehement denials are, if not excusable, at least understandable given the feeding frenzy that is under way. Jesus's arrest has put blood in the water, and the group is therefore primed to order itself around a victim associated with him. That this ordering would result in death is not the least bit lost on the hapless apostle, and so he loses his nerve. The ensuing crow of the cock (predicted devastatingly by Jesus) is not as dramatic and theologically important as the gaze of Jesus: "the Lord turned and looked at Peter" (Luke 22:61). Though certainly a look of reproach and sadness, it is also a gesture of identification, a silently indication that those who side with Jesus will face a fate similar to his.

With the breaking of dawn, another group, of much higher status, comes together, but Luke shows us how the dynamics by which they organize themselves do not significantly differ from those that governed the petty mob around the fire. The council of the Sanhedrin asks whether Jesus is the Messiah, but Jesus refuses to answer: "If I tell you, you will not believe, and if I question you, you will not answer" (Luke 22:67). When a dysfunctional group is bent on scapegoating, it is utterly indifferent to questions of truth or falsity, for all it wants is a victim. What Jesus's response indicates, once again, is the breakdown in real communication that inevitably accompanies group formation around victimization: no listening, no believing, no reasoning—in a word, no intellectual responsibility.

There follows a chilling confirmation of the Girardian dynamic: "Then the assembly rose as a body and brought Jesus before Pilate" (Luke 23:1). Like the body of Christ, this blaming assembly is now a cohesive and determined unity of interdependent organs and cells, but it is drawn together demonically, becoming thereby the mirror opposite of Christ's church. Their properly Satanic purpose is revealed the moment they arrive in the presence of Pilate: "They began to accuse him saying, 'We found this man perverting our nation, forbidding us to pay taxes to the emperor, and saying that he himself is the Messiah, a king" (23:2). They find their unity in blaming.

At a climactic moment in the book of Revelation, the devil is supplanted, and his fall is accompanied by these words: "The accuser of our comrades has been thrown down, who accuses them day and night before our God" (Rev. 12:10). Jesus's kingdom of coinherent compassion battles with any collectivity that organizes itself around accusation. Note that the Sanhedrin's frenzy of blaming has led, again, to a fudging of the truth: to be sure, Jesus is the Messiah, but they know full well that his messiahship has nothing to do with forbidding taxes or claiming political primacy. The need for a victim trumps all obligation.

To his credit, Pilate initially resists the blind enthusiasm—"I find no basis for an accusation against this man" (Luke 23:4)—but when he senses the resistance of the chief priests and the crowds that they have stirred up, he fears that he may lose political control, so he has Jesus delivered to Herod, the tetrarch of Galilee.

If truth is the first victim of the scapegoating mob, justice is the second. Herod more or less toys with Jesus, hoping that he will amuse him with a miracle, and all the while, the scapegoating mob is intensely at work: "the chief priests and the scribes stood by, vehemently accusing him" (23:10). Finally, after belittling Jesus, Herod sends him back to Pilate, realizing that he is effectively securing Jesus's execution.

There follows—and this is unique to the Lukan account—a wonderful Girardian detail: "That same day, Herod and Pilate became friends with each other; before this they had been enemies" (Luke 23:12). When a common victim is found, even the worst rivals can find solidarity with one another. Aristotle taught that true friendship is possible only in the measure that two people come together in loving some transcendent third; Girard indicated the perversion of this friendship in the coming together of two people dysfunctionally around a scapegoated, victimized third. Such is the pseudofriendship of Herod and Pilate.

In his *Mysterium Paschale*, Hans Urs von Balthasar argues that the incarnation had an essentially downward momentum, God's Son coming into flesh and going to the limits of Godforsakenness. I have expressed much the same idea through the invocation of the icon of the warrior: Jesus came to fight all those powers—Barth's *das Nichtige*—that stand opposed to the creative purposes of God.

In the Lord of the Rings trilogy, J. R. R. Tolkien employs a number of Christ figures, but the most obvious is Frodo the hobbit. The mission of this curious hero is not, as it is for many other epic heroes, to find something, but rather to get rid of something: he must throw the Ring of Power into the fires of Mt. Doom, and that mountain is found deep within the confines of the evil nation of Mordor. A basic conviction of Tolkien, born of his Christian faith, is that evil has to be actively engaged on its own ground; if it is to be defeated, it must be fought at close quarters, disempowered as it were from within. Jesus's embrace of the cross is the culmination of his saving mission, his coming to Mt. Doom, his final *agon*. What has been on view throughout the Gospels is Jesus's consistent decision not to engage the scattering powers on their own terms and through the use of their weapons. Rather, like water putting out fire, he addressed the darkness by shining a light into it. This method of meeting hatred with compassion, violence with coinherence, comes to its fulfillment on the cross.

After his condemnation by Pilate—made possible by a furiously scapegoating mob—Jesus is led through the streets of Jerusalem and then outside the city walls to a place called "the Skull." Like the ritual scapegoat described in the Old Testament, Jesus, bearing the sins of those who hunted him down, is driven outside the encampment. It is only appropriate that the organizer of the rightly ordered city finds no place within the walls of the sinful city—an exclusion, as we saw, anticipated in the infancy narrative. At Skull Place, they "crucified Jesus there with the criminals, one on his right and one on his left" (Luke 23:33). As we saw in our consideration of the infancy narratives, it is only fitting that at the culminating moment of his life and work Jesus finds himself in between two sinners and, for all practical purposes, reckoned as one of them. The icon of the invisible God is a friend of sinners. This means not simply that he wishes them well from a distance or, even less, that he merely provides them with a norm of right behavior; it means that he moves into their world, staying where they stay, feeling what they feel, enduring what they have to endure. He desires to go into the far country with the prodigal son and to share his alienation. Moreover, his position in the center of this iconic presentation is hardly accidental, for in his compassion he is the gatherer, the central point to which sinners are summoned.

Immediately after being fixed to the cross, Jesus said, "Father, forgive them; for they do not know what they are doing" (Luke 23:34). Violence thrives when it is met with violence; evil grows when met with more evil. One of the most important elements of Jesus's kingdom ethic was, accordingly, the praxis of forgiveness: "If anyone strikes you on the right cheek, turn the other also; and if anyone wants to sue you and take your coat, give your cloak as well. . . . Love your enemies and pray for those who persecute you" (Matt. 5:39–44). As Walter Wink has pointed out, these recommendations have nothing to do with passivity in the face of evil; rather, they embody a provocative but nonviolent manner of confronting evil and conquering it through a practice of coinherent love. By forgiving his direst enemies—those putting him to death in the vilest way—Jesus is drawing them onto new metaphysical ground, or better, awakening them to the truth in which they already stand: their connectedness to him and each other in God. The father of the prodigal son forgave (continued to give) even in the face of insults and rejection, inviting both of his sons into the loop of grace despite their insistence on living in the realm of *ousia*. These simple words from the cross constitute, therefore, one of the most effective acts of Jesus the warrior.

In accordance with the Scriptures, "they cast lots to divide his clothing" (Luke 23:34). We saw that at the root of sin is fear, especially fear of death. To counter that fear, people aggrandize the ego, decorating it with the approval of others or stuffing it with material things. Thomas Aquinas said that the good life is tantamount to loving what Jesus loved on the cross and despising what he despised on the cross. As he approached his death, Jesus was stripped of everything that might protect, bolster, or puff up the ego: reputation, comfort, esteem, food, drink, even the pathetic clothes on his back. And since he is nailed to the cross, he cannot grasp at anything at all. What he remains attached to is nothing but the will of his Father. So ordered, he is ready for the final battle.

"There was also an inscription over him, 'This is the King of the Jews'" (Luke 23:38). The Old Testament authors reveled in the warrior kings that Yahweh had sent them—Saul, David, Gideon, Joshua, the Maccabees—but they especially rejoiced that Yahweh himself was the true warrior fighting through the secondary causality of those figures. One of the principal hopes of the prophets was that Yahweh, through his Messiah, would establish himself as King of Israel and, by extension, King of all the nations. Thus if there was a definitive sign that a claimant to messiahship was deluded, it would be his execution at the hands of an alien power. The irony of the sign over the cross of Jesus is therefore so thick that twenty centuries later we are still unpacking it, still amazed by it. Jesus, the icon of the invisible God, is indeed the king of the Jews (*ho basileus ton Ioudaion*) and, as such, the King of the world, but his lordship consists not in military conquest or cultural dominance but rather in love unto death. What was anticipated in his humble birth, far from the court of Augustus Caesar, was completed in his death as an official victim of Augustus's successor.

In the book of Revelation, John the visionary is invited to look into the court of the heavenly King, and he sees the Holy One seated upon a throne and holding in his hand a scroll with seven seals. The scroll, with writing on both sides, stands for the meaning of history, the heavenly account of time and space, the knowledge of good and evil. It becomes clear that no one in heaven or earth has the power to open those seals and reveal the secrets. But then one of the elders, an attendant at the divine throne, speaks up: "See, the Lion of the tribe of Judah, the Root of David, has conquered, so that he can open the scroll and its seven seals" (Rev. 5:5).

Who is this fierce beast, this warrior king (from the root of David)? "Then I saw between the throne and the four living creatures and among the elders a Lamb standing as if it had been slaughtered" (Rev. 5:6). Here is the same irony, the same paradox. The key to the meaning of history is not one of the rulers of this world, not a paragon of power in the ordinary sense of the term, but rather one of the meekest of animals, a lamb of sacrifice. Moreover, this lamb, though standing, bears a mortal wound. There is an exact parallel between this extremely odd Lion of Judah and the comical King of the Jews hanging on his cross: both are mockeries of the phony power of the world; both are affirmations of the true *potentia* of God.

The reversal of value and meaning represented by the cross of Jesus is reflected symbolically in certain upheavals in the cosmic rhythms. In Matthew's account, the death of Jesus is accompanied by earthquakes and the rising of the dead, while Luke tells us, "It was now about noon, and darkness came over the whole land until three in the afternoon, while the sun's light failed" (Luke 23:44–45). What we take to be light is in fact the darkness, and what we take to be life is really death. The sinful universe is upside down; the warrior came to right it. Also, our sense of rightly ordered religion is revolutionized: "and the curtain in the temple was torn in two" (23:45). The curtain in question is that which guarded the holy of holies in the Jerusalem temple, that which protected—and hence defined—the sacred. The tearing of the curtain thus calls to mind Jesus's promise that he would tear down the temple, putting an end to the old cultic practices and the inadequate theology associated with it. ("The day is coming when you will worship neither on this mountain nor in Jerusalem . . . [but] in spirit and truth," John 4:21–23) It also indicates, relatedly, that the authentic holy of holies—the love unto death of the Son of God—is now, on the cross, visible to all, publicly available to Jew and Gentile alike.

In the midst of this upheaval—the birth pangs of the new world—the warrior speaks for the final time: "Then Jesus, crying with a loud voice, said, 'Father, into your hands I commend my spirit.' Having said this, he breathed his last" (Luke 23:46). As we have seen in many different contexts, the New Testament sense is that the suffering of the world is produced by the breaking of the loop of grace, the insistence that one's life should be one's own. When this attitude dominates, when we want the knowledge of good and evil for ourselves, when we want what is coming to us, *charis* hardens into *ousia*, and we end up losing the little that we think we have. John Calvin said that Jesus saved us by the whole course of his obedience. His savior's life was an obedient response to the will of God, a displacement of his own concerns in favor of the Father's: "the Son can do nothing on his own, but only what he sees the Father doing" (John 5:19). So here, at the last moment, he signals his willingness to live in grace, commending his life-spirit to the Father in the confidence that the Father, whose whole way of being is grace, will return it to him. Once more, we sense the unbearable lightness of the loop of grace: divine Spirit is breathed in precisely in the measure that it is breathed out; divine being is had exactly in the measure that it is let go of.

And in this, the warrior wins the ultimate battle. Herod, Augustus, Pilate, Herod Antipas, the scribes and Pharisees were but henchmen of the scatterer, the elusive power behind the more obvious purveyors of dysfunction. But the matrix for the work of the scatterer is, as we have seen, the fear of death. Therefore, having engaged the powers and the Power, Jesus tales on the energy source that animates both. Breathing out his spirit in the assurance that even death can't interrupt the loop of grace, Jesus sums up his warrior's life and effectively dissolves the final enemy.

Girard teaches that the violent pseudocommunity is sustained by negative mimesis, each person looking rivalrously at the desire of the others. The positive, redeemed community, on the other hand, is animated by a positive mimesis, people learning how to desire by imitating the wholesome desire of those around them. Throughout the passion narrative, we have seen examples of the dysfunctional community; now, at the end, the seeds of the beautiful community are evident. Joseph of Arimathea, a secret admirer of Jesus, comes courageously to ask for the body of the Lord, and a group of women who had accompanied Jesus from Galilee watch carefully to see where he is buried. As his enemies closed in on him and even his most intimate disciples fled in fear, these people have stayed with Jesus until the end. Luke aptly speaks of the women as having "followed" the body of Jesus to its resting place, their discipleship (following) of the Lord complete and consistent.

What becomes unmistakably clear in all the Gospels is that Jesus wants to go to the cross because he loves his Father's will. And therefore, those who love him—who want what he wants—will go to that same bitter end. "If any want to become my followers, let them deny themselves and take up their cross and follow me" (Matt. 16:24). Jesus's desire to share in the will of his Father can be imitated positively and without rivalry because the object of that desire is inexhaustible, and consequently a beautiful community can spring up around it. With the birth of that *communio*—however small in numbers and influence at first—Jesus the warrior has won.

6

King

The earliest and most basic form of the kerygma is *Iesous Kyrios* (Jesus is Lord). We can find this formula in a number of the evangelical speeches in the Acts of the Apostles, and we see it stated and expanded upon frequently in the Pauline letters. It is, furthermore, assumed throughout the four Gospels. What the first Christians endeavored to tell the world was that Jesus of Nazareth, crucified and risen from the dead, is the true *Kyrios*. This was, as we have seen, a clear challenge to all the earthly potentates, including and especially the Roman emperor, who claimed lordship, and it was a proclamation that was thoroughly conditioned by a biblical imagination. Throughout the Hebrew Scriptures, we discover the conviction that the Messiah would gather the scattered tribes of Israel and would then, as properly constituted king of Israel, become, by extension, the gatherer of the nations, thereby embodying and realizing Yahweh's lordship of creation, which had been compromised by sin. When Peter and Paul went, respectively, to Jews and Gentiles with the good news that Jesus is Messiah and Lord, they were operating out of this clear biblical assumption.

Now throughout his public ministry, Jesus acted as the Messiah of Israel. In his prophetic preaching and healing, in his praxis of inclusive table fellowship, in his condemnation of the religious establishment and cleansing of the temple itself, in referring to himself as the indispensable embodiment of the kingdom, Jesus consistently acted in the person of

Yahweh the gatherer of Israel. The challenge to his legitimacy came at the crucifixion. As we saw, if there was one indisputable indicator that a claimant to messiahship was mistaken, it would be his death at the hands of the Israelite religious leaders and with the collusion of a foreign power. No matter how inspiring he was or how impressive his words and actions, a pretender to the title of Messiah would be ipso facto discredited by a shameful execution. Therefore, even from a neutrally historical perspective, there is a very serious problem of interpretation in regard to the beginning of the Christian movement: how could people have possibly begun to declare a crucified man the Messiah and Lord? The only finally satisfactory answer is the one provided by the New Testament: Jesus's bodily resurrection from the dead.

To be sure, from ancient to modern times, a wide variety of alternative explanations have been offered, but none can adequately make sense of the enthusiastic claim that a crucified and buried man is the Lord. Jews of Jesus's time had a plethora of titles, concepts, and ideas capable of conveying the conviction that Jesus had been taken up to God (like Elijah or Enoch), or that he was fondly remembered by his followers (as were the Maccabean martyrs), or that his soul had left his body (as in Platonism). But they relied on none of these concepts, employing instead the precise term *resurrection*, to designate what had happened to him three days after his death. As N. T. Wright has thoroughly demonstrated, the word *resurrection* was never used by a biblical Jew to designate a nonbodily event. On the contrary, it referred to the eschatological occurrence—anticipated by some but not all Jews of the New Testament period—whereby the dead would be restored to a transformed and vibrant physical existence. The novelty of the resurrection of Jesus consisted in the fact that this eschatological act had taken place in time and for a particular person. Because of this altogether surprising historical anticipation of the final victory of Yahweh over sin and death, because of his resurrection from the dead in a transformed physicality, Jesus was, despite the folly of the cross, declared to be the Messiah and Lord of Israel and, by implication, *Kyrios* of all the nations.

Having analyzed a cluster of icons of Jesus the gatherer and Jesus the warrior, I will bring this christological section to a close by looking at three sacred pictures of Jesus the Lord, the King who galvanizes, governs, and commissions his people. These icons will all be depictions of the glorified and resurrected Jesus, the crucified one whom God has made *Kyrios* of the world. If Jesus the gatherer corresponds to our finding of the center, and Jesus the warrior to the deep knowledge that we are sinners, Jesus the Lord corresponds to the conviction that our lives are not about us, that we belong to a power beyond ourselves.

The Road to Emmaus

The twenty-fourth chapter of Luke's Gospel, which deals with the resurrection appearances of Jesus, is a literary and theological *chef d'oeuvre*. At the heart of this beautifully crafted text is the narrative of the meeting of the risen Jesus with two of his disciples on the road to Emmaus. In its concision, subtle characterization, drama, humor, and profound theological penetration, it is rightfully judged to be one of the greatest stories ever told, a masterpiece within the masterpiece.

The narrative begins with two people going the wrong way. In the Gospel of Luke, everything moves toward Jerusalem, for that is the site of the cross, the resurrection, and the sending of the Spirit. Mt. Zion is the place where the Messiah gathers the lost sheep of Israel and where the ultimate battle is fought, and so it was to Jerusalem, the true pole of the earth, that Jesus had led his people. But "two of them" (*duo ex auton*), presumably two of Jesus's number, "were going to a village called Emmaus, about seven miles from Jerusalem" (Luke 24:13). We have heard that Jesus's closest disciples, at the moment of truth, "all fled," some denying him, others betraying him, all opting for their own safety rather than following the Master. These two figures—probably not among the Twelve—followed suit, moving away from the dangerous city. If Buddhism is a sitting religion, Christianity is a religion in motion (as can be seen with special clarity in the Gospel of Mark); the all-important issue is to determine which way one is moving.

As they walked, they talked "about all these things that had happened" (Luke 24:14) in the holy city the past several days. There is a great deal in this story about words and the interpretation of words, about speaking, hearing, and properly understanding. While they walk away from Jerusalem, away from the gathering point and the final battlefield, away from where Jesus led, their speech about the recent events is bound to be skewed and misleading. Jean-Luc Marion has distinguished between *Theo*logy and theo*logy*, the former a type of speech about God that is determined by God's own logic, the latter God-talk that draws the divine mystery into conventional categories. He implies that too much of the theological tradition trades in the second mode of predication, devolving, at its worst, into useless human chatter about God. A bit like the friends of Job—theologians explicitly chastised by God for their misleading speech—the disciples on the road to Emmaus talk but say little of value. The inadequacy of their theological discussion is indicated not only by their direction (away from Jerusalem) but also by the closed quality of their conversation. They are discussing these matters among themselves, away from the wider Christian community and away from Jesus himself, whom they had abandoned. The Greek hints at this self-containment in the word that we render "discussing": *syzetein* (lit. "seeking together").

At this moment, "Jesus himself came near and went with them" (Luke 24:15). As we have repeatedly seen, since Jesus's mission was to gather the lost sheep of the house of Israel, he did not stand aloof from sinners, expecting them to come to him; on the contrary, he went were they were, searching them out, tracking them down even when they wanted nothing to do with him. So here, the resurrected Jesus seeks out his two errant disciples, joining them even as they walk in the wrong direction and talk about him in the wrong way. As he quietly, unobtrusively slipped into the waters of the Jordan to stand next to sinners, and as he willingly suffered alongside two other crucified criminals, so here he, without fanfare, falls into step with the two journeyers.

"But," says Luke, "their eyes were kept from recognizing him" (24:16). There is at least a double sense to this mysterious statement. In almost all of the resurrection accounts, there is the implication that the body of the risen Jesus is in both continuity and discontinuity with his preresurrection body. Though he is clearly physical—in John, able to be touched, in Luke, able to eat—his body seems to possess unusual qualities: passing through walls, vanishing and appearing, etc. And though he is recognized by many of the recipients of the appearances, others doubt or wonder or fail to recognize. Thus, one explanation of the lack of recognition in the Emmaus story is the uncanniness of the risen Jesus's transformed physicality. A second sense is more symbolic and is in accord with the line of interpretation I have been developing. To see Jesus is to understand him aright, and to understand him aright is to set him in the proper hermeneutical grid. Thus we could say that the eyes of their minds are prevented from recognizing him because they are in the wrong spiritual space and employing a faulty interpretive lens. Like the native people who literally did not *see* the Spanish caravels that has suddenly appeared in their cove because they had absolutely no frame of reference for them, the disciples on the road to Emmaus do not recognize Jesus because they are hermeneutically incapable of taking in what is in front of them.

Then the stranger speaks. His words are not those of a judge but those of a seeker: "What are you discussing with each other while you walk along?" (Luke 24:17). Walking with them, he joins them physically; with his question he seeks to enter their spiritual and intellectual world. In both cases, he does so gently and by invitation.

The immediate reaction to Jesus is both physical and psychological: "they stood still, looking sad" (24:17). His question stops them in their tracks, and this is all to the good, since they have been moving away from Jerusalem; the presence of the Lord (even disguised) serves to arrest their negative momentum. Their sadness is a function of their cowardice and blindness. Jesus told his disciples at the Last Supper that his purpose was to share with them the joy that he and his Father experience. Joy is the consequence of having entered into the loop of grace, the gift-giving and gift-receiving characteristic of the divine life. Walking away from Jerusalem—the city of Jesus's total self-offering to his father—is a refusal to live in grace and hence an exclusion from joy. To remember Jesus through a self-contained conversation and while walking in the wrong direction is thus to recall him in sadness.

In response to Jesus's faux-innocent question, Cleopas speaks: "Are you the only stranger in Jerusalem who does not know the things that have taken place there in these days . . . the things about Jesus of Nazareth?" (Luke 24:18–19). The irony, of course, is that Jesus is precisely the only one who does understand what went on, while everyone else fails, to varying degrees, to see. Cleopas's manner of misunderstanding becomes clear as he recounts for his interlocutor the "things" about Jesus: "a prophet mighty in deed and word before God and all the people, how our chief priests and leaders handed him over . . . and crucified him," and how his disciples had "hoped that he was the one to redeem Israel," and that some had even reported that he was alive (Luke 24:19–24). Cleopas has clearly been attentive, for he has taken in most of the relevant data concerning Jesus of Nazareth. He knows him correctly to be one who had acted in the role of the Messiah, who had awakened in the people the hope of salvation, who had, consequently, been put to death by the keepers of the established order, and who, if the reports are credible, has possibly risen from the dead. He is operating altogether adequately at Bernard Lonergan's first level of epistemological perception. But none of his ruminations and conversations have produced anything like insight, the perceiving of the pattern that is characteristic of the second degree of perception. He sees the facts but not the form; he takes in everything and takes in nothing. And this is why Jesus quite aptly replies, "Oh, how foolish you are, and how slow of heart to believe all that the prophets have declared!" (24:25).

Now the Word is ready to speak. "Beginning with Moses and all the prophets, he interpreted to them the things about himself in all the scriptures" (24:27). The Greek word behind "interpreted," *diermeneusen*, could be construed as "applied the hermeneutic." Employing the sacred texts of the Jewish people, the Word made flesh reveals the pattern that runs through the data of his life, death, and resurrection. Significantly, he does not simply pick out a few relevant passages from the Torah and the Prophets that bore upon him; rather, he shows that the Scripture as a whole is "about him," that in its totality it provides the clarifying lens for what has transpired in him. What is this pattern that Jesus uncovers in the Scriptures? We don't know it in precise detail, but we know its general thrust: "Was it not necessary that the Messiah should suffer these things and then enter into his glory?" (Luke 24:26). The disciples have been walking away from Jerusalem because the cross convinced them that Jesus must have been deluded, but in point of fact, the cross is the solution to the puzzle. The glory of the Messiah is the light that flows from his suffering and self-emptying love; the *doxa* of Israel's God is the splendor of coinherence, of being-for-the-other.

After this hermeneutical exercise—conducted in the walking Aristotelian manner—they come close to their destination. Though they were going the wrong way, the Messiah has walked all the way with them, just as he had accompanied sinful humanity all the way to the limit of sin and death. As always, the Bible tells the story not so much of our quest for God as of God's passionate quest for us. When Jesus indicates that he means to go on further, they press him: "Stay with us" (*meinon meth emon*, Luke 24:29). The verb *meinen* (to stay or to remain) is frequently used in the Gospel of John. When the two disciples of the Baptist are confronted by Jesus, they ask him, "Where are you staying?" and when the Lord replies, "Come and see," they stay with him for the rest of that day (John 1:38–39). Furthermore, Jesus says that he remains in his Father and his Father in him, indicating thereby the mutual participation that constitutes his being at the deepest level. These two disciples in Luke, with their plaintive "stay with us," give voice to the pleading of the church that Jesus might continue to be the source of its being, its lifeblood. They have begun to sense that without the hermenuetical grid of his presence, they will not see.

If the first part of this narrative describes something like a liturgy of the Word, the second part delineates a liturgy of the Eucharist. The risen Lord does what he did the night before he died: "when he was at table with them, he took bread, blessed and broke it, and gave it to them" (Luke 24:30). We saw in the last section that the intense coinherence of the Last Supper—the gathering of the disciples around Jesus, the identification of Jesus's own self with the elements of bread and wine, the eating and drinking of the Lord's body and blood—was interrupted by the forces of the scatterer. It is as though that lost moment is recovered here in the quiet of the Emmaus evening. The gatherer uses his most characteristic gesture in order to bring back to him two who had wandered from the center. When Jesus performs the act that had anticipated and now recapitulates his love unto death, "their eyes were opened, and they recognized him" (24:31). Through the hermeneutics of the Word, the disciples, on the road, had begun to see; now through the hermeneutics of the Eucharist, their vision is clarified and completed. The words of the Torah and the Prophets—interpreted by the speech of Jesus—had brought them close; now the gesture of the Word made flesh brings them to the end. The self-offering of the Son of God is therefore the "place" where authentic *theology* can alone flourish.

One wonders why Jesus made meals so central to his kingdom praxis. Perhaps it is because, in the biblical vision, divine friendship was lost through a dysfunctional meal and can be regained only through a properly constituted one. Adam and Eve ate the fruit of the tree of the knowledge of good and evil, hoping thereby to seize divinity for themselves and to hold off the threat of a rivalrous God. In this, like the prodigal son and his brother, they broke the loop of grace, taking what can only be received as a gift. And so the new Adam, the one who embodies divine friendship with the human race, invites sinners to gracious meals that symbolize God's invitation to reenter the circle of coinherence. So, at the end of the story of revelation, two friends of God sit down with Jesus to eat what God offers to them in love, thereby undoing the anxious grasping of the meal described at the beginning of the story. After the graceless repast of Eden, the eyes of Adam and Eve were opened and they saw themselves as threatened, vulnerable, and alienated from God. After the graceful meal of Emmaus, the eyes of Cleopas and his companion are opened, and they recognize the divine coinherence made flesh.

At this point, at the moment of recognition, Jesus "vanished from their sight" (Luke 24:31). This sort of sudden coming and going, appearing and disappearing, on Jesus's part is commonly mentioned in the resurrection accounts. It certainly signals the freedom of the risen Jesus from the ordinary constraints of space and time, but it also points symbolically to the spiritual "space" opened up by the resurrection. In all the appearance stories there is a moment of commissioning and sending: those who see the risen Christ know that they must go, announce, act. What makes this mission possible is the disappearance of Jesus, for if the physically risen Lord were permanently "there," available in the ordinary confines of space and time, his followers would be locked in a finally unproductive aesthetic arrest. His leavetaking opens up the "acting-area," in Balthasar's phrase, that permits his disciples to do what he did and be who he was. And so in the Emmaus account, once the two disciples have adequately applied the hermeneutic, recognizing him fully in the sacred meal, Jesus clears a space for them to act. His disappearance is his wordless commission.

Therefore "that same hour they got up and returned to Jerusalem" (Luke 24:33). The narrative commenced with movement in the wrong direction; as it came to its central, tensive point, movement halted; and now, in its denouement, there is a reversal of momentum. Having seen properly, the disciples return to the place they never should have left, the city of the cross, Zion, true pole of the earth.

Once in the holy city, they search out the community of Jesus, the Eleven who have been forged as a coinherent family through the Last

Supper and the resurrection. Before the Emmaus pair can even speak their good news, they hear it from the others: "The Lord has risen indeed, and he has appeared to Simon!" (24:34). Having taken in the *evangel* of the others, they articulate their version of it: "they told what had happened on the road, and how he had been made known to them in the breaking of the bread" (24:35).

This play of announcing and listening, this mutual sharing of the good news, is the characteristic life of the body of Christ, each member strengthening the other through a declaration of the resurrection. As they share the body and blood of the Lord in the fellowship of the table, so they share the truth of the Paschal Mystery in the coinherence of speech and understanding. This authentic church—even here in seminal form—is the creation of Christ the King, the risen Lord who has commanded his disciples into mission.

The Appearance to the Eleven

Luke's account of Jesus's appearance to the eleven remaining core disciples follows immediately upon the Emmaus story; in fact, the two stories mirror each other thematically in a number of ways. They are chronologically linked through a narrative device reminiscent of the book of Job: "while they [the Emmaus journeyers] were talking about this, Jesus himself stood among them" (Luke 24:36). Once more, we notice that Jesus's appearance is tied to a dynamic of ecclesial life: in the Emmaus story the breaking of bread and here the sharing of resurrection faith. But another dimension of ecclesiality is signaled symbolically in the positioning of the characters. The risen Jesus stands in their midst (*este en meso auton*), so that he functions as the center around which the others gather in a kind of circle. Here is the shepherd at work, the divine power that orders and arranges the lost sheep of the house of Israel around himself. Just as he had summoned the wandering Emmaus disciples back to Jerusalem, so here he draws the still frightened apostolic group together.

In medieval rose windows, the central medallion is invariably a representation of Christ, and around that still point all the other images are arranged in harmonious patterns. This icon is, accordingly, an image of the properly functioning cosmos (centered on the creative power of God), the well-ordered soul (all of its energies focused on Christ), and the adequately constituted church (all of the members of Jesus's body drawing their energy and purpose from him).

Having organized his church ontologically, Jesus articulates in speech what he has accomplished: "Peace be with you" (Luke 24:36). In Jerusalem (the city of peace), the Prince of Peace offers *shalom* to his disciples and, through them, to the scattered tribes of the world. As we have seen, peace breaks down in the measure that sinners turn in on themselves, rupturing the loop of grace, refusing to give as a gift what has been received as a gift. By going to the limits of Godforsakenness and fighting the effects of sin through nonviolent love, Jesus effectively drew fallen human beings back into *communio* with God and hence into connection with one another. Abiding in their midst, like a heart in the midst of a body, he can communicate his *shalom*, like blood, like a life force, to all of them.

Their reaction is not, immediately, joyful acceptance but rather apprehension and confusion: "They were startled and terrified, and thought that they were seeing a ghost" (Luke 24:37). The fear of the disciples can be read at several levels. In the most obvious sense, they are afraid because they are witnessing something wholly strange and unexpected, an event outside conventional categories. That a shade of a dead man, who had gone to Sheol, might rarely and under extraordinary circumstances make an appearance in this dimension of space and time was not unheard of, for it happened in the case of the specter of Samuel, called up through the machinations of the witch of Endor. Or that a ghost might manifest itself was, similarly, deemed a possibility (as the disciples' initial reaction to Jesus's appearance suggests). Even that, as in the cases of Lazarus and the daughter of Jairus, a dead person might be resuscitated was, though rare, at least understandable to a Jew of Jesus's time. But that someone who had died would return after his death in an eschatologically transformed but still embodied state, a harbinger of the general resurrection of the dead expected at the end of time—that was utterly unexpected. And so, understandably, the disciples are terrified, flummoxed.

But there is, I submit, another and more spiritually significant reason for their fear. These are the very men who had, in the moment of crisis, abandoned, betrayed, and denied their Master, fleeing for their lives rather than standing in solidarity with him. Thus, when they see him alive and in their midst, they rather naturally assume, in accord with the standard haunting story, that he is back for vengeance. In the ordinary practice of the fallen world, the breaking of relationship, the shattering of the peace, is paid for through a kind of retributive violence. The imbalance caused by a rupturing of the community is restored through an answering violence: "an eye for an eye and a tooth for a tooth." This is the sort of justice favored by the older brother in the prodigal son story: the offender against *communio* should be compelled to pay before being readmitted to the family. And it is recommended in myths, legends, and sacred stories from ancient times to the present day—from the Epic of Gilgamesh to *Dirty Harry*. When order is lost through violence, it is restored through a greater violence. And so the disciples stand in the presence of the crucified and risen Lord in an attitude of fear, convinced that he is an avatar of worldly *ordo*.

But central to the teaching and practice of Jesus is forgiveness, the restoration of order not through violence but through compassion and nonviolence. Essential to his vision that the heavenly *ordo* become the *ordo* here below is the hope that we might learn to share the forgiveness that we have, together, received from God: "Forgive us our debts, as we also have forgiven our debtors" (Matt. 7:12). Thus, when confronting those who have drastically violated his friendship, the risen Jesus says, "Shalom," a word of pardon, and in so doing creates an entirely new spiritual space and introduces a revolutionary understanding of God.

We saw earlier that Jesus consistently acted in the very person of Yahweh, claiming an authority that belonged exclusively to Israel's God. And so, in going to his death on the cross, he was expressing Yahweh's solidarity with sinners and Yahweh's willingness to endure the resistance of those whom he wished to gather into friendship. Therefore in putting Jesus to death, his executioners—both direct and indirect—put Yahweh to death, expressing their definitive rejection of the mercy offered to them by God. This awful truth, paradoxically, is the ground for salvation, though we appreciate it only in light of the resurrection. When the crucified Jesus returns alive to his disciples, stands in their midst, and says, "Shalom," he is once more speaking in the very person of Yahweh, and what he implies is that even the killing of God is not enough to block the divine forgiveness.

According to the standard interpretation of justice and the traditional theology, this greatest of crimes would call for the greatest of retributions, but instead it is met with nonviolence, compassion, *shalom*. This in turn shows us that authentic justice is much different from what we had imagined and that God is much stranger than we had thought. God's love is such that it can swallow up, absorb, and conquer even the most pointed resistance, and this becomes clear in the manner in which the murdered God restores order to the broken circle of his disciples. They (along with many others) contributed to the killing of God, the most egregious violation of justice imaginable, and God answers this injustice with forgiving love. In light of this compassion that swallowed up the greatest of sins, Paul could exclaim, "I am certain that neither death, nor life, nor angels, nor rulers, . . . neither height, nor depth, nor anything else in all creation, will be able to separate us from the love of God in Christ Jesus our Lord" (Rom. 8:38–39). Human beings committed the unsurpassable sin—not only turning from God but actively opposing him, even to the point of putting him to death—and they were met with forgiveness. The only conclusion is the one that Paul drew: that nothing is powerful enough to turn back the relentlessness of the divine mercy.

In many of the fathers of the church, one can find an account of redemption that Gustaf Aulén, in the twentieth century, characterized as the Christus Victor theory. Though it is presented with slight variations and accents, it has the following basic structure: Sinful human beings are held captive by the devil; God compels the devil to release sinners by luring him toward the particularly enticing object of the perfect human being, Jesus Christ; the devil "takes" Jesus through his death on the cross but then finds himself captured by the hidden power of Jesus's divinity, much as a fish is caught by a hook concealed behind an alluring piece of bait. The end result of this process is a freed humanity and a disempowered devil—in a word, salvation. Now many have over the centuries quarreled with this theory, finding it either theologically superficial or simply fantastical, but I wonder whether, properly demythologized, it might still prove illuminating. That God is forgiving and merciful had certainly been a central proclamation in the Torah and the Prophets, but those very texts reveal that the full extent of that forgiveness was not apparent to Israel, for there seem to have been numerous qualifications and conditions set on the divine mercy. How could Yahweh convince his people of the absolutely unqualified nature of his compassion? First, he had to become one with us, condescending to exist at our level and on our terms, but second, he had to accept from our hands a rejection so total that, in forgiving it, he could surround it and disempower it. Following the main lines of the Christus Victor theory, then, could we say that the devil is Sin itself (that which holds humanity captive) and that the divine forgiveness (hidden as it were under the guise of Jesus's humanity) is the hook that "captures" it? Sin had, as it were, to be lured out into the open, and this took place through the provocative quality of Jesus's life, ministry, and death; then, thus exposed, Sin could be undermined and adequately dealt with. Prior to the incarnation and the cross, in other words, humans could never know the height, breadth, depth, and length of God's forgiveness and were hence still held captive.

It is certainly a patristic commonplace that the sin of Adam was a *felix culpa* for humanity in the measure that it won us a savior, but Balthasar has reminded us that for some of the fathers, it could even be seen as a *felix culpa* for God, since it allowed him to demonstrate so dramatically the extent of his forgiveness. Only when we had done our worst (through killing the Son of God) could God reveal his best (forgiving even that act). The full meaning of Christ the warrior comes into focus only here, when Christ the Lord demonstrates his victory-through-forgiveness over sin.

Concerned that they still think they are seeing only a ghost (*pneuma*), Jesus said, "Look at my hands and my feet; see that it is I myself. Touch me and see; for a ghost does not have flesh and bones as you see that I have" (Luke 24:39). It is extremely important in Luke's account that the risen Jesus is, despite the strangeness and numinosity of his presence, stubbornly, objectively, and physically *there*. If the resurrected Christ were but a projection of the disciples' desires, a fantasy, a fond memory, a vague "sense" of being forgiven (as in Schillebeeckx), or the content of a spiritual "experience," we would still be in our sins. For any of those psychological phenomena would be, necessarily, infected by the fallenness of the world, by the violence and lack of coinherence that mark both community and subjectivity. It is essential that something new, unexpected, and objective *happened to* the Eleven; without this exteriority and surprise, the excitement that is apparent on practically every page of the New Testament would be unintelligible. From the beginning, human beings have longed for and fantasized about salvation, but the power and point of the New Testament witness is that this dream has been concretely and historically realized.

But there is more to it. Jesus invites his followers to look specifically at his hands and his feet (*idete tas cheiras mou kai tous podas mou*), which is to say, the wounded extremities of his body, those parts of his body most immediately affected by the crucifixion. There can be no mistake that the risen Christ—again, despite all of the obvious transformation that he has undergone—is none other than the crucified Jesus. This continuity preserves the link between Jesus as warrior and Jesus as Lord: the one who stands before them as the embodiment of the divine forgiveness is, simultaneously, the one who mediates the divine judgment. In the *shalom* of the risen Christ, they know they are forgiven, and in the wounds of that same Christ, they know the intensity of the sin that required forgiveness. Were the two separated, the salvifically delicate balance between sin and grace would be compromised.

The dense physicality of the risen Jesus (*sarka kai oseta*, flesh and bones) indicates that the whole drama of salvation has to do with real, embodied human beings. There is nothing in authentic Christianity of the Platonic-Gnostic myth of descending and reascending souls, of the imprisonment of spirit in matter and subsequent escape. When this form appeared in Origen's speculations, it was quickly appreciated as repugnant to the intuitions of orthodoxy. The God described in Genesis made all things good, including matter, and therefore salvation affects the human being at all levels. Whatever resurrection life means (and it remains certainly mysterious and ambiguous throughout the New Testament), it does not mean the career of a disembodied soul. Rather, it must have something to do with the elevation of the entire person and the intensification of her physical, psychological, and spiritual powers.

Though we do not know from the text itself whether the disciples responded to Jesus's invitation to touch him, the fact that he *could* be touched has important ecclesiological implications. Since the Word became flesh, it is with and in our flesh that we contact him. The objective physicality of the risen Lord grounds, therefore, the sacramental imagination of the church, the conviction that we find God's presence unabashedly in things such as water, oil, bread, relics, vestments, saints, candles, and pictures, and not by fleeing to a realm of sheer interiority or sheer transcendence. The touch of the disciples signals the electrical energy of the coinherence of Jesus and his church.

The reaction of Jesus's followers to all of this is deliciously described: "While in their joy they were disbelieving and still wondering . . ." (Luke 24:41). We have seen that joy is the mark of anyone who is caught in the loop of grace, since joy is a concomitant of ecstasy. Joy must be the principal "emotion" shared by the trinitarian persons, since their life is nothing but self-forgetting love, and joy is the greatest gift that Jesus gives to his church: "I speak these things in the world so that they may have my joy made complete in themselves" (John 17:13). Sadness of soul follows from the heaviness of self-regard, and precisely this sadness is conquered in the surprise and facticity of the resurrection.

So accustomed to processing the world through the receptive powers of the fallen mind, the disciples are dazzled by what is before them. Jesus therefore brings them rather comically down to earth: "He said to them, 'Have you anything here to eat?" (Luke 24:41). Again, I would read this request as an insistence on realism and embodiment precisely when the witnesses to the resurrection might be tempted in a Platonizing or spiritualizing direction. The joy that Jesus offers to his church happens in and to bodies. But we see more when we press things symbolically. As we have seen, meals figured prominently in Jesus's ministry as an expression of coinherent inclusivity, and a meal of broken bread was for the Emmaus disciples the occasion for their breakthrough of awareness into the reality of the risen Christ. That particular repast is now complemented by another postresurrection meal, this time featuring fish. It would be difficult to miss the symbolic reference to the supper of miraculously multiplied loaves and fishes that is featured in all four Gospels and that serves as a prime expression of Jesus's mystical fellowship with his church. What is particularly powerful in this Lukan resurrection narrative is that the church, as it were, returns the favor, since it is the disciples who give Jesus fish to eat. Here, on vivid and beautiful display, is the loop of grace, the giving and receiving and returning of gift, which, on the Christian reading, is the heart of reality.

Having shared the meal that signals the divine-human coinherence, Jesus repeats what he did at Emmaus—applies the hermeneutic: "Then he said to them, 'These are my words that I spoke to you while I was still with you—that everything written about me in the law of Moses, the prophets, and the psalms must be fulfilled'" (Luke 24:44). As before, this does not mean so much that certain sections of the Hebrew Scriptures concern Jesus but rather that the Hebrew Scriptures in their entirety anticipate him, relating to him as question to answer, as anticipation to fulfillment. And as at the Emmaus supper, Jesus here specifies the interpretive key: "Thus it is written, that the Messiah is to suffer and to rise from the dead on the third day" (24:46). In other words, Jesus himself, in his movement from death to new life, is the lens through which the whole of biblical revelation is to be seen. The God who is a love that death itself can neither destroy nor deter is the key that "opened their minds to understand the scriptures" (24:45).

Having understood, what are they to do? "Repentance and forgiveness of sins is to be proclaimed in his name to all nations, beginning from Jerusalem" (24:47). The Emmaus disciples were sent back to Jerusalem, because they had been running away from the city of the cross in fear and doubt. Having been gathered with the others and galvanized by the presence of the risen Jesus, they are now commissioned to go out from that central place, the city of peace, in order to draw everyone into the circle of grace.

The proclamation of the forgiveness of sins is central to the work of the church, for it is the richest expression and application of the ontological change affected by the Paschal Mystery. The church's task is to tell the world that the meaning of being has shifted, since we know that even the worst sin cannot separate us from the love of God made manifest in the dying and rising of Jesus. Through the sheer graciousness of God, the rupture of sin has been mended and the loop of grace reestablished. Jesus the Lord, the Prince of Peace in the midst of the city of peace, sends the core group to carry that message.

I commenced this iconic Christology by considering Jesus under the title Gatherer, and we close by studying him under the title Lord. Jerusalem was reverenced by the prophets and psalmist as the true pole of the earth, the place where, at the time of the Messiah, the scattered tribes would be reunited. So it happened, in seminal form, in this gathering of the apostles on Easter night around the body of the risen Jesus. Christ the Lord then scattered them—not as the *diabolos* would, as an attack on unity, but as a sower would, scattering seeds. And they went forth with the power of Christ the warrior, the one who faced down sin, death, and the devil; they went forth with a message of victory or, which is saying the same thing, the forgiveness of sins.

PART III

The Epistemic Priority
of Jesus Christ

7

The Scriptural Warrant

One of the characteristic marks of the modern style of philosophizing is the predilection for commencing the intellectual project with epistemology. Most moderns hold that the limits and capacity of knowledge must be firmly established before one can fruitfully endeavor to explore issues in politics, ethics, or metaphysics. I have purposely resisted this modernism by commencing my project with an investigation of the narrative icons concerning Jesus Christ. It is my conviction that we don't read Jesus through the lens of a predetermined epistemology, but rather that we understand the nature of knowledge in general through those narratives.

But is this coherent? Do Christians know in a distinctive way? Are both the object of their intellectual investigation and their manner of rational procedure unique? Do Christians become aware of the centrality of Jesus Christ after a long and epistemologically neutral inquiry, or does that awareness condition all modes of their intellection from the beginning? The questions fix us on the horns of a dilemma. To answer them affirmatively seems to place Christians in an irresponsibly fideistic and sectarian position, compromising their capacity to enter into conversation with those outside their community of discourse; but to answer them negatively seems to force Christians to abandon their claim that Christ has primacy in all things, including, presumably, what and how we know.

This tension is, of course, not new. It is a defining problematic in the roiled history of Christian theology, having given rise to the numerous

battles between "Athens" and "Jerusalem" played out in the writings of
Tertullian, Origen, Aquinas, Bonaventure, Jacques-Bénigne Bossuet, Newman, Barth, Rahner, and many others. What I shall endeavor to do in the
this chapter and those following it is to address this problem, not so much
in the hopes of "solving" it as in the desire to show a way forward. I am
convinced that one form of the liberal-conservative dispute is a function of
an awkward handling of this old and knotty tension and that a consistently
and generously christological approach opens a more promising path. I will
try to show that a mind radically conditioned by the narratives concerning
Jesus Christ—gatherer, warrior, and Lord—actually grasps reality most
richly and thus, paradoxically enough, makes possible the most creative
conversation with the non-Christian culture.

Scripture's Claims for Christ

It is difficult to read the New Testament and not be struck by the
maximalist claims constantly being made about Jesus Christ. He is "Lord"
(Matt. 21:3), "Son of God" (Heb. 1:2), "Son of Man" (Matt. 12:8), "Messiah"
(Mark 8:29), "Son of David" (Luke 18:39), "the Alpha and the Omega"
(Rev. 1:8), "Author of life" (Acts 3:15), and, in the ecstatic words of Thomas
the former doubter, "My Lord and my God" (John 20:28). But there is
no more extraordinary and far-reaching description of Jesus's significance
than the one found in the first chapter of the letter to the Colossians.
There we read that Jesus is "the image [*eikon*] of the invisible God, the
firstborn of all creation," the one in whom "the fullness of God was pleased
to dwell" (Col. 1:15, 19). Lest we miss the power of these statements,
their implications are clearly spelled out: "in him all things in heaven and
on earth were created, things visible and invisible, whether thrones or
dominions or rulers or powers" (v. 16). In this Jesus, all things have come
to be; he is the prototype of all finite existence, even of those great powers
that transcend the world and govern human affairs. If we are tempted to
understand his influence as only a thing of the past, we are corrected: "in
him all things hold together" (v. 17). Jesus is not only the one in whom
things were created but also the one in whom they presently exist and
through whom they inhere in one another. And if we are inclined to view
the future as a dimension of creation untouched by Christ, we are set
straight: "through him God was pleased to reconcile to himself all things,
whether on earth or in heaven, by making peace through the blood of his
cross" (v. 20). Individuals, societies, cultures, animals, plants, planets and
the stars—all will be drawn into an eschatological harmony through him.
Mind you, Jesus is not merely the symbol of an intelligibility, coherence,
and reconciliation that can exist apart from him; rather, he is the active

and indispensable means by which these realities come to be. This Jesus, in short, is the all-embracing, all-including, all-reconciling Lord of whatever is to be found in the dimensions of time and space.

A text that parallels the first chapter of Colossians in the intensity and range of its claims is, of course, the prologue to the Gospel of John. If in Colossians the particular figure Jesus of Nazareth is identified with the creative power of God, in the Johannine text the process is reversed: now the transcendent Logos of God is appreciated as the one who became concretely available in this Jesus: "The Word became flesh." But the assertion of Christ's absolute ontological priority remains the same: this Jesus is the Word that was with God from the beginning and through whom all things that exist came to be and continue in being.

Now what follows from these breathtaking descriptions is a centrally important epistemic claim: that Jesus cannot be measured by a criterion outside of himself or viewed from a perspective higher than himself. He cannot be understood as one object among many or surveyed blandly by a disinterested observer. If such perspectives were possible, then he would not be the all-grounding Word or the criterion than which no more final can be thought. If we sought to know him in this way, we would not only come to incorrect conclusions but also involve ourselves in a sort of operational contradiction. To be consistent with these accounts, we must say that Jesus determines not only what there is to be known (since he is the organizing principle of finite being) but also how we are to know what is to be known (since the mind itself is a creature, made and determined through him).

A Christ-illumined mind in search of Christ-determined forms seems to be the epistemology implicit in Colossians and the Johannine prologue. Further, as Bruce Marshall has argued, this primacy implies that the narratives concerning Jesus must, for Christians, be an epistemic trump, that is to say, an articulation of reality that must hold sway over and against all rival articulations, be they scientific, psychological, sociological, philosophical, or religious.[1] To hold to Colossians and the prologue to John is to have a clear negative criterion concerning all claims to ultimate truth: whatever runs contrary to the basic claims entailed in the narratives concerning Jesus must certainly be false.

---

1. Bruce Marshall, *Trinity and Truth* (Cambridge: Cambridge Univ. Press, 2000), 44–47.

8

Modern Foundationalism

Before defending and exploring further the implications of the claim that Jesus Christ has epistemic priority, we must consider two serious counterproposals: modern foundationalism and neoscholastic "natural" theology. Both of these seem to suggest that there is a realm of rationality outside of, or at least prior to, the dimension determined by Jesus Christ, and hence both appear to call into question the exclusivity and radicality of Jesus's epistemic priority.

To understand foundationalism in at least one of its peculiarly modern forms, we turn than the writings of René Descartes. In his great autobiographical and programmatic text *Discourse on Method*, Descartes tells us that he was frustrated by the deep ambiguities and uncertainties that ran through all the sciences of his day (with the possible exception of mathematics).[1] On even the most basic issues, the best philosophers, poets, and theologians across the centuries were in fundamental disagreement, and worse, there seemed to be no coherent criteria by which to adjudicate their disputes. What's more, when Descartes looked to the moral practices of the various European cultures, he found a similar multiplicity and confusion: what was considered rational and morally upright for one people might be lightly valued or condemned outright by another.[2] In short, the Christian and classical culture of his time,

1. René Descartes, *Discourse on the Method*, in *The Philosophical Works of Descartes* (Cambridge: Cambridge Univ. Press, 1979), 1:86–87.
2. Ibid., 86.

bequeathed to him by the late Middle Ages, proved deeply unsatisfactory precisely from an epistemological viewpoint. It was, according to his famous image, like a cluttered, dangerous, and poorly constructed seaside city, full of dead ends and circuitous streets and lacking any coherent organization.

The solution that Descartes proposed, after his solitary meditation in a heated room in Ulm, is the prototype of subjective foundationalism. In order to avoid all possible confusion, Descartes resolved to doubt whatever can be doubted. In the process, he eliminated most of what had been taken as basic: sense experience (so often illusory), received traditions (so thoroughly contested even by the best minds), abstract concepts (so often unclear or unreliable). What he was left with was the stubborn fact that, as he doubted everything around him, he couldn't doubt that he was doubting. The skeptical self could shake off everything but itself: *cogito* [or *dubito*] *ergo sum*. Thus the lonely but unassailably secure Cartesian ego, standing amidst the ruins of culture, intelligence, and sense experience, emerged as the sure foundation for knowledge. In the great reversal that effectively defines modern philosophy and science, Descartes then proceeded to build his knowledge of the objective world on the basis of his certitude regarding his subjectivity, or better, he brought all claims to knowledge before the bar of the self-validating ego for adjudication. In this he anticipates the Copernican revolution in Kant's epistemology and Hegel's apotheosis of the subject, and, as we will see, much of modern theological liberalism.

Convinced that he had found intellectual *terra firma*, Descartes endeavored to reconstruct the edifice of knowledge or, to stay with his more elaborate metaphor, to build up a city that is rational, clear, and practically satisfactory. First, he brought God before the bar. Because he found in his mind the clear and distinct idea of a perfect being, and because he, in his admitted imperfection, could not possibly have given rise to that idea, God must exist in fact. Though Emmanuel Levinas has helpfully indicated the important decentering or relativizing of the ego involved in this claim, nevertheless Descartes' God is affirmed only *through* the ego.[3] Thus the subject's humility in the presence of the perfect reality seems a bit strained, a false piety. Once God in his goodness and perfection has been confirmed—placed, like a slightly smaller stone, on the foundation stone of the *cogito*—then the rest of the structure is rather easily built. Since God would not allow us to be consistently deceived in our perceptions and intellectual acts, it follows that the world as we sense it and consider it is real. And therefore

3. Emmanuel Levinas, *Basic Philosophical Writings*, edited by Adriaan Peperzak (Bloomington: Indiana Univ. Press, 1996), 11–12.

the scientist can investigate and ruminate, unhampered by doubt and insecurity.[4]

Thus, for Descartes, valid knowledge is either the self-evident or that which is grounded in the self-evident; it is either the *cogito* itself or what can be justified through appeal to the *cogito*. This subjective foundational-ism is presupposed throughout the *méthode* that Descartes proposes. The responsible knower proceeds on the basis of clear and evident foundations and moves to a further claim only when a certain logical relationship can be established between that claim and its ground. To operate otherwise is to invite the confusion that had bedeviled European science and from which Descartes so obsessively tried to extricate himself.

Now there is another form of modern foundationalism, one that grants epistemic priority not to subjective consciousness but to sense expe-rience. This was the approach of empiricists such as John Locke and David Hume.[5] On Locke's reading, all valid ideas are grounded finally in indubitable sense data, and thus forms of reasoning are determined to be legitimate only in the measure that they can be referred to a sensible foundation. Inexact thinking ensues when ideas are allowed to become unmoored from these empirical bases. Like many of the moderns, Locke cultivated an exquisite distaste for scholasticism, a system he took to be particularly marked by fuzzy and irresponsible speculation. Like Des-cartes, Locke sought to articulate a method that was simple, testable, unprejudiced, and in principle universally available. Just as anyone can realize the truth of the *cogito*, so anyone can have access to knowledge through the senses. In neither case is the mediation of tradition, church, or philosophical authority strictly necessary. Descartes makes a remark at the very beginning of the *Discourse on Method* to the effect that all people are equally gifted in matters of reason.[6] Though contrary both to the universal philosophical consensus that preceded him and to common sense, this claim is congruent with the typically modern/foundationalist wish for a universally accessible method.

As I've suggested, both of these forms of foundationalism had a huge impact on the development of modern philosophy and physical science, and the practical success of the latter has certainly helped to validate foundationalism in the minds of many. It seems obvious, a banality, that knowledge is legitimate only in the measure that it can be justified through evidence and finally through appeal to indubitable starting points. To argue otherwise seems to place one outside of the circle of responsible

4. Descartes, *Discourse on the Method*, 106.

5. William Placher, *Unapologetic Theology: A Christian Voice in a Pluralistic Conversation* (Louisville, KY: Westminster John Knox, 1989), 25–26.

6. Descartes, *Discourse on the Method*, 81.

conversation and to invite all varieties of superstition and obscurantism. Not to be a foundationalist of some stripe appears both epistemologically problematic and morally questionable. And therefore, what I have proposed—that Jesus Christ ought to have epistemic priority, that truth is best discerned not through appeal to subjective states or empirical experience but through him—seems the height of folly. How could a religious claim—arbitrary, unjustified, believed by a particular community—be the proper ground for intellection in the general sense? Again, how could one claim epistemic priority to Jesus without falling into sectarianism and the rankest fideism? And wouldn't accepting some form of modern foundationalism be the only way to establish a meaningful and peaceful interreligious conversation? In responding to these questions, I will try to show, first, that foundationalism is problematic precisely on foundationalist grounds, and second, that it in point of fact has much more in common with religious claims than its proponents would like to admit.

The simplest and best argument against modern foundationalism is that it is inconsistent with itself. The claim (to combine the two forms discussed) is that valid knowledge is that which is either self-evident (through sense experience or subjective intuition) or based upon what is self-evident. But how is this assertion itself either sensed or subjectively intuited? Where has one seen or heard the foundationalist dictum itself, or how has one appreciated it as intuitively given? Or, if it is not itself immediately given, how has this principle been deduced logically from self-evident grounds? In short, it appears that the radicality and universality of the foundationalist claim rules out the heuristic device that governs and defines foundationalism itself.

There are many other reasons as well to question this position. The foundationalist assumption is that the foundations—subjective or empirical—are easily known and not themselves rooted in any deeper ground or situated in any wider context. They are "properly basic," given. But is the Cartesian experience of the doubting self in fact known in such a tidy manner? Is it not the case that Descartes looked to the *cogito* precisely because he was instructed by the tradition to look there? In his battles with the skeptical "academics" of his time, Augustine formulated a dictum strikingly similar to Descartes': "Si fallor sum" (if I am mistaken, I am). And antecedents to Augustine's claim can be found in classical philosophical schools as well. More to the point, the very capacity to feel and to formulate the power of the *cogito* depended on the languages that Descartes was using (both Latin and French), and these in turn were dependent upon myriad assumptions, conceptual frameworks, cultural contexts, and complex histories. Thus, the tradition that Descartes felt he was placing in epoche while he sought for epistemic *terra firma* was, willy-nilly, conditioning that search at every point. It was Wittgenstein who commented that a programmatic doubt is for any philosopher strictly impossible, since if it were really taken seriously it would preclude even the ability to raise a question.[7] Therefore, one can (and I would say should) accept the truth of the *cogito*, but one should never be under the illusion that the perception of the doubting self's existence is somehow basic or foundational. Rather, one should appreciate how that particular truth situates itself in a preexisting web of interdependent insights, assumptions, and desires.

But what about the other type of modern foundationalism, the empirical form associated with Locke? Shouldn't we see sense experiences as elemental, properly basic, simply given? And would it not be appropriate to ground legitimate knowledge finally in such sensible intuitions? Certainly the empiricist strain of modernity has had staying power. Beginning with Locke and Hume, it stretches through the nineteenth century and can be seen on clear display in the work of the logical positivists well into the twentieth century. Rudolf Carnap, Moritz Schlick, and A. J. Ayer all felt that there was a discernible and verifiable level of sense experience that was prior to all interpretation and that provided the only viable foundation for the claims of science. But here again, this take has met with a great deal of criticism. Researchers from a variety of fields both practical and theoretical have concurred that sense experiences are never simply and uncomplicatedly given; rather, they are conditioned by perspective, expectation, context, the assumptions of one's community, etc. They are, in the technical phrase, "theory-laden" from the beginning.

Wittgenstein's duck-rabbit illustrates this point simply but effectively. The philosopher loved to show a figure that, viewed from a particular angle and with the right suggestion in one's mind, looked like a duck and that, squinted at from another perspective and with a different set of expectations, resembled a rabbit: same figure but remarkably varying perceptions. The later Wittgenstein was both fascinated and frustrated by this knotty problem of seeing something *as* something. If sense data were simply basic, this problem would not arise. Once more, this is not to call into question the *truth* or reliability of sense experiences, but it is to question the claim that they are foundational in any kind of exclusive or privileged way; like the *cogito*, they participate in a much wider and more complicated ontological and epistemological nexus. Wittgenstein commented that when he found what he took to be the foundations of the epistemic edifice, he discovered that they were being supported by the rest of the house. Similarly, R. O. Quine said that seeking the unambiguous foundations of thought is like looking for the places in Ohio that are

7. See Ludwig Wittgenstein, *On Certainty*, edited by G. E. M. Anscombe and G. H. von Wright (New York: Harper and Row, 1969), 33, no. 248.

starting places.[8] Obviously, there are no such places; it all depends upon where you happen to be situated and where you want to go.

So we can see that the modern foundationalist enterprise itself has quite a bit in common with the supposedly irrational religious perspective from which it was trying to escape. Though its advocates claimed that it was pristine, without prejudice, and hence capable of generating reliable and universal truth, in fact it was shot through with as many assumptions and presuppositions as any classical philosophy or theology. The question is not whether one system has prejudices or not, but rather which ones does it have and what do they make possible. I have been arguing that the Christian approaches the world with a particular type of mind—and I will say much more about this below—but what I hope is becoming clear is that modern foundationalists also see the world through an interpretive lens, with a type of mind. The problem is that they often effectively blind themselves to this truth, pretending that they are knowing simply as such, or as one ought to know.

Even a cursory glance at *Discourse on Method* reveals that Descartes is favoring a type of intellection and, if I may push things a bit, training a type of knower. In urging methodical doubt as a starting point, Descartes assumes that the ideal philosopher is basically, even radically, skeptical. Doubting what can in principle be doubted is not a sign of mental illness (as it might be seen in a different cultural setting) but an indication of intellectual health. In insisting on the primacy of the *cogito*, Descartes is privileging a subjectivist and inward mode of knowing. In making a sharp demarcation between the *res cogitans* (knowable through immediate intuition) and the *res extensa* (belonging to the dubious realm of the sensible), Descartes implicitly encourages his disciple to be epistemologically wary of the historical, the physical, the particular. And by embarking upon a systematic undoing of the received cultural and intellectual heritage, he encourages an iconoclastic antitraditionalism in the one who seeks wisdom. Now all of these Cartesian stances may be helpful in certain circumstances, but it is by no means obvious that they are the attitudes of the unprejudiced knower, simply seeking the truth. In fact, they come up out of Descartes' own desires, life history, frustrations, and cultural setting—and they should be assessed as such. They should certainly not be compared favorably to the prejudices and assumptions of the Christian knower.

Now it should come as no surprise that when Christian theologians, eager to dialogue with modernity, adopted foundationalist positions, the epistemic priority of Jesus, implied in the New Testament, would be com-

8. See Hilary Putnam, *Realism and Reason* (Cambridge: Cambridge Univ. Press, 1983), 37.

promised. Earlier in this book I sketched the outlines of Schleiermacher's theology, emphasizing how his method involved the correlation of Christian doctrines to an underlying subjective state, characterized as either "the sense and taste for the infinite" or "the feeling of absolute dependency." What I hope is clear in this context is just how like the Cartesian *cogito* is this Schleiermacherian "feeling" of complete dependency. It is the indubitable, immediately intuited, interior perception on the basis of which the entire project is undertaken. Or to switch the metaphor, it is the subjective bar before which the whole of (in this case) theological objectivity is brought for adjudication. Thus God is to be understood as the source of the feeling of absolute dependency; miracles are events that awaken or confirm the feeling, and as we saw, Jesus Christ himself is to be interpreted as the human being in whom this feeling and consciousness was most fully realized.

Schleiermacher, of course, became a sort of "church father of the nineteenth century," and his theology became a watershed, the dividing point between so-called *Alt-Protestantismus* and *Neu-Protestantismus*.[9] He has inspired innumerable imitators in the past two centuries, from Albrecht Ritschl and Ernst Troeltsch to, as we saw, Rahner, Schillebeeckx, and especially Tillich. From his early German writings, especially the *Dogmatik* of 1925, through *The Courage to Be* and culminating in his great *Systematic Theology*, Tillich articulated what he called a method of correlation.[10] The anguished questions that arise naturally from human finitude must be coordinated with the "answers" that are found in the scriptural and theological tradition. On this reading, theology breaks down either when it ceases to listen to the right questions or when it loses confidence in its answers. To be sure, Tillich stands in a venerable tradition when he says that human life is a sort of question, an unresolvable tension. Paul's cry "Who will rescue me from this body of death?" (Rom. 7:24) is echoed by Augustine's "Quaestio mihi factus sum" and by Søren Kierkegaard's insistence that to be aware of one's finitude is to be anxious. What is new in him is the typically modern tendency to assess the meaningfulness of the objective data of Christian revelation in terms of that question. Thus Tillich holds that God ought never to be named outside of the creature-Creator correlation and that "God" signals the "answer to the question implied in being."[11] Accordingly, the trinitarian nature of God (the play in him between the one and the many) is the answer to the question implied in the human tendency to oscillate dangerously between the poles of individualization

9. See Brian Gerrish, *A Prince of the Church: Schleiermacher and the Beginnings of Modern Theology* (Philadelphia: Fortress, 1984), 11.

10. See especially Paul Tillich, *Systematic Theology: Three Volumes in One* (Chicago: Univ. of Chicago Press, 1967), 3–10.

11. Ibid., 163.

and participation. The coming together of liveliness and faithfulness in God is the solution to the terrible finite tension between dynamics and form; the eternity of the divine is affirmed in the measure that it calms the anxiety that comes from being situated in time and hence having a being toward death; God's ubiquity is ratified inasmuch as it soothes the fear that any space-bound creature feels.[12] And Jesus is the New Being, which is to say the proper relationship between divinity and humanity, appearing under the conditions of sin and estrangement.

A defender of Tillich might argue that the method of correlation in fact refuses to grant primacy either to the anxious subject or to the scriptural symbols but holds them in a sort of tensive equality. But this seems naive or disingenuous. In the Platonic dialogues there is no doubt as to who controls the conversations between Socrates and his various interlocutors. It is always the one who asks the questions who shapes the conversation, determining its rhythm and direction. So the Tillichean subject, despite its anxiety and humility, is in fact the dominant element in the correlation, and therefore, even granting a degree of mutuality in the relationship, it is still Christ who is fitted to the subject and not vice versa. But as Colossians insists, it is in Jesus that all things, including subjectivity, hold together. Barth criticized the theological method of Tillich with the sardonic observation that it would work in paradise or in heaven, but not here below. What he meant was that in a state of union with God, we would spontaneously ask the right questions and find the proper correlative answers. The problem is that our minds are so cramped and compromised by sin that we tend to ask the wrong sorts of questions; as a result, the answers that we derive from those interrogations are similarly distorted and inadequate.

David Tracy critiques the correlationalist method of Tillich, but not on Barthian grounds. On the contrary, he insists that Tillich does not adequately account for the complexity and multivalence of the existential situation that is brought into correlation with the biblical message. For Tracy, Tillich's reading is too neat inasmuch as it lines up the "questions" of the situation with the "answers" of the Bible, forgetting that the former proposes plenty of its own answers and the latter is rife with its own unanswered questions.[13] "Philosophy" does not wait docilely for theology to resolve its problems, and theology does not eagerly look to philosophy to articulate the questions that it will answer. Thus, whatever correlation is effected between experience and revelation (and Tracy feels that there can and should be one) is far more subtle and complex than Tillich imagined. On Tracy's own reading, the correlation takes on a more Ricoeurian flavor as the two "worlds" of the Scripture and the interpreter

12. Ibid., 186–201.
13. David Tracy, *The Analogical Imagination* (New York: Crossroad, 1981), 340–41.

are allowed playfully to overlap and interact, the questions and answers of each contributing to mutually transforming conversation.

But here again we face a difficulty. If Jesus Christ is the one in whom all things were created and hold together, and through whom all things will be reconciled to God, what precisely is the realm or dimension with which his word could possibly be correlated? What stands outside his influence and determination as a properly "secular" sphere? If Colossians is correct, can there be the sharp demarcation between "philosophy" and "theology," or between "the situation" and "the message" that correlational-ism requires? To be sure, in the biblical framework there is an area "outside" of Christ, viz., the arena of sin and death, but this is a form of nonbeing and hence is not in the strict metaphysical sense separate from him. And it certainly could not constitute in itself a "pole" of conversation. Further, who precisely is coordinating the mutually enhancing correlational con-versation and where is she standing as she does so? Clearly, the effecter of the correlation must in some sense hover above both elements of it, making the requisite judgments, assessments, connections. But this person would then be above not only the purportedly secular realm but Christ as well, and her decisions would have primacy over both. Once more, we face our problem of epistemic priority. In line with its fundamentally Cartesian assumptions, correlationalism assumes that, at the end of the day, the questioning or adjudicating subject has the final word, and this seems impossible to reconcile with the extraordinary claims made in the New Testament about the centrality and unsurpassability of Jesus Christ.

9

Natural Theology

Before we can turn to a detailed analysis of the nature of the Christ-mind, we must consider a second challenge to the proposition that I have made concerning the epistemic primacy of Christ. Because it comes up from the heart of the Christian church, this challenge is at once less threatening and more subtle than that posed by modern foundationalism. This is the perspective of so-called natural theology, or a discourse about God that rests not upon revelation but upon the workings of unaided reason. Most natural theologians took as their scriptural warrant the Pauline claim that "ever since the creation of the world his eternal power and divine nature, invisible though they are, have been understood and seen through the things he has made" (Rom. 1:20). Paul, it appears, asserts that certain truths about the Creator can be known on the basis of an honest intellectual investigation of creation. The "purely rational" character of this knowledge seems confirmed by the setting for Paul's claim. He is telling the Roman Christians that the pagans, who obviously have in no way benefited from revelation, finally have no excuse for their ignorance of God and concomitant immorality, since they have this ordinary rational grasp of the things of God.

Therefore it seems, in principle, not only possible but desirable to engage in an investigation of the things of God using ordinary philosophical or scientific tools. But it was Karl Barth (who certainly could not be accused of insufficient appreciation of Paul's letter to the Romans) who gave voice to a standard objection to such a reading: "The natural theologian either has no faith or is in bad faith." What Barth implies is that a Christian who practices a purely rational form of theology either has bracketed the epistemic claims of Colossians and the Johannine prologue (he has no faith) or is playing coyly with them, pretending for the sake of addressing a particular audience that they have not been made (he is in bad faith). Is there a way past this dilemma?

The formula I employed above to characterize natural theology—a discourse about God based upon unaided reason—is one that was frequently used in the neoscholasticism of the nineteenth and twentieth centuries. At the heart of the argument that I will make is that this account of what the great practitioners of Christian philosophical theology were doing is, in fact, quite inadequate and that a more proper description will conduce toward a resolution of our dilemma. As we turned to Descartes as the most representative figure in subjective foundationalism, so now we turn to Thomas Aquinas as undoubtedly the most authoritative and important figure in the tradition of "natural" theology.

It is well beyond the scope of this chapter to explore the history of interpretations of Aquinas's work on this topic, but a few remarks may prove helpful.[1] Far too many readers of Aquinas restrict themselves to a consideration of his technical work in the two *Summae*, especially the *Summa theologiae*. But when Thomas became a *magister* in Paris, his primary responsibility was the proclamation of the Word of God; hence, commentary on the *sacra pagina* was basic to his theological work. In the course of doing biblical commentary, of course, numerous problems of interpretation arose, and therefore Thomas was compelled to engage in public disputations and discussions of theological questions. From these flowed his voluminous written accounts of the conversations—what we know as the *quaestiones disputatae*—covering topics as varied as the power of God, the nature of evil, the meaning of the incarnation, and the nature of truth. Finally, in an attempt to summarize and systematically organize the material of theological investigation, Aquinas composed the two great *summae* as well as the *Commentary on the Sentences of Peter Lombard*. It is most important to note that the second *Summa* was written precisely for *incipientes* or beginners in the field. Therefore, it can be extremely misleading to read only the treatments found in the *summae* without attending to the more basic, and in many cases more thorough, analyses in the disputed questions and the biblical commentaries. The interpretation of Aquinas on the nature of theology is a case in point.

When neoscholastic commentators turned to the *Summa contra gentiles*, they found a rather exaggerated demarcation between what can be known

---

1. For an extremely helpful and thorough discussion of this issue, see Michel Corbin, *Le chemin de la théologie selon Thomas d'Aquin* (Paris: Beauchesne, 1974), esp. 643–93.

of God through natural reason and what can be known only through revelation. The argument for God's existence based upon the phenomenon of
motion is developed at great length, and much of the discussion of God's
attributes and powers is drawn from that rational demonstration.[2] In fact,
in the *Summa contra gentiles*, Thomas treats the trinitarian nature of God
only in book 4, after discussing God both directly and indirectly through
the course of three lengthy books. It appears as though a great deal can
be said about God on the basis of purely philosophical arguments before
coming to a distinctively Christian or revelation-based description.

Similarly, neoscholastics drew attention to the language of *preambula
fidei* that can be found in the later *Summa theologiae*. Thomas claims that
there is an entire range of data that can be known about God purely on the
basis of reason prior to, or overlapping with, what can be known through
the articles of faith.[3] These "preambles," including the existence, goodness,
perfection, unity, love, providence, and creativity of God, are the rather
ample grist for the mill of natural theology. More to the point, Jesus Christ,
the incarnation, and the Paschal Mystery are explicitly brought into the
discussion only in the third part of the *Summa theologiae*, after thousands
of pages of theological analysis. Perhaps later critics from Luther to Barth
can be forgiven for complaining that such a program seems hardly to be
based upon the epistemic priority of Jesus Christ.

But as I have suggested, such a reading is superficial. During the 1260s,
which is to say around the same time that he was composing the second
Summa, Thomas was also writing a massive commentary on the Gospel
of John. In the course of his interpretation of the prologue—one of the
texts that I have used to argue for Christ's epistemic priority—he makes
some key remarks about the nature of knowing, both theological and
otherwise. After examining the Johannine claim that all things were made
through the power of the Word, Thomas turns to the evocative text that
runs, "What has come into being through him was life, and the life was
the light of all people. The light shines in the darkness, and the darkness
did not overcome it" (John 1:4–5). This light, he tells us, signifies the
power of the Word in regard to human beings, especially their capacity
to see and know. Following Augustine, Ambrose, and others, Thomas says
that the image of light is used metaphorically to describe any event of
manifestation, drawing on the prime analogue of seeing sensible things in
the light of the sun. Thus the mind comes to know through the light of
intelligibility and the soul comes to proper spiritual awareness through
the light of grace. Both of these forms of "vision" are dependent upon the

---

2. Thomas Aquinas, *Summa contra gentiles*, bk. 1, *God*, translated by Anton C. Pegis (Notre
Dame, IN: Univ. of Notre Dame Press, 1975), 85–96.

3. Thomas Aquinas, *Summa theologiae* (Torino: Marietti, 1952), 1a, q. 2, art. 2 ad. 1.

light of the Word, and in a double sense. First, the light of the divine Logos must fall upon the object of vision, and second, the one who sees must share to some degree in that same light; there must be a correspondence, based upon mutual participation, between the knower and the known. In the case of rational knowing, the subject participates in what Thomas calls, here, the *lux intellectiva* and elsewhere the *lux agentis intellectus* (the light of the agent intellect). Lest we miss the theological implication, he tells us, quoting the Psalm, that this light is the "light of your face, that is, of your Son, who is your face by which you are made manifest." In short, just as the Logos of the Father is the power through which all things are intelligible, so that same Word is the power through whom all things are known. Accordingly, it is in Christ and through Christ that even the simplest act of cognition takes place; "natural" reason is thoroughly christological. "Whatever of the truth is known by anybody is totally through participation in this light . . . because all truth, said by anybody, is from the Holy Spirit."[4] To be sure, a given knower need not be explicitly aware of this, but the one who accepts the truth of the prologue realizes it.

Aquinas next considers the phrase, "and the light shines in the darkness." *Tenebrae*, he says, can be taken to designate either the ordinary weakness of a finite mind in the presence of the divine light or the intellectual debility produced by sin. In the first case, the mind—even the mind of a saint—is to God as air is to the sun, that is to say, possessing a kind of capacity to receive the light of God, but in itself, and by comparison, remaining nothing. In the second instance, the sinful mind, crippled and blinded by pride, envy, and the other deadly sins, fights actively against Christ and is hence even less capable of receiving the light. Only when such a mind is converted, remade from within, will it be capable of seeing divine things. Thus sinners require the illumination of the Christ, but so to a lesser extent do saints, even sinless saints, since even the ordinary functioning of the mind is based upon participation in the Word. Both Adam before the fall and his descendants afterward are, to varying degrees, in the *tenebrae*.

The theme of participation is even more clearly emphasized as Thomas turns to the interpretation of the verse "The true light, which enlightens everyone, was coming into the world" (John 1:9). The Word is described as "true light" because it is not a light through participation but is rather the sheer intelligibility of God, beyond which there is nothing further that can be known. All forms of knowing, from the most elemental sensible perception, to human intellectual insight, to the vision of God had by the saints and angels, are a function of participating in this unsurpassable

---

4. "Quia quicquid veritatis a quocumque cognoscitur, totum est participatione istius lucis . . . quia omne verum, a quocumque dicatur, a Spiritu Sancto est." Thomas Aquinas, *In evangelium Ioannis* (Torino: Marietti, 1952), caput 1, lectio 2, n. 2.

luminosity. "Natural" reason, therefore, is not to be sharply demarcated from theology; rather, both are to be placed on a spectrum of seeing, running from less intense to more intense. Hans Urs von Balthasar, one of the great opponents of the neoscholastic reading of Aquinas, saw that for the mainstream of the Christian tradition, philosophy and theology are not so much separate epistemological forms but instead are born of the selfsame eros for vision and communion and hence are best understood as existing, like the trinitarian persons, in a sort of *circumincessio*.[5]

But what precisely would induce someone to use this lesser mode of seeing, once she is in possession of the higher? Why, for example, does Thomas Aquinas himself bother with "natural" theologizing when, through revelation, he is more than capable of deeper vision? We have to look for the answer in those *tenebrae*. Later in the Johannine commentary, Thomas remarks on the story of the man born blind. In the well-known account, Jesus spits on the ground and makes a sort of paste, which he then smears on the blind man's eyes. After washing in the pool of Siloam, the man returns able to see. Following Origen and Augustine, as is his wont in matters scriptural, Thomas comments that the spittle of Jesus, coming from his head and mouth, represents the divinity in him, while the earth represents his frail humanity. When the two mix—in the incarnation—they produce a salve, a healing balm, able to produce vision in finite and sinful human beings. What I wish to draw attention to here is the *debilitas*, the weakness of mind, that Thomas assumes to exist universally in fallen people, those who have "the eyes of their minds directed to the things of the earth." Less intense forms of knowing are a desideratum not so much in themselves but as a pedagogical tool in service of such minds. As we have seen, "natural" theology is not outside the Word or prior to it, not on a parallel track to revelation-based theology; it is a less intense participation in that Word and hence easier for weakened minds to take in.

This glance at the Johannine commentary helps us to appreciate and to interpret more accurately the texts on the relationship between theology and philosophy in the *Summa theologiae*. Lest there be any confusion concerning the type of project he is undertaking, Thomas specifies, in the opening article of the opening question of the *Summa*, that he will be exploring *sacra doctrina* (holy teaching) and that this enterprise is based not on the speculations and principles of philosophical reason but on revelation.[6] Mind you, this is a description of the entire project, not of something undertaken once the work of "natural" or philosophical theology is completed. Properly speaking, the subject matter of *sacra doc-*

5. Hans Urs von Balthasar, *The Glory of the Lord: A Theological Aesthetics*, vol. 1, *Seeing the Form* (San Francisco: Ignatius, 1982), 134–35.

6. Aquinas, *Summa theologiae*, 1a, q. 1, art. 1.

trina is "outside of the philosophical disciplines which are investigated by human reason,"[7] but this does not compromise the scientific or rational character of theology. In the second article of this first question, Aquinas teaches that *sacra doctrina* is scientific precisely in the measure that it proceeds from first principles known in the light of a higher *scientia*, viz., that knowledge of God enjoyed by God himself and the saints. Through revelation, human beings are allowed to participate in a luminosity that would otherwise surpass them—the intense vision of the saints—and this participation amounts not so much to an abstract knowledge as to a "science" by way of shared experience. How redolent of the John commentary, of course, is this language of light and participation. Theology draws out in a disciplined and logically focused way the implications of this experience.

But what precisely is the rapport between *sacra doctrina* and the philosophical investigation of God? Thomas realizes as he commences his work of summarizing theology that he will make almost constant use of the vocabulary and conceptual frameworks of philosophy; thus, having established the independence of *sacra doctrina*, he must show the relationship between this unique science and properly human science. To this issue, on which the discussion of "natural" theology finally hinges, he turns in article 5. The question formally posed there is the following: "Whether *sacra doctrina* is more dignified than the other sciences."[8] The first objection calls attention to the relative certitude of philosophy vis-à-vis theology: "But the other sciences, whose first principles cannot be doubted, seem to be more certain than *sacra doctrina*, whose principles, namely the articles of the faith, are subject to doubt."[9] What is more certain seems more dignified; therefore theology, derived from extremely dubitable first principles, ought to cede its primacy to the more reliable philosophical sciences. It is intriguing how exactly this objection anticipates the attitude of the Enlightenment regarding religion, especially the view of Hegel on the relative dignity of philosophy and religion. But it can also seem to anticipate Thomas's own method throughout the *Summa*, giving pride of place to philosophical argumentation and using Scripture (it appears) as mere ornamentation.

Aquinas's response is quite congruent with the analysis in the Johannine commentary: "Nothing prevents that which is more certain according to nature to be less certain for us, due to the weakness of our mind. . . . Hence the doubt that comes to some with regard to the articles of the

7. "Praeter philosophicas disciplinas quae ratione humana investigantur" (ibid.).
8. Utrum sacra doctrina sit dignior aliis scientiis.
9. "Sed aliae scientiae, de quarum principiis dubitari non potest, videntur esse certiores sacra doctrina, cuius principia, scilicet articuli fidei, dubitationem recipiunt" (*Summa theologiae*, 1a, q. 1, art. 5).

faith is not due to any lack of certitude in the articles but is due to the weakness of the human intellect."[10] The *debilitas* of the human mind in this discussion corresponds to the *tenebrae* in the John commentary. As the owl is blinded by excess of light, so the weakened, darkened minds of sinful human beings are overwhelmed by the clarity and certainty of the divine light given in revelation. What appears to us as more certain is not objectively greater but simply easier to take in; and what seems to us doubtful is not objectively less, just too much to absorb.

In the play between the second objection and its response, we see the precise nature of the rapport between these higher and lower forms of knowing God. The objector states that it is appropriate for a lower science to borrow from the principles of a higher, just as music derives its structure from mathematics. However, theology borrows amply from various philosophical disciplines. Therefore it seems to follow that theology is inferior to natural reason. One anticipates here not the concerns of the Enlightenment but the objections of Luther and the other Reformers concerning the lordship that secular Aristotelian conceptuality seemed to exercise over the language of the Bible in scholasticism. Thomas responds to this powerful objection with his customary laconicism: "This science [theology] can accept something from philosophical disciplines, not that it requires them out of necessity, but rather that it might make more manifest those things that are treated in this science."[11] Philosophy is not a foundation or preparation for theology, nor does it clarify the language that theology uses; rather, it is employed for pedagogical purposes in order to make its subject matter more accessible. But to whom? Once more, it is to the entire human race, which suffers from a *defectum intellectus nostri* (a defect of our mind), like the man born blind and like those who walk in the *tenebrae*. What we fallen knowers require is, to use Thomas's charming image, a leading by the hand (*manuducitur*) to orient us toward the realm of pure light. It is just this *manuductio* that the philosophical sciences provide; it is in performing this pedagogical task that they are the *ancilla*, the handmaid, of theology. Once more we are struck by the prominence of the image of light. Philosophy leads the fallen seeker to the light, much as a rescuer might lead a lost spelunker out of a deep cave, only very gradually introducing her to the full intensity of the daylight.

What is emerging here is the balanced vision so typical of Aquinas. Natural reason is given its full due as a participation in the light of the

---

10. "Nihil prohibit id quod est certius secundum naturam esse quoad nos minus certum propter debilitatem intellectus nostri. . . . Unde dubitatio quae accidit in aliquibus circa articulos fidei non est propter incertitudinem rei sed propter debilitatem intellectus humani" (ibid.).

11. "Haec scientia accipere potest aliquid a philosophicis disciplinis, non quod ex necessitate eis indigeat, sed ad maiorem manifestationem eorum quae in hac scientia traduntur" (ibid., ad. 2).

Logos and as an ancilla of theology, but it is certainly not placed either in opposition to or on a par with theology. In fact, it emerges as a requirement in the theological enterprise only because of the inherent limitation of the fallen intellect. And thus one would never be justified in drawing the conclusion that the practice of natural theology compromises the epistemic priority of revelation. Perhaps the best that one could say is that there is an essential nondualism between theology and natural reason, even as the two retain their differences in intensity.

Is Thomas Aquinas therefore caught on the horns of the Barthian dilemma? Is he a man of either no faith or bad faith? Hardly. Aquinas's project in the *Summa theologiae* is, from beginning to end, theological and thus conditioned by and dependent upon revelation. He does not bracket the faith in order to test it, nor does he translate the data of revelation into more accessible categories, nor does he seek some rational realm with which he could affect a correlation to faith. Rather, he stands in the great Augustinian and Anselmian tradition of faith seeking understanding. And like his predecessors, he knows that whatever means of perception or communication he employs in this quest, he will never be leaving the confines or influence of the Word.

And here we come close to the heart of my argument in this part of the book. It is precisely the epistemic priority of Jesus Christ, the Word made flesh, that warrants the use of philosophical and cultural tools in the explication and propagation of the faith, since those means come from and lead to that very Word. Because Jesus Christ is the Logos incarnate—and not simply another interesting religious figure among many—signs of his presence and style are to found everywhere, and he can relate noncompetitively to them. The paradox then is this: the lower the Christology, the more problematic the dialogue with philosophy and other cultural forms becomes; the higher the Christology, the more that conversation is facilitated. Modern foundationalism is indeed irreconcilable with the epistemological primacy of Christ, but the philosophically flavored theologizing practiced by Aquinas and his colleagues is not.

10

The Nature of the Christ-Mind

Having considered two possible challenges to my central assertion, we are now in a position to look more carefully at the epistemic claim implied in Colossians and the Johannine prologue. What precisely is the Christ-mind, and what does it mean to say that we approach all of our knowing through this mind? What is at stake in having, as Paul put it in Philippians, "the same mind . . . in you that was in Christ Jesus" (2:5)? It means, to state it in most basic form, that what we know and how we know is conditioned by what was revealed in Jesus Christ. It is my conviction that the Christ-consciousness displays itself in terms of seven dimensions.

The Intelligibility of Coinherence

Colossians tells us that in Jesus all things have come to be and that all things hold together and find their fulfillment in him. He is before, during, and after all finite existence, creating, surrounding, and pulling it to completion. Further, the John prologue informs us that this Jesus is the incarnation of the Word by which the Father has made all that is, without exception. Therefore to acknowledge the epistemic primacy of Jesus Christ is, first, to assume the intelligibility of all that

153

is.[1] Since all has been made through, and will be ordered by, a divine rationality, there must be form in all finite being as a whole and in each particular thing that exists; what comes to be through Logos is, necessarily, logical. This implies, of course, that there is an unavoidable correspondence between the activity of the mind and the structure of being: intelligence will find its fulfillment in this universal and inescapable intelligibility.

Many have pointed out that it is no accident that the physical sciences—astronomy, physics, chemistry, biology—developed and flourished in the Christian West.[2] People formed in the biblical conviction that finite reality is intelligible, made through the divine Logos, will rather naturally move out to meet that the physical world with confident rationality, and their investigations will proceed without hesitation to the farthest reaches of the macrocosmic and the microcosmic realms. Without this intuition, which can only be called mystical, none of the sciences would get under way. Of course, this correspondence can be turned in the opposite direction and used as a *manuductio* for scientific seekers after God. One could argue that the universality of objective intelligibility (assumed by any honest scientist) can be explained only through recourse to a transcendent subjective intelligence that has thought the world into being, so that every act of knowing a worldly object or event is, literally, a re-cognition, a thinking again of what has already been thought by a primordial divine knower. Hence, every scientific act is, ipso facto, an affirmation of God's existence. This kind of argument, obviously, is shaped by the same insight that we found in Thomas's Johannine commentary: natural reason is a participation in the pure intelligibility of the Logos and thus is necessarily congruent with the deepest perceptions of theology.

We find a similar intuition in the curiously equivalent claims of Jacques Derrida and George Steiner that to know anything at all is, implicitly, to know that God exists, for it is to accept the reign of the Logos or transcendent intelligibility. To be sure, Derrida denies just this type of logocentrism, and his denial is a function of his assertion of the permanently open-ended and undecidable nature of human knowing. Steiner accepts it, precisely because he affirms the possibility of real speech and knowledge. For our purposes, what is most interesting is the logical connection that both see, from different sides and with opposite intentions, between knowledge and what can only be called "faith."[3]

---

1. See Joseph Ratzinger, *Introduction to Christianity* (San Francisco: Ignatius, 1990), 106.

2. John Polkinghorne, *Faith, Science, and Understanding* (New Haven, CT: Yale Univ. Press, 2000), 18–19.

3. See George Steiner, *After Babel: Aspects of Language and Translation* (Oxford: Oxford Univ. Press, 1998), 110.

But there is more to it than this. In the language of the John prologue, the ground of the world's intelligibility is a Word spoken by a speaker. Further, it is an utterance that bears the full power of the one who utters it: "the Word was with God, and the Word was God" (John 1:1). This Word cannot be identical to the one who speaks it, for then there would be no real speech. At the same time, there must be an unsurpassable closeness between the two, even to the point of oneness of essence, since the communication is so complete. This implies that the primordial intelligibility is a being-with-the-other, or better, a being-in-the-other, a coinherence. Now it is through this Word that the entire world is made, and hence it is by this Word that all things are intelligibly marked. Therefore relationality, being-for-the-other, must be the form that, at the deepest level, conditions whatever is *and* the truth that satisfies the hunger of the mind. It is not simply reasonability that characterizes the real, but this type of reasonability. And how congruent this claim is with the narratives concerning Jesus Christ—especially those dealing with Christ the gatherer—that we explored earlier.

This principle becomes even clearer when we follow the narrative of the prologue to the point of the enfleshment of this Word. The primordial divine conversation partner becomes a creature in order to draw creation into the embrace of the divine life, to be a light in the darkness. In dialogue with Nicodemus, the Logos personally delineates the nature of this mission: "God so loved the world that he gave his only Son, so that everyone who believes in him may not perish but may have eternal life" (John 3:16). Through the incarnation, the coinherence of the Father and the Logos seeks to provoke a coinherence of creation with God and of creatures with one another. In light of the entire Gospel, we know that the momentum of this enfleshment is toward the total self-gift of the cross: "When I am lifted up from the earth, [I] will draw all people to myself" (John 12:32). In the Colossians hymn, we find that the final unification of all things will take place through Jesus, but the description is made precise: "through the blood of his cross" (Col. 1:20). Consistently therefore, Christian revelation insists that the most radical sort of being-for-the-other—self-donation—is the nature of the Logos that has marked all created reality. Invoking Marshall's negative formulation of the epistemic priority of Christ, we must say then that any philosophy, science, or worldview that does not see relationality, being-for-the-other, as ontologically fundamental must be false. To state it more positively, we can assert that what the mind correctly seeks as it goes out to meet the intelligibility of the real is always a form of coinherence.

In the thirteenth century, Bonaventure maintained that all of the non-theological arts and sciences taught in the university find their proper center in theology, the science that speaks directly of Christ the Logos.[4] As the rationality of God the Creator, Christ is the physical, mathematical, and metaphysical center of the universe and hence the point of orientation for all of the sciences dealing with those dimensions.

In the nineteenth century, at the high-water mark of modern foundationalism, John Henry Newman felt compelled to call for the reinsertion of theology in the circle of university disciplines. Following the inner logic of Christian revelation, Newman, like Bonaventure, saw that theology not only should be around the table but must be the centering element in the conversation, precisely because it alone speaks of the Creator God who is metaphysically implicit in all finite existence.[5] Thus the sciences become hypermaterialist and reductive when they are severed from their theological ground, and the arts, when celebrated for their own sake, apart from a theological purpose, become morbid, sentimental, or bizarre; even abstract mathematics devolves into a fussy and self-preoccupied rationalism when its link to sacred geometry is lost. And Newman saw that once theology is displaced, some other discipline necessarily takes its position at the center and thereby disturbs the proper harmony among the sciences, for no other discipline has the range or inclusiveness properly to hold the center.

I stand in this tradition as I call for the epistemic primacy of Christ, and I see the same implication for the other intellectual disciplines. Though theology obviously does not determine the particular methods, strategies, and techniques of the individual sciences, it does legitimately name their fundamental orientation as a quest for the intelligibility of coinherent relationality.

A Praxis of Epistemic Participation

If relationality is the basic form of the real, then it follows that the optimal mode of knowing is through relation with the thing or event to be known. If mutual participation is the fundamental form of intelligibility, then the subject's participation in the object, and the object's sharing in the subject, is the most correct epistemic method. This insight corresponds to the ancient dictum that like is known by like. How odd all of this sounds to one shaped by the concern for sheer objectivity in knowing. On such a reading, a thing is properly known in the mea-

4. St. Bonaventure, "Unus est magister noster Christus," in *Le Christ Maître*, edited by Goulven Madec (Paris: J. Vrin, 1990).

5. John Henry Newman, *The Idea of a University* (Notre Dame, IN: Univ. of Notre Dame Press, 1986).

sure that the distorting perspective and prejudice of the subject are eliminated. But such an epistemology assumes just the conflictual and atomistic metaphysics rendered otiose by the claim that mutuality is the ultimately real.

A tour of a few aspects of Thomas Aquinas's deeply Christian account of knowledge helps to illustrate the principle I have invoked. In the light of the New Testament, Thomas, as we have seen, held that all things are intelligible because they are thought into being by the Creator God. God doesn't know things because they exist (as we do); rather, they exist because he knows them. There is, therefore, a correspondence at the deepest level between knower and known in the very constitution of finite reality: being known by another, namely God, is the ontological perfection of a created thing. This correlation, this mutuality, is played out *mutatis mutandis*, at the level of purely finite knowing. For Thomas, the intelligibility of an object calls out to a potential knower, and the knower seeks out the intelligibility of the object, each one finding its perfection in the other. The intelligible thing is lit up and brought to fulfillment in the act of being known, and the knower's desire is fulfilled in the same act. It is decidedly not the case for Thomas that the knower imposes an intelligibility on the object that it otherwise wouldn't have (as in more typically modern construals), but at the same time, the knower is not distanced from the object in the act of knowing—just the contrary. A sort of harmony or consonance is established between knower and known in any act of real intellection. Fergus Kerr comments that Aquinas's epistemology is not of the "subjective-observer" type but of the "objective-participant" variety.[6]

All of this is caught in the wonderfully understated scholastic adage *Intellectus in actu est intelligibile in actu*: the intellect actualized by the object *is* the actualization of the intelligibility of that object. This is neither the imposition of meaning on the object by the subject nor the total bracketing of the subject in favor of brute objectivity; rather, it is the mutual illumination of both subject and object in the coinherent act of knowing. The mystical dimension of ordinary knowing becomes clear when we recall that the mutuality between finite knower and finite known is a participation in that elemental mutuality between divine knower and creature that constitutes the very being of the creature. That is, the intellectual coinherence of God and creature—the relationality that the creature *is*—is mimicked in a real though imperfect way in the coinherence between the ordinary act of intelligence and ordinary intelligibility.

In the eighteenth century, Goethe voiced a critique of the regnant Newtonian form of reason, which is to say, a rationality fiercely analytical,

---

6. Fergus Kerr, *After Aquinas: Versions of Thomism* (Oxford: Blackwell, 2002), 27.

experimental, and invasive.[7] The Newtonian scientist rather aggressively drew the object into the world of the subject, compelling it to respond to the subject's concerns and questions. Goethe proposed in its place a more contemplative form of rationality, one that respected the otherness of the object, carefully following its rhythms and structure, refusing to impose itself. Hence the Goethean knower would not rip the plant from the ground in order to dissect it but would instead sit with the plant in its own environment, draw it, document its movements, etc., allowing it to ask and answer its own questions.

Thomas's account, with its roots in the New Testament and not in modernity, goes beyond the split between Newton and Goethe. It is not a matter of privileging either subject or object but rather of seeing the essential link between them, born of the unbreakable bond between knower and known, which itself is grounded in the even more basic connection between divine knower and creaturely existence. That mind, object, and Creator coinhere is assumed by Aquinas. When that coinherence is questioned, as it was in the modern period, we face the finally unresolvable dilemma between Newtonian and Goethean epistemology, between the demands of the subject and the integrity of the object. What Thomas proposes is an active mutuality of knower and known that can be properly described as a type of love. It is not as though the subject utterly effaces itself in the presence of the object or that the object surrenders utterly to the demands of the subject. On the contrary, each, in a way proper to itself, gives itself to the other and finds its own perfection in that coinherence.

It is against this background that we should understand Aquinas's definition of the truth as *adequatio rei et intellectus*, the correlation of thing and intellect. This has been taken as a classical expression of the correspondence theory of truth frequently and gleefully attacked by its critics from William James to Richard Rorty.[8] The difficulty, of course, is that the critics read the Aquinas definition through the lens of the modern demarcation of subject and object and thereby misinterpret it. They assume that Aquinas imagined a self-contained subject trying to effect a correspondence with the objective world through a mental picture or proposition, as in the early Wittgenstein. In fact, the *adequatio rei et intellectus* that Aquinas speaks of is the mutually enhancing coinherence of objective intelligibility and the subjective act of intelligence. *Res* is not a "thing" dumbly out there but an actuality oriented to real and possible knowers, and *intellectus* is not so much a mental space that is to be filled with adequate representa-

7. See Hans Urs von Balthasar, *The Glory of the Lord: A Theological Aesthetics*, vol. 5, *The Realm of Metaphysics in the Modern Age* (San Francisco: Ignatius, 1982), 362–63.

8. See Richard Rorty, *Philosophy and the Mirror of Nature* (Princeton, NJ: Princeton Univ. Press, 1979), esp. 44–45.

tions of objects as an operation of the mind called into actuality through participation in the intelligibility of the objective realm.

Lonergan comments that there are two types of emptiness: that of the box and that of the stomach. The box is dumbly empty, whereas the stomach is, if you will, intelligently empty, since it knows what it wants. The mind, prior to experience, is empty (hence a *tabula rasa*), but empty like a stomach, since by its nature it seeks participation with being. And as the word itself suggests, existence is a standing out from itself (*ex-istere*). To exist is to emerge into the light of intelligibility, to show up, to become available to a possible knower. The truth as *adequatio* that Thomas insists upon is the meeting of these two other-oriented, "extraverted" dynamics of knower and known.

Here we might actually effect a link between this Christian idea of epistemic participation and William James's account of knowing. Basic to James's epistemology is the conviction that the categories of subject and object have to be transcended in favor of a unified notion of experience.[9] The knower, for him, is not a detached observer, hovering outside of the world of objects and seeking an adequate account of them; on the contrary, the knower is a swimmer in the never-ending and always unfolding current of life, plunging, coasting, floating, diving into the stream, sometimes navigating it with relative success, often carried away by it. Or to shift the metaphor, the knower is like a bird that flies along the air currents of existence, now perching, now looking, now being carried aloft against its will. So tight in fact is the connection between knower and known that the usual distinctions we make between them break down and they become aspects of one totality. For James, the seer is affected by what he sees, and what he sees is changed in the act of being seen, each one conditioned by the moves of the other. "Experience" is the name that James gives to this irreducible unity that can be examined, for the sake of argument and according to one's purposes, under the aegis of either subjectivity or objectivity. It is on the basis of this radical *Ineinander* of subject and object that James objects to the classical "correspondence" theory of truth, but what is his own account but a particularly dramatic assertion of knowing through epistemic participation?

A real advance in epistemology effected by James, but one in continuity with the participation view I have been proposing, is his claim that emotion is as involved in the act of knowing as is intellection. James was concerned that a one-sided valorization of the rational effectively cuts one off from enormously important dimensions of experience that can be accessed only in nonrational ways. This principle, of course, guides much

---

9. William James, *The Principles of Psychology* (Cambridge, MA: Harvard Univ. Press, 1981), 262–75.

of his work in the philosophy of religion, but it can and should be applied more generally to all forms of knowing. Indeed, most of the great advances in the sciences have taken place not through plodding rational analysis but through intuitive insights, hunches, feelings, emotionally charged gropings in the direction of things only vaguely seen.

James has been echoed recently by Martha Nussbaum, who insists that feelings such as jealousy, sadness, loss, and longing have a cognitive value in the measure that they amount to an assessment of the importance of a given object. In the involving account of her mother's death, Nussbaum shows that her intense feelings of anxiety and grief in the wake of her mother's passing indicated, far more clearly than did her thinking, just who her mother was and what she meant.[10] The emotions are, in a sense, the body's way of knowing the truth.

None of this, it seems to me, is the least bit incompatible with the Christian doctrine of knowing through coinherent participation. What it adds is the clear sense of emotion and body as vehicles of a more intense participation in the object to be known.

Intersubjectivity

We have already seen that one of the principal illusions of Descartes was the conviction that he could find epistemic *terra firma* by retreating into the privacy of his own subjectivity. Turning away from the world (which he took to be a realm of incertitude) and from his fellow seekers (who did nothing but disagree with each other), Descartes turned toward the *cogito*, the stubbornly private "I think." But this, as we saw, is operationally self-defeating. Descartes couldn't even make the moves that he did without the intensely intersubjective facts of language and culture, and his very willingness to write down what he experienced witnesses to his clear interest in other minds as a test of truth. Lonergan gave voice to much of postmodernity's dissatisfaction with this side of the Cartesian project when he implied that the *cogitamus* matters much more than the *cogito*. Whenever a mathematician cogitates, she is assuming a whole range of truths—from the multiplication tables to the value of pi—that she has never verified for herself. Rather, she is relying on the work of others in the tradition, work furthermore that has been independently verified by the theorizing and practical applications of thousands upon thousands of researchers, teachers, builders, etc., across the centuries. Were she intent upon Cartesian certitude, grounded in her own verification of truth, she

10. Martha Nussbaum, *Upheavals of Thought: The Intelligence of Emotions* (Cambridge: Cambridge Univ. Press, 2001), esp. 19–49.

would never get a serious project off the ground. The same can be said, of course, of any scientist. Every astronomer, physicist, chemist, or biologist assumes unquestioningly in his own work a staggering number of observations, calculations, and measurements that have been made by others. Every act of knowledge that the mathematician or scientist achieves is, inescapably, intersubjective, a *cogitamus* much more than a *cogito*.

But the one who assumes the epistemic priority of Jesus Christ should be perfectly at home with this assertion of the dimension of intersubjectivity in knowing. We have already seen that for the Christian the form of objective intelligibility is coinherence and that the method of accessing the truth is radical and mutual participation of knower and known. For the Christian, authentic knowledge comes not through isolation or objectification but rather through something like love. Therefore it should not be surprising that the fullness of knowing would occur through an intersubjective process, with knowers, as it were, participating in one another as each participates in the thing to be known. If, as the Johannine prologue implies, the ground of being is a conversation between two divine speakers, it seems only reasonable that the search for intelligibility here below takes place in the context of a steady and loving conversation.

In a lyrical and compelling section of *Truth and Method*, Hans-Georg Gadamer reminds us that a healthy conversation is something like a game.[11] As two players surrender to the movement and rules of the game of tennis, they are carried away beyond themselves in such a way that the game is playing them much more than they are playing it. In a very similar way, when two or more interlocutors enter into the rhythm of an intellectual exchange, respectful of its rules and of one another, they are quite often carried beyond their individual concerns and questions and taken somewhere they had not anticipated, the conversation having played them. The fundamental requirement for this sort of shared self-transcendence is a moral one: each conversationalist has to surrender her need to dominate the play for her purposes; each must efface herself, not only before the others but, more importantly, before the transcendent goal that they all seek. To have a conversation is humbly to accept the possibility that one's take on things might be challenged or corrected, that the other's perspective might be more relatively right than one's own.

David Burrell has argued in a very similar vein that friendship must provide the matrix for any productive intellectual exchange. This means more than mere mutual respect, as indispensable as that is. Drawing on Aristotle, Burrell states that a friendship will endure only in the measure that the two friends have given themselves to a transcendent third, to the good, or the true, or the beautiful that surpasses both of them and that

11. Hans Georg Gadamer, *Truth and Method* (New York: Continuum, 1990), 101–34.

both seek together. As long as their love is centered on one another, it will dissipate; when it is directed beyond them, it will, paradoxically, thrive. So the truth is best sought by friends, because friends, by definition, will efface themselves before it. Obviously, two or more people locked in antagonism, each trying to refute the other and defend his own claims, will rarely move toward the truth, since concern for the truth has become subordinate to their animosity and egotism. By the same token, two or more people infatuated with one another will rarely discover the truth, since it has similarly been subordinated to their interest in one another.

In his remarkable studies of ancient philosophy, Pierre Hadot has shown that the philosophical schools of antiquity were not so much academies where a doctrine was learned as training grounds where a form of life was inculcated. "Philosophy" was a way of being in the world, and the ancient masters—Pythagoras, Socrates, Plato, Aristotle, Epicurus—were the personal embodiments of that way.[12] Students came to them not so much to learn their objective teaching as to apprentice to them, learning the lifestyle that would conduce to wisdom and ethical excellence. Thus, the Platonic dialogues should not be read primarily as repositories of Plato's key philosophical ideas but as instruction manuals for how to engage in a constructive philosophical conversation. In the *Republic*, for example, we apprentice to the master Socrates in his calm detachment, his concentration on the issue at hand, his use of apt metaphors—and most important, his subtle and respectful manner of engaging his interlocutors. And we take as a negative model Thrasymachus in his anger, rashness of judgment, arrogance, and lack of respect for a truth that transcends his self-interest. The clear implication is that one is invited not so much to think like Socrates as to be like him.

One senses much the same thing in the writings of Thomas Aquinas. We have seen that Thomas's first responsibility as a master of theology was the preaching of the Word and that this obligation led to Scripture commentary and the holding of disputed questions on controversial issues. These *quaestiones disputatae* were public debates, lively exchanges between master and students, the latter posing objections of all varieties and the former compelled to respond respectfully and with persuasive counterarguments. The dynamism and style of these public dialogues were mimicked (to greater or lesser degree of fidelity) in the literary form adopted by Aquinas in practically all his writings. A question is posed (even one as basic as *utrum Deus sit*), objections are brought forward in a logically coherent way, a citation from a scriptural or patristic authority is given, a definitive answer is laid out, and finally the objections are

12. Pierre Hadot, *Philosophy as a Way of Life: Spiritual Exercises from Socrates to Foucault* (Oxford: Blackwell, 1995), 81–108.

carefully reconsidered in light of the answer. Hardly ever does Aquinas brush an objection aside as simple-minded or irrelevant; in point of fact, usually the response shows the validity of some element of the objection.[13] Chesterton said that a love for the tradition is a willingness to embrace "the democracy of the dead," giving those long gone a voice in the living conversation.[14] This valorization of the tradition is everywhere apparent in Aquinas's method: he quotes biblical authorities, fathers of the church, pagan philosophers, Muslim commentators, and Jewish rabbis—always with reverence. Aristotle is "the Philosopher," Averröes is "the Commentator," and Maimonides is always "rabbi Moyses." Thomas's page is thus characterized not by authoritarian diktats but by a vivid back-and-forth movement of question and answer, a disciplined and respectful give-and-take of objection and response. We might press the matter and say that Thomas's method encourages the virtue of friendship necessary for a productive pursuit of the truth. Now just as Platonists transformed the dialogues into doctrine, Thomists distilled Thomas's conversations into clear and distinct ideas. Yet one senses that for Aquinas the ultimate purpose was not indoctrination but the inculcation of method, a radically intersubjective way of thinking.

This picture would remain crucially incomplete if we did not clarify further the limits and rules of a productive intellectual conversation. As we have seen, humility, openness to the other, a willingness to be corrected, and inclusion of challenging perspectives are all necessary for dialogue, but conversation devolves into shrill chattering unless certain restrictions are in place. Obviously, Gadamer respects the table of conversation, but he doesn't invite absolutely everyone to the table. Were there too many conversants, no one could cogently hear an argument. Were there people incapable of fluent and coherent speech, the discussion would never get under way. And most important, were there people around the table who did not share the moral convictions of the community of conversation, a sort of verbal violence would hold sway. Similarly, Aquinas attends to an impressive array of perspectives, and he listens to an extraordinarily diverse community of scholars, but he doesn't entertain every objection, and he doesn't listen to every voice. Some arguments are just silly, which is to say, they don't participate, even in an elementary way, in the truth of the Logos; and some arguers are stupid or disrespectful, which is to say, they don't allow themselves to be conformed, even marginally, to the moral demands of the Logos.

13. Robert Barron, *Thomas Aquinas: Spiritual Master* (New York: Crossroad, 1996), 32, 60.
14. G. K. Chesterton, *Orthodoxy*, in *Collected Works* (San Francisco: Ignatius, 1986), 1:251.

Thus, it is an intellectually and ethically disciplined intersubjectivity that honors the Christ-mind.

We find something similar in the writings of John Henry Newman, a thinker who in many ways inherited the virtues of both the ancient philosophical and the classical Christian traditions. In his *Essay on the Development of Doctrine*, which he wrote during the time of his transition from Anglicanism to Roman Catholicism, Newman pulls the neat trick of using the fact of doctrinal development to validate a more ancient and "conservative" version of Christianity. Protestantism, he argues, solves the problem of development in teaching and practice by essentially ignoring it, radically valorizing the form of Christian life discernible in the scriptural witness.[15] Whatever deviates from that norm is a corruption; whatever imitates it is a valid expression of Christianity. But Newman was profoundly uneasy with this proposal, since it required the believer to bracket practically the whole of church history from the earliest patristic period until modern times. Councils, lives of the saints, speculations of theologians, innumerable practical developments would all have to be seen, ipso facto, as corruptions. Anglicanism employed a more subtle method with roots in the speculation of Vincentius of Lerins. Vincent had said famously that legitimate Christian teaching is that which has been held *semper, ubique, et ab omnibus* (always, everywhere, and by everybody). Deviations are, of course, many, but the truths of the faith enjoy a discernible universality across time and space.[16] But here again, Newman balked. For if this Vincentian principle were consistently applied, one would have to say that the doctrines of the Trinity and the divinity of Christ are not valid Christian teaching, since they have certainly not been believed everywhere and by all: think only of the lengthy period during which Arianism held sway.

What Newman proposed, in line with the *Lebensphilosophie* of his time, was the notion of the development of doctrine. Any idea, he said, is a living thing, since it exists only in a lively mind. The mind is not what Hume thought it was, an empty theater in which ideas dumbly appear; rather, the mind is a restless, curious instrument that constantly turns ideas over and around, sifting, weighing, assessing them, wondering about them and comparing them to other ideas. An idea is like a multifaceted diamond, and the fullness of it is "the sum total of its possible aspects."[17] In accord with his deep anti-Cartesianism, Newman holds that this manifestation of the totality of an idea is not possible simply through the efforts of one mind, however subtle and vigorous. On the contrary, it is only when an

15. John Henry Newman, *An Essay on the Development of Christian Doctrine* (Westminster, MD: Christian Classics, 1968), 8.
16. Ibid., 10.
17. Ibid., 34.

idea has been brought to the far richer and more powerful sifting process of an entire community of minds that it begins fully to show itself.

Now if this is true with regard to ideas in general—even relatively simple ones—how much truer when one of the master ideas of Christian faith is under consideration. The incarnation, for instance, is so inexhaustibly rich a concept that its aspects, implications, dimensions, and applications can only appear gradually and through an especially concentrated play of lively minds. No one thinker, no one community of discourse, no one school, no one time could possibly exhaust such an idea. This is, of course, precisely why the idea of the incarnation has had a rich history, stretching from the biblical period, through the roiled debates of the early councils, to the speculations of Augustine and Aquinas, to the ruminations of the mystics, and finally to the work of the political and liberation theologians of our time. Without this process of intersubjective weighing, turning, and assessing, the notion of the incarnation couldn't even have begun to present itself with relative adequacy. Rahner suggested this evolutionary quality of the idea of the incarnation in his programmatic essay "Chalcedon: Beginning or End." Obviously, the Chalcedonian formula ended the christological debate in a significant sense by precluding certain interpretive possibilities. In Newman's language, it closed off certain corrupt readings. At the same time, in the very laconicism of its expression, it called forth further development, amplification, and explanation.

Newman was uneasy with both modernity and Protestantism in regard to this living quality of ideas. In its Cartesian and Newtonian forms, modernity seemed to suggest that the private knower, through an immediate intuition or a disciplined empirical analysis, can unambiguously grasp the truth of nature, and Lutheran Protestantism held that the individual believer, reading the Bible without the interpretive aid of the church, can understand the deepest truths of salvation. Both assumed a certain stasis at the level of ideas and a subjectivism at the level of epistemology. For Newman, knowing is more like a disciplined game involving a ball perpetually in motion and a team of lively players, in accord with definite rules, alternately tossing, holding, passing, and kicking it.

A Mind in Love

The first words out of the mouth of Jesus in Mark's Gospel are these: "The time is fulfilled, and the kingdom of God has come near; repent, and believe in the good news" (Mark 1:15). The term translated by the moralizing "repent" is *metanoiete*, derived from two words, *meta* (beyond) and *nous* (mind). Jesus is urging his hearers not primarily to change their behavior but to go beyond the mind that they have, to see things in a new

way, to adopt a different attitude.[18] Essential to this epistemic conversion
is faith (*pistis*), for he implies that the *metanoia* will make possible the
trusting acceptance of the good news: *pistuete ton euangelion*. This is not
so much acceptance of new data as willingness to enter into the world
opened up by the novelty of Jesus himself, to believe what has become
a possibility in him. As becomes clear in the course of the Gospels, the
kingdom of God is not primarily social reform, ethical renewal, or political
transformation (though it gives rise to all of these); the kingdom, first, is
Jesus himself, the coming together of divinity and humanity, the Word
made flesh.

What is the opposite of this trust? What is the quality of mind that
must be transformed in the course of *metanoia*? At the close of the narrative of the calming of the storm at sea, as the disciples, half-afraid,
half-fascinated, look up at Jesus, the Master says to them, "Why are you
afraid? Have you still no faith?" (Mark 4:40). The implication is that the
opposite of trust is fear, a turning in on oneself, a refusal to move into
the power of Jesus's way of being. To have the Christ-mind is to know
the world not through the distorting lens of one's self-absorption and
fear but through the clarifying lens of the kingdom, which is to say, the
coming together of divinity and humanity. To enter trustingly into that
surprising coinherence of Creator and creature is to adopt the right way
of seeing all that can be seen.

At the very beginning of the *Summa theologiae*, Thomas Aquinas, as we
have seen, holds that theology is a discipline that goes beyond the range
of the philosophical sciences. Revelation-based *sacra doctrina* orients us
to the properly supernatural end that, in a curious paradox, is naturally
ours. And if we turn to the beginning of the third part of the *Summa*, we
find that the culmination of revelation is the event of the incarnation.
Theological vision is, accordingly, an ecstatic form of seeing, conditioned
by the novelty of the enfleshment of God, and the theologian, by definition, is someone who is willing to be drawn up beyond herself in an
attitude of trust in the power of that miracle. In terms of Mark's Gospel,
the theological knower is one who has undergone *metanoia*, a radical
transformation of vision through the incarnation. But if, as I have been
arguing, the theological mind is the paradigmatic mind, then all forms of
human knowing are, at their best, marked by this same trust, this same
capacity for ecstasy, this same willingness to see the world in terms of an
incarnational teleology.

In one of his sharply worded attacks on Aristotelian scholasticism,
Martin Luther said that the fatal flaw in Aristotle's metaphysics and epis-

18. Robert Barron, *And Now I See: A Theology of Transformation* (New York: Crossroad,
1998), 4.

temology is their focus on being, which is to say, the present constitution of a thing. Though he remained interested in past and future (efficient and final causality), Aristotle held that the proper object of philosophical investigation is substance (*ousia*). But this, says Luther, from the biblical perspective, is distorted, for God is far more interested in the future, the ultimate destiny, of things. This appears most plainly in the renaming of key figures throughout the biblical narrative: Abram becomes Abraham, Jacob becomes Israel, Simon becomes Peter, Saul becomes Paul. Through this shifting of names, God signals that he reads each of these figures from the perspective of the future. He is interested in them in the measure that they serve the divine purpose of bringing about the transformation of the world through grace. Furthermore, when the philosopher makes the present the focus of his intellectual concern, he labors under the illusion that he is in control of the object to be known, when in point of fact it is only the Lord of the future who truly knows. Therefore, a trusting decentering of the ego is an essential element in a Christian epistemology. Luther's criticism can be seen as an extremely prescient anticipation of a modern science that would almost completely bracket questions of teleology and divine intentionality, rendering a scientistic, immanentist view of the universe. The mind that has undergone *metanoia* reads all things through the lens of the incarnation, which is to say, from the perspective of the absolute future that God holds out to his world.

We see something related if we consult the much-commented-upon hymn text that Paul integrates into his letter to the Philippians. The author urges his readers to "let the same mind be in you that was in Christ Jesus" and then proceeds to spell out the nature of this attitude: "though he was in the form of God, [Jesus] did not regard equality with God as something to be exploited, but emptied himself, taking the form of a slave, being born in human likeness" (Phil. 2:5–7). Like Jesus in his inaugural address in Mark's Gospel, Paul is inviting his listeners to *metanoia*, a transformation of mind, more precisely, a taking on of the mind that characterizes Christ himself. If in the Markan context, this conversion was a matter of moving from fear to trust, here it amounts to the transition from arrogance to humility or autonomy to obedience. Jesus's mind (which remains the absolute criterion for all correct knowledge) is, in a supreme paradox, a mind that obeys, that does not cling to its own prerogatives but rather looks to the direction of another—the Father. And this obedience is total, for he "became obedient to the point of death—even death on a cross" (Phil. 2:8). This is the mind that Paul urges us to adopt, one capable of total other orientation, complete self-denial, one that looks stubbornly to the purposes of the other who is God.

In line with his Thomist intuitions, Bernard Lonergan appreciated God (the fullness of being) as the lure for the mind, even in its simplest acts of cognition. Whenever the mind seeks truth, it is operating under the impulse and aegis of the Truth itself; whenever it endeavors to see, it is implicitly seeking the fullness of the beatific vision, the act that would be, in Lonergan's famous phrase, "knowing everything about everything."[19] God's intelligence has grounded the intelligibility of the world and hence animated the intelligently seeking human mind. This entails, first, that the dynamisms of the mind must be fundamentally extraverted, oriented to the other. The cognitive act corrupts when it turns inward, thwarting its own natural tendency outward toward the fullness of all that can be known. It implies, second, that any cognitive act is a sort of obedience to God, for God is the Truth that suffuses all that can be known. In light of these basic epistemic assumptions, Lonergan formulated his imperatives to any and all knowers: "Be attentive, be intelligent, be reasonable, be responsible."[20] All four of these are calls to overcome self-absorption, to look outward, to conform oneself to the demands of the all-surrounding divine truth. As such, they are directives to habituate the mind toward love and trust in God. They are a summons toward *metanoia*.

To be attentive—to see, hear, taste, smell, and touch what is before us—is much more difficult than it may seem. If the mind were simply a *tabula rasa*, it would but have to rest passively before being and allow itself to be written on. But the mind is, as we saw, alert even in its emptiness. It has consequently to look in a focused and disciplined way, avoiding the lazy tendency to accept the "obvious." It is required to take time before an object or event, seeing its many aspects, watching it unfold across time and space. Above all, it must overcome its tendency toward selective perception, seeing only what it wants to see, only what it might be convenient to see. To be attentive is to take in the novel, the strange, the deeply disconcerting, the dangerous. It is to respect what God has chosen to create in all of its uniqueness and specificity and not presume that one knows the physical world a priori.

To be intelligent, in Lonergan's sense, is to look for formal patterns, to seek out the intelligible structures that run through whatever exists. The summons to intelligence corresponds to the assumption of universal reasonability that I spoke of earlier, the mystical intuition that undergirds the sciences. But this assumption is only the beginning, the condition for the possibility of real intelligence. The actual seeing of the pattern is as difficult and demanding as real attentiveness, involving a perception that is both penetrating and playful.

19. Bernard Lonergan, *Understanding and Being*, in *The Collected Works of Bernard Lonergan*, vol. 5 (Toronto: Univ. of Toronto Press, 1990), esp. 146–55.
20. Bernard Lonergan, *Method in Theology* (Toronto: Univ. of Toronto Press, 1990), 18.

When a scientist has been sufficiently attentive to the data before her, she begins to formulate a series of hypotheses, likely explanations for their unique arrangement. She senses a number of possible intelligible patterns that undergird the phenomenon under investigation—some simple, others complex, still others quite speculative and unlikely. This arraying of intellectual possibilities—hypotheses to be tested—is what Lonergan means by *intelligence*. It is contained in a series of often interrelated "aha" experiences, insights, graspings of form.

In *A Portrait of the Artist as a Young Man,* James Joyce gives a wonderful description of aesthetic intelligence. In the context of a lively discussion of the nature of beauty, Stephen Daedalus asks his friend Lynch to consider "a basket which a butcher's boy had slung inverted on his head."[21] He then invites him examine the basket more closely, "passing from point to point, led by its formal lines, apprehending it as balanced part against balanced part, feeling the rhythm of its structure." To see at this level, to participate with the mind in the rhythm of a thing's formal complexity, to sense what Aquinas called its *consonantia*, is to be intelligent. In both the scientific and aesthetic contexts we sense a similar demand and commitment: the seeing of the form calls one outside of himself into a sort of ecstatic participation in the thing or event under investigation. The "rhythm of structure" has a primacy, compelling the mind into imitation.

The third Lonerganian imperative is "be reasonable." This is a summons to the mind to be decisive, to make a judgment among the various hypotheses presented to it, to determine which of many admittedly bright ideas is the right idea. Finally there is only one relatively adequate explanation for a phenomenon, one rational structure that truly informs it. This emerges at the end of a long process of experimentation, reflection, discussion, the marshaling of evidence, and the arrangement of argument and counterargument. At the level of judgment, the determination of this truth is made. As the word itself suggests, decision is always a bloody business, involving a cutting off. It is enticing to contemplate a range of interesting suggestions and ideas, reveling in their possibilities, aspects, and implications; it is painful to opt ultimately for one, since it entails the leaving behind of all the others, intriguing as they are. In judgment, the knower is called to accept the hard truth, to draw the reasonable conclusion even if it goes against his hopes and expectations.

In the Christian vision, the truth of a thing is a reflection of the Truth that made it, a participation in the Logos that informs it. Making a judgment is, accordingly, honoring the will of the Creator God, following his more elemental decision. Lonergan speaks frequently of the properly

---

21. James Joyce, *A Portrait of the Artist as a Young Man,* in *The Portable James Joyce,* edited by Harry Levin (New York: Penguin, 1987), 479.

functioning mind as having the "unrestricted desire to know." To have this desire is to want the truth above all, without cavil or hesitation, and hence it is to love God with one's mind, to seek God even at the greatest cost. Here we see the connection to the Pauline hymn in Philippians. To have the same mind that was in Christ Jesus is to have a desire to follow the will of the Father even to the total emptying out of one's self. Jesus judged that the will of the Father was that he come to the cross. Though every emotion and inclination in him veered away from that fate (as is recounted in the Gethsemane narrative), he perdured in his judgment. The Christian knower is the one who, in a similar way, honors God through her judgment, overcoming the self-absorption that would blind her to the truth.

The final of the Lonerganian imperatives—"be responsible"—is a call to live out the implications of one's judgments. Having seen things in a particular way, having decided, now one must adjust one's body, feelings, and actions to that vision. This could take the form of publishing certain findings, undergoing a moral conversion, resolving to pray, seeking reconciliation with a former friend, going to war, or going to confession. Some people are remarkably attentive, sparklingly intelligent, even decisive, but remain incapable of living out their decisions. But those who lack the courage of their convictions are, despite their intellectual achievements, alienated from a participation in truth, for as the Gospel of John suggests, the truth is finally something that one does. This final imperative draws the knower out of herself into an ecstasy that involves the totality of her existence. To follow it is to participate in the truth with body, will, mind, and heart. If the four imperatives are followed habitually and the mind is thereby allowed to develop in accord with its deepest intentionality, one grows into the state of being "unconditionally in love with God," which is to say, unrestrictedly conformed to the demands of the truth. This is the mind and heart of the saint; this is the Christ-mind in its fullest expression. It is the mind that has undergone *metanoia*.

The central tension of this chapter comes once more to the surface: How is the particularity of the Christ-mind related to the mind as such? Can someone who has surrendered to the Christian form of cognition enter into conversation with a non-Christian? Or to turn the question around: wouldn't a non-Christian happily admit that the well-functioning mind operates according to something like Lonergan's imperatives? Could there be a Buddhist, a Hindu, an agnostic scientist, an atheist social commentator who would not say that it is a desideratum to be attentive, intelligent, reasonable, and responsible? And if that is true, then how are any of these imperatives distinctively Christian?

Lonergan helps us to see how these are finally only pseudoproblems. Christians maintain that the Logos that became incarnate in Jesus Christ is the Logos by which all things, including the mind, are made. Hence it should not be surprising that what appears explicitly as an epistemic implication of the incarnation is participated in to varying degrees by anyone who exercises his mind in a responsible way. Here we are close to Aquinas's treatment of the relation between theology and the "natural" reason that explores the *preambula fidei*: both are participations in the Logos, the former being far more intense and complete than the latter, but both stemming ultimately from the same source. Lest this sound too bland, too much like a mere distinction in degree and not kind, we must consider that the Christian is called to a love of the truth that mirrors the Truth's love of him or her, and that this love is manifested as a gift of self unto death. The Lonerganian "saint," the one unrestrictedly in love with God, is someone marked by the Christ-pattern, the kenosis of the mind and self in the presence of the truth.

If we combine the two insights that I have been developing in this section, we might say that the mind by which all things came to be, through which they subsist, and by which they will be reconciled, the mind, furthermore, by which a knower properly understands all things, is one of other orientation, trust, and obedience. It is a mind that looks with uncompromising attention to the present and future intentions of God in the world. The perspective that cannot be contextualized or positioned by any higher perspective—the Christ-mind—is a mind of love and in love.

The Fallen Mind

It is a commonplace of the Christian tradition that the fall had implications at all levels of a person's being. Original sin affected not only the will but the body, the passions, the imagination, and the mind as well.[22] Because of sin, each of the powers within a person has become corrupt, and more to the point, they have fallen into disharmony with one another. What God intended to be a smoothly functioning and well-integrated organism has become a diseased body—able to operate but slow, disjointed, awkward, at cross-purposes to itself. Nowhere is this disjointedness more powerfully described than in chapter 7 of Paul's letter to the Romans: "So I find it to be a law that when I want to do what is good, evil lies close at hand. For I delight in the law of God in my inmost self, but I see

---

22. "And if one were to deny . . . that the whole Adam, because of that sinful disobedience, was changed in body and soul for the worse, let him be anathema." *Decree concerning Original Sin*, para. 1, in *Decrees of the Ecumenical Councils*, edited by Norman Tanner (London: Sheed and Ward, 1990), 666.

in my members another law at war with the law of my mind, making me captive to the law of sin that dwells in my members" (Rom. 7:21–23). To some degree, Paul would have realized this inner disharmony through the Greek philosophical tradition to which he was heir. As we have seen, the philosophical schools of the ancient world were moral training grounds, places where one passed through a strict discipline in order to learn how properly to think. It was a basic assumption among these philosophers that there is something wrong with the way most people naturally act and reason. But Paul knew the depths of the problem from the biblical tradition, which puts the dysfunction of human beings—even heroes such as Moses and David—on constant display.

Paul bequeathed this sense of the fallen self to the subsequent Christian tradition, where it was especially developed by Augustine. The *Confessions* is the story of how a darkened mind comes very gradually and painfully to a glimpse of the light; *The City of God* is the account of how a corrupt and perverted civilization is called to conversion; and *De Trinitate* is an account of how a poorly ordered soul achieves integration through an alignment with the persons of the Trinity. All three works are unintelligible without the undergirding assumption of the fall and its effects.

From Augustine, this notion was transferred to the medieval Christian consciousness. We have already seen how for Thomas the sinful mind is sunk in the *tenebrae*, unable properly to see, appreciate, or evaluate the world. But the theme of the fallen mind is even more clearly emphasized in Thomas's colleague Bonaventure, who, anticipating Luther, remained extremely wary of what he took to be the overconfident and immanent-ist speculations of the Aristotelians of his own time. What particularly bothered Bonaventure was the blithe assumption that a Christian could uncritically take in the thinking of a philosopher whose mind was fallen and untransformed by grace. Among the thinkers of the Reformation, this theme was taken up but in a somewhat exaggerated way. Luther's perhaps legitimate suspicions of rationalist scholasticism devolved into a complete contempt for "whore reason," and this led in turn to his embrace of the *sola scriptura* principle and his suspicion of all forms of natural theologizing.

Perhaps this very exaggeration of the motif of the fallen mind contrib-uted to the counterreaction of the Enlightenment. All the major Enlighten-ment figures took for granted that there is something the matter with the mind, but they tended to see the problem as exterior rather than interior. They acknowledged that the European intellect was not functioning at full capacity, but they felt that this was not because of intrinsic weakness but because it had been shackled by uncriticized dogmatisms, clouded by religious obscurantism, and infantilized by political authoritarianism. In the mathematical method of Descartes, the strict geometry of Spinoza's ethics, and the rationalism of Kant's religion, we get some idea of what the *Aufklärers* believed the enlightened mind could produce once these various hindrances were removed. In his programmatic essay "What Is Enlightenment?" Kant calls for European intellectuals to achieve their majority, to dare to know on their own, free from the tutelage of religion and tradition.[23] The basic assumption is that the mind is good and strong but simply underdeveloped. Having witnessed the moral outrages of the twentieth century, postmodern thinkers, as we have seen, are far less impressed by the intrinsic goodness and integrity of the mind and far more willing to reconsider the Christian view of an intellect that is kinky, twisted, at odds with itself.

Once more, Lonergan helps us to grasp the nettle of this issue. As a Jesuit, Lonergan was immersed in the spiritual tradition of Ignatius of Loyola, for whom conversion was an essential lifelong preoccupation. As a philosopher and theologian, Lonergan placed special stress on this dynamic in relation to the functioning of the intellect. Throughout his writings on epistemology he asserts that the mind must be summoned to conversion, precisely because it has a tendency to dysfunction. The term *conversion*, with its religious and moral overtones, is quite apt, for the problem with the mind is not simply technical but rather personal and spiritual. The poorly operating mind is one that has turned in on itself (*curvatus in se*) and in its self-preoccupation lost contact with the objective world. It is a mind, in our terminology, insufficiently in love. Lonergan sums up his position in the wonderfully pithy observation that authentic objectivity (contact with the real) is a function of properly constituted subjectivity (the converted mind).[24] Traditionalists who complained that Lonergan's interest in the dynamics of subjectivity amounted to a surrender to Cartesianism missed the centrality of the theme of the fallen mind. If the mind were uncompromised, one could simply "turn to the things themselves," but it is the weakened intellect that prevents the "things in themselves" from properly appearing.

A return to the four imperatives explored in the last section—"be attentive, be intelligent, be reasonable, be responsible"—will be helpful here. A first mark of the fallen mind is inattentiveness: it does not contact the real because it is not alert enough to see. I mentioned above the tendency toward selective perception—seeing only what one wants or is predisposed to see—but we might also point to simple perceptive laziness. We don't take in the world because perception requires too much effort. Thus a scientist might not collect all the necessary data

23. Immanuel Kant, "What Is Enlightenment?" in *The Foundations of the Metaphysics of Morals*, translated by Lewis White Beck (Indianapolis: Bobbs-Merrill, 1978), 85.
24. Lonergan, *Understanding and Being*, 173–74.

before launching into a theoretical explanation; a commentator might not notice all the details of a given political battle before proffering an explication; a golfer might not take in all the vagaries of his situation before choosing a particular club. In each case, a person is willing to assert himself—theoretically or practically—without a sufficient attention to the objective. Another reason for this imperative is fear: sometimes we don't or won't see because we have been told not to look. There are, of course, innumerable examples of this kind of censorship and restriction over the centuries. Religions, cultures, political regimes, schools of philosophy, and scientific establishments have all, for various reasons, placed certain areas outside the purview of attentive minds. Here we can appreciate the moral courage that is required of someone who would, in a fallen world, carry out the command to look.

A second quality of the compromised mind is unintelligence, stupidity. To be intelligent is to have insights, which is to say, to penetrate to the level of form, to appreciate the ontological patterns that characterize a given thing or situation. When asked what he took to be the essence of his artistic genius, Pablo Picasso said that it was the capacity to appreciate visual analogies: this bicycle seat is like the head of a bull; the curve of this pear is like the curve on the body of a guitar, which in turn is like the curve of a woman's figure. This sort of seeing of related patterns—Tracy's analogical imagination—is a mark of intelligence. Thus the unintelligent person is someone who is dazzled by surfaces and never seeks to look deeper, who sees light, color, and movement but never attends to texture, structure, and interconnection. To be stupid is not to raise questions such as "Why is this so?" and "What makes these many one?" and "How is this like that?" We have seen that simple attentiveness requires effort, but intelligence calls for an even greater level of engagement and self-transcendence. To seek after patterns is to ask questions relentlessly (think of Aquinas's almost manic piling up of questions in the *Summa*), to follow the evidence where it leads, to participate in endless conversation, to entertain novel perspectives. The fallen mind is marked, in Tillich's phrase, by "self-complacent finitude." Blandly at home with the superficial and the familiar, it rests in itself and thus becomes sluggish, dull-witted, uncurious. It cannot summon the moral or intellectual energy to raise even one good question, much less a series of them. Again, intimidation can play a role here. Many curious minds are cowed into complacency by the threat of punishment or ostracization.

The third mark of the fallen mind is unreasonability, the incapacity to make a judgment. In the course of a lively and curiously intelligent investigation, a thinker will entertain a number of intriguing possibilities and likely hypotheses, but, as we saw, only one can be relatively adequate. To be reasonable is to be able to discriminate from among these many the one that corresponds to the truth. The unreasonable mind stays fixed on the fence of ambivalence, unable to decide. There can be a variety of grounds for this indecision. First, a person might be entertained by the sheer beauty and multiplicity of the intellectual options on display and be unwilling to close off any of them. In that case, the aesthetic improperly triumphs over the noetic. Second, a person might, in her incertitude, be terrified to choose; or she might be concerned that a particular decision will hurt and disappoint those she loves or relies upon. Third, someone might realize that a given decision would involve a major change in her life, a change she is unwilling to make. In these cases, the desire for self-protection would improperly trump the desire for the truth. For these and many other reasons, the fallen mind, even if it has become relatively attentive and intelligent, can settle into self-regarding unreasonableness.

Finally, the mind in the *tenebrae* is irresponsible, unwilling to carry out the practical and ethical implications of a judgment. If something has been determined to be true, then the life of the one who has made the determination must be shaped in accord with that truth. Thus the responsible person makes the objective truth the norm of his subjectivity. When John Paul II calls for a clear correspondence between freedom and truth, he is responding to the fourth of Lonergan's imperatives. It is perhaps in terms of this imperative that we appreciate most readily the tragedy of the fallen mind, for the irresponsible mind is equivalent to the unintegrated self, the riven subject. Hamlet, who knows precisely what he must do but cannot do it, is irresponsible in this sense, as is Pilate, who knows full well the innocence of Jesus even as he sends him to the cross. All of Jesus's own condemnations of the Pharisees and keepers of the law hinge upon the irresponsible disconnection between their stated convictions and their concrete practice.

Therefore the fallen mind, the mind in the shadows, has a tendency toward inattentiveness, stupidity, unreasonability, and irresponsibility; it is *curvatus in se*, self-absorbed, fearful, pusillanimous. The central paradox is this: only those who have been touched by the Christ-mind, the intellect in love, realize the limitation of the minds they have. Only those who have begun to stand in the light recognize the smudges and shadows on what they had taken to be the clear transparent pane of the intellect. Just as the saints—Augustine, Francis, Thérèse of Lisieux—are most aware of their sinfulness, so those illumined by the Christ-mind are most conscious of the fallenness of their intellect. Saints of the mind realize that perfect attention, intelligence, reasonability, and responsibility are only asymptotically approached through grace, and thus they cultivate a becoming epistemic humility.

The Incarnate Mind

The prologue to John unambiguously celebrates the transcendence and divine majesty of the Logos ("the Word was with God, and the Word was God"), but it just as clearly states the immanence and humility of that same Logos ("the Word became flesh and dwelt among us"). Colossians certainly stresses the sublimity and transhistoricality of Christ ("he is the image of the invisible God"), but it just as clearly posits his particularity and historicity ("he is head of his body, the church"). In the first letter of John, we find the same juxtaposition in an even more jarring expression: "We declare to you what was from the beginning, what we have heard, what we have seen with our eyes . . . and touched with our hands, concerning the word of life" (1 John 1:1). The Word of life, existing with God from the beginning, is *touched with human hands*.

This incarnation of the Logos, celebrated in the New Testament and defended throughout the history of the church, gives to Christians a distinctive epistemic style. The Word, which has made all things and which illumines properly functioning minds, is oriented to flesh and, by implication, is at home with all of the messy particularity of time, space, history, language, and culture. This means that Christians don't seek intelligibility, even of the highest sort, apart from matter and history, and that they are consequently uneasy with epistemological dualisms and angelisms of any kind. Because the Word did not despise the flesh, Christians prefer to know, in Wittgenstein's phrase, "on the rough ground."

In a classical context, both Plato and Plotinus advocated a praxis of separation from the body as a condition for the possibility of authentic knowing. Until one manages to escape from the shackles of materiality and particularity, one is destined to remain epistemologically at the level of mere opinion; only upon effective dissociation of mind from matter (achieved through various practices) can an adept access the forms and hence attain authentic knowledge. Insight is possible but at the cost of a severe disciplining of sense and imagination. The solitariness of this process became especially clear in Plotinus. If the body is the problem, then association with other bodies, with all their attendant distortions and prejudices, simply exacerbates the difficulty. Hence, at the highest pitch of Plotinian intellection, one finds himself "alone with the Alone." In the modern framework, we find a similar dualism and subjectivism. For Descartes, since the mind is known through a clear and distinct intuition while the body belongs to the dubious realm of the sensory, there must be a radical demarcation between body and mind. And the latter must be able to function (indeed function better) in separation from the distortions and ambiguities of the former. A similar preference for the pure mind and a concomitant distrust of the physical can be seen in the austere ethics of Spinoza and in both the epistemology and religion of Kant.

An especially interesting locus of modern epistemic angelism is Locke's philosophy of mind. In his empiricism, Locke seems innocent of any charge of Platonism, Cartesianism, or epistemological dualism, but if we attend to his account of the dynamics of assent, we can pick up the strain that I have been exploring. Like most moderns, Locke was deeply concerned with clarifying and policing the process of thought, so that the obscurantisms of the past might be avoided. Descartes's cluttered city was the result of sloppy thinking, and it could be rebuilt on the basis of a more careful intellectual procedure. Locke identified the key problem as the often faulty relationship between inference and assent.[25] In a word, too many people give to propositions an assent out of proportion to the quality of inference offered as a foundation for the assent. Thus, though I might have only a somewhat convincing argument, or perhaps even no argument at all, for a given claim, I nevertheless give my full assent to it. Or, to turn it around, though I have a very clear inferential support for a particular assertion, I only give it mild assent or no assent at all. The problem can be effectively addressed only when it is seen as a properly moral one: for Locke, it is *unethical* to give to a proposition an assent that is disproportionate to its inferential support. Thus, if one has a poor argument for a claim, he ought to give it mild assent; if he has a fairly good argument for it, he ought to give it middling assent; if he has a clinching inferential demonstration for it, he ought (in the fully moral sense of "ought") to give it full and unhesitating assent. How is one to know whether he is an authentic seeker of the truth? Locke can think of only one valid test: "there is one unerring mark of it, viz. the not entertaining any proposition with greater assurance than the proofs it is built on will warrant."[26]

John Henry Newman, though he guarded throughout his life a deep respect for Locke, made his disagreement with this Lockean proposal the centerpiece of his epistemological masterpiece *An Essay in Aid of a Grammar of Assent*. His fundamental complaint was that the tight linking of assent to inference made sense only on the assumption of some sort of epistemological angelism, "a view of the human mind . . . which seems theoretical and unreal."[27] In point of fact, says Newman, we fully assent to numerous propositions for which there is, at best, vague inferential support. We know from direct experience, for example, that numerous assents endure even long after their logical substructure has vanished or

---

25. See John Henry Newman, *An Essay in Aid of a Grammar of Assent* (Notre Dame, IN: Univ. of Notre Dame Press, 1979), 136–137.

26. John Locke, *An Essay concerning Human Understanding*, chap. 7, quoted in Newman, *Essay in Aid of a Grammar*, 138.

27. Newman, *Essay in Aid of a Grammar*, 139.

been forgotten. So many of our most basic convictions and beliefs about the world—what Newman calls "the clothing and furniture of the mind"—are accepted unquestioningly and implicitly, though we could only in rare cases articulate the logical arguments upon which they are grounded. On the other hand, sometimes assent gives way even when the inferential arguments used to justify it are still vigorously in place. Though the reasons for a conviction remain unassailed, the conviction itself fails. "Sometimes our mind changes so quickly, so unaccountably, so disproportionately to any tangible arguments . . . as to suggest the suspicion that moral causes, arising out of our condition, age, company, occupations, fortunes, are at the bottom."[28] We no longer accept a proposition because someone we deeply admire does not accept it; we fail to subscribe to a point of view because we are no longer children; we stop believing something because we have suddenly lost our money and good name. In none of these cases does the transition from belief to disbelief have anything to do with shifts in the argumentative base.

Then again, sometimes assent is never given even in the face of well-crafted and persuasive arguments. Newman remarks that at times "we find men loud in the their admiration of truths which they never profess."[29] Though the mind might grasp the truth of a demonstration immediately, it can take years for the act of assent to develop, or though the intellect might see a necessary connection between proposition A and proposition B, the body, emotions, and heart remain unconvinced. In other cases, pressure and coercion can play a dissuasive role: Newman cites the couplet "A man convinced against his will / Is of the same opinion still." And this applies even in regard to mathematical demonstrations that play themselves out over a series of steps and logical inferences. Though each move be impeccably made, the mathematician is sometimes unable to give her assent to the proof until a number of other nonrational factors come into play.

Now on Locke's reading, these ruptures between inference and assent would be signs of moral and intellectual dysfunction, but for Newman they should not be so construed; instead they should be taken as evidence that the mind in fact does not operate according to the rationalist strictures that Locke has set for it. The mind finds itself inescapably embodied, conditioned by emotion, and situated in a social network, but this context is not a problem to be overcome; rather it is to be appreciated as itself a contributing factor to the intellectual process.

To make his critique of a one-sided rationalism more pointed, Newman examines the advantages and limitations of the classical syllogism. Newman admired Aristotle even more than Locke, but he felt that the

28. Ibid., 142.
29. Ibid.

logical tool developed by Aristotle contributed only in part to the act of assent. In its standard form, the syllogism displays itself in a tripartite way: if A and B, then C, A taken as a universal, B as an instance of A, and C as the explication of the implied relationship between A and B. What allows the syllogism to work is that symbols are substituted for words, or abstractions for individuals. Symbols and abstractions stand for pure notions, stripped as far as possible of all particularization, and it is this very streamlining that enables them to be manipulated with such compelling logical force. Words, on the other hand, are indicative of individuals in all of their peculiarity, and they accordingly carry with them a whole set of connotations, implications, connatural senses, and poetic overtones. This undisciplined, unfocused, untamable quality of words—which makes them uniquely apt in the description of the particularly real—disqualifies them from use in syllogisms. In his setting aside of words, "the logician for his own purposes . . . turns rivers, full, winding, and beautiful, into navigable canals."[30]

This means that the premises of a syllogism will effectively catch universal qualities and general trends but will tend to miss the individual exceptions to the rule. "All men have their price; Socrates is a man; therefore Socrates has his price" will be a correct calculation precisely in the measure that the unique individual Socrates is like all or most other men. In the measure that he is not, the syllogism will, despite its impressive logical structure, fail to generate the truth. Newman concludes that the syllogism is "open at both ends," implying that the nondefinitiveness of the necessarily abstract premises conduces to the nondefinitiveness of the conclusion.[31] Again, this is not to say that such a form of reasoning does not have its uses: it is, in fact, an extremely helpful indicator of the direction in which particular truth lies. But it is to say that syllogistic inference in and of itself is never enough to bring the mind to assent in concrete matters. What we notice here is the correlation between the abstract logical form of the syllogism and a purely disembodied mode of intellection. If we were pure minds (angels), the syllogism would be enough; inasmuch as we are embodied spirits in search of an incarnate truth, more is required.

This "more" Newman refers to as "informal inference." This mode of reasoning includes the formal element of syllogistic ratiocination but supplements it with a range of intuitions, feelings, hunches, and above all, an instinct for the convincing power of convergent probabilities. Newman gives several examples of the actual functioning of this mode of thinking, but the best known is his account of how we come to the unambiguous

30. Ibid., 215.
31. Ibid., 227.

assent that Great Britain is an island.[32] No sane person doubts the claim that Great Britain is an island or would hesitate even for a moment in making practical judgments on the basis of that claim. Anyone who would seriously maintain the opposite would be considered not only intellectually deficient, but mad. But when we look for the set of clear, logical inferences upon which this assent is based, we are frustrated. We assent to the insularity of Great Britain without hesitation or cavil, even though there is no syllogism that has generated the assent. How then has the mind in forming this judgment actually operated? It has done so through the sifting and assessing of a range of probable arguments, some clearly formulated, most felt and intuited rather than explicitly thought out. That Great Britain is surrounded by water "we have been taught in our childhood, and it is so in all the maps; we have never heard it contradicted or questioned, . . . every book we have read invariably took it for granted, our whole national history, the routine transactions and current events of the country . . . imply it in one way or another."[33] None of these arguments or observations amounts, obviously, to a clinching demonstration; any and all of them could be questioned or doubted by a stubborn skeptic. If Locke were correct in his assumption that assent should be strictly tied to the quality of inference, these numerous probabilities ought to lead to a mitigated or only partial assent: we are nearly or for the most part sure that Great Britain is an island. But in point of fact, our assent to this claim is not mitigated or qualified.

Now what is to prevent this embrace of informal inference from devolving into sheer irrationality? Here Newman introduces the controversial notion of the illative sense, the epistemological innovation for which *The Grammar of Assent* is perhaps best known.[34] We speak rather naturally of an aesthetic sense, that which makes one capable of good judgments in matters of beauty; we also are well aware of the moral sensibility, that which enables one to determine the right course of action *in concreto*, what Aristotle called *phronesis* and Aquinas *prudentia*. These are both faculties of discrimination and assessment, and both orient one to the particular case rather than to general principles. Though she carries a wealth of aesthetic convictions and ideas in her mind, the aesthete determines that *this* sculpture is beautiful through her feel for art, born of thousands of experiences, past judgments, and intuitions. And though he is possessed of numerous moral laws and guiding axioms, the good man knows what to do *here and now*, not through a dispassionate appeal to those general norms but through his feel for the situation, his varied experience in mak-

32. Ibid., 234.
33. Ibid., 234–35.
34. Ibid., 270–99.

ing nuanced judgments. Newman asserts that there is a parallel capacity in regard to determinations concerning what is true. This is the illative sense, from the Latin *latus*, implying a carrying or bringing over. The illative sense is that feel for the truth which allows one to sift through, assess, and assemble a number of probable arguments that are converging in the same direction. It is the power to take those hunches and intuitions that fall short of absolute persuasiveness and "carry them over" to assent.

One strand of steel cannot lift a massive load, but if a hundred strands of the same size and density are wrapped one around the other, they will constitute a cord more than powerful enough to lift the weight. One bucket with a hole in it will not efficiently transfer water from one receptacle to another. But that bucket placed within a series of equally defective buckets will be a perfectly adequate bearer of the water. Similarly, one flawed or merely probable argument will not bring the mind to assent, but a conglomeration of probable arguments, each imperfect but conducing to the same conclusion—as in the "Great Britain is an island" case—will move the mind to acquiescence. The illative sense is the intuitive power that presides over this process, reading and directing it. As I have been hinting, this capacity is largely unconscious, a matter of feel more than ratiocination, and it is honed through wide experience. Newman says that a judge should announce her decision clearly and unambiguously but should refrain from giving the reasons for her determination, for the judgment is probably correct, though the reasons consciously given are almost certainly inadequate as an explanation. In a similar way, through the illative sense one can be perfectly right in his epistemological judgment but utterly incapable of telling precisely how or why this is so.

When *The Grammar of Assent* was published in the early 1870s, it was met with fierce resistance on the part of some traditional Catholic philosophers who felt that it advocated, against the regnant neoscholasticism of the day, an irresponsible emotionalism or relativism in matters of knowing. After all, how does one adjudicate a dispute between two highly responsible and intuitive people who, through the exercise of their respective illative senses, have come to precisely opposite conclusions on a key issue? As I hope I have made clear in this presentation, the illative sense is by no means irrational or disconnected to the exigencies of formal inference. Thus one can show through appeal to syllogistic-style reasoning that a given position is inconsistent or incoherent. But what the illative sense adds is the necessary complement to pure reason, the role that the nonrational dimensions of body, emotion, experience, and intuition undoubtedly play in the process of coming to judgment. Here it can be seen as congruent with my earlier reflections on the cognitive quality of emotion. Perhaps it tells us that when seeking to resolve a dispute with an interlocutor, one simply has to be more patient, more careful, more willing to attend to the extrarational but by no means irrational elements that contribute to intellection.

In terms of the central argument of this part of my book, Newman has presented an epistemology that is incarnational and therefore christological in style. The Word—the rational truth in all of its forms—manifests itself in the vagaries and particularities of history and is received according to the capacity and complexity of an embodied mind. Truth is come to neither through escape from the body (Platonism) nor sequestration of the mind from the body (modern Cartesiansism and Lockeanism), but through a rough, incarnate interaction of matter and spirit. If classical and modern epistemologies are relatively dualist, Newman's Christian epistemology is one of coinherence, stressing as it does the *Ineinander* of reason and emotion, cognition and intuition, body and soul.

One of the deftest moves that Newman makes is to show that this illative way of knowing—which rationalist critics had seen to be an irrationalism typical of religious thinking—is in fact characteristic of all manners of intellection, from the scientific through the psychological to the philosophical. Anticipating Lonergan, he says that every type of knowledge develops from an array of assumptions, received traditions, creative intuitions, leaps of faith. Like Aquinas, Newman realizes that all forms of intellectuality are participations in the Logos and are, as such, incarnate in their mode and finality.

The Prophetic Dimension

In the first chapter of the Gospel of Mark, we find the account of Jesus's confrontation with the demoniac in the Caparnaum synagogue. While Christ is preaching, the possessed man furiously shouts, "What do you want with us, Jesus of Nazareth? Have you come to destroy us?" (Mark 1:24). It is most important to note that Jesus's initial encounter with the demonic takes place in a synagogue, a formally sanctioned place of prayer. This foreshadows the long and intense struggle that he will have throughout his public life with the representatives of the official religion of his time: the Pharisees, scribes, rabbis, and elders of the people. This shouldn't surprise us, since Jesus is consistently described as a prophet, and prophets—from Amos to Jeremiah—were antagonists of the religious-political establishment. In the Old Testament tradition, the *nabi* is a truth-teller and religious visionary, someone who speaks the word of God and stubbornly reads the world through the interpretive lens of that word. And this mission implies opposition, confrontation, and critique, since the keepers of worldly order are frequently looking through other lenses and listening to other words.

Now Jesus is not simply a speaker of the divine word; he is the incarnation of that Word, the personal embodiment of the divine purpose. Thus he is prophetic to the depth of his being, and his prophetic vocation will manifest itself in all of his speech, gestures, and actions. This entails that his confrontation with fallen powers and dysfunctional traditions will be highly focused, intense, and disruptive.

An episode recorded in all four Gospels is the Jesus's paradigmatically prophetic act of cleansing the temple. Standing at the heart of the holy city of Jerusalem, the temple was, as we saw, the political, economic, cultural, and religious center of the nation. Turning over the tables of the money-changers and driving out the merchants, shouting in high dudgeon, upsetting the order of that place was to strike at the most sacred institution of the culture, the unassailable embodiment of the tradition. It was to show oneself as critic in the most radical and surprising sense possible. That this act of Jesus the warrior flowed from the depth of his prophetic identity is witnessed to by the author of John's Gospel: "His disciples remembered that it was written, 'Zeal for your house will consume me'" (John 2:17). Many of the historical critics of the New Testament hold that this event—shocking, unprecedented, perverse—is what finally persuaded the leaders that Jesus merited execution.[35]

The crucifixion itself is presented in the elegantly crafted narratives of the Gospels as the supreme prophetic gesture of Jesus. Christ is put to death not by minor officials but by a coterie of the leading religious and political authorities of the time, both Jewish and Roman. Standing before Pilate in the ludicrous get-up that the soldiers have dressed him in, Jesus is a sort of court jester, commenting ironically, in the manner of King Lear's fool, on the corruption of the one passing judgment on the Judge. Over the cross Pilate places the notice, in the major languages of the culture, that this man is the king of the Jews. Meant as jest and mockery, it is in fact an indictment (readable by any and everyone) of the corrupt powers that put to death the author of life. In the letter to the Colossians, upon which we have been so reliant throughout this chapter, we find Paul's magnificent summation of the prophetic significance of the crucifixion: "He [Christ] disarmed the rulers and authorities and made a public example of them, triumphing over them in it" (Col. 2:15). Like a conquering Roman general dragging his captives through the streets, Jesus publicly displays the powers of the world whom he had defeated through his cross.[36]

35. See N. T. Wright, *Jesus and the Victory of God* (Minneapolis: Fortress, 1996), 335–36.

36. See William Placher, *Narratives of a Vulnerable God* (Louisville, KY: Westminster John Knox, 1994), 10–20.

Now how does all of this impinge upon questions of epistemology? It does so in the measure that, in this prophetic quality of the incarnate Logos, the central epistemic category of the capacity for self-criticism emerges. What becomes unavoidably clear in the course of the New Testament narratives (I have considered just a few obvious cases) is that there is nothing acquiescent, passive, or uncritically accepting in the attitude of Jesus, especially in regard to his own most sacred traditions. That Jesus reverences the traditions of his people is indisputable, but that he is willing to turn on them dramatically when they have become corrupt or self-contradictory is equally incontestable. Even when threatened by the coercive power of the state, Jesus refuses to back down and maintains his critical integrity. And as Paul insinuates in Colossians, the risen Jesus, bearing the wounds of his crucifixion, stands as a permanent criticism of those powers that so marked him.

But it is most important to attend to precisely *how* Jesus questions and criticizes. He does so not by standing outside the tradition but by appealing to a forgotten strand or a deeper intuition of the tradition itself. Thus in the cleansing of the temple, as we saw, he is able to see and excise the rot because he has thoroughly immersed himself in the monotheistic mysticism of classical Judaism. He can go to the cross—implicitly critiquing the keepers of the tradition who sent him there—because he is personally rooted in the will of his Father, that will which informs the tradition as a whole. In the Sermon on the Mount, Jesus is able blithely to reinterpret some of the most sacred words of revelation—"You have heard it said, 'You shall love your neighbor and hate your enemy,' but I say to you, 'Love your enemies and pray for those who persecute you'" (Matt. 5:43–44)—because he speaks from the deepest and most abiding assumptions of the revelation tradition itself. He does not assume a perspective outside of revelation and then affect a critique from that abstract space; rather, he moves from place to place within the whole of revelation, positioning himself now here, now there, and seeing from those various points of vantage the signs of corruption, the indications that the tradition is out of line with itself. What he embodies thereby is the paradox of the fiercest loyalty giving rise to the fiercest self-criticism.

A major emphasis of the *Aufklärers* is the need for hoary traditions to submit to analysis and critique. This accounts for the pointed, skeptical, edgy quality of much Enlightenment epistemology, and it explains its often strongly antireligious bias. One of the most consistent defenders of the Enlightenment tradition today, especially in its epistemological implications, is Jürgen Habermas. A brief analysis of his philosophy might help us to assess the relationship between the prophetic critique characteristic of the Christ-mind and the critique of tradition and institution associated with the Enlightenment. With his roots in the Frankfurt school, throughout his career Habermas has maintained a deep interest in the dynamics of dysfunctional societies—more precisely, in the ways that social groups engage in oppressive and distorting praxis.[37] He has recognized that, like individuals, societies and cultures can become neurotic and self-destructive through repressions born of fear. Thus the violent imposition of one political viewpoint leads to silencing, self-loathing, and antagonism throughout a society—and all of this conduces to a profound distortion of speech. People in oppressive political situations are so afraid to give voice to their convictions that they lose confidence in the very category of truth and in the power of speech to bring clarity and liberation. This is why, in his later writings, Habermas has focused thoroughly on the nature of speech acts, in both their ideal and distorted forms.

Taking seriously J. L. Austin's distinction between the locutionary (declarative) and illocutionary (performative) dimensions of the speech act, Habermas remarks that every declaration made in the course of a conversation has at least a rudimentary illocutionary force.[38] When someone says to a conversation partner even something as banal as "It's a nice day," she is implicitly eliciting her partner's agreement, seeking common ground. In a properly functioning conversational environment, one's interlocutor is free to respond, "Yes, it is," or "Actually no, it's a rather gloomy day." But the illocutionary dimension breaks down, collapses in on itself, if one speaker is holding a gun to the head of the other as she makes her statement. In that case, the "Yes, it is" of the respondent has no real significance, even if it accurately reflects his views.

All of this becomes even more pointed and complex when it is a question not of comments about the weather but of constructing arguments and counterarguments. If I were to formulate an argument in favor of George W. Bush's policy on Iraq while threatening you with dismissal from your job in the case of your disagreement, neither my argument nor your response would have any real illocutionary force. Conditions permitting real conversation would have collapsed because of profound inequality and implied violence among the conversants. Obviously, the means and modes of intimidation in dysfunctional societies are usually much subtler than the brandishing of a gun or the direct threat of unemployment, but the effect remains the same.

In light of these observations, we can begin to sketch the contours of the ideal speech situation as Habermas envisions it. A properly functioning communicative society is one in which the equality of the conversation

37. See especially Jürgen Habermas, *The Theory of Communicative Action*, vol. 1 (Boston: Beacon, 1987), and *Communication and the Evolution of Society* (Boston: Beacon, 1979).

38. See J. L. Austin, *How to Do Things with Words* (Cambridge, MA: Harvard Univ. Press, 1962), 98–107.

partners is guaranteed, where there is no threat of coercion or violence, where appeals to special revelation and privilege are disallowed, and where only ordinary or commonly accepted canons of reasonableness may be invoked in the adjudication of disputes. Paramount is the capacity of each conversant to engage in criticism of any institution—religious or secular—that threatens his or her integrity and freedom in self-expression. Only under these strict conditions will speech acts retain their illocutionary power of persuasion and fair exchange.

How can someone who has accepted the epistemic primacy of Jesus Christ assess this Enlightenment-based proposal? A Christian response to Habermas's program might serve (happily enough) as a summary of all that I have developed throughout this section. In their willingness to raise a critical voice against any form of corruption, even in the most sacred places, Christianity and the Enlightenment at their best come together. Jesus cleansing the temple and hanging from his cross is a figure infinitely more radical than any of the *lumières*, revolutionaries, and *philosophes* of the Enlightenment, and *ecclesia semper reformanda*—a foundational dictum of the community of Christ—is a call to institutional reform easily as disturbing as any slogan of the *Aufklärung*. More to the point, in their repudiation of all forms of violence, the Christ-mind and Habermas's ideal speech community coincide.

Now, it is painfully obvious that actual Christian communities throughout history have rarely if ever lived up to this ideal of non-coercion, but of course the same could be said of those varied political systems that have emerged from the Enlightenment. As I have presented it, the Christ-mind is one that looks for and relies upon coinherence as it goes about its work. One-in-the-other, a balance of identity and community, is the basic form of Christian intellection, and hence an epistemic praxis of violence would be radically out of step with such a form. Moreover, I have argued that the proper setting for the Christ-mind is a community of dialogue, an intersubjective conversation, since the God who grounds intelligibility is himself a conversation of coinhering persons. Habermas and the committed Christian, then, come together in their suspicion of excessively subjective and privatized views of truth and their embrace of lively exchange as the optimal matrix for truth seeking.

At this point, though, the differences become evident. In the Habermasian ideal speech community, claims to special revelation or privileged insight are precluded. But practitioners of the Christ-mind have accepted the revelation of God in Christ and have, in light of that event, committed themselves to seeking forms of coinherence. They take as their epistemic starting point not a neutral "quest" for truth but the ontological priority of Jesus Christ, crucified and risen from the dead.

Do the two sides here simply fall into antagonism and mutual suspicion? Perhaps one way to avoid that outcome is to show that Habermas's program is not, in point of fact, so different from the Christian program in its acceptance of certain basic and uncriticized assumptions. Without making a case for it, Habermas assumes that "secular" reason—free from the taint of the supernatural—is the sole model of rationality. But why, the Christian might ask, does the bracketing of all claims to revelation or religious insight make a conversation necessarily more reliable? Might such arbitrary exclusion not in fact skew the quest irredeemably in an immanentist direction, guaranteeing a secular conclusion in advance? Thus it is finally a question not of revelation versus reason but rather of two competing claims to revelation, two competing sets of elemental presuppositions.

Another key difference emerges around the issue of egalitarianism. As we saw, in Habermas's ideal speech community the equality of all the conversants is respected, and all claimants to special insight or privileged status are excluded. But those who claim a fundamental revelation can have no truck with this sort of radical leveling. The Christian holds that what is ontologically and epistemically ultimate arrived in a historical revelation witnessed by certain privileged individuals and that these receivers in turn passed on to their successors—official and otherwise—the power of the revelation. Thus Paul says, "I handed on to you as of first importance what I in turn had received: that Christ died for our sins in accordance with the Scriptures, and that he was buried, and that he was raised on the third day" (1 Cor. 15:3–4), and the author of the first letter of John claims, "We declare to you what we have seen and heard so that you also may have fellowship with us" (1 John 1:3). What is on display here is not a community of coequal conversants, each on a disinterested quest for the truth, but a hierarchically organized and epistemically disciplined society, in which the passing on of a central conviction is absolutely essential.

From the beginning, Christian communities—with the possible exception of certain groups of the Radical Reformation—have recognized the indispensability of order and authority and have been consequently suspicious of appeals to radical egalitarianism. If everyone has equal access to the truth and equal claim to authority, then the conversation loses its direction and devolves into chatter. And again, the Christian is likely to peek behind the façade of the Habermasian system and spy the various forms of ordering, hierarchy, and exclusion that go on there. She will notice that her distinctively religious voice has been silenced and that her equality as a conversation partner has hardly been acknowledged, and she will also see that the secular discussion itself is necessarily policed and disciplined by authority figures, keepers of the revelation, such as Habermas himself. She will conclude that the Enlightenment critique of religious authoritarianism rings just a tad hollow.

So can the Christ-mind meet the demands of the Enlightenment? In its call for respect among all conversation partners, its insistence upon non-coercion and nonviolence in discussion, and its summons to criticize the corruptions of even the most sacred institutions, the answer is assuredly yes. But in its egalitarianism and antiauthoritarianism, in its rejection of any claim to revelation, in its embrace of a purely immanentist construal of rationality, the answer is just as assuredly no.

Conclusion

What I hope to have shown in the course of this chapter is the coherence of an unabashedly Christoform epistemology. I have tried to demonstrate that those who assume the epistemic priority of the narratives concerning Jesus Christ are neither insane nor irresponsible, or at the very least, no less sane or responsible than those who assume the purportedly neutral epistemic stance of modernity. Cartesians, Humeans, and Kantians presumed certain principles in order to clarify their thinking; so, I have argued, Christians presume certain principles flowing from the Scripture and theological tradition in order to clarify their reflection on the world. The battle, therefore, is not between the prejudiced and the unprejudiced but between two camps, each prejudiced in a distinctive manner. This acknowledgment does not lock us into sectarianism or relativism; rather, it opens the door to an argument far more fruitful than the one that held sway between Christian and secular thinkers throughout most of modernity.

PART IV

The Noncompetitively Transcendent
and Coinherent God

11

Thomas and James

Jesus Christ, the Word made flesh, is the hermeneutical lens through which the whole of reality is properly viewed, and the narratives concerning him function, perforce, as an epistemic trump: whatever runs fundamentally counter to them must be false. In him, therefore, we understand most adequately both ourselves and God. The examination of ourselves—especially in the moral dimension of our existence—will be the topic of the fifth major section of this study, but the subject of this fourth section is God.

In line with the christocentric epistemology that I've defended, I choose to begin this analysis with the distinctively Christian theology of Thomas Aquinas. One of the most remarkable features of Aquinas's doctrine of God is its agnosticism. In the prologue to question 3 of the first part of the *Summa theologiae*, dealing with the divine simplicity, Thomas says, "Since we are not able to know what God is, only what God is not, we are not able to consider in regard to God how he is, but rather how he is not."[1] Though we speak often and at great length about God, we don't quite know what we are saying. Because our language is drawn from the realm of creatures, we use it in connection to God awkwardly and always with a keen sense that it is always more misleading than clarifying. In Aquinas's technical language, though the *res significata*—God's goodness, God's perfection, God's justice, etc.—can be indicated adequately enough with

---

1. Thomas Aquinas, *Summa theologiae* (Torino: Marietti, 1952), 1a, q.3, prologue.

191

ordinary speech, nevertheless, the *modus significandi*—precisely *how* those words mean in regard to the divine—remains highly mysterious. Many have used the image of sculpting to convey this largely negative theological way: as the sculptor carves away from the stone what his figure is not, so the theologian removes creaturely qualities from the concept of God. The problem with this comparison, of course, is that the terminus of an act of sculpting is usually a piece of some distinctness, whereas the terminus of a process of theological carving is necessarily something strange and uncanny. Perhaps the metaphor could be salvaged if we thought of some of the statues that Michelangelo executed for the tomb of Julius II, those rough-cut, unfinished "captives" whose forms are only vaguely indicated and whose contours are shrouded in shadows reminiscent of Leonardo da Vinci's *chiarascuro*.

The ground for this theological agnosticism is the great anti-idolatry principle that Aquinas inherited from the biblical tradition. When Moses inquired as to the name of the numinous power that had addressed him from the burning bush, God replied, "I AM WHO I AM" (Exod. 3:14), a description utterly lacking in conceptual content but full of rhetorical force. It was as though God were saying, "Stop asking such inappropriate questions!" Since God is not a reality that can be caught in the net of any intellectual scheme or defined by even the sublimest denomination, the very act of seeking his name is fraught with spiritual danger. Isaiah expressed this same insight when he said, in the voice of Yahweh, "As the heavens are higher than the earth, so are my ways higher than your ways and my thoughts than your thoughts" (Isa. 55:9).

The parables of Jesus himself are often exercises whose purpose is to confuse and confound the hearer, overturning her expectations and upsetting her theological convictions. God is just, but in light of the parable of the vineyard owner who pays out the same wage to those hired at different times of the day, one realizes that the ordinary notion of justice only vaguely indicates what divine justice is like. God is compassionate, but after hearing the story of the prodigal son, one knows that divine compassion infinitely surpasses even the most radical mode of human love. We recall that the original sin was an act of grasping at knowledge of the deep things of God, the knowledge of good and evil. And cannot the whole of the Bible be understood as the story of God's relentless attempt to undo the ill effects of that unfortunate and finally self-defeating reach?

But why, we still wonder, is the biblical God so elusive, so resistant to description and nomination? Why is the anti-idolatry principle so central to the scriptural tradition? One key answer is found in the opening line of the book of Genesis: "In the beginning . . . God created the heavens and the earth" (Gen. 1:1). Because God brought the whole of the finite universe into existence, God must be other in a way that transcends any and all modes of otherness discoverable within creation. Spatial distance, modal diversity, differences in grade, degree, kind, species, variations in speed, temperature, or density—none of these can begin to indicate the type of difference that obtains between God and anything that God has made. To the theologian who glimpses it, this otherness is vertiginous, disorienting, which is all to the good both intellectually and spiritually. John Henry Newman commented that the mind is never so strong as when it has recently been overthrown.[2] For the biblical and classical theological tradition, the revelation of the Creator God fortifies the mind precisely because it constitutes a permanent overthrowing of it, a salutary *bouleversement*.

I indicated in the introduction to this book that this healthy agnosticism began to be undermined through the work of late medievals such as John Duns Scotus and William of Occam, both of whom stressed the univocal character of the concept of being. A principal consequence of that epistemological decision was that God and worldly things can be compared, since they can be gathered together under the same general metaphysical category. Though God remains infinite and creatures finite, nevertheless, both God and creatures, on this reading, are beings and hence mutually commensurable. As the late medieval world gave way to the modern, this conception of the God-world relationship became solidified. As a result, a great confidence that one could speak of God in a rationally clear manner took hold of many moderns. Even when they emphasized the transcendence of God, they tended to do so in more or less "spatial" terms, seeing God as distant from, or set over and against, the world yet still mappable on the same set of coordinates as creatures.

Nowhere is this tendency on more evident display than in the philosophy of God developed by the founder of modern thought, René Descartes. In both the *Discourse on Method* and *The Meditations on First Philosophy*, Descartes holds that the idea of God is "clear and distinct" and comparable to other ideas with the same qualities.[3] Moreover, he is convinced that God is "a substance that is infinite, eternal, immutable, independent, all-knowing, all powerful."[4] John Locke, Isaac Newton, and others in the deist camp similarly hold to a rationalist conception of God, conceiving of him as a supreme being whose existence can be established by arguing mechanistically from effect to cause. How far we have come from

2. John Henry Newman, *Apologia Pro Vita Sua* (New York: Doubleday, 1956), 328.

3. "For on the contrary, as this idea (of God) is very clear and distinct. . . . so that the idea which I have of Him may become the most true, most clear, and most distinct of all the ideas that are in my mind." René Descartes, *Meditations on First Philosophy*, in *The Philosophical Works of Descartes*, translated by Elizabeth Haldane (Cambridge: Cambridge Univ. Press, 1979), 1:165–66.

4. Ibid., 165.

Aquinas's cautious agnosticism in regard to what and how God is. Just about the last thing that Thomas would have said about the "idea" of God is that it is either clear or distinct, and he explicitly denies, again and again throughout his career, that God is a substance or *ens summum* comparable to similar substances within the genus of existence.

There is a second strain of modern thought about God that also flows from the late medieval turn to univocity and rationalism. It is the pantheist view, common to Spinoza, Schleiermacher, Hegel, and many others, that God is substantially identical to what the Bible called the created realm: *Deus sive natura*. Though they quite correctly maintain that God is not a being alongside of the world, the pantheists undermine the divine transcendence, collapsing God into creation. We can hear this philosophy ecstatically stated in Schleiermacher's second speech on religion: "The whole of religious life consists of two elements, that man surrender himself to the Universe and allow himself to be influenced by the side of it that is turned towards him."[5] Later in the *Speeches* he speaks, with similar romantic fervor, of the religious person lying on the bosom of the *Universum* and becoming its soul. Though at first glance it seems quite distinct from the God-as-supreme-being philosophy we have just considered, romantic pantheism has in common with that view a compromising of the strangeness and radical otherness of God assumed throughout the Bible. "God" becomes but the collectivity of creatures considered as a totality. In this sense, modern pantheism is the logical fulfillment of Scotus's adoption of a univocal conception of being: God and the world can be spoken of univocally because there is finally no difference between them.

This sort of modernism couldn't be further from Thomas's understanding of God. Though he opted typically for the phrase *ipsum esse subsistens* (the sheer act of being itself) when describing God, Thomas was extremely careful to draw a distinction between that notion and *ens commune* (being in general). The divine act of existing is in no sense identical to the generic "being" in which all created things share, or to the totality of creatures, which Thomas customarily compared to an army under the divine command. Any sort of pantheism would have egregiously violated Aquinas's dictum that we cannot know what God is or how God is.

A Jamesian Interlude

One of the best articulations of the two modern approaches to God that I have been sketching is a series of lectures that William James gave

5. Friedrich Schleiermacher, *On Religion: Speeches to Its Cultured Despisers* (New York: Harper and Row, 1958), 58.

at Oxford in 1908, just two years before his death. Though they have been gathered together under the title *A Pluralistic Universe*, the central concern of these essays is the existence and nature of God.[6] What James presents with his customary clarity and elegance is, first, a characteristically modern caricature of classical theism and, second, the two rationalistic views of God that followed from the rejection of that purportedly inadequate theology. To grasp what is at stake in a postliberal doctrine of God, it is particularly instructive to follow the twists and turns of James's archetypically liberal analysis.

In his opening essay, James first contrasts the "materialist" and the "spiritualist" approaches to metaphysics and then states that the latter is subdivided into "monist" and "dualist" branches. Most of his attention in the subsequent lectures is given to a consideration of the differences between these two forms of spiritualism. The dualist form he identifies with scholastic theism, describing it as the view that "God and his creation are entities distinct from each other."[7] The altogether deleterious consequence of this philosophy is that it leaves "the human subject outside of the deepest reality in the universe." More to it, the classical dualist conception of God implies that God is not in real relation to his creation, remaining totally unaffected by it even as he exercises his sovereignty over it. Like most moderns, James finds this arrangement deeply alienating: "man being an outsider and a mere subject to God, not his intimate partner, a character of externality invades the field."[8] James then gives voice to numerous concerns about the classical God's "non-relationality" and "impassibility" that would become the staples of process theologians and philosophers seventy years later. He concludes by stating that this conception of the divine conduces to a fundamentally rivalrous understanding of the God and creatures: "God is not heart of our heart and reason of our reason, but our magistrate."[9]

Since I will return to these issues in great detail in the next section, I will not make a lengthy rejoinder here, but suffice it to say that this notion of God and the world as radically distinct "entities" is the result, as we have seen, not of Aquinas's analogical conception of being but of late medieval univocity. The paradox is that the very attempt to gather God and creatures together under one metaphysical canopy effectively separated them, turning them, as James rightly sees, into rivalrous "beings." In protesting against this "external" and legalistic view of God, James is wrestling not with Aquinas but with a corrupt form of medieval theism.

6. William James, *A Pluralistic Universe* (Lincoln: Univ. of Nebraska Press, 1996).

7. Ibid., 25.

8. Ibid., 27.

9. Ibid.

In point of fact, as I will show later, there could scarcely be a better way to express Thomas's understanding of the God-human relationship than to say that he is "heart of our heart and reason of our reason." Like most moderns, James champions the prerogatives of the individual over and against an oppressive deity. If only he could have spied behind late medieval voluntarism the theology that advocated as radically as anyone could want the noncompetitiveness of God and the created world.

At any rate, instead of the alienating dualist understanding of God, James prefers a "monist" view that makes the divine more "organic and intimate" to creation. This approach, which he somewhat curiously calls "pantheist," is a "vision of God as the indwelling divine rather than the external creator, and of human life as part and parcel of that deep reality."[10] We notice immediately the anomaly that creation is described as the act of a God "external" to the world, whereas on the classical reading, the Creator God, precisely as radically other, could never be characterized as contrastive to the world that he makes. But we sense that James, quite rightly, wants a God who does not compete with human flourishing, who can coinhere with human life at all levels: "from a pragmatic point of view, the difference between living against a background of foreignness and one of intimacy means the difference between a general habit of wariness and one of trust."[11] The problem is that, still operating within a stubbornly modern framework, he will propose only pseudosolutions.

Now James's "pantheism," which affirms the basic identity of human and divine substance, falls into two categories, a more all-embracing monistic type and a relatively pluralist type. These Jamesian options correspond quite closely to, respectively, the Cartesian-Lockean account and the Spinozan-Schleiermacherian account that I sketched above. The "all-form" is the mystical *Identitatsphilosophie* according to which the individual finds itself only in the measure that it is assimilated to the One. This is expressed in Spinoza's monism of *natura naturans et natura naturata*, and it is given a more contemporary application in Ralph Waldo Emerson's transcendentalist account of the Over-Soul. The sage of Concord (whom James both revered and teased) told his readers to lift up their eyes and their minds to the infinite and participate in it and in that way to find spiritual satisfaction. James also presents the absolutism of his friendly rival Josiah Royce, the American Hegelian. Royce had argued that the connnectedness and mutual influence that can be found universally among things are evidence of a primordial unity that is more basic than any differentiation. But with this sort of universalism James has little sympathy. Finally, the Spinozan or Roycean or Emersonian absolute is as cold and

10. Ibid., 30.
11. Ibid., 31.

unfeeling as the distant God of classical theism, and for the same reason:
"it has no history."[12] We can relate on a personal and experiential level
only with a God who suffers, loves, responds, and moves, but the Over-
Soul, the Universum, the Eternal has none of those qualities. Emerson
might tell us to raise our minds to the One, but he provides no clue as
to how we, rooted in history and particularity, can possibly manage the
trick. "The absolute's own perfection moves me as little as I move it,"[13]
James concludes.

We remark an intriguing progression. Having ruled out the Creator God
as hopelessly alien and threatening (a mere magistrate), James moves to a
more immanent conception of God, something confirmable by personal
experience. Schleiermacher too, uneasy with metaphysical accounts of the
divine, opted for an experiential approach, finding God in the feeling of
absolute dependency. The truly religious man, on Schleiermacher's reading,
requires neither dogma nor rational demonstration to believe in God; on
the contrary, he feels God's existence as surely as he intuits his own. For
James, such an experience of God—intimate, immediate, organic—is far
superior to the "knowledge" of a distant God had through classical theology.
But this intuition of the Universum was still problematic precisely in the
measure that the modern All retained many of the objectionable qualities
of the theistic God—impassibility, unresponsiveness, perfection, etc.—and
was, as a result, still not sufficiently "friendly" to human concerns. And
this is why James finally turns to the other great modern option, a view of
God as a being among others—but a being somehow accessible through
experience and with none of the alienating and overbearing features of
the classical God.

It is this pluralist version of "pantheism" that James sets out in the
final essays of this collection. As a sort of bridge to his own philosophical theology, James considers the work of Gustav Fechner, a relatively
obscure nineteenth-century German physician and philosopher who,
James assures us in a bit of questionable prophecy, will "wield more and
more influence as time goes on."[14] It becomes clear that what attracts
James to Fechner, at least in part, are the striking similarities between the
life experiences of the two thinkers. Like James, Fechner was trained in
medicine and the physical sciences and turned only later in life to a consideration of philosophy, and again like James, the German suffered from
a series of psychosomatic illnesses, "terrific attacks of nervous prostration,
with painful hyperaesthesia of all the functions."[15] The most remarkable

12. Ibid., 47
13. Ibid., 48.
14. Ibid., 135
15. Ibid., 147

similarity between James and Fechner, however, is that both found a solution to their psychological and physical maladies through a kind of "faith," a decision to believe. The immediate connection to the divine, especially as this connection has a psychologically ameliorative power, is key to James's sense of God.

At the heart of Fechner's metaphysics is the conviction that "the whole universe in its different spans and wave-lengths, exclusions and developments, is everywhere alive and conscious."[16] Our greatest intellectual folly is to presume the dualist hypothesis that the spiritual is not the rule but the exception in the order of nature. Just as the parts of the human body move at the prompting of the spiritual power of the will and intellect, so the myriad elements on the earth—trees, plants, sea, wind—move through the influence of a higher mind and desire, viz., the consciousness of the earth itself. But then our tiny planet finds itself moved in turn by higher systems and orders of knowledge, the spiritual consciousness of the solar system and the galaxy. This mystical panpsychism would, partially through James's own mediation, find its way into the thought of Teilhard de Chardin and, most notably, Alfred North Whitehead. That every actual entity desires, seeks, "prehends" the world around it and that actual entitites themselves are arranged in various societies and hierarchies that prehend in their own way are ideas central to Whitehead's process metaphysics. At any rate, Fechner maintains that God is best described as the "totalized consciousness of the universe" as a whole, that mind which is using the all of the material elements of creation as its body and means of expression.

James comments that just as our "eye-sensations" realize nothing of the larger conscious life of which they are a part, so the particular movements, events, and persons within the cosmos are, for the most part, unaware of the divine mind into which they are drawn and to which they contribute. Our individual minds and bodies are contiguous to this higher Mind, and the key to the spiritual life, for Fechner, is to make this connection to the divine spirit clear, explicit and operative.

Now one might suspect that James would find this talk more than a little gassy and overly abstract, even redolent of the absolutism that he had just criticized, and one would be, to a degree, right. James comments, "He [Fechner] posits a complete God as the all-container and leaves him about as indefinite in feature as the idealists leave their absolute."[17] Though he chides the German for quasi-monist tendencies, he remains nevertheless convinced that Fechner also shows us a way forward theologically, because "he provides us with a very definite gate of approach . . . in the shape of

16. Ibid., 149.
17. Ibid., 174.

the earth-soul, through which in the nature of things we must first make connexion with all the more enveloping superhuman realms."[18]

That the divine impinges on us without crushing us or absorbing us is crucial for James, and he thinks that Fechner's consciousness theory opens up a hopeful path in the right direction. Just as the soul operates thoroughly throughout the body without compromising its integrity, so the World-Soul can act through particular consciousnesses without overwhelming them. Once stripped of its absolutist husk, this theory, James thinks, can account for the noncompetitiveness between God and the world that most moderns value so highly.

This stripping takes place in the eighth of James's lectures, titled "The Continuity of Experience." Motifs from *The Varieties of Religious Experience*, "What Is Consciousness," and *The Principles of Psychology* are rehearsed and given a new focus in this culminating essay, including and especially that of the metaphysical density of relationality. What has crippled ontologies from Plato's to Royce's is what James takes to be the irrational prejudice against relation as such and the ungrounded valorization of the substantial. This favoring of the termini of a relationship over the rapport itself is possible for those who analyze the world abstractly, but those who examine "the sensible life *in concreto* must see that relations of every sort, of time, space, difference, likeness, change, rate, cause, or what not, are just as integral members of the sensational flux as terms are."[19] Those who appreciate this are adepts of what James approvingly calls "radical empiricism," and he distinguishes them from those who are blinded by monist and absolutist dogma. Radical empiricists know that, if anything, relationality has metaphysical pride of place, since all things are constituted by their relationships: "the tiniest feeling that we can possibly have comes with an earlier and a later part and with a sense of their continuous procession."[20]

An honest survey of the flux of experience reveals that it is impossible finally to isolate one thing from all others or one sensation or feeling from what surrounds it, or, as Augustine recognized long ago, to specify the present moment as anything other than a blend of past and future. In language that strikingly anticipates Whitehead's, James declares: "In every crescendo of sensation, in every effort to recall, in every progress towards the satisfaction of desire, this succession of an emptiness and a fulness that have reference to each other and are one flesh is the essence of the phenomenon."[21] This, of course, is the "stream" of experience that James had insisted on throughout

18. Ibid.
19. Ibid., 279.
20. Ibid., 282.
21. Ibid., 283.

his philosophical career. Though the analyst can cut that stream into discrete moments, events, and "things," those demarcations remain abstract and artificial, less real than the flow in which they are enfolded: "their *names*, to be sure, cut them into separate conceptual entities, but no cuts existed in the continuum in which they originally came."[22]

The purpose of this ontological explication is to introduce the quasi-Fechnerian idea of God as the mind coimplicated with the moves of human minds. What we call "consciousness" at any given moment is our explicit awareness, the act of focusing in on what is at the center of our intellectual attention. But this attentive intellect is not so much a discretely existing substance as a "field" surrounded by a fringe that stretches "insensibly into a subconscious more."[23] The "whole" self is that entire range of interests, preoccupations, influences, passions, and experiences that surround the central act. This leads James to speculate that "every bit of us at every moment is part and parcel of a wider self,"[24] so that our thoughts (which are really ours) are at the same time ingredient in a higher consciousness. Though Fechner thought of God in an absolutist manner, might it be possible to adapt his insight so that a more universal mind be seen as coexisting with a variety of particular minds in a sort of ordered hierarchy or complex nexus? This in fact is James's wager. He wants a God who is neither external creator nor abstract absolute, but fellow sufferer, one who thinks, feels, and acts in congruence with us. This hypothesis, in line with James's preference for the "each-mode" over the "all-mode," would allow us to speak of God in the context of a pluralistic and open-ended worldview.

There is, I think, much to recommend this view, and I will attempt to make the positive aspects of it clearer as I go on, but we see the fatally modern quality of James's reflections as he specifies the details of the relationship between higher mind and lower mind. In accord with his empiricist prejudice, James looks for concrete "experimental" evidence of this rapport, and he suggests that it might be found in the phenomenon of "divided or split human personality," as this has been described by Pierre Janet, Sigmund Freud, and others. "Automatic writing and speech . . . mediumship and 'possession' generally," unrecognized in Fechner's time and all the rage in the early twentieth century, might prove that a "superior consciousness" can think in and through a lower mind.[25] What is happening in these cases remains quite mysterious, but one could speculate that the higher mind of God, in which all of the experiences and memo-

22. Ibid., 285.
23. Ibid., 288.
24. Ibid., 289.
25. Ibid., 298–99.

ries of the universe are somehow gathered, from time to time opens up
and actively informs certain individuals of a mystically perceptive cast
of mind. These moments of influx from the divine consciousness are the
specifically "religious" experiences that James detailed so carefully in *The
Varieties of Religious Experience* and that, he maintained, were irreducible
to other types of psychological or physiological happenings.

That these empirically verifiable, occasional interventions of a higher
being upon a lower being could be described as specifically "religious" is
possible only for someone who has an attenuated sense of God as the
creator, radically other than any of the things in the world that he has
made. The surest indication of the modern quality of this theory is its
rationalism. The interactions of two beings, quantitatively but not qualitatively different from one another, are being surveyed by an observer
who stands within a framework of space and time presumably shared by
all three. Every detail of this would be ruled out by Aquinas's creation-
based agnosticism.

Let us follow James to the end of his argument. In the final lecture
of the series, James spells out more clearly the nature of the God who
is implicated in the pluralistic play of finite things. In accord with his
father's speculations and his own meditations in *Varieties* concerning the
"twice-born," James says that the properly religious experience is that of
"an unexpected life succeeding upon death."[26] This has, he clarifies, nothing to do with the immortality of the soul, but rather with the birth of a
keener and deeper sense of life after an experience of despair. It is well
known that James himself went through just such a process during his
young manhood, and therefore it is not surprising that he should use it as a
general template. There is something clearly Protestant in the emphasis on
a stark contrast between the two states: "sincerely to give up one's conceit
or hope of being good in one's own right is the only door to the universe's
deeper riches."[27] It appears as though a person's self-complacency has to
be shattered, and her own mind and will have to be stymied, in order to
initiate commerce with the higher mind.

Adapting language from the *Varieties*, James says of the believer's experience that "the tenderer parts of his personal life are continuous with
a *more* of the same quality which is operative in the universe outside of
him. . . . In a word, the believer is continuous, to his own consciousness,
at any rate, with a wider self from which saving experiences flow in."[28]
Whereas the absolutist and the monist prefer "thinner" descriptions of
the contact with God, James opts for this relatively "thick" account that

26. Ibid., 303.
27. Ibid., 305.
28. Ibid., 307.

can be verified through the "unwholesome facts of personal biography," his own and others. So concerned is James for a vital sense of God that he draws the divine into the confines of the flow of experience.

To make this description even more vivid, James employs a delicious analogy. Just as a cat or dog might wander into a library, see all of the books, and hear the hubbub of conversation while having no inkling as to the meaning of it all, so most of us, due to our spiritual obtuseness, make our way through the universe seeing everything but "getting" very little of it. The things of nature, political events, relationships, etc., are all part of a far larger and more complex pattern of meaning which remains opaque to ordinary awareness. The mystic, the "twice-born," the saint is like James's dog suddenly able to participate in a higher consciousness and to sense thereby the full meaning of the library in which he had previously cavorted rather dumbly.

Thus James holds that there is a superhuman mind with which the religiously aware are able to establish contact. But how (and here we come near the heart of it) exactly is that higher consciousness to be conceived? In order to avoid the inconveniences of the various types of absolutism, the divine mind—however vast it may be—must be thought of as something finite. As such, it can enter into the pluralistic universe, interacting with the many other minds alluringly but uncoercively. "The line of least resistance . . . both in theology and in philosophy is to accept, along with the super-human consciousness, the notion that it is not all-embracing, the notion, in other words, that there is a God, but that he is finite, either in power or in knowledge, or in both at once."[29] James's influence can clearly be seen in Whitehead's insistence that God, the greatest actual entity among other actual entities, be construed not as the exception to the rules of metaphysics but rather as their supreme exemplification. In their interpretation of God, both James and Whitehead are the intellectual descendants of William of Occam, for like Occam, they hold that God and creatures are situated under the canopy of an overarching metaphysical structure, mappable on the same ontological grid, and hence comparable one to another. James states this commonality with admirable directness: "Yet because God is not the absolute, but is himself a part when the system is conceived pluralistically, his functions can be taken as not wholly dissimilar to those of the other smaller parts."[30] How like Scotus's claim that God and creatures are both beings, though the former is infinite and the latter finite, one the biggest part, the other smaller parts. God, in sum, is a being among others, capable of influencing lower realities without compromising them, existing in the same universe as they and subject to the same metaphysical constraints.

29. Ibid., 311.
30. Ibid., 318.

The modernity of James's religious imagination becomes especially apparent in his construal of otherness in regard to God: "Let God but have the least infinitesimal *other* of any kind beside him, and empiricism and rationalism might strike hands in a lasting treaty of peace."[31] All of the foregoing, in many ways, has been but a preparation for that statement. What bothered James so much about classical theism is the sheer externality of the God-world relationship, and what concerned him about modern forms of theological absolutism is the crushing quality of the God-world rapport. The only solution that he sees is a pluralistic theism whereby God and what is not God enjoy a sort of side-by-side equilibrium, enabling each to affect the other in a real but unintrusive way. God and the world are conventionally and not noncontrastively other.

And here we are left by modernity, forced to choose between Schleiermacher's absolutized collectivity and James's supreme being, caught in the nexus of conditioned relationality. What has been misconstrued (or in most cases altogether forgotten) by modern thinkers is the dynamic biblical view of God which had held sway in Christian thought through the High Middle Ages and which allows one to affirm both the full godliness of God and the full flourishing of the free human subject in relation to God. This is the understanding of God as the Creator of all that is, a reality existing in a modally different way from any creature or collectivity of creatures, otherly other than the nondivine and hence capable of the most intimate and noninvasive relationship with the nondivine.

One reason that this distinctive point of view had been occluded is that it flows, ultimately, not from philosophical speculation but from the unique and densely textured narratives of the Bible, especially those concerning Jesus Christ. Both Michael Buckley and William Placher have argued that in the measure that Christian theologians and philosophers lost confidence in the power of those narratives, they began to adopt more generically philosophical accounts of God. And it was these philosophies of God that became, unfortunately, the subject of modern debates and discussions. The wager that I will make in the next chapters is that a vibrantly recovered biblical and christocentric theology of God is far more rationally compelling than any of the competing religious philosophies of modernity and, in point of fact, more capable than they of responding to typically modern concerns about the independence of the human subject.

31. Ibid., 312.

12

The Distinction

In accord with the antifoundationalist and unapologetically Christian epistemology outlined in part III, I will attempt now to lay out a doctrine of God conditioned by the distinctive revelational forms contained in the biblical witness as a whole and more pointedly in the event of Jesus Christ. As I suggested in the epistemology section, this approach is hardly a novelty but is instead congruent with the method employed by the great theological masters of the Christian tradition: Irenaeus, Origen, Augustine, Aquinas, Newman, and so on. It was a neoscholasticism tainted by Cartesian assumptions that proposed a purely rational, neutrally philosophical account of God as a foundation for a theological superstructure. Among the masters, including and especially Aquinas, philosophical language was employed, as we saw, according to theological discipline and for theological purposes. Whatever truth was arrived at through proofs and demonstrations was positioned by, and in service of, the fullness of truth made plain in the biblical witness. Michael Buckley has highlighted a fatal weakness in traditional neoscholasticism by drawing our attention to Étienne Gilson's claim that in regard to knowledge of the existence of God, the Christian theologian can only wait for the natural philosopher to deliver up his findings! How far this is from Aquinas's extremely measured assessment of the ancillary and pedagogical role played by philosophy in theology.

What then do we Christians know of God? As I suggested in the Christology chapters, much hinges upon the disquieting claims made about Jesus of Nazareth. Though the first proclaimers of the Christian message—Peter,

Paul, John, and their attendant communities—were profoundly shaped
by the theology of the Hebrew Scriptures, they nonetheless were saying
something new and distinctive about God, precisely in the measure that
they were describing him as the Father of our Lord Jesus Christ. Though
they liberally employed Old Testament forms—evident on practically
every page of the Gospels and Epistles—and though they were willing at
times to adopt philosophical categories (Paul's speech on the Areopagus
is a good example), these early preachers and theologians of the Christ
event were communicating a truth about God that earlier thought forms
couldn't encompass.

The author of Mark's Gospel implies this novelty when he portrays Jesus,
to the dismay of those surrounding him, confidently forgiving the sins of the
paralyzed man; Matthew insinuates it when he places in the mouth of Jesus
the statement "You have heard it said [in the Torah is the implication] . . . ,
but I say . . ."; Luke makes it clear when he presents Jesus as the gatherer
of the tribes of Israel and as the one who hosts a meal of divine welcome
for the alienated and forgotten; John makes it unmistakably evident when
he says, "The Word became flesh and lived among us"; and Paul hints at
it when he says that we can see the glory of God shining on the face of
Jesus Christ. The God already revered as the one powerful Lord of the
universe and as the compassionate/demanding elector of Israel is now
declared to be the one who has become personally present in the life,
teaching, career, death, and resurrection of a very particular first-century
Jew. God must be otherwise than was thought.

As we recall from the Christology chapters, the coming together of
divinity and humanity in Jesus was given classical doctrinal expression in
the two-natures formula of the Council of Chalcedon. Because in Christ
God becomes a creature without ceasing to be God or undermining the
integrity of the creature he becomes, God must not be a worldly or finite
nature. His otherness to the world is, simultaneously, radical and noncontrastive. We might express this difference with the classical idea of God's
transcendence, but we would have to nuance the notion immediately by
insisting that this transcendence is noncompetitive. God's otherness from
the world cannot be construed in such a manner that God and what is not
God are comparable within a common frame of reference or according
to shared properties univocally interpreted. Contrary to the assumptions
of James and other moderns, God is neither one being among many nor
the sum total of creatures understood collectively. Nor is he a supreme
being squatting outside the world and intervening in it on occasion. In
relation to the created universe, God is, as I stated earlier, otherly other.
That God transcends/inheres in this way must be affirmed, even as we, in
line with Aquinas's reticence, don't know quite what we're saying when
we affirm it.

All of the above leads to the conclusion that the God disclosed in the incarnation is a reality that can let the other be even as he draws close. God is capable of a noninvasive and noninterruptive intimacy with that which he has made, though we have no way of understanding precisely *how* this is possible. The mutual exclusivity that we noticed among creatures is not, therefore, ontologically basic but represents instead a sort of falling away from what is metaphysically prior. Another way to state this principle is that God is nonviolent in his dealings with what stands outside of him. His noncontrastive and noncompetitive quality allows him to be present to another in such a way that the other is enhanced by the intimacy of the divine presence. In a word, God's qualities of immanence and transcendence in regard to the created world must be seen not as mutually exclusive but as mutually implicative.

This divine coinherence and nonviolence is disclosed not only in the dynamics of the incarnation but also, as we saw, in the drama of the Paschal Mystery. We recall that when the risen Jesus appeared to the Eleven, to those who had betrayed, abandoned, run from him in his hour of need, he offered not retribution but forgiveness. To those who had killed God, God extended *shalom*, proving thereby that the antagonistic way of the world, the restoration of order lost through violence by answering violence, is contrary to the deepest grain of reality. The behavior of the risen Jesus is but the "ethical" manifestation of the metaphysics of nonviolence that undergirds the incarnation. Thus the claim of the author of the first letter of John that "God is love" is perfectly congruent with the assertion of the author of the Johannine Gospel that "the Word became flesh." Both are expressions of the letting-be of the other that characterizes the God disclosed in Jesus Christ.

The coinherence of God and creation is nothing other than the loop of grace manifested in the stories of the woman at the well and the prodigal son. What is at issue in both those narratives is the transition from an antagonistic relationship with the divine grace to a relationship of receptivity, nonviolence, and mutuality. A very similar dynamic is at play in the account of the appearance of Christ on the road to Emmaus. Those who had been sent by fear away from the holy city (much as Adam and Eve had been expelled by their fear from the Garden) find themselves in communion with God in the measure that they allow themselves to be fed by the divine grace.

It is this unique modality of the divine existence that the great theologians and spiritual teachers of the tradition attempt to make plain. In coming to understand, however inadequately, the nature of the divine "difference," the spiritual seeker grasps how his life must change. In appreciating, however inchoately, God's capacity for noninvasive coinherence, one walks more perfectly the path of discipleship. Prior to 1300, there was no distinction between what we now call theology and spirituality, but after that date, a rupture occurred, the former becoming a university discipline and the latter a concern of mystics and seekers after the interior life. What I shall endeavor to do next is to show how the nonviolence and unique transcendence of God are on display in the writings of two medieval masters, Anselm of Canterbury and Thomas Aquinas. My hope is to demonstrate that the carefully crafted philosophical accounts of these two thinkers are determined through and through by a biblical form and that their ultimate purpose is to effect a gospel-inspired transformation in those who appropriate them. The "spirituality" of Anselm and Aquinas is contained precisely in the still surprising theology in which they describe the divine reality disclosed in Jesus.

Anselm's God

It is regrettable that almost all treatments of St. Anselm's doctrine of God focus exclusively on the demonstration of God's existence from the second chapter of the *Proslogium*, the so-called ontological argument, while ignoring both the highly charged prayer that precedes it and the illuminating elaboration that follows it. Michel Corbin, one of the most insightful contemporary analysts of Anselm's work, has commented that the famous *ratio* offered in chapter 2 is, despite its traditional appellation, *ni argument, ni ontologique*. This becomes clear, however, only when we attend to the setting and context in which the demonstration is situated. It will be my contention that what Anselm endeavors to show us throughout the *Proslogium*, and most pointedly in the "proof," is the strangeness of God's way of being, a distinctiveness that calls forth from us a radical spiritual realignment. In this sense, his work is in continuity with mode and style of the Gospels.

Anselm was not primarily a philosopher, and he was certainly not a modern-style skeptic puzzling over the existence of God. He was a monk and a man of prayer, united by both obligation and affection to his brothers in the monastic life. Both the *Monologion* and the *Proslogion*, composed between 1075 and 1078, the period just before Anselm became abbot, were products of deeply recollective prayer and a desire in charity to help those who needed guidance in the spiritual life.[1] Therefore, the arguments that unfold in both texts, conditioned by Anselm's immersion in the world of the Bible and in the practices of a Benedictine monastery, are invitations to a deeper love of God. Anselm's wager seems to be that the condition

---

1. R. W. Southern, *Saint Anselm: A Portrait in a Landscape* (Cambridge: Cambridge Univ. Press, 1990), 113–16.

for the possibility of awakening such love is a correct understanding of who and how God is.

Anselm's best-known work commences with an autobiographical pre-amble, the general lines of which are echoed in Eadmer's biography of the saint. He tells us that, having published at the promptings of his mo-nastic brothers a work of meditation on the reasonability of the faith (the *Monologion*), he began to search for a single, elegant demonstration that would, of itself, "guarantee that God truly is, that he is the sureminent good having need of no other, which all other things require for their existence and well-being."[2] Our theologian is not seeking angelic intuition, for it is an *argumentum* that he is looking for; nevertheless, he wants insight into God that is simple, clear, unifying, and as direct as possible for one here below. Now the biblically minded person is put immediately on guard, for she knows that a quest to seize a type of knowledge paved the way to the originating sin, and Anselm, as we shall see, becomes aware of the precarious ground on which he is standing. He goes on to inform us that he ardently sought this *argumentum* and at times thought that he had it, while at other times he found it fleeing completely from his mental grasp (*aliquando mentis aciem omnino fugeret*). This tantalizing oscillation be-tween half-seeing and total blindness conduced toward a state of despair and the desire simply to leave the question aside. But Anselm discovered that the more he tried to ignore the quest and to lose himself in practical considerations, the more this thought forced itself on him with a kind of importunity (*se coepit cum importunitate quadam ingerere*).[3] Worn out finally by resisting, agonizing in the "conflict of his thoughts," he let the idea come to him. What he had despaired of gave itself to him, and with ardent heart he embraced that which he had previously been pushing away.

This psychological and spiritual account, which echoes some crucial moves in Augustine's *Confessions*, is remarkably penetrating, and it pro-vides the hermeneutical key to the reading of the rest of the *Proslogion*. Anselm wanted a particularly clear and illuminating knowledge of God, in the manner of a geometrician seeking an elegant demonstration of a point that he had already proved with a complex and convoluted chain of reasoning. To seek such insight in regard to geometrical figures is one thing, but to seek it in regard to the true God is precisely what tripped up Adam and Eve. They were forbidden to eat of the tree of the knowledge of good and evil, not because God was opposed to their full flourishing or

2. "Ad astruendum quia deus vere est, et quia est summum bonum nullo alio indigens, et quo omnia indigent ut sint et ut bene sint." Anselm of Canterbury. *Proslogion* in *L'Oeuvre de S. Anselme de Cantorbery*, vol. 1, *Monologion/Proslogion*, edited by Michel Corbin (Paris: Editions du Cerf, 1986), 228.

3. Ibid.

cultivated a perverse anti-intellectualism but rather because the knowledge of the deep things of God cannot in principle be grasped by a created mind. When one tries to effect such a grasp, he necessarily turns the true God into an idol, a phantom of the intellect, for the mind can seize only that which falls in the nexus of conditioned relationality. And this is why Anselm is blocked and tantalized in his initial attempt. In his biographical sketch, Eadmer suggests that Anselm, during this painful period, became convinced that his desire to find the one clinching argument was a temptation from the devil.[4] There was something quite right in that conviction. For to seek God in the manner that Anselm was seeking him—through an aggressive grasp of the intellect—is indeed a temptation redolent of the primal temptation. Therefore, the saint's experience of deep frustration was altogether salutary.

But the route he chose in the wake of that experience—turning away from the quest altogether—was equally dysfunctional. In the Genesis account, Adam and Eve, having failed in the their attempt to seize God, fled from the divine presence, but this strategy was as hopeless as the first, for the true God can be neither grasped nor hidden from.[5] In a similar way, Anselm, having realized the futility of his efforts at knowing, turned away but then discovered that God wouldn't allow him to remain hidden: the *argumentum* began to press upon him, invading his thoughts, refusing to leave him at peace.

Another extremely important interpretive lens emerges here. What characterizes worldly natures is that they can, at least in principle, be seized by the mind. Aristotle said that the soul is in a certain sense all things, because all finite realities can be represented and categorized there. A second mark of worldly things is that they can be, at least to a degree, set aside, ignored, turned away from. Every and any finite reality, including a highest being, can concern me to a point, but none of them can concern me ultimately. Anselm's roiled interaction with this *argumentum*, which he alternately desired and despised, sought after and ran from, is a hint that he is in relation with the true God, that radically nonworldly reality which can be neither seized nor avoided.

The turning point for St. Anselm was the moment of surrender. Frustrated by his attempt to grasp and tired out from his attempt to avoid, he let go, and into his conflicted soul came a gift. The very thing that he was seeking and fearing *se obtulit* handed itself over to him. God forbade Adam and Eve to take from the tree of the knowledge of good and evil, to seize at divinity, but this was not because he did not want them to have a share

---

4. Southern, *Saint Anselm*, 117.
5. See Robert Barron *And Now I See: A Theology of Transformation* (New York: Crossroad, 1998), 91–106.

in his life. Rather, he did not want them to *seize* it. The divine life—as the Gospels make clear over and again—can only be received as a grace and can be maintained only by being given away in turn. Anselm realized this same truth when, at the end of striving, he took in a gift.

Now this taking in is by no means one-sidedly passive. It was with ardor that Anselm embraced what was offered to him, "ut studiose cogitationem amplecterer," just as it was with engaged enthusiasm that the prodigal son accepted his father's hospitality and that the woman at the well cooperated with her interlocutor. Once she had taken in the gift of the divine life welling up within her, the Samaritan woman ran into the town and became an evangelist, spreading the good news that she had received. In a very similar way, Anselm, having embraced the gift, endeavored immediately to give it away: "Thinking therefore that what I had rejoiced to have found could, if written down, please some reader, I have written the present work."[6] The writing of the *Proslogion* itself is the act by which Anselm maintained himself in the loop of grace. What becomes clear in this preamble is the nonworldliness and graciousness of the divine reality and the dynamics of both the false and true human responses to God. The rest of the work, including and especially the famous "proof," constitutes an explication of these intuitions.

But before coming to the *argumentum*, we must pass through the first chapter of Anselm's masterwork. Again, most commentators ignore this portion of the *Proslogion* or perhaps, at best, dismiss it as the sort of boilerplate one would expect of a medieval monk, a bit of pious decoration. But these are mistakes. Just as an aspirant to Anselm's Benedictine way of life would be compelled to move through a trying period of novitiate training, so the reader of the *Proslogion* must endure a kind of purification of heart and clarification of spirit before reading the theology that Anselm will offer. Approached in the wrong frame of mind, the God disclosed in the *ratio* of chapter 2 will be misconstrued. In order to see the truth of this, all we have to do is consult the rationalizing misinterpretations of the "ontological argument" down the ages, from Gaunilo to Descartes, Kant, and Charles Hartshorne.

The first chapter of the *Proslogion* bears the title "Excitatio mentis ad contemplandum deum" (The Awakening of the Spirit toward the Contemplation of God). The clear implication is that the mind, in relation to God, tends toward sluggishness, indifference, and groggy misperception and must accordingly be shaken out of its slumber. So Anselm's first words are "Eia nunc" (up now, pay attention), and they are addressed to *homuncio* (man of nothing), the human being who has lost the essence of who he should be, who, like the prodigal son, has squandered his substance

6. Anselm, *Proslogion*, 230.

and become ontologically poor. The *homuncio* is urged to flee for a time his *occupationes* and to hide a bit from his "tumultuous thoughts."[7] His engagements with the world of conditioned things, as manifested both interiorly and exteriorly, must be broken so that a contact with the one unconditioned reality can be affected.

He is then told to enter "in cubiculum mentis tuae" (into the cell of his mind) and to exclude everything except God and what will help him to find God. The reference is, obviously, twofold. On the one hand, it recalls Jesus's recommendation that when we pray we should go into our room, close the door, and contact the heavenly Father in secret, and on the other hand, it is redolent of the Benedictine tradition of the holiness of the monastic cell, the place where the solitary one (*monachus*) communes with God. Again, the many conditioned things are set aside in favor of the unconditioned one.

Having been urged to make these basic preparations of the spirit, the *homuncio* is then told to pray wholeheartedly, "Quaero vultum tuum; vultum tuum, domine, requiro" (I seek your face; your face, O Lord, I search out).[8] The God who is not an idol of the mind can only be received as a gift, and therefore it is essential that the seeker after God ask and ask again. Whatever can be seized by the spirit through its own efforts is a conditioned form and not the radically other. It is only within the loop of grace, the giving and receiving of gifts, that one experiences the true God.

Then Anselm, in the spirit of Abraham, Moses, and Job, rouses God to action: "Eia nunc ergo tu, domine deus meus, doce cor meum ubi et quomodo te quaerat, ubi et quomodo te inveniat" (and you, Lord my God, rise up and teach my heart where and how to seek you, where and how to find you). How far we are here from a modern confidence that all is fundamentally well with the mind! We have within us the desire for God, but we cannot entirely trust it to lead us to God, for it has become distorted. Therefore we must pray, not only for the content of what we seek but also for the grace that is the condition for the possibility of seeking in the right way. Anselm's own awkward lunging after God and subsequent hiding from him are sufficient demonstration of the necessity of this prayer.

Like many other Christian thinkers—Augustine, Kierkegaard, and Blaise Pascal come to mind most readily—Anselm argues for the existence of the fall on the basis of the painful split in the human spirit. We desire God with all our hearts, but we are unable to find him; we seek to see the divine face, but we are stranded in a land of exile; we have been made

7. Ibid., 236.
8. Ibid.

for union with God, but we never do what we were made for: "Denique ad te videndum factus sum, et nondum feci propter quod factus sum" is Anselm's theological anthropology in summary form.[9] Since God could never have directly desired such a state of affairs, we must have fallen away through sin from our natural condition and orientation, so that we are miserable and God seems sequestered in a far country. Anselm's lament at the general condition of the children of Eve is one of the most moving and honest in the tradition, in part because it is addressed so frankly to God:

> Why has he taken life away from us and inflicted death? Wretches that we are, from where have we been expelled and where are we being led? From where have we been cast down and where have we been buried? From the homeland toward exile, from the vision of God toward our blindness, from the joy of immortality into the bitterness and horror of death. Miserable change! From such good into such evil! Heavy loss, heavy sorrow, heavy is everything.[10]

The agony that Anselm described in the preamble is a consequence of this dire condition, while the revelation that came to him and his subsequent response are indications of the way out. None of us can move from exile to the homeland, but the homeland can, as it were, move toward us; none of us can see with our blind eyes, but those eyes can be filled with light through the power of the Light. And this is why, after the lament, Anselm prays, "Look at us, Lord, hear us, illumine us, show us yourself."[11] Once more, the only possible relationship with the Creator is one of grace—receiving and then giving away.

Toward the end of the first chapter, St. Anselm utilizes the language of Augustine to disclose the precise nature of the fallen condition: "Lord, turned in on myself, I can only look downward; lift me up that I might tend toward the heights."[12] The fundamental problem—and cause of the terrible heaviness complained of earlier—is none other than the tendency to become collapsed around the infinitely boring space of one's own ego. When this occurs, the self becomes a substance cut off from the flow of grace, and God becomes a projection of that self, the supreme substance. The two confront one another across a terrible abyss. This illusion of a self-sufficient ego cut off from a supreme being is

---

9. Ibid., 238.

10. "Ut quid nobis abstulit vitam et inflixit mortem? Aerumnosi, unde sumus expulsi, quo sumus impulsi! Unde praecipitati, quo obruti! A patria in exsilium, a visione dei in caecitatem nostram. A iucunditate immortalitatis in amaritudinem et horrorem mortis. Misera mutatio! De quanto bono in quantum malum! Grave damnum, gravis dolor, grave totum" (ibid., 240).

11. "Respice, domine, exaudi, illumina nos, ostende nobis teipsum" (ibid.).

12. "Domine, incurvatus non possum nisi deorsum aspicere, erige me ut possim sursum intendere" (ibid., 242).

what Scotus, Occam, and, after them, moderns from Descartes to James took as metaphysically basic. And therein lies the principal problem in interpreting the famous *argumentum* that Anselm presents in chapter 2. What he will try to show is that seeing God with at least relative adequacy and being in the right spiritual attitude are correlative and mutually implicative.

As we turn to the second chapter of the *Proslogion*, we confront one of the most studied and controverted texts in the Christian tradition. As I have been suggesting, it is indispensable that we leave behind the prejudices and interpretations born of modernity's preoccupations and try to read the argument from the perspective of a medieval monk, which is to say, with biblical eyes. Well aware of the fallenness of his own mind, cognizant of his tendency to create idols and mistake them for the true God, Anselm prays: "Therefore Lord, you who give understanding to faith, give me as far as you judge it to be good to recognize that you are as we believe you to be and that you are what we believe."[13] In an attitude of receptivity and trust (faith), Anselm asks for the kind of understanding that will not alienate him from the true God but will in fact increase his faith. And the key is donation: he requests that God *give* him this insight, and on God's terms. Even when he moves into technical philosophical language, acceptance of grace will be, he prays, the controlling element throughout the exercise in theological understanding. What he asks for is a ray of light from the inaccessible light that is sensed only in the darkness of faith, knowing full well that the understanding he thereby acquires will lead him deeper into the darkness. Properly thrown off balance intellectually, he commences.

In the preamble, Anselm told us that what he had been seeking came to him as a gift. Now we discover that the content of that gift was a name: "And indeed we believe you to be that than which nothing greater can be thought."[14] Moses sought a name and was given a surprising and disconcerting response, a kind of nonanswer. Something similar is at work here, for the name that Anselm receives has no positive content and provides no conceptual clarity. To say that God is that than which nothing greater can be thought is tantamount to saying that whatever you think is less than God. Any idea of God, even that of the highest being, can necessarily be trumped, thought beyond, overshadowed. Hegel taught us that to think a limit is to be already beyond the limit. Thus to think of God as the unsurpassably highest reality is already to be beyond God and in a position to judge him and categorize him. Even as one pays the high-

---

13. "Ergo, domine, qui das fidei intellectum, da mihi, ut quantum scis expedire intelligam, quia es sicut credimus, et hoc es quod credimus" (ibid., 244).

14. "Et quidem credimus te esse aliquid quo nihil maius cogitari posit" (ibid.).

est possible metaphysical compliments to God, one is, in point of fact, declaring one's own implicit superiority. What Anselm's name rules out is just this sort of intellectual move. It is hence perfectly in accord with Augustine's radically apophatic dictum *si comprehendis, non est Deus* (if you understand, it is not God that you are understanding) and with the generally biblical prohibition against the making of idols. What this name assuredly is not is a definition or description of God, since both of those linguistic operations imply delimitation, specification, and contrast. It is therefore extremely important that we call "that than which nothing greater can be thought" a name, just as "I AM WHO I AM" is a name. Names are disclosures offered by someone who remains mysterious and uncontrollable even in the act of self-disclosure; as such, they can only be given and received by persons. How alien Anselm's name is to Descartes' clear and distinct idea of a perfect reality, on the basis of which the father of modernity constructs, in awkward imitation of Anselm, what he takes to be a clinching argument for God's existence. Just about the last thing that one could say about *aliquid quo nihil maius cogitari possit* is that it is clear and distinct, and therefore just about the last thing that one would presume to construct on its basis is a rational demonstration in the accepted sense of the term.

A further implication of Anselm's mysterious name for God bears quite directly on the argument that I have been making concerning God's noncompetitive transcendence. Any and all of the supreme beings proposed by either philosophers or the concocters of myth would exist competitively over and against other lesser beings in the world. No matter how many impressive attributes we ascribe to Zeus, he remains one god among many and, in relation to lower things, one being among many. And no matter how loftily we describe a first principle of nature, such as Aristotle's first mover or Heraclitus's universal logos, it remains one power in or alongside of the cosmos as a whole. Consequently, Zeus plus anything else in the world would be greater than Zeus alone, and the prime mover plus anything else in nature would be greater than the prime mover alone. None of these supreme realities could, accordingly, be "that than which nothing greater can be thought." Anselm's name for God signals the absolutely unique form of transcendence that we saw in connection with the Chalcedonian formula. That which neither competes with nor contrasts to a worldly nature (or the whole complex of worldly natures) is that than which no stranger can be thought. One must say (though it is impossible to know precisely what one is saying when one says it) that God plus the world is not greater than God alone, that the whole of finite reality adds nothing to God's perfection. Whatever God is, God must be so modally different from anything else that exists that any comparison between him and the rest of reality is impossible.

I do not think that it is merely coincidental, by the way, that there is a close relationship between Anselm's mysterious name for God and a "naming" of Christ that takes place in Paul's letter to the Philippians. Because, Paul tells us, Jesus accepted the incarnation and endured the passion, he has received "the name above every other name." That than which no greater can be thought is tightly correlated to the one than whom no greater can be named. In designating God as he does, Anselm is giving expression to the elemental Christian conviction that the divine power disclosed in Jesus Christ, precisely in the measure that it comes so close, must be utterly strange.

Now, having clarified (as far as possible) the meaning of the sacred name, we may still wonder, with Anselm, whether it corresponds to anything real, whether it names something outside the mind. Perhaps, after all, the fool mentioned in Psalm 14 is right when he says in his heart that there is no God. Anselm's opening move is to observe that even the one who denies the existence of God has the idea of God in his mind, since if that were not the case, he wouldn't know what he was denying. This might seem to be a banality, but we must remember that it is this unique and distinctive idea of God as "that than which no greater can be thought" that Anselm is placing, for sake of argument, in the mind of the doubter. Presumably, the idea of Zeus or of the prime mover could never ground the argument that Anselm is going to launch, since such ideas could indeed exist only in the mind. But "that than which nothing greater can be conceived" cannot be a concept sequestered merely in the intellect, precisely because it is greater to exist both inside the mind and outside the mind than in the mind alone. If we were to say then that God is but a fantasy or clever idea, we would be caught on the horns of a dilemma, for we would be saying that we are thinking about something greater than that which no greater can be thought about. And therefore a denial of God's existence involves us in a hopeless logical conundrum.

It would of course be well beyond the scope of this book to rehearse the innumerable debates that have swirled around this simple demonstration for the past nine centuries, but I would like to engage, however briefly, a few of the classical criticisms, in order to clarify the nature of Anselm's project and purpose in developing this *argumentum*. Anselm's monastic colleague Gaunilo inaugurated a long tradition of misreading when he stated that the actual existence of a perfect being could no more be proved from the idea of such a being than the existence of a perfect island could be demonstrated from the idea of such an island. Not only does Gaunilo overlook the fact that Anselm takes the idea of God to be utterly unique and not the least bit comparable to any other notions, but more important, he misconstrues "that than which no greater can be thought" as a perfect being. As I have tried to show, just about the last thing that Anselm's curious designation indicates is a perfect or highest being. On the basis of such a concept precisely nothing can be demonstrated, as Gaunilo quite rightly points out.

Another standard objection is raised by Thomas Aquinas. With his customary laconicism, Thomas claims that Anselm makes the elementary logical mistake of moving from the notional to the real, from the intramental to the extramental. No matter how impressive and distinctive an idea is, it remains an idea and cannot warrant, on its own, the claim that it corresponds to something real. This sort of interpretation follows from a setting aside of the preamble to the *Proslogion*. Anselm told us that at the end of his searching, he was given this argument through the grace of God. It is not, therefore, an idea that he starts with but rather an experience of God summed up in a sacred name. The experience, moreover, was made possible by Anselm's setting aside of his desire both to grasp at God *and* to hide from God. In brief, when he abandoned the sorts of spiritual attitudes that would make the divine into a conditioned object, he was given the name above every other name, that than which no greater can be conceived.

What occurs in the course of the *argumentum* is not the drawing of extramental conclusions on the basis of intramental premises, but rather the showing forth of the implications of that experience and that name. The one who says in her heart that there is no God is a fool, because she thinks that the unconditioned reality can be isolated in the dimension of subjectivity. But anything that is sequesterable in one finite category is set necessarily over and against another finite category and thus cannot possibly be the unconditioned. Were God "this" rather than "that," he would be something caught in the web of finite things, and hence contrastable, in the ordinary sense, with anything else. It should be clear that, by the same token, the claim that God is a supreme object "out there" would be equally problematic and for the same reason. "That than which no greater can be thought" couldn't possibly be, as we've seen, a supreme or perfect being, since such an object would be contrastable not only to other beings but to the entire dimension of subjectivity. It is indeed "greater" to exist both in the mind and outside the mind than in the mind alone, or for that matter, in the objective realm alone, and thus Anselm is showing us, through his argument, *how* the true God exists.

To understand the spiritual dynamics of the *argumentum*, we must make constant reference back to the grounding experience. Whatever is locatable within categories descriptive of finitude can be either grasped or hidden from. Thus to say that God is only an idea (as opposed to an object) or only an object (as opposed to an idea) is, *eo ipso*, both to grasp him intellectually and to find a way to avoid him. If God is in only one dimension of being, one can catch him in the web of the mind, and one can escape from him by running to the contrasting dimension of existence. To objectify or subjectify God is thus to be in sin, to be thinking with the fallen mind. And this is why Anselm took us through the discipline of chapter 1 before getting to the *argumentum*: we had to come to grips with our tendency toward idolatry before we could glimpse the ungraspable and unavoidable quality of that than which no greater can be thought.

Many of the Christian masters have observed over the centuries that Jesus Christ is the breaker of idols. Anselm is demonstrating that the God who comes to us in the incarnation is not in, above, or alongside the world and, as such, cannot be turned into a conditioned object. As we have seen, this very strangeness of the true God is what allows him to operate in the world so peacefully and so noninvasively.

Aquinas's God

In the epistemology section of this book, I indicated the christological character of Thomas's overall project. Despite the distortions of the neoscholastics and the caricatures presented by the moderns, authentic Thomism is conditioned through and through by the person of Jesus Christ, the one whom Thomas was, as a Dominican, obliged to preach and proclaim.[15] Though it might not be apparent to the superficial surveyor of Thomas's texts, Aquinas's doctrine of God is an explication of the difference upon which I have been insisting. The God he seeks to explain is the God and Father of our Lord Jesus Christ, the strange power capable of effecting a hypostatic union with a creaturely nature, that puzzling reality that can be neither grasped nor hidden from. The unique mode of the divine otherness appears on practically every page of Aquinas's treatment of God, but I will focus on three key areas: the simplicity of God, God's creativity, and God's direction of the world through secondary causality. My overall purpose, once again, is to show that the modern concern for the integrity and freedom of the creature over and against God is far better honored in medieval theology than in the constructs of the modern religious philosophers.

Though he argues for the divine simplicity throughout his career and in a variety of his writings—in fact it is a kind of master idea for him— Thomas's most thoroughgoing and detailed treatment of the theme is in the disputed question *De potentia Dei*, a text he composed in the mid-1260's, around the same time as he was producing the *Summa theologiae* and the commentary on the Gospel of John. Many have smiled wryly at Thomas's

---

15. See here Nicholas Healy, *Thomas Aquinas: Theologian of the Christian Life* (Aldershot, UK: Ashgate, 2003), esp. 24–47.

own characterization of the *Summa theologiae* as a text for beginners, but his claim becomes a bit more credible when we compare the second *Summa* with the *De potentia*. Whereas the former contains articles with relatively pithy *respondeos* and a play of perhaps three or four objections and responses, the latter features lengthy and densely complex *respondeos* and up to eighteen or twenty objections and responses. In general, the arguments in the disputed question are more fully developed and nuanced than those in the *Summa*, suited for advanced students and professors.

The overarching issue that Thomas considers in the *De potentia* is the divine power or God's capacity to give rise to what is other. Accordingly, both the trinitarian processions (the *ad intra* othering within God) and the act of creation (the *ad extra* othering outside God) are analyzed. But the ground for both acts is the peculiar nature of God as that which simply is. Hence in question seven of the *De potentia* Thomas explores the divine simplicity, using, as we've come to expect, the path of negativity and removal, stripping from the idea of God any trace of creatureliness. After rehearsing in article 1 certain basic arguments for the divine simplicity, Thomas turns in article 2 to the metaphysical heart of the matter, namely, the question of the identity of essence and existence in God: "utrum in Deo sit substantia vel essentia idem quod esse." The argument that Thomas unfolds in the *respondeo* is quite distinctive inasmuch as it constitutes indirectly a proof for the existence of God, in many ways more elegant and convincing than any of the five famous demonstrations from the first part of the *Summa theologiae*. When, he says, a variety of causes producing diverse effects come together in giving rise to one common effect, this must be due to the influence of a higher cause. As is his wont, Aquinas provides a surprisingly homely illustration of this rarefied ontological principle. Many particular causes—pepper, zanzibar, other spices—produce their distinctive flavors in the stew, yet all unite in contributing to the heating of the dish. In order to explain this phenomenon, one must appeal beyond those particular influences to a cause whose proper effect is heat: the fire that warms the whole stew.

In a similar way, he continues, all finite causes, despite their enormous diversity, come together in producing *esse*, the act of being. Hence, "heat makes something to be hot, and a builder makes the house to be."[16] Though they produce at the relatively superficial level widely diverging effects, they come together, at the most substantial level, in giving rise to the same effect, namely, be-ing. But this can be explained, in accord with Thomas's principle, only through appeal to a higher or more elemental cause that works through them and whose proper effect is to-be. And

---

16. "Calor enim facit calidum esse, et aedificator facit domum esse." *De potentia*, q. 7, art. 2.

this fundamental cause, which must operate in and through any and all worldly causes, is God. This argument for God's existence has particular effectiveness: unlike the first, second, and fifth of the *quinque viae*, it points to a properly creative power and not simply to a mover or cause among many, and unlike the third of the five ways, it displays a certain economy and elegance of expression.

At any rate, this demonstration of the existence of a cause whose proper effect is to-be is but a preliminary step in Thomas's overall argument for the identity of *esse* and essence in God. The proper effect of a given cause, he argues, proceeds as a similitude to the very nature of that cause, just as the heating of the many elements in the stew flowed ultimately from the fire whose nature is heat. It therefore follows that God, the cause whose distinctive effect is to-be, must himself *be* to-be. If God were anything other than the sheer act of to-be, he would be a type of being and hence capable of giving rise only to a particular mode of existence. But if this were true, we would have to appeal beyond him to a still higher, unifying cause capable of grounding the modified being that he produces, and this would involve us in an absurdity.

Does this naming stand in tension with the agnosticism that I empha-sized at the outset of this chapter? By no means, for in saying that to be God is to be to-be (to borrow David Burrell's phrase), we aren't really making any sort of positive claim; we are rather gesturing toward the darkness of what we do not know. As the sheer act of *esse*, God cannot be qualified, defined, delimited, or specified, and he cannot be compared with anything else. He is not up rather than down, or in rather than out, or great rather than small, or here rather than there. He cannot be placed, positioned, or indicated. This is why, of course, in the two *Summae* and elsewhere Thomas is so careful to clarify that God is not a body, not material, not composed of substance and accident, and not in any sort of real relationship with something outside of him. If God were any of those things, he could be caught in the net of conceptual knowledge, and the prohibition of such a "catching" is the practical purpose of the claim that he is to-be itself.

This negativity is even more clearly emphasized in the next article, which considers the question whether God might be categorizable in any genus. Given the Aristotelian framework in which Thomas was working, this question is tantamount to the following: can God be known scientifi-cally? Transposed into a more biblical frame of reference, it is tantamount to "when the Israelites ask me your name, what am I to tell them?" (see Exod. 3:13). We are on sacred and dangerous ground. Thomas offers three arguments against the claim that God is placeable in a genus, and the third is the most telling. Since God is simply perfect (*simpliciter perfectus*), he must contain within himself the perfections of all genera. If he were in a particular genus, he would be determined according to the perfections of that one category of reality and thus would not be simply or inclusively perfect. Thomas states the result of this bit of reasoning with disconcerting clarity: "From this it appears that God is not a species, nor an individual, nor does he have a difference or definition, for a definition is made from genus and species."[17] Because God is not namable even according to the most generic of categories, he cannot be circumscribed, defined, or grasped. Nor can he be in any sense *a being*, an individual, since this would make him comparable to other individuals. As *simpliciter perfectus*, God must be prior to and beyond any and all customary ontological divisions and contrasts. Thomas's simple God is therefore identical to Anselm's "that than which no greater can be thought," the one who is neither subjective nor objective, neither a mere idea nor a mere object.

And both theologians, in making these claims, are ruling out the grasping and hiding tendencies of the sinner. The first move of Adam is rendered absurd by God's essential incomprehensibility and incommensurability, but Adam's second move is equally problematized by God's infinity: where precisely would one be able to run from that which contains the perfections of all genera, that which includes and envelops all of reality? As we saw, there is about these descriptions something deeply disconcerting and disorienting, but this is because the human consciousness is fallen. Having taken these theologies in, we don't quite know what to do or where to go, but this is precisely because our ordinary modes of thought and action are so determined by sin.

As for Anselm so for Thomas: this strange God, who is not an individual or a specifiable reality, cannot possibly be in competition with the world. Even as he enters most intimately into creation, grounding it and sustaining it, he must allow it to be itself, for to do otherwise would be to compromise his own otherness. The example that Thomas used in the previous article shows this delicate play of closeness and distantiation: even as God exerts his primary causality and gives rise to being, he does so through a practically infinite variety of secondary causes, each of which retains its integrity and uniqueness as cause. If God were a supreme being alongside those other agents, his causality would necessarily compete and interfere with theirs, but because God is somehow else, both immanent and transcendent in the highest degree, he can be, vis-à-vis secondary causes, both everything and nothing. Paul Tillich argued that God's existence is permanently and not simply provisionally mysterious, by which he meant that there is no way, in principle, that God's to-be could ever be illumined through thought categories applicable to finite things. And Karl Rahner

---

17. "Ex hoc ulterius patet quod Deus not est species, nec individuum, nec habet differentiam, nec definitionem; nam omnis definitio est ex genere et specie." *De potentia*, q. 7, art. 3.

intensified this assertion by saying that in heaven the blessed would see for the first time just how incomprehensible God is. Following Thomas, he claimed that the divine mysteriousness is not so much a function of our noetic limitations as an essential attribute of God. Once more, behind this metaphysics is the distinctive relationship that obtains between the divine and human natures in Christ, anchored noncompetitively to the unity of a divine person.

This christologically oriented metaphysics, as we saw, unraveled at the beginning of the modern period, allowing for the various types of "supreme being" doctrines presented by philosophers from Descartes to William James. Even James's carefully nuanced account centers on a conception of God as a being among beings, a mind over other minds. Saddled with a caricature of medieval philosophy, James couldn't see past a fundamentally competitive God obliged to withdraw into finitude in order to allow other beings freedom to move and act. Unable to appreciate how the God of Aquinas is some*how* else, James had to make God some*where* else. The irony is that the God who retreats into finitude is in point of fact more competitive with other finite things than the God who remains properly infinite.

In my analysis of the story of the prodigal son, I emphasized that when the younger son wandered off into a far country, effectively severing his graced relationship with his father, his wealth disappeared. When he abandoned the loop of grace and clung to the *ousia* that was coming to him, he became lost, hungry, homeless. So the modern person, having escaped from the clutches of the supreme being and desperately clinging to her freedoms and prerogatives, becomes a sojourner in the far country, her liberty turning to dust. In terms of Jesus's great parable, true freedom and joy are discovered in the act of surrendering completely to the Grace who cannot, even in principle, undermine the integrity of the one who surrenders.

The other-enhancing quality of the one whose very nature is to-be emerges forcefully in Aquinas's still surprising discussion of the act of creation. Recent debates concerning evolutionist and "creationist" accounts of the origins of nature are marked through and through by modern assumptions about a distant, competitive, and occasionally intervening God, whether the existence of such a God is affirmed or denied. Thomas Aquinas would have said something like "A plague on both your houses," for his doctrine of creation rests upon the metaphysics of the strange God who lets the other be in the very act of constituting that other as other. We will explore Thomas's premodern theology of creation by looking, once more, at the densely textured disputed question *De potentia Dei.*

Of the ten questions in the *De potentia*, question 3, which deals with creation, is by far the longest, comprising nineteen separate articles. It seems safe to assume that Aquinas considered the proper treatment of this issue crucial. Article 1 raises the hinge question: "whether God can create something from nothing."[18] What becomes clear in the course of the discussion is that this formulation of the query is actually redundant, since *creatio*, for Thomas, means exclusively to make something from nothing. At the beginning of his *respondeo*, Aquinas asserts that we must firmly hold (*tenendum est firmiter*) that God not only can but does create *ex nihilo*, and his justification for this assertion rests upon God's nature as purely actual. Every agent acts in the measure that it is in act, which is to say in possession of some perfection of being. Thus a finite cause—fire, sunlight, a carpenter—produces a finite mode of existence, being *secundum quid*, determined in this way or that (*ens . . . determinatum ad hoc vel ad aliud*). Another way to state this same principle is to say that any natural or finite cause acts by moving another, by changing or further specifying its being in some manner. But God, the simple reality, must be totally in act (*totaliter in actu*), and hence he produces the whole of finite being, not acting as a mover on something preexisting but rather bringing forth the existence of the world in its entirety. Nothing other than the simple reality can stand, as it were, over and against it, influencing or being influenced by it; God does not enter into the nexus of conditioned relations, interacting with other similar things. On the contrary, the web of interdependent realities as a whole is brought into being by that which remains necessarily other.

Therefore creation is not a change or a motion. In any *mutatio*, there exists some substrate that remains the same from beginning to end of the transition. Thus in a substantial change, a fundamental materiality remains, and in an accidental change, some substrate moves from potency to act while remaining substantially identical. But neither of these types of change obtain in the case of creation, since there is nothing preexisting that could even in principle receive or endure the act of creation. We cannot maintain that unformed matter is the recipient of creation, since matter is a creature. And even if we stay at the more abstract level, we cannot say that time is a substrate or condition of creation, since time itself is a creature; and we cannot maintain that space is the unchanging theater in which creation takes place, since space itself is created. When we say that time began or that space emerged into existence, we are speaking, says Thomas, on the basis of primitive imaginative representations, not exact metaphysical ideas.[19] Creation is not in any ordinary way an influence or activity, and it could certainly never appear to the senses, because it is the fundamental condition for the possibility of any influence, activity,

18. "Utrum Deus possit aliquid creare ex nihilo." *De potentia*, q. 3, art. 1.
19. Ibid., q. 3, art.2.

or sense event. When trying to describe creation positively, we come up against the same problem we did when attempting to speak positively of the divine existence: we know roughly that it is, but we have no real idea what it is.

This anomalous, elusive quality is made plain in the third article of question 3, which raises the following issue: "whether creation is something really in the creature, and if it is, what it might be."[20] Some have said, Aquinas tells us, that creation is a sort of *via media* between God and creatures, a mediating principle that is "in" neither the Creator nor the creature. But this cannot be the case, for if it were, there would be something—namely this "creation"—that has not been created, and thus the principle of *creatio ex nihilo* would be violated. Others have argued that creation is not really in creatures but only in God as an active principle. But this would run counter to the metaphysics of real and logical relationality. For Aquinas and his medieval colleagues, a real relationship is one that involves dependency, whereas a merely logical relationship is one that involves no change or contingency. Thus, a cathedral wall is really related to a flying buttress, inasmuch as the stability of the former is dependent upon the influence of the latter, whereas a pillar is only logically related to one who stands now to its left and now to its right. In the case of creation from nothing, we have an instance of a mixed relation, for the creature is, in the most thoroughgoing sense, dependent upon the causal influence of God, whereas God, even as he gives rise to the world, is in no sense contingent upon the world.

If we take the term *creation*, then, to mean the creative act, we must say that it is "in" God, since it is the same as the divine essence; however, if we take it in the passive or relational sense, we cannot say that it belongs to God, though we must ascribe it as fully as possible to the creature. Now even here, we have to move carefully. In the strict sense, creation cannot be construed as something passively received, since there is no receptacle outside of creation capable of receiving it. It is more correctly described as a relationship, but one unlike any that we know in ordinary experience. The best we can say therefore is this: creation is "only the beginning of being and a relation to the creator from whom it has being, and thus creation is nothing other really than a kind of relation to the God with newness of being."[21] In speaking of the "beginning" of being, Thomas obviously does not mean chronological inception, but rather something like the ongoing grounding of the deepest center of a creature's existence. This is

20. "Utrum creatio sit aliquid realiter in creatura, et si est, quid sit." Ibid., q. 3, art. 3.

21. "Sed solummodo iceptio essendi et relatio ad creatorem a quo esse habet; et sic creatio nihil est aliud realiter quam relation quaedam ad Deum cum novitate essendi." *De potentia*, q. 3, art. 3.

the "freshness" or "newness" of being that he speaks of. Thomas Merton had this metaphysics in mind when he said that contemplative prayer is realizing that place where one is here and now being created by God.

We notice as well that Aquinas refers to creation as a "kind of relation," implying that it cannot be described in Aristotelian terms as a rapport between two already existing things. In point of fact, the creature, according to this radical ontology, does not so much have a relationship; it *is* a relationship. The Zenlike quality of this affirmation is confirmed in the play between the seventeenth objection and response in article 3. The objector argues, reasonably enough, that in order for God to give being, there must be something preexisting in order to receive the gift. But if this is the case, then God does not, strictly speaking, create *ex nihilo*. In answer, Thomas says that "in giving being, God simultaneously produces that which receives being."[22] I would challenge anyone to grasp the nettle of that observation within the framework of ordinary being-to-being relationships. Coinherence is built into the very structure of creaturely existence.

At this point in the argument, are we not forced to wrestle with the familiar objections of James, Whitehead, and their process theology disciples that this absolute God, not really related to the world, is cold, unresponsive, heartless, and domineering? In some ways, it is Thomas's Latin usage that makes him vulnerable to this charge. For when he says that God's rapport with the world is not "realis," the contemporary person hears this as implying distance, whereas Thomas means simply lack of contingency and dependency. As I have just demonstrated, the Creator God's involvement with the creature could hardly be more intimate. Since God is responsible for the entire to-be of the creature, God cannot be said to "respond" to what the creature does or to have feelings in reaction to what he has made. Rather, he is the ground of any and all creaturely activities, emotions, reactions, and passions and hence is more, not less, connected to the creature than he would be if he were merely an outside actor. In the *Summa theologiae*, Aquinas comments that God is *in* all things by "essence, presence, and power," and he adds, "intime," intimately so. Were God a being among others—and hence not the simple Creator—his relationship to other realities would necessarily be limited, reactive, and extrinsic and thus less "real" in the ordinary acceptation of the term.

Furthermore, were God a finite thing, his relation to others would be interruptive and invasive. But the simple one who gives being *ex nihilo* stands, as John Milbank has observed, in a relationship of radical nonviolence vis-à-vis the world that he makes. When God gives rise to the universe, he does not wrestle any recalcitrant matter into form, nor does he subdue divinities outside of himself, nor does he order a stubborn

22. "Deus simul dans esse, producit id quod esse recipit" (ibid.).

chaos—for none of these things or states could exist outside of God's creative power. Rather, in a sheerly peaceful act, God allows the other to be. James Alison has observed that traces of a mythological account of creation can still be found in the book of Genesis's story of God's Spirit hovering over the *tohu va bohu* of the primal waters. The doctrine of *creatio ex nihilo*, so carefully spelled out by Aquinas, came into the Christian tradition, Alison continues, because of the nonviolence of the Paschal Mystery. As we saw in the Christology chapter, when the risen Jesus met the violence of the disciples' rejection with the *shalom* of his forgiveness, he showed that the divine way of establishing order is peaceful rather than coercive. This resurrection *shalom* forced a reconsideration of the theology of God, conducing toward the claim in the first letter of John that "God is light; in him there is no darkness," which is to say, in him there is a love utterly untainted by violence. And if God is sheerly nonviolent in his dealings with creation, the very nature of the creature has to be rethought, precisely along the lines indicated by Aquinas. If God *is* nonviolent love, then the creature must *be* a pure relationship to its creative source.

One more question has to be addressed under the rubric of the divine creativity: why precisely does God create? If, as Thomas never tires of reminding us, God is utterly self-sufficient, why would he feel obliged to give rise to beings outside of himself? One way to solve this problem is to dissolve it and say that God creates because he has to. In the Aristotelianism of the Arab commentator Avicenna, for example, creation is seen as a sort of automatic emanation from God. In this regard, Avicenna anticipated by eight centuries the dialectical theology of Hegel and by nine centuries the process speculations of Whitehead. But with this sort of emanationism Aquinas has no truck. While natural causes that act through necessity are determined toward the production of one type of effect (think of a plant giving rise predictably to seed after seed), causes that act through intelligence and will produce a wide diversity of effects (think of Picasso or James Joyce). God's production is supremely diverse and multifaceted, and thus it follows that his mode of creativity is not automatic but intelligent, purposive, and artistic. Moreover, as the pure act of existing, God must be in possession of all ontological perfections, including mind and will. Therefore whatever he does in regard to the world that he makes is conditioned by mind and mediated by choice. Thus God chooses, with artistic intent, to give rise to the universe, but he does so in utter freedom from self-interest. And this implies that God's creative act is a gesture of love, since love is the willing of the good of the other as other. The pseudo-Dionysius (whom Thomas devotedly and frequently quotes throughout his writings) said that God's creative act is like the shining of the sun; just as the sun gives light because it is its nature to do so, so God gives being since it is his nature to share himself with the

other. To be sure, we must purge this image of its "automatic" and excessively naturalistic overtones, but nevertheless it accurately communicates
the sheer effervescent generosity with which God gives rise to the world.
Indeed, in the Sermon on the Mount, we find a variation on this image,
when God's love is compared to the sun that shines indiscriminately on
the good and the bad alike. God creates because he is good and the good
is diffusive of itself. In response to certain Hegelianizing tendencies in
nineteenth-century theology, the First Vatican Council reiterated this
point, stating doctrinally that God creates not out of any sort of need but
out of a desire to share his goodness and glory.

Having sketched Aquinas's treatment of the simplicity and creativity of
God, I would like to examine one more major motif in Thomas's doctrine
of God; his teaching concerning the relationship between divine causality
and creaturely causality. This is a vexed problem, and much hangs on its
resolution. Once more, the modern mind reacts against any claim that
God interferes with either the movements of nature or the movements
of the mind and will. The objection is theoretical (for don't the natural
sciences and psychology adequately account for these phenomena?) but
also existential (a competing supernatural cause is an intolerable restriction of human freedom). What has been explored more abstractly to
this point now becomes focused and concrete: how exactly does the
noncompetitiveness of God play itself out in terms of specific interior
and exterior events?

I would first observe that Thomas speaks of God as both Creator (the
one who gives rise to the whole of the universe from nothing) and as
mover (the one who directs particular creatures and creation as a whole
to their appointed ends), and he sees no contradiction or tension between
the two characterizations. God affects creatures at the deepest possible
level of their existence and in relatively secondary ways as well. When God
moves or otherwise affects a creature, he is not in the strict sense creating,
but he never ceases to be the Creator. We might say that God is able to
bring his actualizing power to bear on a creature to varying degrees of
intensity. In question 22 of the first part of the *Summa theologiae*, which
deals with divine providence, Aquinas joins these dimensions of God's
causality neatly together. He argues for the absolute universality of God's
providential reach precisely on the basis of God's status as all-embracing,
all-grounding Creator. What this shows is that the same noncompetitiveness that obtains in regard to the unique act of creation holds, analogously,
in regard to less dramatic instances of divine influence.

The most pointed discussion of this problem of the coincidence of
divine and nondivine agency is found in the seventh article of our by-
now-familiar third question of the *De potentia*. The query posed by
Thomas—whether God operates in the operation of nature—is a natural

one. If God, consciously and with intention, creates the whole of finite reality from nothing, what room is left for the free exercise of creaturely activity? Would the presence of God not simply absorb any purposeful agency outside of himself? The biblical citation that Thomas offers in the *sed contra* to this article could function as the leitmotif of my entire discussion of the God-world relationship in this section: "O LORD, . . . all that we have done you have done for us" (Isa. 26:12). There it is stated clearly and unapologetically, the dimensions of created and uncreated causality placed side by side without the slightest attempt to explain the anomaly of their juxtaposition. We have really done certain things, and yet they have been accomplished in us by God. To be sure, there is an asymmetricality between the two, since it is God who gets the praise, but nevertheless, our real agency is unhesitatingly affirmed.

Thomas works out the details of this assertion in the remarkably complex *respondeo* to article 7. He begins by considering the radical position of Moses Maimonides that natural agents do not in fact communicate effects, since they do not operate according to their own power. Thus, as Aquinas draws out the implications of the rabbi's position, "fire does not heat, but God creates heat in the thing heated."[23] It is important to note the play between this claim and Maimonides' consistent teaching that words used of God and worldly objects are applied in a purely equivocal manner. There is no common language concerning God and creatures, because there is no metaphysical point of contact between the two. But Thomas finds this point of view repugnant not only to reason and common sense but also to the dignity of God. If it is not the fire that is heating the kettle poised over it, our most ordinary perceptions and judgments about these simple objects are incorrect, but what is even more disconcerting is that our sense of God's goodness would thereby be contradicted. As we have seen, God creates out of a desire to share his being with what is other. If God therefore refused causal integrity to the whole of his natural creation, he would, to that degree, be withholding his goodness from what he has made, fussily interfering with it and lording over it, rather than giving it to itself.

How therefore does the universal divine agency work? Thomas lays out several models for understanding. First, one thing can operate in another in the measure that the former provides the latter with its *virtus* or power to act, as, say, the sun influences a solar heating device. God certainly operates in this way, since as Creator he continually provides not only power but being to all of his creatures. Second, a thing can cause the agency of another inasmuch as it moves it to act, as, in Thomas's typically homely example "A man is the cause of the cutting of the knife inasmuch as he

---

23. "Ignis non calefacit, sed Deus creat calorem in re calefacta." *De potentia*, q. 3, art. 7.

applies the sharpness of the knife for cutting by moving it."[24] God operates in this way constantly, since he is the first unmoved mover by whose
influence every change in the cosmos can eventually be traced. Third,
and related, one cause can act in another in the measure that the former
is the principal cause and the latter the instrumental cause, as the soul
moves the body by using it for its purposes. God is the highest and most
all-embracing principal cause, since he sustains all things into existence
and thus uses all finite realities instrumentally. Indeed, Thomas specifies,
"the higher, a cause is, the more common and efficacious, and the more
efficacious, the more profoundly it can penetrate into the effect."[25]

With this last remark, we come to the heart of the matter. All of the
scenarios that Thomas has displayed for us are borrowed from the ordinary realm of being-to-being relationships, the way one thing moves,
influences, empowers, or uses another. In all these cases there is a curious tensive balance. The "using" cause invades the being of that which is
used, but because the "invader" in question is limited in being, the scope
of his influence is restricted, and to that extent the integrity of the effect
is maintained. But when we apply this to God, the equilibrium seems to
break down, since God is unlimited in being and hence, one would assume,
utterly invasive in his influence. In order to allow finite causes to have
their integrity, it seems as though God must join them metaphysically as
one being among many. But if that is the case, everything that Thomas
has said about God is compromised.

If we attend to the adage just cited, though, things begin to clear up.
Aquinas told us that the higher and more all-embracing the cause, the
more ingredient that cause can be in those things that it effects. Therefore
the highest cause of all must be able to influence another not invasively
from without but noncompetitively from within. Because the highest
cause is not a being among many, it can operate in the realm of beings
nonviolently, or as the book of Wisdom has it, "sweetly." Once more, the
very otherness and simplicity of God is what permits God to operate so
thoroughly for and among creatures. So indeed, "all that we have done
you have done for us."

Nowhere is this paradoxical principle more clearly on display than in
the play between human freedom and divine causality. God, says Aquinas,
moves the human will so as to accomplish his providential purposes, but
this in no way interferes with human freedom, since God does not so much
push or pull the will from without as energizes it from within. Freedom

24. "Homo est causa incisionis cultelli ex hoc ipso quod applicat acumen cultelli ad inci-
dendum movendo ipsum" (ibid.).
25. "Quanto enim aliqua causa est altior, tanto est communior et efficacior, et quanto est
efficacior tanto profundius ingreditur in effectum" (ibid.).

is not unmitigated spontaneity but the ordered pursuit of the good in accord with the deepest desire of the free subject. The otherly other God can operate at the level of the ground of the will, luring it in accord with its ownmost nature, and hence can enable the subject to be itself through surrender. God's very capacity to become noninvasively ingredient in the creature in whom he operates is the resolution of the tension between the two freedoms, human and divine. Once more, the incarnational dynamic stands behind and informs the metaphysical principle.

William Placher and others have incisively indicated how, with the breakdown of the classical Christian worldview and the emergence of the more mechanistic modern perspective, this delicate resolution was forgotten, and the problem of God's involvement with the universe took on a new urgency for both the natural scientist and the humanist. For the former, the difficulty was reconciling divine causality with the seemingly closed system of worldly causes and effects presumed by the burgeoning and remarkably successful sciences of physics, astronomy, and chemistry. The preferred solution for those who still desired to retain a connection to the theological tradition was some form of deism: God as designer and occasional corrector of the great machine. For the latter, the problem, as I have been arguing throughout this book, was reconciling divine influence with human freedom. The favorite escape route of theologically minded modern humanists was to envision God as an inspiration and model for the heroic human project. But, of course, in time even this benign God, cheerleading from the sidelines of history, proved too interfering and was relegated by the great atheists to the status of neurotic projection. What Placher and his colleagues have seen so clearly is that this way of framing the question is utterly foreign to the premodern theological tradition. As we have seen with Aquinas, it is never a matter of a zero-sum game, an ontological competition between God's causality and the world's. On the contrary, both are robustly defended and appreciated as utterly compatible. The moment that God was demoted to the level of a being, the inevitable problems ensued.

In all its ramifications and implications, this teaching concerning the existence, creativity, and providential agency of God shows that the possibility so feared by modern philosophers—the overbearing supreme being's posing a threat to human freedom and integrity—is, as far as Thomas Aquinas is concerned, an idol, a fantasy of the sinful mind.

13

God as Giver and Lover

In his account of creation, Thomas speaks of God frequently as the one who *dat esse* (gives being). This description corresponds, of course, to the deeply Christian intuition that God is gracious, full of *gratia*, a giver of good gifts. One of the most intriguing conversations in contemporary philosophy has to do with the supposedly aporetic, self-contradictory quality of any and all gift giving. Theologians and philosophers of religion have not been slow in picking up the implications of this problem for much fundamental religious speech. In my view, the difficulties in regard to gift giving, especially as they apply to divine graciousness, flow from the peculiarly modern description of God and creation that I have been criticizing throughout part III. The resolution of these aporias will come only when an understanding of God as simple and noncontrastively transcendent holds sway. Therefore, engaging with this thorny postmodern problem will help to bring the premodern notion of God that I have been exploring into sharper focus.

The aporia of the gift has been taken up by, among many others, Jacques Derrida, Jean-Luc Marion, and John Milbank, but the problem has its roots in the anthropological work of Marcel Mauss.[1] In his studies of the societies of primal peoples, Mauss observed that an economy of exchange held sway in which the ostensible giving of gifts served as a cover for an elaborate system of obligation and coercion, one "gift" compelling the giv-

---

1. See especially Marcel Mauss, *The Gift: The Form and Reason for Exchange in Archaic Societies*, translated by W. D. Halls (London: Routledge, 1990).

ing of another. This sociological analysis—applicable, to be sure, as much to developed cultures as to primal ones—has led to an enormous amount of philosophical speculation concerning the very possibility of gift giving. In the *Oxford English Dictionary* one reads that a gift is "the voluntary transference of property without consideration," where "consideration" connotes something like "compensatory reward."[2] A spirit of generosity and disinterestedness on the part of the giver seems to be an essential feature of a true gift. Indeed, if I were to receive something from another and it were clear that strings were attached, that the reception of the object obligated me to respond in kind or made me in some other way beholden to the giver, I would be immediately convinced that I had been not "gifted" but manipulated or imposed upon. Even a gift as seemingly simple and benign as a birthday present from one's close relative devolves into a burden if it awakens in the recipient the obligation to write a compensatory thank-you note. To be truly a gift, the relative who gives it would have to be utterly uninterested in receiving an acknowledgement of thanks from the receiver or even the praise of a third party, and the receiver would accordingly feel no obligation to express her gratitude. We could sum this up by saying that the first indispensable condition of the gift is that it be free—on the part of both the giver and the receiver.

A second condition for the possibility of the gift is presence, which is to say, the appearance of the gift qua gift. It is worth noting that in English the terms *gift* and *present* are functionally interchangeable, indicating that a true gift is something that must clearly appear as such. To be more precise, this "presentation" means that an object becomes a "gift-object" only inasmuch as it is either formally offered as a gift or taken in as one. It is possible for a gift to be purely anonymous, but *to be* a gift, it must, at the very least, be accepted by someone as a gratuitous offering. Thus freedom and presence seem to be the essential features of any true donation.

It is at this point that Jacques Derrida enters into the conversation. Granted the essential and ideal structure of the gift, Derrida wonders whether there *can* be such a phenomenon, whether in fact the conditions for authentic donation can ever in principle be met. The problem is that the criteria of freedom and presence seem mutually exclusive. The moment the gift appears as gift, it tends to awaken in the recipient, as we've seen, a terrible obligation to reciprocate, thus involving her in an economy of exchange. And by the same token, it awakens in the giver a consciousness of his own generosity, which, in justice, would seem to call for some reciprocation, thereby drawing him willy-nilly into an economy of debt and obligation. We could avoid this "economic" danger if the gift remained

2. See here the very helpful discussion in Robyn Horner, *Rethinking God as Gift: Marion, Derrida, and the Limits of Phenomenology* (New York: Fordham Univ. Press, 2001).

unknown to both giver and recipient, but it would cease, precisely in that measure, to be a gift. This is why, in a famous bit of linguistic gymnastics, Derrida relates the English word gift to the German term *Gift* (poison). Any gift is, finally, poison to both giver and receiver, since it involves both of them in an oppressive game of superiority/inferiority, debt/obligation. Gifts seem to devolve, almost despite themselves, into measurable commodities, "monetary" tokens that have a disastrous psychological effect on those who manipulate them. Robyn Horner nicely summarizes this dilemma: "In Derrida's analysis, the gift cancels itself by being elemental in an economy, a cycle of return. The gift cancels itself because as a present, it is never completely free."[3]

Emile Benveniste has drawn attention, in a Derridean vein, to a similar tension in regard to the act of hospitality. To receive another into one's home, to offer him food, drink, and shelter, seems to be an act of pure generosity, but in many cultures, both ancient and contemporary, this gesture dramatically implicates both host and guest in a mutually obliging exchange. There are well-known anthropological accounts of communities in which host and guest—each trying to outdo the other in generosity and hospitality—effectively ruin each other. Accordingly, Benveniste, à la Derrida, comments that hospitality is related to the Latin term *hostis* (enemy). Once again, the very conditions for the possibility of generosity appear hopelessly at odds with one another. Our neediness and ontological insufficiency, it seems, compel us to enter these debilitating rhythms of exchange, rendering authentic love an ideal impossible of realization.

Now as I suggested above, all of this comes to a head when it is applied to the properly theological question of God's capacity to give good gifts. God's gracious offer of being appears, above all, to subject his creatures to an awful obligation of reciprocity and thanksgiving, awakening in them the deepest kind of resentment, locking them into the most brutal type of economic exchange. Indeed, in Thomas Aquinas's account of the liturgy, we find a justification for liturgical practice that corresponds almost perfectly to the contours of the Derridean dilemma. Thomas tells us that we must offer praise and thanksgiving to God as an act of justice, rendering to God what is due to him because of his gift of existence. But does this arrangement not implicitly undermine the divine graciousness and quite explicitly compromise the purity of the human response of gratitude, turning both into fundamentally "economic" moves? In obliging us to respond to his gift, does God not reveal himself as simply the biggest player in this finally pathetic and tyrannizing game? And is the modern criticism that God is the most dangerous threat to human flourishing not thereby justified?

3. Ibid., 8.

At this point, it might prove very helpful to recall the narrative of the prodigal son. The theme of economic exchange is central to the story, since the younger son asks for the *ousia*, the hard currency, the measurable portion, of his father's estate that is owed to him, and the elder son complains that he has been compelled to "slave" for his father for many years while receiving nothing in recompense. The sons go wrong spiritually in the measure that they assume they are in a relationship of strict economic justice with their father. The parable demonstrates quite effectively that this attitude leads to the commodification of the father's love and hence to spiritual famine for both sons.

The gestures of the father toward both his children reveal that his love does not have to be earned, because it cannot be earned: even before the prodigal can finish his speech of repentance, his father embraces him and puts the ring on his finger, and in response to the desperate economic calculations of his older son, the father says, "Everything I have is yours." The father needs neither repentance nor gratitude; his gifts do not have to be returned. In fact, it is when the sons forget this truth that they exit the loop of grace and enter the world described by Derrida, the far country of *ousia*, exchange, carefully calculated reciprocation.

Thomas Aquinas's doctrine of the simple God who creates the entire universe *ex nihilo* is the technically theological description of the father in Jesus's parable. Because he is the sheer act of to-be itself, *actus purus*, God, as we saw, stands in need of nothing outside of himself. There is no other reality, actuality, or perfection that could in any way complete or add to his being, since he himself is the ground of whatever exists or could exist outside of him. What follows from this is that God neither creates the universe nor relates to it in order to gain something for himself, and therefore, God cannot even in principle be involved in an economic exchange with his creatures. He cannot give in order to receive, nor can he be gracious in order to be thanked. This kind of reciprocity is possible only among and between *beings*, which is to say, created things existing interdependently. God's relation to the world that he creates and sustains can only be one of sheer generosity, a being-for-the-other. The universe characterized by economic exchange—analyzed with precision by Derrida and displayed devastatingly in the parable of the prodigal son—is a product of the sinful imagination and of the distorting effects of myriad sinful acts. At the center of that fallen milieu is the projection of a supreme being who enters into the mix through domination and manipulation, precisely the god imaged by modernity and the idol exposed through the parable of the prodigal son.

When we try to relate to this false god, we enter metaphysically anomalous space, much like the *chora makra* envisioned in the parable, and we necessarily lose contact with the loop of grace, the stream of uncompromised generosity that flows from the true God. Whatever we have from the illusory god turns quickly to dust in our hands, and whatever we think we owe him awakens in us only resentment and bitterness.

Only with these metaphysical and spiritual clarifications in mind can we properly grasp Thomas's teaching on the "obligatory" quality of the liturgy or put it in a broader context, the general Christian insistence that our lives must be acts of praise and gratitude to the Creator. Such obligations would indeed be burdensome and dehumanizing if they proceeded from a competitive and needy supreme being, but since they come from the one who cannot compete with us and who stands in no need, they are in fact liberating. The gratitude that we offer to the true God is not absorbed by God, but rather breaks against the rock of the divine self-sufficiency, redounding to our benefit. In one of the prefaces to the eucharistic prayer in the Roman rite of the Mass, we find this remarkable observation directed toward God: "You have no need of our praise, yet our desire to thank you is itself your gift. Our prayer of thanksgiving adds nothing to your greatness, but makes us grow in your grace." It is precisely because God has no need of our praise that our act of gratitude is a gift and not a poison; it is precisely because God's plenitude cannot be increased that our prayer intensifies rather than compromises our participation in the loop of grace. The solution to the Derridean dilemma is, paradoxically, a God who has no real relation to the world.

I would like now simply to hint at a theme that I will develop at greater length in the final section of this book. Love is described in the Christian tradition as a theological virtue, which is to say, a habit or capacity that comes not from the cultivation of natural potentialities but as a gift from God. This is true because love is a participation in the divine life. What I hope has become clear in the preceding analysis is that the simple Creator God is uniquely capable of love in the complete sense, since he alone can fully will the good of the other as other. As Derrida helpfully points out, love—the real giving of gifts—is practically impossible among us creatures, compromised as we are by ontological neediness, self-interest, and violence. What makes real love possible among humans is only a sharing in the love with which God loves, some participation in the divine to-be. When we root ourselves in the God who has no need, who exists in radical self-sufficiency, we can begin to love the other as he does, for our needy, grasping ego has been transfigured by proximity to the divine way of life. Without this elevation, our desire will always be tainted by finitude and sin and hence will tend toward "economic" modes of relationship.

Paul's ecstatic exclamation in Galatians 2:20, "It is no longer I who live, but it is Christ who lives in me," presupposes a liberating transformation: because the old self has given way to the Self-in-God, Paul is capable of the love characteristic of the divine to-be. Augustine states the same truth when he says that we don't truly love the other until we love him "in God" and for the sake of God. This recentering of the ego on the simple God is the only escape from the far country.

A Marion Interlude

Throughout this section, I have been relying on the Thomistic notion of God as the sheer act of to-be in order to counteract the modern understanding of God as a competitive supreme existent among existents. In the course of my discussion of creation and of the aporia of the gift, I shifted the optic a bit, focusing not so much on God in himself as on God the giver of being. Is there a smooth transition from the one angle of vision to the other, or does the move from considering God as being itself to looking at him as giver of good gifts signal a major change in the understanding of the divine? In raising this question, we move once more into the thought world of Jean-Luc Marion. The Christology section examined Marion's famous distinction between idol and icon, between that which exhausts itself in being seen and that which, in being seen, guides the eye beyond itself to what is essentially invisible. At the heart of Marion's argument in *God without Being* is the claim that the description of God as being itself stands in danger of devolving into intellectual idolatry, whereas the qualification of God as the good—as the one who gives—remains properly iconic. In order to clarify further the antimodern notion of God—specifying more exactly what God is not—it will prove helpful to follow the sinuous lines of Marion's analysis.

As a young man, Marion studied under the great Thomist Étienne Gilson, who at the end of his career had become embroiled in a controversy over the so-called metaphysics of Exodus. Following the classical tradition, Gilson argued that the self-description of God in the third chapter of Exodus—*ehyeh asher ehyeh*—effectively grounded a metaphysics of God as the sheer act of existing. But numerous biblical scholars and theologians challenged this reading, arguing that the mysterious Hebrew expression should best be rendered in a more personalist and less explicitly ontological register. Many suggested something like "I will be with you" as a more accurate translation than either the *ho on* of the Septuagint or the *Ego sum qui sum* of the Vulgate. Marion comments that even if we set aside these objections and accept Gilson's traditional ontological reading of Exodus 3:14, we are still left with the problem of determining whether this name is primary, especially vis-à-vis the privileged name of God disclosed in the first letter of John: *ho theos agape estin* (God is love).

Thomas Aquinas explicitly raised this question of primacy in his early *Commentary on the Sentences* as well as in the first part of the *Summa theologiae*, in both cases fully aware of the Dionysian claim that the divine name of the "good" (*bonum/agathon*) is higher than the divine name of "being." Of course, Dionysius stood in the Platonizing tradition, which held that the form of the good (that which gives) is "beyond the beings" which it gives, that it is like the sun in whose light all existing things are seen. But Aquinas disagrees, postulating that "the good does not add anything to being either really or conceptually" and hence that *qui est* (the one who is) remains God's highest and most proper name. He can say this because he has moved from a Platonic to an Aristotelian thought world, in which the good is not so much "that which gives" as "that which is desirable." Because the desirable is the perfect and because the perfect is tantamount to existence, *being* and *the good*, Thomas can consistently maintain, are convertible terms.

At almost the same time that Aquinas was answering this question one way, his colleague Bonaventure was answering it the other way. In the *Itinerarium mentis in Deum*, Bonaventure considers the two most sacred and mystical names of God—being and the good—under the symbolic rubric of the cherubim that face one another on either side of the ark of the covenant.[4] *Being*, drawn from the *Ego sum qui sum* of Exodus, effectively designates the unity of the divine essence and stands as the highest title of the Old Testament revelation. But *the good*, derived from the New Testament claim that God is love, signals the plurality of the trinitarian persons, each one of whom gives himself to the others in love. Lest there be any confusion about which of the names is more sacred, Bonaventure reminds us that Jesus himself, in his conversation with the rich young man, used the designation of *good* when naming God: "Why do you call me good? No one is good but God alone" (Luke 18:19). And then he makes things even more explicit: "Damascene therefore, following Moses, says that 'he who is' is the first name of God; Dionysius, following Christ, says that 'good' is the first name of God."[5]

Now I realize that this disagreement between these two doctors can seem the worst and most pointless kind of medieval hair-splitting. What precisely is at stake? Marion analyzes the issue in terms of his distinction between idol and icon. Marion shares the Dionysian and Bonaventurian concern that the name *being*, precisely as relatively comprehensible, can function as a sort of conceptual idol, exhausting the "gaze" of the mind. Evidence that this concern is not ungrounded comes from the pen of Aquinas himself. In the body of the article dealing with the naming of God

---

4. St. Bonaventure, *Itinerarium mentis in Deum*, in *Itinéraire de l'Esprit vers Dieu* (Paris: Vrin, 1990), 96.

5. "Damascenus igitur sequens Moysen dicit quod qui est est primum nomen Dei; Dionysius sequens Christum dicit quod bonum est primum nomen Dei" (ibid., 82).

in the *Commentary on the Sentences*, Thomas justifies the primacy of the title *being* as follows: "For the first term that falls within the imagination of understanding is *ens*, without which the understanding can apprehend nothing."[6] And in the later *Summa theologiae* he mounts much the same argument: "Now the first thing conceived by the intellect is being; because everything is knowable only inasmuch as it is in actuality. Hence being is the proper object of the intellect and is primarily intelligible."[7] What particularly worries Marion here is the stress on a concept that can be so immediately known, that indeed "falls" under the apprehension of the human mind, or even more alarmingly, into the imagination of the intellect. Precisely as so readily "knowable" and "imaginable," does the notion of *ens* not come dangerously close to taking on the quality of a conceptual idol? The good—that which gives—stands necessarily prior to any and all beings that may appear as its effects, and hence it remains permanently elusive, properly iconic. As we have seen over and again, Thomas Aquinas is acutely aware of the dangers of using idolatrous language in connection with God, but might we not sympathize with Marion's rather Bonaventurian worry that unless the name *being* is subordinated to the name *good* in theological speech, we will run the risk of making God an object susceptible to the too searching gaze of the mind?

There are two ways that one might attempt a response on behalf of Aquinas. First, in light of the dictum *Nemo dat quod non habet*, it seems a bit naive or disingenuous to claim that the act of giving has a clear priority over the being that is given. To be sure, divine giving is ontologically prior to creaturely being, but what is it that enables God to give if not the divine being? Even the Platonic sun gives light because it first *is* light. Further, Aquinas consistently argues that we do not see the divine being directly or with anything like conceptual clarity; we appreciate it only as it is reflected in those finite beings to which it has given rise. This means that the concern about excessive "visibility" in regard to the idea of God is unfounded. Any knowledge that we have of God, for Thomas, is thoroughly iconic, since it is mediated through visible effects (creatures) that are supersaturated with the invisible power in whom they participate. The moment theological description even hints at the creaturification or the rendering visible of God, Thomas objects vehemently.

And second, one might show that being and the good must come together in God, since God's very capacity to give in the full sense of the term is predicated upon the unique quality of the divine to-be. Though,

6. "Primum enim quod cadit in imaginatione intellectus est ens, sine quo nihil potest apprehendi ab intellectu." Thomas Aquinas, *Commentary on the Sentences*, 1, d.1, q.8, a.3 *solutio*.

7. "Primo autem in conceptione intellectus cadit ens: quia secundum hoc unumquodque cognosciblile est, inquantum est actu. Unde ens est proprium obiectum intellectus." Thomas Aquinas, *Summa theologiae*, Ia, q. 5, art. 2.

as we saw, Thomas typically opts for the Aristotelian notion of the good over the Platonic, he is not unaware of the Dionysian tradition of the *bonum diffisivum sui* and uses it, in fact, to explain the wherefore of creation. But as I made clear in the Christology section, it is in relation to the question of the fittingness of the incarnation that Thomas makes most provocative use of the principle, arguing that God, as the highest good, must give in the most generous way. Yet what is it that enables God to give in this manner if not his utter ontological self-sufficiency? As I tried to demonstrate in regard to the Derridean aporias of the gift, it is because God does not need anything outside of himself that his acts of generosity can be so complete, so unsullied and unselfregarding. Creaturely being is indeed the effect of divine giving, but divine giving is a function of the peculiar texture of divine being, the two qualities existing in a sort of circumcession.

And yet there still seems something too neat about all this; there is something that still nags in Marion's critique. One way to get at the difficulty is to wonder why, if the Old Testament name of God is the highest, we had any particular need for a New Testament name. Further, if the term that points to the unitary essence of God (Being itself) is unsurpassable, why does Christian theology fuss with trinitarian speculation? Though we should never practice a crude supercessionism whereby the New Testament theology trumps the Old, we must honor the novelty of what was disclosed to us about God in the supreme icon of Jesus Christ. The Gatherer, the Warrior, and the Lord was, above all, the One Sent. "God so loved the world that he gave his only Son, so that everyone who believes in him may not perish" (John 3:16). "For this I came into the world" (John 18:37). Jesus appeared among us as the supreme Gift of the divine Giver: "Long ago God spoke to our ancestors in many and various ways by the prophets, but in these last days he has spoken to us by a Son" (Heb. 1:1–2). He was, in a word, a gift ontologically commensurate with the Giver, "the exact imprint of God's very being" (Heb. 1:3).

This told us something that we did not know before—that there must be within the structure of the divine to-be a play of giver, gift, and giving. Prior to the event of Jesus Christ, it might have been possible to see that God, due to the simplicity of his existence, could give with unalloyed generosity to creatures, but it was not possible to see that the divine being is itself a play of generosity. That God loves can follow from the simplicity of his being and the fact of creation, but that he *is* love appears to us only through the icon of the incarnation and its display of a manifold within the divine reality. Now we begin to see more clearly: what the simple God gives with utter generosity is the giving that he is. The to-be of God is to-give, is to-be-for-the-other. We could not have grasped this by meditating on creation alone, since God does not need the world; he

might, in principle, be fully himself without his self-emptying relationship with what he has made. But in the ecstatic play of Sender, Sent,
and Sending (Giver, Gift, and Giving), we see that coinherence is not an
accidental modification of God, but very God. And with this insight, we
are ready for a final step, a meditation on the trinitarian dynamics that
obtain in the Simple One.

The God Who Is Love

It is with an understandable trepidation that I approach the question
of God's triune nature. Even after gazing at the trinitarian face of God at
the end of his journey through paradise, Dante's pilgrim can say, "How
my weak words fall short of my conception / which is itself so far from
what I saw / that 'weak' is much too weak a word to use." Joseph Ratzinger
claims that trinitarian language has much the same function as incense at
a liturgy: to obscure one's vision, precluding the possibility of clear seeing
and description. If any overeager and potentially idolatrous searcher has
managed to slip past the intellectual defenses established by the term
simple, he is definitively stopped by the puzzle of the term *trinity*.

At the same time, as we have seen, even the most negative formulations
shape, almost despite themselves and however inchoately, some sort of
positive conception. The idea of God as a trinity of persons is rooted in
the biblical narratives concerning the dying and rising of Jesus and the
sending of the Holy Spirit into the church. As such, it is the uniquely Christian account of God. Though the notion of God as simple flows, in fact,
from the event of the incarnation and the compatibility of the divine and
human natures in Jesus, nevertheless this notion has been entertained and
developed by other philosophical and religious schools. But the doctrine
of the Trinity is unarguably distinctive to Christianity. Stanley Hauerwas
has remarked that when someone invokes upon him the blessing of God,
he responds, "Which God are you talking about?" The Christian God is
the God who, in the Spirit, sent Jesus Christ for the salvation of the world.
The abstract dogma of the Trinity is the necessarily halting attempt to
indicate the mystery implicit in that narrative.

Most modern philosophical accounts of God are distinctively nontrini-
tarian. Descartes, Spinoza, Locke, Kant, James, and many other moderns
carefully develop philosophies of God, but they refer at best only occasionally to the Trinity. One of the most telling examples of this tendency
to marginalize the Trinity is Schleiermacher's treatment of God in the
Glaubenslehre. Though he treats of God across nearly one thousand pages
of text, he turns to a consideration of the three persons only in a brief
appendix at the end—and then only reluctantly, since that doctrine is not

directly related to the feeling of absolute dependency. The great exception to this general rule is, of course, Hegel, but his "trinitarianism" is tied to the peculiarities of his philosophical system and scarcely draws at all on the particularities of the biblical revelation.

The postmodern Christian theology of God that is being developed here reflects an impatience with this marginalization of the Trinity. I see in the strange symbol of the three persons in one essence the summation and intensification of all that has been said to this point about the simple, self-sufficient, and impossibly generous ground of all that is. The coinherence that God is able to achieve with created natures is rooted in the even more radical coinherence that obtains among the Father, Son, and Holy Spirit. The being-for-the-other apparent in God's rapport with creation falls into shadow when compared to the being-for-the-other that marks the very to-be of the triune God himself.

Though a fully developed doctrine of the Trinity is not explicitly presented in the Scripture, the New Testament is filled with the seeds from which that doctrine would eventually grow. At the end of Matthew's Gospel, the risen Jesus commands his disciples to spread the good news to all nations and to baptize people in the name of the Father, the Son, and the Holy Spirit. Sprinkled throughout the Pauline literature are references to the triunity of God: in the letter to the Romans, Paul reminds us that the Father has sent his Son in the fullness of time in order that we might all become his sons and daughters, and he specifies that it is only in the Spirit that we can call God "Abba" or father. In that same letter, he says that Jesus has been established Son of God by the Father in the spirit of holiness. In 1 Corinthians 12:4–6, Paul makes use of an at least seminally trinitarian formula: "There are varieties of gifts, but the same Spirit; and there are varieties of services, but the same Lord; and there are varieties of activities, but it is the same God who activates all of them in everyone." We find something similar in the first letter of John: "By this you know the Spirit of God: every spirit that confesses that Jesus Christ has come in the flesh is from God" (4:2). In some sense, the entire Gospel of John is a meditation upon the Trinity, since at its heart is the *communio* between the Father and the Son, the love that binds the Sender and the One Sent. All of this New Testament witness to the triune nature of God is summed up in the implicitly trinitarian formula in 1 John 4:16: "God is love." If love is not simply an activity in which the one God engages but rather what God essentially is, then God must be in his nature a play of lover, beloved, and active love.

The most sustained and theologically rich prototrinitarian meditation is found in chapters 14 through 16 of John's Gospel, the Last Supper discourse of Jesus. In this meandering and haunting speech, Jesus lays out the dynamics of the coinherence that obtains between himself and his Father, a *communio* into which he is inviting his disciples. The mutual implication of Father, Son, and Spirit is nowhere in the New Testament more fully explored than in the course of this farewell address. It therefore behooves us to examine it with some care.

Many commentators have noted a connection between this speech of Jesus the night before his death and the rambling farewell discourse of Moses in the book of Deuteronomy, delivered on the eve of the Israelites' passage into the Promised Land. Jesus, the new Moses, is preparing his followers for entry into an entirely novel way of being, marked by the coinherence and mutuality of the divine persons. James Alison has remarked that the old form of life ("the world" in Johannine argot) from which Jesus is calling his followers is the one conditioned through and through by enslavement to the power of death. The promised land that he offers them is a participation in the to-be of God, a mode of existence that knows nothing of the fear of death.

The discourse begins then, appropriately, on a note of reassurance: "Do not let your hearts be troubled. Believe in God, believe also in me" (John 14:1). The faith that Jesus speaks of here has little to do with assenting to propositions; rather, it is a call to existential trust, a placing of the "heart" in the care of God. The extraordinary thing is that Jesus urges that his followers have the same confidence in himself as in God. He is not simply the prophet/teacher who awakens in them the proper attitude toward God; instead, he is the object of their deepest religious feeling and aspiration. It is as though the very act of trusting in God is ingredient in a concomitant act of trusting Jesus, and vice versa. Not only are God and Jesus coequal, but they are coimplicative to such a degree that having ultimate confidence in one is tantamount to having ultimate confidence in the other. The coinherence of Jesus and God is further stressed in the next assertion: "In my Father's house there are many dwelling places" (14:2). As we saw in the Christology section, Jesus referred to the temple as "my Father's house" and identified his own body as the new and purified temple, the place where the tribes of Israel would properly gather in prayer. The Father's house, therefore, is Jesus himself; he is the place where the Father dwells, the locus of the divine *shekinah*. There are many dwelling places in him because he is coextensive with the Father's to-be, because he is a temple large enough to contain the whole of divinity. How perfectly this confirms the pastoral praxis of Jesus, which was a sustained attempt to bring people into the circle of the divine life.

When Jesus promises his disciples that he is going to prepare a place for them in the house of God, Thomas wonders how they will know the way. Jesus responds: "I am the way, and the truth, and the life. No one comes to the Father except through me" (14:5). With Balthasar, I have to insist that Jesus claims not simply to know the path (as any of the other great religious founders from Muhammad to the Buddha claimed) but rather *to be* the path, so that there is no full access to the Father apart from him. Further, he is not simply a teacher who has a particularly rich grasp of the truth or a saint who in a particularly striking way shows forth the spiritual life. Rather his to-be *is* the truth that any religious seeker wants, and his to-be *is* the life to which any spiritual person aspires. Indeed, if he were merely a human mediator of the sacred or symbolic representative of God, the statement that no one can come to the Father apart from him would be, to say the very least, presumptuous. But if being Father entails necessarily a relation to Jesus, and if being Jesus necessarily entails a relation to the Father, then the statement is perfectly valid. If, in short, the to-be of God is essentially and not just accidentally relational, then the paradoxical language of Jesus remains coherent.

When Philip presses the issue, asking the Lord to show them the Father, Jesus responds, with a hint of exasperation: "Have I been with you for so long a time, Philip, and you still do not know me? Whoever has seen me has seen the Father" (14:9). The icon of the invisible God, Jesus is supersaturated with the divine presence of the Son, who is utterly reflective of the Father's being, so that to see Jesus is to see the Son and to see the Son is to see the Father. The display of coinherence here—the Father in the Son, the Son in the Father, God in Jesus—is almost dizzying, but this is the mode of existence that the author of the Gospel wants us to see: a being-for, a being-with, a being-in-the-other.

The noncompetitiveness between God and the world that I have been exploring and insisting on is seen now to be rooted in the even more basic noncompetitiveness of the Father and the Son: "The words that I say to you I do not speak on my own; but the Father who dwells in me does his works" (14:10). The works, of course, are those of Jesus, but since Jesus and his Father are so radically coinvolved, they belong to the Father as well and function as vehicles of his presence. Recall that in the context of John's Gospel, the works of Jesus—the healing of the man born blind, the curing of the royal official's son, the raising of Lazarus, etc.—are acts of re-creation, redolent of the primal creation effected by the Father. The same being-for-and-with-the-other evident in the latter are reconfirmed and elevated in the former. The creature is most itself precisely in surrendering to the noncompetitive God, just as the Son is nothing but the reflection of the being of the noncompetitive Father.

At this point in the speech, reference is made to a mysterious third. "If you love me, you will keep my commandments. And I will ask the Father, and he will give you another Advocate, to be with you forever. This is the Spirit of truth" (14:15–17). Just a moment before, Jesus had identified himself as the Truth and as, essentially, one with the Father. Thus we find in this first reference to "the Advocate," the *parakletos*, a fairly clear prototrinitarian formula. As Jesus reflects the Father's being, so this third seems to reflect the mutuality of Jesus and the Father, since both are involved in his sending. The *parakletos*'s role is to animate the church, which Jesus, at least in the ordinary sense, is about to leave. More precisely, the *parakletos* will lead the followers of Jesus into the fullness of truth, maintaining a vibrant continuity with the Lord and hence with the Father: "The Advocate, the Holy Spirit, whom the Father will send in my name, will teach you everything, and remind you of all that I have said to you" (14:26). Once more we notice the densely packed coinherence that obtains among the three, a one-in-the-otherness into which the church itself is being invited.

The fifteenth chapter of John commences with a beautifully organic image: "I am," Jesus says, "the true vine, and my Father is the vinegrower" (15:1). The church, he insists, is made up of those who are grafted onto this vine, remaining in Jesus and sharing his life, a life that in turn comes to him from the Father: "I am the vine, you are the branches. Those who abide in me and I in them bear much fruit" (15:5). The Lord is urging on his disciples a decentering of the ego that mimics the being-in-the-other of the Father and the Son: by remaining in Jesus, they will, *eo ipso*, remain in the One in whom Jesus remains, and so the divine life will flow from the Father through the Son into the church.

When this organic relationship is interrupted, life fades: "Whoever does not abide in me is thrown away like a branch and withers" (15:6). As we have seen over and again, the loop of grace—the giving and receiving of gifts—is the key to a Christian ontology and morality. When, like the prodigal son, we turn away from the Father's love and seek to ground our lives in our own projects and desires, we necessarily wither, losing the little that we have.

To live the good life is not finally a matter of autonomy but of obeying commandments: "If you keep my commandments, you will abide in my love, just as I have kept my Father's commandments and abide in his love" (John 15:10). Mind you, listening to commands is tied closely to love on the part of the one who commands, and since love is nothing but the willing of the good of the other, the obedience that Jesus speaks of is not an alienating heteronomy but a theonomy, a surrender to the one who massively wants what is best for the surrenderer. The entire to-be of the Son is a listening to the command of the Father, a command that is nothing other than the to-be of the Son, and the creature, consequently, is meant to be nothing but a listening to the command of the Son.

This is why Jesus says, "You are my friends if you do what I command you. I do not call you servants any longer . . . I have called you friends" (15:15). This statement is, it could be argued, the climax of the biblical revelation. What was lost in the Garden of Eden was precisely friendship with God, symbolized by the easy fellowship enjoyed by Adam and Yahweh as they walked in the cool of the evening. As I have been arguing throughout this book, the original sin—a sort of preemptive strike against a threatening God—resulted in a deeply distorted conception of the human relationship with God, so that friendship devolved into fear and resentment of an alien divinity. The whole of the biblical revelation—culminating in Jesus—could be construed as the story of God's attempt to restore friendship with the human race. In the Last Supper discourse we hear the conditions for this restoration: coinherence with God, which is tantamount to an insertion into the coinherence that God is. Adam and Eve—and all of their descendants—decided, to one degree or another, that the safest and best-defended mode of being is egocentric; on the night before he dies, Jesus shows the folly of that decision. To be in such a way that even death is not fearsome is to be in Jesus whose to-be is in the Father. This is why the teaching concerning the Trinity is utterly crucial for the right ordering of one's life.

Now the Johannine Jesus could not state more clearly the fact that this risky and other-oriented manner of existing strikes most people as utterly wrong: "If the world hates you, be aware that it hated me before it hated you. If you belonged to the world, the world would love you as its own. Because you do not belong to the world . . . the world hates you" (15:18–19). "The world" is that collectivity of persons, institutions, armies, and nations predicated upon the loss of friendship with God. That network will hate the followers of Jesus because it cannot frighten them, and its success depends upon fear. Jesus is about to be swallowed up by the forces of the world, but he is not held captive or entranced by them, because he does not live in himself, and hence in fear, but rather in the Father, the power that conquers the world. Jesus wants his followers to experience that same freedom and insouciance, but, once again, it is participation in the coinherent dynamics of God's being—insertion into the loop of grace that God is—that makes such liberating detachment possible.

In the course of chapter 16, Jesus speaks again of the *parakletos*, identifying him as "the Spirit of truth" who will guide the church into the fullness of truth. This Advocate is, once more, presumed to be ontologically one with the Father and the Son. Jesus says, "He [the *parakletos*] will glorify me, because he will take what is mine and declare it to you. All that the Father has is mine. For this reason I said that he will take what is mine and declare it to you" (16:14–15). In receiving the Spirit, the church, throughout the course of its history, will take on the identity of the Son, an identity rooted, in turn, in the Father. Every saint across the centuries represents a unique living out of this fundamental to-be of the Son, reflective of the Father and made possible by the indwelling of the *parakletos*. The work of the Spirit is the making present and visible, in an infinitely variegated way across space and time, the coinherent manner of being that characterizes the Father and the Son.

In the Synoptic accounts of the Last Supper, the breaking of the bread and the sharing of the cup anticipate the divine drama that would unfold the next days. In the Johannine Gospel, the washing of the feet and the delivery of this mystical speech serve much the same function. The play between Father, Son, and Spirit, described verbally in Jesus's discourse, would become historically visible in the crucifixion and resurrection. As Hans Urs von Balthasar has emphasized, the sending of the Son by the Father reaches a sort of climax as Jesus enters into the unsurpassable spiritual suffering of Godforsakenness ("My God, my God, why have you forsaken me?") and the unsurpassable darkness and silence of death itself. In these moments the "separation" or the mutual letting-be of Father and Son becomes sacramentally apparent. However, that the Son and Father never exist apart from one another as separate beings becomes clear in the resurrection of the Son from the dead through the power of the Holy Spirit. The *parakletos* of whom Jesus spoke the night before his death is none other than the love that essentially binds Father to Son, the shared being-for-the-other of Sender and Sent. Therefore, when the Father in the Spirit calls Jesus back from death, we see that the otherness that obtains between Father and Son is not one of alienation or over-and-againstness but rather of love, willing the good of the other.

The great salvific achievement of the Paschal Mystery (besides revealing the inner dynamics of the trinitarian life) is the inclusion of the world into the to-be of God. Having gone to the limits of Godforsakenness, Jesus embodied the divine outreach to all those aspects of creation that had wandered into alienation from God. Drawn back to the Father in the Holy Spirit, Jesus effected the gathering unto God of all of those he had embraced on his downward journey. The participation in the differentiated divine life that Jesus spoke of so evocatively the night before his death is, in principle, accomplished through his dying and rising.

14

Augustine, Aquinas, and the Trinity

Augustine's Argument with the Arians

In the attempt to probe the peculiar metaphysics of the Trinity, we now leap forward, three hundred years following the composition of the Gospel of John, to the *De Trinitate* of Augustine. It is obviously far beyond the scope of this book to explore the myriad twists and turns in Christian speculation about God that took place during those intervening centuries. Suffice it to say that many a subtle mind wrestled with the seemingly conflicting data of revelation bequeathed to the Christian church by the Old and the New Testaments. On the one hand, the Shema ("Hear, O Israel: the LORD is our God, the LORD alone"), the paradigmatic expression of Hebrew faith, clearly insists on the unity of God, and on the other hand, the event of the Paschal Mystery (the dying and rising of Jesus, accompanied by the sending of the Holy Spirit) indicates, as we have just seen, a play of diversity within God. Monarchian, subordinationist, and tritheist explanations were proposed but finally rejected as inadequate to the complexity of revelation. In the wake of the Council of Nicaea (325), the great fourth-century theologians of the East—especially Athanasius, Basil, and Gregory of Nyssa—began to articulate a nuanced and carefully balanced metaphysics of the Godhead. Their work was mirrored in the West by Augustine, whose *De Trinitate* remains, by common consensus, the most masterful articulation of the rules of the language game used by Christians when speaking of God.

After laying out a number of hermeneutical directives in the first several books—including the *communicatio idiomatum*, the absolute primacy of the scriptural witness over the conceptuality of philosophy, and the correspondence between missions *ad extra* and processions *ad intra*—Augustine turns in book 5 to a consideration of a vexing logical conundrum presented by Arian challengers to standard orthodoxy. It behooves us to follow Augustine's extremely careful argument, for in the course of articulating a response to this objection, he pushes classical metaphysics into a new key, effecting a shift in the understanding of being comparable to the one effected several centuries later by Anselm and Aquinas. That Augustine knows he is moving into uncharted intellectual waters becomes clear in his opening statement in book 5: "From now on I will be attempting to say things that cannot altogether be said as they are thought by a man—or at least as they are thought by me."[1]

The argument proper begins with the observation that God is a substance or essence, indeed the fullness of being, since he says of himself, "I am." Now other things that we call "substances" admit of accidents, by which they are rendered capable of change, but God cannot be of this type, since his to-be is fully realized and hence incapable of either increase or diminishment. From this metaphysical claim follows a rule of speech, viz., that one may never predicate qualities accidentally of God or speak of God as though he were in possession of accidental modifiers.

In light of this principle, however, the Arians formulate an objection to trinitarian talk which Augustine himself qualifies as "cunning and ingenious" (*calidissimum*).[2] Orthodoxy, they say, speaks of God in an incoherent way, since it characterizes the Father as "unbegotten" and the Son as "begotten," while maintaining that Father and Son are both God and hence of the same substance. But mutually exclusive terms can be logically predicated of a substance only if they are in reference to that thing's accidental modifications. Thus one can say coherently enough that a person is both in the room and not in the room, in the measure that one is speaking of that person according to the accidentality of her existence in time: now here, then not here. Or one can say that the same man is both nude and clothed, as long as one is qualifying him according to the accidentality of his vesture: nude in the morning, clothed later in the day. But one could not claim legitimately that the same person is both a human and a dog, or simultaneously rational and irrational, since in those cases one would be speaking of him substantially. Thus, continue the Arian objectors, when

---

1. "Hinc iam exordiens ea dicere quae dici ut cogitantur vel ab homine aliquo vel certe a nobis non omni modo possunt." Augustine, *De Trinitate*, bk. 5 in *Corpus Christianorum, Series Latina, Aurelii Augustini Opera*, pars 16, 1 (Turnholti: Brepolis, 1968), 206.
2. Ibid., 208.

orthodox theologians say that the one God is both begotten and unbegotten, they must be speaking of God in an accidental way, yet, as Augustine himself concedes, it is always inappropriate to predicate things of God accidentally. What follows is that this kind of talk is incoherent, unless it is being used to describe two separate substances. But in that case, it appears as though orthodoxy has fallen into the Arian camp, since central to Arianism is the assertion that the Father and Son are indeed two distinct essences. Orthodox Christianity is therefore, it seems, caught on the horns of a dilemma: either it holds that "begotten" and "unbegotten" are accidental predications and thus that God is not absolute, or it holds that they are terms descriptive of substances and thus that God is not one.

Compelled by the exigencies of revelation and the pointedness of this objection, Augustine searches for a metaphysical category beyond the pair of substance and accident. He notices that *accident* and *modification* are names given to dimensions of a substance that can be changed or lost, as color in hair for instance, or that wax and wane within a substance, as the life of the soul. But as we have seen, none of this obtains in regard to God, who can in no sense change, develop, gain or lose. However, says Augustine, the negation of accidental predication of God does not "mean that everything said of him is said substance-wise."[3] At this moment he is speaking, from the standpoint of classical philosophy, so much nonsense, just as Anselm does in saying that God is that than which no greater can be thought, and just as Aquinas does in claiming that God makes the world *ex nihilo*.

To be sure, in regard to ordinary created things, Augustine continues, this customary either-or remains in force, but in regard to God, things get more complicated. For the Father is spoken of only in the measure that he gives rise to the Son, and the Son only inasmuch as he is generated by the Father: in both cases, the one is described necessarily *ad aliquid*, in relation toward some other. At the same time, neither Father nor Son can be named accidentally, since neither one comes into being or could ever pass out of being or develop in any sense. It is not as though the Son is "born" or emerges in an ordinary natural sense, or that the Father subsisted as Father "prior" to the appearance of the Son. On the contrary, both are, without change, modification, or evolution *ad aliquid*, being toward the other. "But since the Father is only called so because he has a Son, and the Son is only called so because he has a Father, these things are not said substance-wise, as neither is said with reference to itself but only with reference to the other. Nor are they said modification-wise, because what is signified by calling them Father and Son belongs to them eternally and unchangeably."[4]

---

3. "Nec tamen omne quod dicitur secundum substantiam dicitur" (ibid., 210).
4. "Sed quia et pater non dicitur pater nisi ex eo quod est ei filius et filius non dicitur nisi ex eo quod habet patrem, non secundum substantiam haec dicuntur quia non quisque eorum ad se

So what precisely are these peculiar nonaccidental relations? Many centuries after Augustine, Aquinas will call them "subsistent relations," since they have something in common with ordinary substances (namely subsistence or existence through themselves) and something in common with accidents (namely being toward another). They are not like ordinary accidental relations, which hover, as it were, in between substances, yet they are by their very nature referred to another; they are utterly subsistent, yet they are ordered *ad aliquid*. Another way to get at this paradox is to say that qua subsistent relations, the Father and the Son are distinct from one another, but qua substance, they are the same, so that the Father is utterly like the Son except that he is the one who gives rise to the Son, and the Son is completely the same as the Father except that he is generated by the Father. What is subsistent in the relationalities that are the Father and Son is grounded in the identical substance that they share.

A bit later in book 5, Augustine will refer to these relations as "persons," but he does so with great hesitancy, for he knows that such usage could easily give rise to the misconception that God is made up of three separate spiritual beings or centers of consciousness, or even that the one essence of God is realized according to three instantiations, much as Socrates, Plato, and Aristotle variously express the one essence of humanity. Thus, in an admirably modest spirit, Augustine comments: "Yet when it is asked 'Three what?' human speech labors under a great dearth of words. So we say three persons, not in order to say that precisely, but in order not to be reduced to silence."[5] Centuries later, Anselm, when asked to designate the nature of the trinitarian persons, replied that they are three *nescio quids* (I don't know whats). It is through the introduction of this admittedly puzzling third category, both beyond and inclusive of the standard qualities, that Augustine manages to extricate himself from the dilemma posed by the Arians: *begotten* and *unbegotten* designate neither accidents nor separate substances, but rather the sheer relations that, while remaining distinct, constitute the unitary essence of God.

Even as he insists that trinitarian language has a negative purpose, precluding by its very strangeness anything like clarity of comprehension, Joseph Ratzinger holds that it has a positive purpose as well. He formulates this positivity in terms of three propositions, the last of which is especially pertinent to the matter at hand: "The paradox *'una essentia tres personae'* is subordinate to the problem of absolute and relative and emphasizes the absoluteness of the relative, of relativity."[6] In an Augustinian spirit,

---

ipsum sed ad invicem atque ad alterutrum ista dicuntur; neque secundum accidens quia et quod dicitur pater et quod dicitur filius aeternum atque incommutabile est eis" (ibid., 210–11).

5. "Tamen cum quaeritur quid tres, magna prorsus inopia humanum laborat eloquium. Dictum est tamen tres personae non ut illud diceretur sed ne taceretur" (ibid., 217).

6. Joseph Ratzinger, *Introduction to Christianity* (San Francisco: Ignatius, 1990), 129.

Ratzinger comments that the words of the formula—one essence, three persons—are less important than the metaphysical tension that they are meant to express. Yet the formula is not simply an arbitrarily constructed string of words. While God's unity at the level of substance must be rigorously maintained, there nevertheless exists in God something like the "dialogue" or differentiation through speech presumed by the use of the word *person*. Whether in its Greek derivation (*prosopon*) or its Latin form (*persona*), *person* indicates a being *ad aliquid*, in the first case a "looking toward" and in the second a "speaking toward." But this means that both being and relationship, as irreducible and mutually implicative qualities of the divine, must be equiprimordial, flatly contradicting the Aristotelian privileging of substance (existence through itself) over relationality (existence for another).

What I hope has become clear is that this highly abstract philosophical language game serves to express the ontology implied in the Last Supper dialogue that I analyzed earlier. We saw that Jesus assumes throughout his discourse that he, the Father who sent him, and the Advocate whom he and the Father will send are coimplicated to the point of identification. Having faith in Jesus is tantamount to having faith in the one who sent him; Jesus is the truth who communicates all that he received from the Father; the Advocate in turn receives everything from the Son and will lead the disciples to fullness of truth. The clear separation of the three, and the constitution of each through something like radical coinherence, is the essential datum of revelation that Augustine articulates through a breaking/transcending of the customary metaphysical categories.

Now we are able to perceive (albeit dimly) the deepest ground for the coinherence that obtains between God and creation. God enters noncompetitively and intimately, "by essence, presence, and power," into the being of a creature, and the creature, without losing its integrity, participates thoroughly in the to-be of God. And though God is in no sense dependent upon the creature—the God-world rapport is in this sense radically asymmetrical—nevertheless there is between the divine and the nondivine a shared being-in and being-for the other. As intimate and differentiated as this relationship is, it is but a shadow of the intimacy and differentiation that are found among the trinitarian persons. As Balthasar has commented, there is no creaturely otherness, no distance of space, time, or quality, that is greater than the "distance" between the Father, Son, and Spirit, for any and all creaturely qualities merely participate in the more primordially divine reality. By the same token, there is no creaturely connection, unity, identity that surpasses the oneness enjoyed by the trinitarian persons. The coinherence in creation is but an iconic representation of the Coinherence that *is* the to-be of God.

Aquinas's Simple God Is Many

I spent a good portion of an earlier chapter arguing, on Thomist grounds, for the simplicity of God, the coming together in God of essence and existence. Following Aquinas, I asserted that only when this metaphysical quality of the divine is maintained can we speak coherently of God as the noncompetitive Creator and Sustainer of the universe. But Thomas and we (like Augustine) face a problem: the Bible rather unambiguously speaks of God as differentiated. How then can we reconcile an uncompromising insistence on nondifferentiation in God (simplicity) with an equally uncompromising insistence on the diversification of Father, Son, and Holy Spirit? To explore Aquinas's resolution of this dilemma, I will examine his complex treatment of the Trinity in the fourth book of the *Summa contra gentiles*.

As did Augustine in the *De Trinitate*, Aquinas begins his analysis with the biblical witness. Both the Old Testament and the New state that there is something like "generation" within God. Thus, in the book of Proverbs we find in reference to God "What is the person's name? And what is the name of the person's child? Surely you know!" (Prov. 30:4), and in reference to the divine wisdom "When there were no depths I was brought forth, when there were no springs abounding with water" (Prov. 8:24). And, of course, the New Testament is rife with assertions of this same intradivine dynamic: "No one knows the Father except the Son" (Matt. 11:27), and "The beginning of the good news of Jesus Christ, the Son of God" (Mark 1:1), and "Long ago God spoke to our ancestors in many and various ways by the prophets, but in these last days he has spoken to us by a Son" (Heb. 1:1–2). We cannot deny this oft-asserted datum of revelation, but, Aquinas knows, we struggle mightily to understand it, given what we already have grasped concerning the divine immutability and simplicity. In chapter 10, book 4 of the *Summa contra gentiles*, he lays out several compelling arguments against generation or procession within God. In our experience, generation invariably involves a mutation or a corruption, but neither of these can be ascribed to the immutable God; what is begotten or generated receives its nature from that which generates it, but this kind of contingency cannot be found in the utterly simple God; if the Father and Son are two separate persons yet one in essence, there must be something in them other than essence by which they are distinguished, but this seems impossible in the one in whom essence and existence utterly coincide; and if one says that what distinguishes them is relationality, this seems to name not something in itself but rather a "to something." Moreover, any relative depends upon its correlative, and any kind of dependency is irreconcilable with the absoluteness of the divine essence.[7]

Chapter 11 is one of the real tours de force in the writings of Thomas Aquinas, for he manages there to show that these extremely powerful arguments can in fact be turned back, once we understand the peculiarly dynamic quality of the divine simplicity. Throughout his career, Aquinas was interested in the question of emanation, both interior and exterior. In many ways, the whole of the *De potentia* is nothing but a meditation on the different modes of "coming forth" that occur both in God and from God as well as among creatures. And in the *Commentary on the Sentences*, the disputed question *De veritate*, and of course in both *Summae*, this issue is thoroughly treated. The opening remark of question eleven in the *Summa contra gentiles* functions as something of a summary statement of Thomas's thinking on this matter: "Following a diversity of natures, one finds a diverse manner of emanation in things, and, the higher a nature is, the more intimate to the nature is that which flows from it."[8] Despite the protestations of the process philosophers, the metaphysics of Aquinas is anything but static. On the contrary, Thomas is convinced that being—both created and uncreated—is constantly giving rise to another; what he deems worthy of investigation is the mode of emanation.

In accord with his commonsense view of things, Aquinas holds that inanimate bodies (*inanimata corpora*) hold the lowest place in the hierarchy of being. The sign of this ontological inferiority is that emanation can occur in such things only in the most extrinsic and imperfect way, as, to use Thomas's own example, fire enflames an object by being pressed to it. Moving to the next level of metaphysical sophistication, we come to plants, the most primitive species of living or self-moving things. The plant can, obviously, replicate itself in the manner of an inanimate object, but it can also effect a more interior and perfect kind of imaging, since it forms a seed within the complex of its own organic structure. To be sure, the seed falls to the earth, and only in that realm exterior to the plant itself does it come to gestation; and for this reason, we reckon the plant less than ontologically perfect. Beyond the vegetative life, we find a higher grade of existence, associated with what Aquinas calls "the sensitive soul," that mode of animation characteristic of animals. An animal is capable of a remarkably intense kind of inner replication in the measure that it can transfer the sensible species of an object from the eye or ear to the imagination and finally to the memory. What is present in the memory of,

7. Thomas Aquinas, "Salvation," in *Summa contra gentiles*, bk. 4, chap. 10 (Notre Dame, IN: Univ. of Notre Dame Press, 1975), 75–79.

8. "Secundum diversitatem naturarum diversus emanationis modus invenitur in rebus; et quanto aliqua natura est altior, tanto id quod ex ea emanat magis est intimum" (*Summa contra gentiles*, bk. 4, chap. 11).

say, a dog is practically identical to the sensed object that gave rise to it, and it is precisely this mirroring quality that enables the animal to navigate successfully through its environment. Yet even this high level of inner replication is far from perfect, since it depends upon external reality as a trigger and because it never reaches the level of authentic self-reflection: no mere animal knows itself as a knower.

Passing from the animal to the human level, we cross a quantum divide, for the human, though participating in the inanimate, vegetable, and sensitive dimensions, also possesses the peculiarly intellectual power of self-presence, making her a participant in a higher mode of existence. Following lines indicated in Augustine's *De Trinitate*, Thomas says that the human *mens* can engage in an act of self-examination through the formation of an image, which Thomas typically calls an "interior word." In this way, it effects an act of emanation that qualitatively surpasses in its completeness and interiority anything found at lower levels of being. But here too we are compelled to look higher, for even the human mind takes its basic data from the outside arena of sense and finds its highest powers of self-knowledge mediated through the work of the imagination. We are indeed spirits, but, as Rahner reminded us, we are "spirits in the world," forced to arrive at self-presence through nature and sense.

Our exploration of the hierarchy of being next takes us to the angelic dimension, a mode of being in which Thomas remained deeply interested throughout his career: the discussion of angels in the *Summa theologiae*, for example, stretches over sixteen rather lengthy questions. Thomas argues that angels possess the capacity for self-replication to a more intense degree than we, since "in them, the intellect does not proceed to self-knowledge from anything exterior, but knows itself through itself."[9] Whereas our knowledge is derived ultimately from sense experience and, in its more refined forms, developed through laboriously constructed syllogisms and acts of ratiocination, the angel's knowledge—including and especially his self-knowledge—is unmediated and luminously intuitive. This is because the angel, as a mind separated from materiality, need not filter his acts of intellection through physical organs of receptivity. What Aquinas noticed in the humble rock—a power of self-replication—is now revealed in its highest creaturely manifestation. The interior word of an angel is the most complete type of emanation, self-as-other, possible within the finite realm. But the angelic mode of is not the highest form of life, because an angel is a creature, which is to say, one in whom essence and existence do not coincide. Like any other creature, an angel derives its being in its entirety from God, and therefore, despite the intensity and immediacy

9. "In quibus intellectus ad sui cognitionem non procedit ex aliquo exteriori, sed per se cognoscit seipsum" (ibid., bk. 4, q. 11).

of its intellection, its act of knowing is not simply identical with its act of existing.

Thus we come at last to the simple God, the one whose to be is to-be. In accord with his customary *via negativa*, Thomas tells us how this unique divine emanation is not to be understood. It certainly cannot be construed along the lines of the generation found in inanimate things, which press their form into matter, since God has no matter; nor is it similar to the process by which plants and animals reproduce themselves, since no divine emanation can be separate from the divine substance: "the very Son begotten by the Father is not outside the generating Father, but in him."[10] It must be interpreted along the lines of the process of intellectual mirroring that we remark in humans and angels. God realizes the unsurpassable form of life because in him the act of intelligent self-replication is nothing other than the divine substance itself. Thomas summarizes as follows: "Since in God, therefore, being and understanding are identical, the intention understood in him is his very intellect. And because understanding in him is the thing understood, it follows that in God, because he understands himself, the intellect, the thing understood, and the intention understood are all identical."[11] Since to be God is to be to-be, every act of God is the same as God, and thus the very act by which God effects a self-othering emanation is utterly interior to God himself. Furthermore, since God is purely actual, this act by which God grasps himself intellectually cannot involve a transition from potency to act; instead, it must always be with God. And since God is perfect, the interior Word by which God knows himself must be a completely faithful reproduction of the divine knower; he must, as St. John tells us in the prologue to his Gospel, *be God*.

But the play of unity and plurality in God cannot stop at this point, since in any rational nature, including and especially God's, will must be found. For Thomas, will is a kind of function of the intellect in the measure that the understanding of the good as good is tantamount to an act of desire: knowing value as value is ipso facto to love it. Therefore God, in knowing himself through his Word as supremely good, necessarily desires that good through an act of love. But this emanation, this act of divine othering, cannot be other than God himself, since all that God does coincides with who God is. Therefore, the love that goes out from the Father to the Son (and from the Son back to the Father) must be one with the divine essence. In Thomas's words: "The being of God in his will by way

10. "Ipse etiam Filius a Deo genitus non est extra Patrem generantem, sed in eo" (ibid.).

11. "Quum ergo in Deo sit idem esse et intelligere, intentio intellecta in ipso est ejus intellectus; et quia intellectus in eo est res intellecta, relinquitur quod in Deo intelligente seipsum sit idem intellectus et res quae intelligitur et intentio intellecta" (ibid.).

of love is not an accidental one—as it is in us—but is essential being. And so it must be that God, when he is considered existing in his own will, is truly and substantially God."[12] This love of the Father and the Son for one another, which is not other than God, is the Holy Spirit.

Having displayed the three divine persons, Thomas is in a position to show, through a series of logical steps, that the play between the subsistent relations within God is not incompatible with the supreme simplicity of the divine to-be. Since God is the simple act of existence itself, God must be perfect; and if God is perfect, God must possess the full actuality of being, including the capacity to know; if God's knowledge (which cannot be other than the divine being) is perfect, God must know himself completely; and if God knows himself utterly, there must be an interior Word that confronts the divine knower as other even as it remains interior to the divine being; furthermore, if God understands himself thoroughly, he must know himself as good, but if he knows himself as good, he must love himself, and this act of self-love, proceeding from both divine knower and divine known, cannot be other than the divine essence. Thus, triunity follows from simplicity.

With this observation, we come, in some ways, to the very center of Christian revelation. The ground of being, the simple God, the Creator of all finite existence, is, in his ownmost nature, the supreme instance of coinherence. The act by which the Father knows himself is other than the Father, but the two inhere so radically in each other that they constitute one reality. The love of the Father and the Son is, in a certain sense, a buffer or guarantor of diversification between them, but at the same time it is the bond, the *vinculum*, that connects them, and more: this love is one with the divine essence, shared by both Father and Son. The one and the many are, in a variety of ways, mutually implicative at the most primordial level of being; relationship and unity are equally basic.

12. "Esse igitur Dei in voluntate sua per modum amoris non est esse accidentale, sicut in nobis, sed essentiale. Unde oportet quod Deus, secundum quod consideretur ut in sua voluntate existens, sit vere et substantialiter Deus" (ibid., chap. 19).

PART V

The Display of the Christian Form:
Ethics by Means of the Saints

15

Deontologism and Proportionalism

By far the longest of the major sections of Aquinas's *Summa theologiae* is the second, which deals with the moral life, the journey of human persons back to the God from whom they came. One could say, with some justification, that the *Summa theologiae* is really a book of moral theology with a lengthy doctrinal introduction (the *Prima pars*, treating of God and creation) and a substantial sacramental postscript (the *Tertia pars*, analyzing Jesus and the sacraments of the church). Indeed, from the late Middle Ages through the Renaissance period, the *Secunda pars* of the *Summa*—of special interest to preachers, confessors, and spiritual guides—was the most copied and widely distributed part of Thomas's *chef d'oeuvre*. For our purposes, what is most interesting is the tight connection between ethics, doctrine, and sacraments that Aquinas assumed as he composed the three sections of the *Summa*. If it had been suggested to him that a coherent account of the Christian moral life could be given in abstraction from the central creedal claims and religious practices of the believing community, he would have been, to say the least, puzzled. From his perspective, if the moral life is the path followed by those who seek God, then a moral theology that proceeds without an adequate description of God would be doomed to failure.[1] Further, if morality is a way (*via*), then a moral account that leaves aside consideration of the one who claimed to be *the* way, Christ himself, would be crippled from the start.

1. See Servais Pinckaers, *The Sources of Christian Ethics* (Washington, DC: Catholic Univ. Press, 1995), esp. 223–29.

The fundamental problem with moralities of a modern provenance is precisely this isolation of ethics from the environment of the church, from the community whose life is disciplined by certain specified beliefs and practices.[2] To begin this final section, I will analyze two typically modern philosophical accounts of the moral life—deontologism and proportionalism—and show how neither is compatible with a vibrantly imagined Christianity. Then I will attempt to demonstrate how a valid postliberal Christian morality must take its bearings not so much from abstract notions as from persons who have sufficiently incorporated the beliefs and practices of the church, namely, the saints.

Kantian Deontologism

As we have already seen, the modern philosophers were preoccupied with finding a universal form of reason, some set of convictions or manner of thinking that would unite a Europe so divided by internecine religious conflict. And we have noted that their customary procedure was, paradoxically enough, to find that universality through an examination of subjectivity. In many ways, Immanuel Kant is the prototypical modern. Just as in the first *Critique* he discovered the unifying form of reason in the a priori structure of consciousness, so in the second *Critique* and the *Foundations of the Metaphysics of Morals* he uncovered the unifying element in the categorical imperative implied in the very nature of the will. The paradigmatically modern opening line of the *Foundations* is "There is nothing on earth or heaven that could be called good without qualification save a good will."[3] Whereas Plato looked for goodness in the forms and especially the form of the Good and Aristotle sought it in the patterns of nature, Kant found it in the interiority of his own capacity for choice.

What precisely is it that makes the will good? It is its self-formation according to duty rather than inclination, that is to say, in accord with the dictates of the moral law rather than in accord with the desire for pleasure or happiness. If a moral agent acts out of a desire for pleasure, the pure goodness of her will is compromised. Thus the shop owner who treats her customers fairly because "honesty is the best policy" and not simply because it is right to be fair is acting from inclination and is hence not morally praiseworthy.

2. See the seminal work of Stanley Hauerwas, *Sanctify Them in the Truth: Holiness Exemplified* (Nashville: Abingdon, 1998), 19–36.

3. Immanuel Kant, *The Foundations of the Metaphysics of Morals*, translated by Lewis White Beck (Indianapolis: Bobbs-Merrill, 1978), 9.

Now if we press the question further, we will see that the ground for dutiful action is in fidelity to the law, and this means a complete conformity to the universal, since exceptionlessness is the mark of law. From this logical sequence of duty, law, and universality, Kant derives the first form of the categorical imperative: "That I should never act in such a way that I could not also will that my maxim should become a universal law."[4] One's resolution in a particular case must never be out of step with what any and all moral agents should (indeed could) resolve in a similar situation. Were one to deviate from this universality, one would, *eo ipso*, be operating for selfish motives, from one's very uniquely inflected inclination. Thus, according to Kant's infamous example, I would be obliged to tell a madman seeking my brother's life exactly where my brother is hiding, lest by lying in that particular case I were to legislate in a logically inconsistent manner. As many commentators have indicated, Kant, in his radical separation of duty and inclination, affects a reversal of Aristotle, for whom the purpose of the moral life is precisely the establishment through virtue of a coincidence between law and personal preference. Susan Neiman has remarked that Kant's moral theory encourages the individual actor to assume a godlike position, creating, as far as possible, a thoroughly consistent moral universe, unaffected by the inconsistencies and distortions of individual inclination.[5] Both observations point up the oddly isolated quality of the Kantian moral self, which legislates free from any connection to nature, the discipline of a community, the practice of virtue, or the consideration of consequences. In fact, Kant would interpret any such conditioning as a compromise of the autonomy of the moral ego, the self-legislation ingredient in the very idea of the categorical imperative.

Now some have seen, in Kant's second formulation of the imperative—"Act in such a way that a human being can never be treated as a means but only as an end"—a nod in the direction of a more classical understanding of the moral life. Indeed, certain Christians have interpreted it as simply an alternate formulation of the golden rule. However, what seems to be at stake here for Kant is not so much the moral obligation to love the other as the intellectual obligation to recognize the irreducibility of another godlike subjective agent who is able, through freedom, to ground his own choices. In other words, to treat another moral subject as a means would be logically incoherent.

What role does God play in all of this? Kant holds that God, construed as a heteronomous source of moral obligation, is not only unnecessary to the

4. Ibid., 18.
5. Susan Neiman, *Evil in Modern Thought* (Princeton, NJ: Princeton Univ. Press, 2002), 64–65.

moral life; but in fact repugnant to it, for the sheer autonomy implied in obeying the categorical imperative would be decisively undermined by the intervention of an overbearing external sanction. However, as a postulate of the practical reason, God—along with freedom and immortality—has a function in the moral enterprise. Obviously, a realm of liberty—outside of the sheer Newtonian determinism of the natural world—must be presumed if the moral life is to be logically coherent, but God and eternity are, similarly, required as presumptions.

Having clearly sundered duty and obligation in order to show the dynamics of the categorical imperative, Kant, somewhat anomalously, brings them together under the rubric of the *summum bonum*, the asymptotically approached ideal that energizes the moral life. Since duty and inclination are never adequately joined in this life, we must postulate both an eternal dimension in which they could conceivably come together and a being powerful enough to preside over their reconciliation. In a word, we must presuppose both immortality and God. But we notice that this postulated God exists only as part of a conceptual apparatus necessary for the support of the autonomous ego in its decisions. God is by no means the privileged object of choice, the good primarily sought by the will, or the one to be loved above all and for his own sake.

This explains why we find such a reductive account of God in *Religion within the Limits of Reason Alone*. At the very outset of that text, Kant declares unambiguously that morality, of itself, requires no support from religion but that, due to this necessary postulation of God, it leads ineluctably to the imagination of God as a supreme lawgiver. The bland Kantian interpretation of the biblical narrative as symbolic depiction of the war between the categorical imperative and inclination—which I rehearsed in the Christology section—follows from this reading of the rapport between morality and God.

What made this ethic of the autonomous self and the marginal God possible? I would urge that, once again, we direct our gaze back to the late medieval period from which modernity sprang. There is, I will argue, a clear link between Occam's nominalism and Kant's deontologism, between the collapse of a participation metaphysics and the emergence of the threatened and assertive self. Much hinges on Occam's radical reconfiguration of the idea of freedom. For the classical, patristic, and medieval traditions, freedom was correlated to definite ends and ultimately to the quest for happiness through union with the ultimate good. Furthermore, it was seen in a necessary and salutary relationship to habituation in virtue and to the disciplines and practices of a community of people sharing common values. In short, freedom was not reduced to autonomy but was seen rather as ingredient in an entire nexus of ends, conditions, goods, and activities, all centering on the desire for God. Servais Pinckaers refers to this understanding of freedom as *liberté de qualité* or freedom for excellence, and he contrasts it to the notion of liberty that emerged in the writings of Occam.

In accord with his nominalist metaphysical assumptions, Occam maintained that freedom is a self-contained absolute, a capacity to say yes or no to any end, even the supreme end of God's goodness. In accord with the more classical understanding, freedom is tightly linked to mind in the measure that the intellect proposes the ends that lure the will; but on the Occamist reading, freedom is prior to the mind because it remains sovereign in regard to anything the mind might propose. "Because the free power is capable of contrary acts, it can determine itself in any one direction or another. The will, as a free power, can will or not will any object whatsoever. If, therefore, it is capable of choosing God, by the same token, it can reject God."[6] Some of Occam's arguments for this isolation and autonomy of freedom have a decidedly contemporary ring. Because there are suicides, even among believers, it is obvious that some people who are fully aware of the ultimate good of God can nevertheless choose against that end. The same conclusion can be drawn from the fact that even those who are fully convinced that mortal sin will lead to the loss of God do sometimes choose mortal sin. Indeed, in order for heaven to be a place of impeccability, the blessed, according to Occam, have to be compelled through grace to choose the God who stands fully displayed before them, for even in that state, they could, in freedom, choose against the ultimate good. Thus, strictly speaking, the saints in heaven are less free than the denizens of earth. In the very perversity of the will, we can discern the independence of freedom.

What follows from the sheer autonomy of the will is the monadic quality of each act of freedom. Since the will is not determined by any good proposed to it or by any set of behaviors or legal prescriptions extrinsic to it, each of its movements is absolute, self-contained. Like one of Whitehead's actual entities, an Occamist free act comes into being and then fades away before another can arise. All sense of character formation through virtue is thus set aside, and all natural inclinations to happiness, truth, and goodness are bracketed in favor of the purity of the will's liberty.

There is a curious mirroring relationship between this autonomous human freedom and the autonomous divine freedom defended by Occam and the other nominalists. As we saw, when the connections between God and creatures assumed by the participation metaphysics of Aquinas fell apart (in accord with the assumptions of nominalism), the only relation possible between God and the world becomes one of will. All of this comes

6. Cited in Pinckaers, *The Sources of Christian Ethics*, 245.

to full flowering in the Kantian ethics that I have sketched: the primacy and autonomy of the will, the absolute separation between the goodness of the will and inclination, the effective marginalization of God. The freedom of indifference, introduced by Occam, became the structuring element in Kant's characteristically modern construal of the moral life.

One could argue that the metanarrative of Western modernity has been the story of progress, defined as an increase in Kantian freedom, the power of self-determination. And the principal enemies, according to this telling of the story, are the nominalist God hovering in a threatening manner over human autonomy and the institutional representatives of this God, namely, the churches. Thomas Jefferson's "pursuit of happiness" is the political expression of the Kantian moral ideal, the will able to define itself apart from external constraints, and a privatized religion is its necessary accompaniment. But an authentic Christian morality, predicated upon the more classical conception of *liberté de qualité*, cannot flourish within such conceptual and institutional constraints, for it assumes at every stage that human freedom develops precisely in correlation to, and not abstraction from, all those elements that Kant construed as heteronomous: religion, tradition, inclination, habituation toward virtue, etc. And it affirms unambiguously that the true, noncompetitive God is everywhere and at all times ingredient in the exercise of real liberty. Within an integrated Christian framework, the decision of the autonomous will is by no means paramount in the determination of ethical uprightness. Rather, moral goodness is a function of an apprenticing process by which the person is gradually won over into surrender to God and God's purposes.

Proportionalism

The proportionalist position in contemporary theological ethics is usually seen as diametrically opposed to the kind of deontologism that I have been outlining. On the standard reading, Kant puts the stress exclusively on the will, whereas proportionalism emphasizes the consequences of a concrete moral act. But there are three typically modern assumptions that these positions have very much in common: the atomistic quality of particular ethical moves, the primacy of what James McClendon calls "decisionism," and the universal nature of ethical reasoning. Like the Kantian, the proportionalist examines discrete acts, without attending to issues of character, community, and virtue. Relatedly, like the deontologist, the advocate of proportionalism concentrates upon the act of making moral decisions, especially in tricky cases, rather than upon the setting, both communitarian and theological, for the moral life. And finally, Kantians and consequentialists come together in their blithe assumption that a rational and universal ethical form can be discovered apart from the conditioning and specifying elements of the Christian tradition.

I will endeavor to make these modernisms clearer and more concrete as I lay out the fundamental moves of proportionalism, using as my guide the remarkably lucid work of the contemporary Catholic ethicist Timothy O'Connell. The starting point for O'Connell, in accord with much of the thinking marked by the Reformation and modernity, is an anthropology that rests upon a sharp distinction between the inner person and the external realm of action. Though personhood and action are always co-implicative, they can, he asserts, be distinguished. Though we are known through our actions, our identity cannot be reduced to acts, for "if you could make a comprehensive list of all the things I do, all the deeds I perform, all the thoughts I think, all the feelings I possess, you would still not have captured the being that I am."[7] The human person, O'Connell argues, is that mysterious subjectivity that undergirds and unites all the relatively superficial dimensions of thought, feeling, and action. The entire self is something like an onion with myriad layers, each one of which has its own identity but no one of which stands by itself. As we move through the levels and aspects of the human being, we pass from the most exterior dimensions that deal with the environment through the far more interior layers of "moods, emotions, and feelings," to the level of conviction and motivation, until we come to the "very center, that dimensionless pinpoint around which everything else revolves . . . the person himself—the I."[8]

In line with the Kantianism that was bequeathed to him by Rahnerian anthropology, O'Connell states that this deepest self—the I—can be known only in a highly paradoxical way. Since the person is the subject by which the external world and all of the dimensions of the self are perceived, it cannot become an object of its own investigation. It cannot, as it were, turn on itself in order to render itself objective. Thus it is known only indirectly or as that which, though implicated in every act of seeing, is never itself seen.

In light of this clarification, O'Connell maintains, we must always distinguish between the human person and the human act: the latter is capable of objective description while the former is irreducibly subjective and hence elusive. This demarcation between the "categorical" realm of action and the "transcendental" realm of being is evocative of Luther's distinction between the inner man and the outer man, of Descartes's split between the *cogito* and the sensible realm of *res extensae*, and of Kant's radical divide between the interior demand of the categorical imperative

---

7. Timothy O'Connell, *Principles of a Catholic Morality* (New York: Harper and Row, 1990), 66.

8. Ibid., 67.

and the exterior arena of inclination and temptation. And like his modern forebears, O'Connell consistently privileges the more mysterious inner self, making it the deepest ground of thought and action.

It is against the backdrop of this theological anthropology that O'Connell addresses the issue of the "fundamental stance." We make thousands of concrete, practical decisions throughout our lives, determining ourselves categorically in various ways and directions: going here rather than there, studying rather than watching television, performing an act of kindness rather than cruelty. But beneath all these moves there is a qualitatively different sort of self-determination, one that obtains at the level of the person. This is the option by which I situate my entire self in the world, assuming the "stance which gives my life direction, significance and definition."[9] This irreducible exercise of transcendental freedom is what O'Connell and his colleagues call "the fundamental option." It is not one decision among many, and since it takes place at the level of the person, it cannot be clearly known; it is not the choice for this or that object but the determination of the mode of one's subjectivity. He is quick to remind us, however, that this option is not "a once and for all reality," not irrevocable or definitive, since our experience tells us that we can reverse the most basic direction of our lives. O'Connell sees this understanding confirmed at the Council of Trent. Over and against their Protestant interlocutors, who maintained that the justified can have clear knowledge of their justification, the fathers of Trent insisted that the final status of one's soul before God remains mysterious, however thorough one's knowledge of one's categorical moral decisions.

Now what is the relationship between the fundamental option and the categorical choices that we make? The latter are the externalizations, expressions, symbols of the former: "The human person that we sense ourselves to be does not stand apart from the actions that we do. . . . The fundamental stance that gives us the identity that we so highly treasure is not to be found in a vacuum but rather is to be found incarnated in the behavior by which we build our lives."[10] Acts instantiate but by no means exhaustively express the fundamental orientation of the self, which always transcends and precedes them ontologically if not chronologically. Moreover, the fundamental stance usually becomes stronger and more clearly perceived as one moves, in the course of life, through a number of categorical decisions. The two dimensions of the self—and their accompanying modes of freedom—exist therefore in a mutually conditioning but asymmetrical relationship.

9. Ibid., 72.
10. Ibid., 74.

With this clarification in mind, O'Connell is able to address one of the more vexing questions for a theological ethics, the nature of sin. In classical Catholic moral thought, there is a distinction between mortal sin and venial sin, and O'Connell neatly resituates this demarcation in the context of his Kantian anthropology. What the church calls mortal sin—a sin that kills one's relationship to God—O'Connell identifies as a shift at the level of the fundamental stance and not, generally speaking, as a particular categorical act. It is an act of transcendental freedom by which one radically resituates one's life away from God and the divine friendship, and as such, it is never something that is performed casually, flippantly, or by accident. Rather, "as the most serious act that we can perform, mortal sin . . . must be something that occurs relatively infrequently, in a sort of peak moment of human experience."[11] Unlike categorical acts, which can become the object of conscious examination, mortal sin can never be clearly known in a reflexive way, though one can, through an honest assessment of one's particular moral choices, have a relatively good grasp of it. Were this obscurity removed, there would be no room in the spiritual life for the third of the theological virtues: "therefore the Christian truly has no alternative except to hope; there is no place for premature judgment."[12]

What then is venial sin? For O'Connell, it is "simply a human act that is not fully so, that does not come from the core of the human person and that does not involve a fundamental option."[13] We can perform acts that are wrong but that do not compromise the fundamental orientation of our lives toward God; these are sins but do not kill our relationship to the ultimate good. They take place at the level not of transcendental freedom but of categorical freedom; they are the result of a decision to do this or that but not to be this or that. On this reading, the difference between mortal and venial sin is one of kind and not merely of degree. In the moral manuals that preconciliar Catholics studied, mortal and venial sin were distinguished in accord with the "gravity of the matter" involved: if a particular act were intrinsically grave, seriously evil, then the choice to do it was necessarily serious and central. But O'Connell finds this inadequate, because he remains unconvinced that the option to perform even a gravely serious act would automatically entail a shift in one's fundamental stance or, on the other hand, that the performance of an objectively trivial act would *not* involve such a shift. This last observation is important, lest we fall prey to the misleading solution of simply placing mortal sins on the "transcendental" side of the ledger and venial sins on the "categorical" side,

11. Ibid., 92.
12. Ibid., 93.
13. Ibid., 97.

tout court. A categorical act can indeed be the expression and bearer of a fundamental option and hence be a mortal sin, though not qua categorical. The "mortal nature" of the sin is not *in* the categorical act as such but in the depth of the moral agent's self-determination.

Having explored the subjective dimension of morality—especially the closely related ideas of freedom and self—O'Connell turns to the objective, to the "world" that confronts the moral person. Following Dietrich von Hildebrand, he insists on the stubbornly objective character of *Wert* or value.[14] Above and beyond the merely subjectively satisfying (what corresponds to private taste) and the objectively useful (what allows a person to attain certain practical ends), there is the level of value, that which is simply good and worthy of reverence in itself and for its own sake. Beethoven's Ninth Symphony, Plato's dialogues, an Alpine landscape, the act of forgiving one's enemy—all of these confront the human subject as values that make an unconditioned demand, that cannot be denied or set aside because of subjective considerations. And of all the values—aesthetic, intellectual, and moral—the last is the most pressing. Though we are merely saddened for someone who cannot produce or appreciate beauty and truth, we condemn someone who fails to respond to the good. Though we admire the aesthete and the scholar, we hold up for unique adulation the saint.

In stressing this objectivity, O'Connell avoids the traps of relativism or subjectivism on the one hand and legalism on the other. Moral worth can never simply be a function of the sincerity of the agent's act of the will nor of the authority of the moral legislator. In the determination of moral quality there is always a densely objective realm with which one must reckon. Real values such as life, prosperity, truth, health, knowledge, and beauty—as well as their accompanying disvalues—confront freedom and are not its product: "Such values are not created by us, they are found by us. And having been found, they must be respected if we are to be our best selves."[15]

As they emerge in the world, these objective goods and evils, furthermore, come into complex relationship with one another, oftentimes clashing and competing. Thus, I cannot simultaneously realize the goods of being a celibate priest and raising a family, or the values of pursuing a career as a concert pianist and as a great thoracic surgeon. Further, the realization of certain goods—say fostering the psychological health of a friend—might involve the acceptance of clear disvalues, such as a rupture in the relationship or the establishment of mutual mistrust. All of these conflicted goods O'Connell refers to as "premoral" values, implying that

14. Ibid., 132.
15. Ibid., 133.

they are ingredient in every moral act in an antecedent way, that they are the "stuff" that the moral subject works with when he or she decides.

What then is a moral act? It is the willed action by which an ethical subject attempts to realize certain premoral goods and avoid certain premoral evils, knowing full well that a perfect realization of the former and a perfect avoidance of the latter are impossible. How does one assess the moral quality of such an act? One does so by making a reasonable calculation of the actual goods and evils that have flowed as consequences from it, determining as far as possible whether the values achieved outweigh the accompanying disvalues: "Actions are judged on the basis of their actual effects on human persons and on the living of human life. Or, to put this another way, actions are judged on their consequences."[16]

From this description, it follows that no act is, strictly speaking, intrinsically evil, for it seems that one could in principle find a proportionate reason to justify any particular decision, even those traditionally seen as *intrinsice malum*. Thus, stealing might be justified in order to feed a hungry family; lying might be defended on the grounds that it protects someone's life; contraception could be allowed in order to preserve a mother's health, etc. What matters finally is not the nature of the act in itself but the quality of the proportionate calculation that informs the judgment. When, in the past, theorists held that certain acts are intrinsically evil, they were, in fact, trading in moral tautologies. Thus, to say that lying is *intrinsice malum* is simply to say that the telling of an unjustified falsehood is always wrong; and to assert that murder is *intrinsice malum* is tantamount to holding that killing for which there is no proportionate reason is always to be condemned. In short, the characterization of an act as inherently wrong depends upon a rather complete moral description of the act and cannot be attempted apart from a consideration of intentions and consequences.

To be fair, O'Connell made a rather significant adjustment in this regard in the revised edition of his book. Where previously he had argued that there is no act that could be categorized as *intrinsice malum*, in the second edition he maintains that there is indeed one such act: the direct killing of the innocent. Now on the surface this appears to be but an instance of the tautological thinking that O'Connell criticized earlier—"direct" and "innocent" serving to specify the motive and circumstances that make an unjust killing unjust. But in the second edition of his text, he suggests that something more basic obtains in regard to this sort of action. The whole of the moral project centers on the maximization of goods and the minimization of evils, and these qualities are determined in the measure that they impinge upon life, enhancing it in the first instance and detracting from

16. Ibid., 203.

it in the second. Therefore, the direct taking of a life cannot be seen as simply one moral move among many but rather as an act that effectively undermines the very foundations of the moral enterprise as such. If one could find a proportionate reason for a direct attack upon life, one would be legitimizing the unraveling of moral thinking as such. There is in all of this something of Kant's suspicion that certain acts would be not so much ethically wrong as ethically incoherent, logically inconsistent with the basic structure of the moral life.

Now this sort of proportionalist program has been criticized from a number of different perspectives, and in the confines of this study I cannot begin to rehearse the counterarguments adequately. I will focus only on those that throw light particularly on the "modern" aspects of proportionalism. Much hinges on the anthropology that undergirds the system. As we saw, O'Connell purposely separates out the realms of action and person and tends to privilege the latter over the former. The transcendental person expresses himself through categorical acts but cannot be reduced to them; categorical acts symbolize the person, but they cannot exhaust him. There is a level of being that is more basic than the level of acting. But this bifurcation allows the moral subject to hide, as it were, behind her acts, maintaining a sort of *cordon sanitaire* around her interiority and freedom. Though there is intercourse between the categorical and the transcendental realms, the deepest self can nevertheless maintain his integrity even in the face of his most egregiously immoral acts, defending himself on the grounds that his fundamental stance remains unchanged, despite massive counterindications at the categorical level.

The classical tradition avoids just this sort of anthropological dualism. Aquinas remains suspicious of a mysterious transcendental knower who abides behind concrete acts of knowing or a transcendental willer who lurks behind particular acts of the will. Rather, he maintains that it is in knowing that we know that we know and in willing that we know that we will. The "I" is not an agent behind the categorical but rather that which is known and constituted through the categorical. In his writings on moral philosophy in the 1950s, Karol Wojtyla wrestled with this problem, concluding that it would be most coherent to speak not of the person behind the action but of "the acting person." Whenever someone chooses in a morally deliberate way, she is, Wojtyla maintains, opting simultaneously for a particular course of action and for the kind of person she will be, for each act inevitably shapes the moral self. Twisting the Kantian language a bit, Wojtyla refers to this self-creating capacity as "transcendental" in relation to the range of concrete choices of action, but that designation by no means implies a bifurcation at the anthropological level. We choose what to do and thereby choose who to be—and there is no metaphysical divide between the two moves. All of this implies that the "fundamental stance" put forward by proportionalists is a deeply problematic assumption. Betraying his Aristotelian-Thomistic predilections, Wojtyla much prefers to speak of the gradual formation of character through virtue rather than of a definitive choice made at the level of transcendental freedom. And if the transcendental-categorical split is unwarranted, so is the proportionalist account of mortal and venial sin that is based upon it.

Moving now from anthropology to the process by which, on proportionalist grounds, the value of a moral act is determined, we confront a number of problems. Many commentators have indicated the difficulty of making a proportional judgment in regard to premoral goods and evils that remain stubbornly incommensurable. Life, beauty, education, health, friendship, and religion are each properly basic, and none can be evaluated in terms of another. How, for instance, is one to determine whether or to what degree the loss of civilian lives in Iraq is proportionate to the good of putting an end to terrorism and assuring the safety of Americans? How is one to know whether the disvalue of embezzling ten thousand dollars is disproportionate to the value of using that money to help a child attain a high school education? Or how is one to measure whether the cultivation of an aesthetic gift is more pressing than the cultivation of a personal relationship? There is something oddly Cartesian about the desire to reduce the complexities and incommensurabilities of life to a sort of rational grid so that one could make relatively confident calculations about them. In point of fact, we make moral decisions all the time, but we do not do so on the rationalist and calculating basis presented by the proportionalists.

A second and related problem: even if we grant, in accord with O'Connell's later speculations, that there is one intrinsically evil act—one act that constitutes a sort of ethical nonnegotiable—we have to admit that the proportionalist moral field is still fairly wide open. Apart from directly killing the innocent, there is no act that could not, in principle, be justified through the determination of a balancing good. If one moral agent, having weighed the relevant premoral goods and evils, decides in the depth of his interiority that such and such an act is morally justifiable, how could another moral agent cogently disagree with him? The interlocutor could point to actual negative consequences that flowed from the act, but the moral agent could reply that he had taken those into consideration and had weighed them against proportionately good consequences. When intrinsically evil acts are relegated to the level of premoral disvalues, when the dense objectivity of the moral project is compromised, this kind of subjectivism and relativism necessarily follows.

But there is an even more basic difficulty, one that follows from another distinctively modern feature of the proportionalist program: universalism. O'Connell is eager to deny the specifically Christian quality of the ethic he proposes. Claiming the classical Catholic natural law tradition as his inspiration, he argues for a human ethic, in principle available to any thoughtful human being. Indeed, what would prevent anyone—Jew, Muslim, secularist, nonbeliever—from making rational judgments about the premoral values and disvalues that present themselves in human experience? What would prevent any moral agent of any cultural background from deciding what is concretely "helpful or harmful to real human beings"? Thus, Christian revelation adds nothing substantial to the humanist moral program, only a distinctive motivation and coloring. In regard to the contribution of the biblical revelation, O'Connell has this to say: "In the pursuit of the moral life, the primary function of biblical testimony is to assist the community in noticing and embracing its values, to challenge and stimulate the community. Anything more, any more definitive role for Scripture, is simply fundamentalism, a sort of biblical idolatry."[17] In other words, the stories, laws, teachings, and prophecies of the Scripture serve only to stir to more explicit consciousness those values that emerge naturally in general human experience. O'Connell makes this even more pointed when he insists that a life of grace is possible outside of the explicit proclamation of the gospel of Jesus: "Whosoever says 'yes' from the depths of his being to anything, says 'yes' to everything. . . . In the deepest sense of the word, they have been saved."[18]

But this cannot be right. God's definitive revelation through the Bible—the showing forth of his unique manner of being—constitutes, as I have been arguing throughout this book, a world of meaning, a new way of imagining ourselves, a matrix of thought, action, and value otherwise unavailable to us. The narratives of the exile, the giving of the law, and the entry into the Promised Land do not just clarify generic truths knowable on other grounds; rather, they make a people. The evangel of Jesus—Word made flesh, preacher of the kingdom, healer of the brokenhearted, crucified criminal, and risen Lord—does not just exemplify an abstract moral sensibility; rather, it shapes a new creation. Commenting sardonically on O'Connell's universalism, James McClendon says, "Saved in this sense without the gospel, without faith in Christ, without discipleship, without the way of the cross!"[19] In the interest of not excluding anyone from the circle of grace, O'Connell has presented a crucially attenuated version of the Christian moral program.

Both deontologism and proportionalism—in accord with their modern presuppositions—present an isolated moral subject, cut off from the

17. Ibid., 246.

18. Ibid., 105.

19. James William McClendon, *Ethics*, vol. 1 of *Systematic Theology* (Nashville: Abingdon, 1986), 53.

influence of tradition and practice, engaging in a rationalist calculus. And in both perspectives, the God of Jesus Christ remains fundamentally marginal, at best a cheerleader from the sidelines, at worst a threat to authentic autonomy. Both are therefore irreconcilable with the consistently christocentric and tradition-oriented approach that I have been arguing for. What is the ethical form that emerges from the narratives and practices centering on Jesus Christ, crucified and risen Lord? To this question we now turn.

16

The Breakthrough

In the fifth chapter of Luke's Gospel, we find an odd story about Jesus and Peter. As the eager crowds press in on him, Jesus spies two boats moored by the shore of the lake. Without asking permission, he gets into the one belonging to Peter and asks the fisherman to put out a short distance from shore. After teaching the crowds a while, he turns to Peter and says, "Put out into the deep water and let down your nets for a catch." Though Simon Peter protests a bit—"We have worked hard all night but have caught nothing"—he acquiesces, and they manage to bring in such a great number of fish that their nets are in danger of tearing. This miraculous draught of fishes convicts Peter of his unworthiness, and he falls at the feet of the Lord in penitence, but Jesus tells him, "Do not be afraid; from now on you will be catching people" (Luke 5:1–11). This seemingly simple account is another of those subtle and religiously rich icons that the Evangelists were so deft at writing. It is, of course, a picture of discipleship and mission, but it is also a depiction of the central dynamic in Christian ethics.

Let us examine the symbolic significance of the boat. For a Galilean fisherman, his boat was everything. It was his livelihood, his work, the means by which he supported his family and put food on the table. Recent archaeological and anthropological research has shown that first-century Galilean fishermen sent their product not only around the towns of Palestine but also to distant cities within the Roman Empire. So Peter's humble vessel represented his contact with the wider world and functioned, if

I may put it this way, as an instrument of his professional creativity. As such, it serves as a symbol of all that Peter can accomplish spiritually and morally through his own power, using his gifts, energy, and creativity.

Now Jesus just gets into his boat. He doesn't seek Peter's approval, nor does he solicit his permission. He simply commandeers this vessel that is central to the fisherman's life and commences to give orders. This represents something of enormous moment: the invasion of grace. Though God respects our relative independence and smiles on the work that we can accomplish on our own, he is not the least bit content to leave us in a "natural" state. Instead, he wants to live in us, to become the Lord of our lives, moving into our minds, wills, bodies, imaginations, nerves, and bones.

We find something similar in the story about Zacchaeus (Luke 19:1–10). When Jesus spots the little man up in the sycamore tree, he says, "Zacchaeus, hurry and come down, for I must stay at your house today." The house in this narrative has the same function as the boat in Luke 5: it symbolizes the natural life of a human being—about to be invaded by transforming grace. As I have been implying throughout this book, this commandeering of nature by grace does not involve the compromising of nature but rather its perfection and elevation. When Jesus moves into the house of the soul, the powers of the soul are heightened and properly directed; when Jesus commands the boat of the natural human life, that life is preserved, strengthened, and given a new orientation. This is signaled symbolically by the Lord's directive to put out into the deep water. On our own, we can know and will within a very narrow range, seeking those goods and truths that appear within the horizon of our natural consciousness, but when grace invades us, we are enticed into far deeper waters. The manner of our knowing and our willing intensifies exponentially, and we find ourselves both enraptured and overwhelmed—which explains the somewhat befuddled reaction of Peter.

This story of the graceful elevation of the human soul is told over and again in the Scriptures. Abram was presumably conducting his affairs successfully in his home city of Ur, seeing to his business and caring for his family, when suddenly he heard a voice calling him to leave everything, take his family and livestock, and undertake a journey to a promised land. This summons introduced Abram to a dimension of experience invisible to the unelevated consciousness. Whatever goals he had set for himself were trumped by the goal that had been set for him; whatever truths and goods he had endeavored to pursue were reconfigured by the divine truth and goodness that were revealed to him. Saul of Tarsus was utterly and confidently in control of his life, convinced that he was serving the living God, when a light blinded him and he was knocked to the ground. The risen Jesus spoke to him, "Saul, Saul, why are you persecuting me?"

In that moment, a good so compelling and a truth so illuminating were proposed to him that his life underwent a massive transformation. From that moment on, the things that he had pursued with such passion were seen as so much refuse; now his life was not his own but belonged to the one who had been revealed to him: "It is no longer I who live, but it is Christ who lives in me." This reversal, this decentering, this turning upside down is the invasion of grace.

Emmanuel Levinas commented that the biblical tradition presents an ethical program that is radically different from those proposed in the classical philosophies, and precisely for the reason that we have been exploring. Whereas Plato and Aristotle conduct their investigations in the nominative case—what shall I do? what goods shall I pursue?—the biblical heroes do their ethics in the accusative case. When Abraham hears the terrible voice that will command him to sacrifice his only son, he responds: "Here I am"—in Levinas's French, "Me voici." It is not Abraham who names the goods; rather he is named, "accused," by the Good. Often, especially in the writings of the great prophets, the accusing voice of God is mediated through the voices of the suffering; the widow, the orphan, the stranger, the exile make a demand on the moral self, compelling it to respond. They are not calmly proposed as moral goods worth seeking; on the contrary, they interrupt the self-absorbed reflections of the moral agent and seek him.

This biblical theme of the *bouleversement* of the self is reiterated in the doctrinal language of the Council of Trent. Nodding vigorously toward the Reformers, the fathers of Trent insist that justification (friendship with God) can never be initiated through the law or through the ordinary moral achievement of the human subject. Instead, it is made possible through the gracious opening of a new world on the part of God: "If anyone says that a person can be justified before God by his own works, done either by the resources of his own nature or by the teaching of the law, apart from divine grace through Jesus Christ, let him be anathema."[1] And as we have seen, we find something similar at the very beginning of the *Summa theologiae*, when Aquinas insists that there must be a discipline of *sacra doctrina* beyond the range of the philosophical sciences and born of grace in order to articulate the truths that have to do with salvation. To argue, as Timothy O'Connell and others have done, that Christian ethics is simply human ethics with a unique set of motivations is to miss the heart of the matter. Revelation is not a decoration to philosophical ethics

---

1. "Si quis dixerit, hominem suis operibus, quae vel per humanae naturae vires, vel per legis doctrinam fiat, absque divina per Christum Iesum gratia posse justificari coram Deo: a.s." *Decretals of the Council of Trent*, canon 1, concerning justification, in *Decrees of the Ecumenical Councils*, edited by Norman Tanner (London: Sheed and Ward, 1990), 679.

but the opening up of a context of meaning and value that revolutionizes natural morality at every level.

The great tradition has described this transformation by speaking of the inrushing of the divine life into the natural person, with its accompanying gifts of faith, hope, and love. Faith is the virtue in us that corresponds to God's opening of the door to the transcendent dimension. The knowing mind can grasp an enormous range of truths concerning the world of ordinary experience, culminating in the scientific programs of Isaac Newton and Albert Einstein and the philosophical speculations of Aristotle, Spinoza, and Kant, but this move of the mind, no matter how successful and aggressive, can never in principle grasp the inner life of God. That can only be received as a grace, and faith is the virtue by which one intellectually accepts this gift. Hope is an aspiration to a good that transcends any of the goods available within the world. It is born in us only when that supreme Good invades our souls and reconfigures them. The desire for a properly eternal value becomes an existential possibility only when the structures of this world no longer appear as ultimate. The theological virtue of hope is that inchoate, aching desire for a good that one cannot in principle understand; it is, accordingly, quite close to what C. S. Lewis names "joy." When Paul makes the peculiar remark that he finds his true citizenship—the highest manner of intersubjective flourishing—in heaven, he is demonstrating that his soul has been raised by hope to a dimension beyond that imaginable by Aristotle or Cicero.

And of the three supernatural virtues, the greatest, as Paul specified, is love, for love is the very life of God. Faith opens the dimension of eternity; hope makes us desire it; but love allows us to participate in it, even now. In heaven itself, faith will fade away (for we shall see God's essence), and hope will evanesce (for we will have attained what we had hoped for), but love will remain, because love is what heaven is. As we saw in the section on the Trinity, the essential dynamic of the divine life is being-with-and-for-the-other. The Father is constituted as Father by his sheer relationality to the Son, and the Son's very sonship is his being with the Father, and the Holy Spirit, as such, is nothing but the mutual interpenetration of Father and Son. To be God is therefore to be love, the willing of the good of the other.

Further, creation, as we saw, cannot be understood as an expression of divine neediness, since God, in principle, can need nothing. It must be conceived as an exercise born of the sheerest desire to be for the good of the other, an overflow therefore of the trinitarian love. The theological virtue of love is a participation in this uniquely divine manner of being and acting. In the Sermon on the Mount, Jesus tells his followers: "Be perfect, therefore, as your heavenly Father is perfect" (Matt. 5:48). The perfection that he urges—which includes a radical love of enemies, the practice of nonviolence in the face of aggression, the refusal to judge one's brothers and sisters, and an embrace of poverty, meekness, and simplicity of heart—is not desirable or even possible within a natural framework. The form of life outlined in the Sermon on the Mount would strike Aristotle as excessive and irrational—and that is just the point. Its viability and beauty will emerge only when one's mind, will, and body have been invaded and elevated by the love that God is. This is not to say that the natural moral excellences perceived by Aristotle and other philosophers are invalidated by grace; as we have seen in other contexts, the invasion of the sacred does not overwhelm or undermine the secular. But it does indeed transfigure it. This transfiguration is the effect of love, working its way through the moral self.

John Henry Newman offers a very helpful illustration of this relationship in *The Idea of a University*. Throughout the lectures that make up that text, Newman holds out the educational ideal of his beloved Oxford, especially its manner of cultivating a liberal or philosophical habit of mind. By this he means the intellectual capacity to see the whole of knowledge—how all the branches of learning relate to one another in a mutually illuminating and conditioning way—in complete abstraction from considerations of practicality and utility. This type of knowledge, he argues, has a bearing as well on morality, inasmuch as it tends to make the one who possesses it fair, balanced, elevated, and loath to associate with people of low mind and bad habits. In a word, liberal education produces the "gentleman," whom Newman memorably defines as "one who never inflicts pain."[2] Broad in his interests, refined in his sensibilities, the university-educated gentleman "avoids whatever may cause a jar or a jolt in the minds of those with whom he is cast. . . . He is tender toward the bashful, gentle toward the distant, and merciful toward the absurd . . . He guards against unseasonable allusions, or topics which may irritate . . . He is never mean or little in his disputes, never takes unfair advantage . . . He is patient, forbearing and resigned."[3]

Now none of this is to be despised, for such is the quality of character praised by the philosophical mind and possessed by some of our greatest heroes. Nevertheless, Newman admits that this gentlemanly form can be present in a St. Francis de Sales or a Lord Shaftesbury, in a Reginald Cardinal Pole or an Edward Gibbon, proving that it does not constitute in itself the life of holiness. Indeed, Basil the Great and Julian the Apostate were fellow students at the Athenian schools, where liberal education was fully on offer, and the first became a saint and the second a fierce

2. John Henry Newman, *The Idea of a University* (Notre Dame, IN: Univ. of Notre Dame Press, 1986), 159.
3. Ibid.

persecutor of the church. The inrushing of faith, hope, and love—the life of Jesus within us—can so transfigure the natural moral form that the authentic saint is anything but gentlemanly, moderate, and refined in his manner, anything but tolerant and unwilling to inflict pain. One only has to think of Francis of Assisi, Joan of Arc, Augustine, Jerome, and Paul the apostle to see the truth of this claim. It is this difference that I find fascinating, this added element that transforms the naturally good person into a friend of God.

Thomas Aquinas assumes this difference throughout his account of the moral life. Though a superficial glance at the second part of the *Summa* might lead one to conclude that Thomas is nothing more than a careful medieval Aristotelian in his ethics, a more attentive reading reveals that he is, in fact, a master of the Christian life. Aquinas readily utilizes the Aristotelian structure of the natural virtues and vices, absorbing thereby much of the wisdom accrued by the classical moral tradition, but what interests him above all is the manner in which the virtues are transfigured by the addition of the theological virtues of faith, hope, and love as well as the infused moral virtues. Under the influence of grace, ordinary courage becomes the boldness of the martyr, ordinary temperance becomes the chastity of the monk, ordinary justice becomes the poverty of the ascetic mendicant, and ordinary prudence becomes the canny attunement to love characteristic of the saint.

This transfiguration, born of the breakthrough of grace into one's life, is the center of his attention, and I want to make it the center of my attention in the remaining chapters of this book. To make clear the essence of the Christian moral life, it is not sufficient to remain, in the modern mode, at the level of abstract exposition and rational calculus. Nor is it sufficient to remain, in the classical manner, at the level of natural moral excellence. We must rather look to concrete exemplars of the life of grace, the people whom the church recognizes as saints. Thereby we see the good life in its densely textured facticity; we see the dynamics of grace on iconic display. Just as Jesus is not made real to us except through textured, iconic narrative, so the moral life is not made vivid except through a similar narrativity. We can *see* the form of Christian ethics only by looking, finally, at those lives that exemplify it across time and in the face of obstacles. Our determination of what we ought to do depends utterly on our determination of who we ought to be. And in the Christian context, that means being a saint.

Therefore, I am now going to offer sketches of the lives of four saints: Edith Stein, Thérèse of Lisieux, Katharine Drexel, and Mother Teresa of Calcutta. I will present Stein as the embodiment of elevated courage, Thérèse as the model of elevated prudence, Drexel as the example of elevated justice, and Mother Teresa as the archetype of elevated temperance. There is no way, obviously, that I can present even barely adequate biographies of these complex women in the space available. What I will offer, instead, are iconic descriptions of each, concentrating on the manner in which the love of Jesus (taking the genitive in both the subjective and objective senses) transfigured a natural virtue into something properly supernatural. I chose these four relatively contemporary figures (only Thérèse died before the twentieth century) in order to make the portraits more compelling to a twenty-first-century audience. It is far too easy to imagine the saints as distant and largely legendary characters. Of these women, however, we have extensive records, writings by and about them that can be critically examined, and perhaps most important, numerous photographs that bring them vividly to the imagination. In showing how these "gentlewomen" became saints, I hope to demonstrate the form of the Christian ethical life as it displays itself dynamically.

17

Edith Stein

Elevated Courage

For the classical tradition that Aquinas inherited, courage (*fortitudo*) is the virtue that enables a person to resist those fears that would prevent him from fulfilling the demands of reason. The performance of the morally right act is relatively easy when it meets no opposition either from within the agent himself or from the external environment. But there are times in the course of life when we are compelled by conscience to take a particular action even though some threat, perhaps mild, perhaps grave, looms over its performance. To do the right thing would result in the loss of one's job, or the harsh criticism of one's peers, or in the limit case, the forfeit of one's life. The *virtus* by which a moral subject is able to face down those fears is courage.

Now what happens when this ordinary or natural courage is transfigured through the inrushing of grace? It becomes a moral resistance of fear, motivated and informed by the love of Christ which the agent has received. I use the genitive here in both a subjective and an objective sense, indicating that there is both a supernatural motivation for the person's courage (love for Christ) and a supernatural power or form to it (Christ's own love now infused in the person). The virtuous soldier willing to face death on the battlefield becomes the soldier of Christ; the martyr accepts death rather than denying the Lord.

What should become clear, even from this sketchiest of introductions, is that a virtue such as courage really becomes intelligible only in the measure that it is displayed biographically. What do the facing, resisting, and conquering of fear out of love for Christ *look like*? That question cannot, as I've suggested, be answered abstractly through the presentation of ideas; it can answered only iconically, through the display of a living form. Accordingly, here I present, however inadequately, an icon of a contemporary martyr: the Carmelite mystic and scholar St. Edith Stein, Sr. Teresa Benedicta a Croce.

Edith Stein was born October 12, 1891, in Breslau, a town situated today in Poland (Wroklaw) but then part of the German empire established, twenty years before, by Otto von Bismarck. She was the seventh and youngest of child of pious Jewish parents. Her birthday was the highest of the Jewish holy days, the Day of Atonement, a distinction never lost on her or her family. In a curious way, this mark of providence would provide a hermeneutical key to her life and mission as a Christian: she would come to see herself as a sacrificial victim, identified with Christ in his work of redemption.

Edith's father ran a fairly successful lumber company, which he had inherited some years before his youngest daughter's birth. In July 1893, while on a tree-inspecting tour in a forest not far from his home, Herr Stein suffered a stroke and died by the side of the road. This wholly unexpected death, when Edith was only a child of two, shocked her family and forced Frau Stein to adjust her life radically, for suddenly there was no breadwinner for her flock of children. Through sheer willpower, she set her mind to master the details of the lumber business (about which she knew practically nothing) and despite enormous obstacles managed to keep it afloat and even, in time, to prosper. In her extraordinarily detailed autobiography, *Life in a Jewish Family*, Edith recounts: "Gradually, step by step, she [Frau Stein] succeeded in working her way up. Even just to provide adequate food and clothing for seven children was no simple matter. We never went hungry; but we did have to accustom ourselves to the utmost in simplicity and thrift."[1] This obvious *fortitudo*—moral tenacity in the face of difficulty—was a virtue that Frau Stein would pass on to her youngest child.

Like Thérèse of Lisieux, the young Edith was treated by her large family like "a cross between a fairy-tale princess and a porcelain doll." Hopelessly spoiled, she would fly into tantrums when the least of her demands was not immediately met. She recalls her earliest memory thus: "I can see myself standing before a big white door, drumming on it with clenched

---

1. Edith Stein, *Life in a Jewish Family, 1891–1916*, translated by Josephine Koeppel (Washington, DC: ICS Publications, 1986), 42.

fists and screaming because my elder sister was on the other side, and I wanted to go to her."[2] Though the childish self-centeredness would leave her in time, the determination in the face of obstacles—the tendency to pound on doors professional, intellectual, and spiritual—would remain with her all her life. When she was still quite young, her elder brother Paul began reading to her regularly from the great works of German poetry and literature, thereby inaugurating her love affair with words. So precocious was she in this regard that her sister Erna could make the astonishing claim that Edith "began to get a grasp of literature when she was between four and five years old."

Along with her literary apprenticeship, Edith was being introduced by her mother into the thought and practice of the Jewish faith: "among the most important events of life at home, aside from the family feasts, were the major Jewish High Holy Days."[3] Though her older children did not seem particularly interested in carrying on the traditional rituals, Frau Stein always performed them with great devotion, and this tenacity in the faith deeply impressed her youngest child. One of the first lessons that Edith received in the theology of grace came when her mother shared with her what she took to be an effective proof for God's existence: "After all, I can't imagine that I owe everything I've achieved to my own ability." Commenting on this statement many years later, her daughter would say, "This of course was correct."

When Edith was passing through the early years of her education, she began to cultivate a sense that she was destined for greatness: "In my dreams I always foresaw a brilliant future for myself. I dreamed about happiness and fame, for I was convinced that I was destined for something great and that I did not belong at all in the narrow, bourgeois circumstances into which I had been born." It became apparent to her that this ambition would be fulfilled in the academic arena, where she was already showing significant prowess: "At the beginning of each new school year, I greedily devoured the new textbooks for literature and history. . . . I loved to write compositions; they enabled me to include some of the thoughts which occupied my mind."[4]

The conviction that she would achieve intellectual distinction coincided with a loss of the faith that her mother had so assiduously endeavored to plant in her. Utterly beguiled by the power of reason, Edith ceased to believe in God when it became apparent to her that she could not con-clusively demonstrate God's existence through logical means. Though she continued to attend synagogue services with her mother, she did so out

2. Ibid., 54.
3. Ibid., 236.
4. Ibid., 79.

of family obligation and with no sense of faith or devotion: "Deliberately and consciously, I gave up praying."[5]

Edith excelled in her studies at the *Gymnasium*, specializing in German literature and psychology. Her mind was not only refined and extraordinarily well informed but also also tenacious, with something of Wittgenstein's uncompromising passion for the truth: "My decisions arose out of a depth that was unknown even to myself. Once a matter was bathed in the full light of consciousness and had acquired a definite form in my thoughts, I was no longer to be deterred by anything; indeed I found it an intriguing kind of sport to overcome hindrances which were apparently insurmountable."[6] She usually found herself at the head of the class, though once she was denied the top academic prize, which she had clearly merited, due to the barely disguised anti-Semitism of one of her teachers—a chilling adumbration of fiercer persecutions to come.

Upon graduation from the *Gymnasium*, she commenced her studies at the local university of Breslau, continuing her concentration on *belles lettres* and psychology. This latter interest led her to the works of Edmund Husserl, the founder of the phenomenological school that was beginning to attract the best minds in Europe. The confrontation with Husserl would change Edith's life. Poring over the dense pages of the *Logische Untersuchungen*, she became a philosopher and an adept of the phenomenological method, which appeared to heal the rupture between the subjective and the objective bequeathed to Western philosophy by Kant. The detached, analytical, and observational cast of her mind was especially suited to the Husserlian style, and she was soon seized with the desire to study with the leading thinker of the age. She burned to leave the comparative backwater of Breslau and to pursue her research at the University of Göttingen, where Husserl and his circle were ensconced. Many warned her that, as a woman and a Jew, she would never be able to rise very high in the world of academe, but the little girl who had pounded her fists insistently on the door had grown into a woman who was not easily dissuaded from a goal she sought.

Edith arrived in Göttingen in 1913 and discovered a rarefied universe of natural beauty and deep intellectual culture. One of the most lyrical passages in her autobiography describes that time and place: "Dear Göttingen! I do believe only someone who studied there between 1905 and 1914, the short flowering time of the Göttingen school of Phenomenology, can appreciate all that the name evokes in us. . . . I was twenty-one years old and looked forward full of expectation to all that lay ahead."[7]

5. Ibid., 148.
6. Ibid., 152.
7. Ibid., 239.

She was rather quickly introduced to the philosophers who constituted Husserl's immediate circle, including Siegfried Hamburger, Hans Lipps, Dietrich von Hildebrand, Max Scheler, and Adolf Reinach. With Reinach, a generous and charming philosopher, she cultivated a close personal relationship, and with Lipps, a young and handsome man, she rather chastely and distantly fell in love. Through Reinach's ministrations, Edith was ushered finally into the presence of "the Master," Husserl himself, who was impressed by the seriousness of this young woman who had worked her way through both volumes of the *Logische Untersuchungen*. Presently, Edith joined in the regular conversations and discussions with the phenomenological group, enjoying the lively give-and-take between the Master and his disciples.

So taken was Husserl with Edith's abilities that he eventually asked her to work with him as an assistant, helping to organize his often disparate notes and jottings. Though deeply flattered at first by this sign of approbation, Edith was soon disappointed that Husserl saw her mind merely as a useful tool and not as a gift to be cultivated for its own sake. One of Stein's more penetrating biographers, Waltraud Herbstrith, has commented rather bitterly, "There were professors who were good to their students but Husserl was not. He just liked using Edith's philosophical gifts to help himself."[8]

Despite these personal frustrations, Edith pressed ahead, with her customary singleness of purpose, toward the achievement of her doctorate. She chose as her topic a theme that was implicit in most of Husserl's major writings but that had not received from the Master an adequate treatment: the problem of empathy, or the feeling-with another knower that must be ingredient in any complete act of intellection. The strain that went into the composition of this paper nearly broke Edith emotionally and intellectually: "This excruciating struggle to attain clarity was waged unceasingly inside me, depriving me of rest day and night. At that time, I lost the art of sleeping and it took many years before restful nights were granted to me again. Little by little I worked myself into a state of veritable despair."[9] So acute became her psychological disequilibrium that she "could no longer cross the street without wishing she would be run over by some vehicle."[10] We must keep in mind that, as she was writing a thesis on an extraordinarily complex topic, she was also preparing for her general examinations in philosophy and striving to master the Greek language. The depression and anxiety that she so vividly describes are

8. Quoted in Joseph M. Malham, *By Fire into Light: Four Catholic Martyrs of the Nazi Camps* (Louvain, Belgium: Peeters, 2002), 212.

9. Stein, *Life in a Jewish Family*, 277.

10. Ibid., 278.

fairly common symptoms among serious students at that highest level of academic intensity. What is perhaps more remarkable than her suffering is that she persevered, passing her examinations with the highest honors and managing to complete her dissertation by early 1915, less than two years after arriving in Göttingen.

A final challenge was to get the distracted Husserl to read the paper. She pressed and pressed (again that little girl rapping on the door comes to mind) until finally the Master relented and, in her presence, read the thesis through, commenting approvingly if a tad condescendingly, "You are a very gifted little girl."[11] By most accounts, Husserl, despite the patronizing remark, indeed saw that his young student had, with great originality, developed an important but overlooked theme in phenomenology. Soon after she completed her doctorate, Husserl received an appointment at the University of Freiburg in Breisgau, and the Master asked Edith to accompany him there as his assistant.

However, before taking up her intellectual responsibilities with Husserl, Edith felt a moral summons. The Great War, which had commenced in August 1914 and had been met with enthusiasm by most patriotic Germans, including Edith herself, was now well into its sixth month. Edith wanted to participate, according to her abilities, in the war effort, and so she signed on for training as a practical nurse. In the spring of 1915, she was called to service at a lazaretto—a hospital for infectious diseases—in the Moravian sector of the Austro-Hungarian Empire. There she cared for soldiers suffering from dystentery, cholera, spotted fever, and typhoid, oblivious to the dangers both physical and moral that accompanied such close contact with her patients. Her sister Erna remembered: "There, as everywhere else, she was engrossed wholeheartedly in her work and was equally popular with wounded soldiers, her colleagues, and her superiors."[12] It appears as though the young woman who moved so effortlessly in the salons of the Göttingen phenomenologists was able with equal aplomb to minister to the commonest of people in the most disagreeable of circumstances.

What began to press upon her during this period was the demand of love, coming, as Levinas would have it, from the suffering face of the other: "I got the impression that the sick were not used to getting loving attention and that volunteer helpers therefore could find endless opportunities to show their own compassion and love of neighbor in these places of suffering."[13] The peacefulness that Edith demonstrated in her work among the very sick in the field hospital was, of course, a species of courage, and

11. Quoted in Malham, *By Fire into Light*, 216.
12. Quoted in ibid., 70.
13. Stein, *Life in a Jewish Family*, 298.

it foreshadowed the peacefulness of Sr. Benedicta of the Cross, moving among her fellow Jews in the squalor of the train conducting them to the death camp.

After six months of service in the hospital, Edith returned to Freiburg and her only mildly satisfying intellectual work with the Master. As he had in Göttingen, Husserl continued to treat Edith more as a glorified secretary than as a real philosophical colleague, and this frustrated her enormously. During this period, Edith also conducted a series of introductory courses in phenomenology, which she referred to playfully as a "philosophical kindergarten." Many who followed these lectures later testified to their enormous helpfulness, but they certainly did little to help the teacher's career or to hone her philosophical acuity. They were offered out of a genuine concern to help those who were bent on following the same intellectual path that Edith herself had embarked upon.

In November 1917, Adolf Reinach, the engaging philosopher who had so charmed Edith upon her arrival in Göttingen, was killed in action at the western front. This tragedy would signal a major shift in Edith's interior life. She visited Reinach's widow, Anna, expecting to find a thoroughly broken woman, and instead she found someone suffering but fundamentally at peace. This serenity, she learned, was the product of Anna's Christian faith. Strangely, it was Edith, who had also felt Reinach's loss very deeply, who was comforted by his faith-filled widow. "It was my first encounter with the Cross and the divine power that it bestows on those who carry it. For the first time, I was seeing with my very eyes the Church, born from her Redeemer's sufferings, triumphant over the sting of death. That was the moment my unbelief collapsed and Christ shone forth."[14]

We have to attend rather closely to this crucial text. The unbelief that Edith had cultivated from the age of thirteen had been under assault for some time, mainly due to the religiosity of many in the phenomenological circle. Scheler, von Hildebrand, and Reinach were all devout Catholics, and the Master himself was a Lutheran. That men of such penetrating intellect could be enthusiastic Christian believers had begun to convince Edith that her youthful rejection of religion as irrational was perhaps unjustified. Further, the phenomenological method, which urged a detached openness to any and all phenomena, had made the phenomenon of religious faith—pilloried by many modern thinkers as infantile or retrograde—available to serious intellectual analysis. But it was the encounter with Anna Reinach—concrete, vivid, emotionally rich—that caused the rickety edifice of Edith's atheism to crumble. It is significant too that she sensed Anna's faith not so much intellectually as viscerally and existentially, as a power

14. Quoted in Waltraud Herbstrith, *Edith Stein: A Biography* (San Francisco: Ignatius, 1992), 56.

capable of conquering the fear of death. It was the cross as a source of courage that especially affected her.

Just after her visit with Anna Reinach, Edith had another experience that served to awaken faith. While strolling through the old section of Frankfurt with one of her friends, Edith chanced upon the cathedral. The two women entered the building as tourists, intent upon admiring the architecture. Edith spied a woman, fresh from her rounds of shopping, kneeling in the empty church, lost in prayer. She had certainly seen people at prayer during synagogue services or around the seder table at home, or at Protestant worship, but she had never seen anything like this: "This was entirely new to me. . . . Here was someone interrupting her everyday shopping errands to come into this church, although one other person was in it, as though she were here for an intimate conversation. I could never forget that."[15] As we shall see, silent adoration of the Eucharistic Christ would become essential to Edith's spirituality. Her fascination with the Presence—how like the phenomenologist's deep attention to the object of contemplation—commenced that day in Frankfurt.

Edith's conversion was not like Paul's sudden transformation on the road to Damascus; it was more like Newman's or Augustine's—gradual, interior, accompanied by much intellectual wrestling. In the years following the conversation with Anna Reinach, Edith continued to teach and to work with Husserl, but she was also trying to understand the meaning of Christian faith, which had begun to fascinate her. In the summer of 1921, she spent time at the home of her Göttingen friends Conrad and Hedwig Conrad-Martius in Bergzabern. While her hosts were away one evening, Edith went hunting for a book in their expansive library, hoping simply to find something with which to pass the time. She stumbled upon one of the classics of the Christian spiritual tradition, *The Life of Saint Teresa of Avila, Written by Herself*, the autobiography of the sixteenth-century Carmelite reformer and mystic. In the course of that one night, she finished the lengthy book and declared simply, "This is the truth!"

What is was precisely in the text of Teresa that so galvanized Edith Stein it is impossible to say. When pressed to explain her conversion, she would typically reply, "Secretum meum mihi" (this secret belongs to me). Some speculate that it was the kinship she felt with her brilliant and forceful predecessor, a woman able to make her way through sheer determination in a man's world. Or perhaps it was the mysticism of Teresa that served to complement Edith's rather austere intellectualism. Maybe the best explanation is the one offered by Carmelite Sister Maria Amata Neyer: "For years Edith had looked for the truth philosophically as a scholar. It was the truth of things, the things themselves, the objects. Now in Teresa

15. Stein, *Life in a Jewish Family*, 401.

of Avila she was filled with the truth of love that is not knowledge but relationship."[16] At any rate, the reading of Teresa's *Life* was the moment when all of the strands came together, all of the converging probable arguments for faith coalesced, and Edith was convinced. The morning after this experience, she bought a missal and a copy of the Catholic catechism.

With her customary concentration and singleness of purpose, Edith devoured these texts, just as she had once mastered the *Logische Untersuchungen*. Within days she felt confident enough to attend Catholic Mass and entered with relative ease into its rhythms and rituals. Undoubtedly, her experience as a worshiper in the synagogue helped to acclimate her to the liturgy. After the service, she approached the priest in the sacristy and asked to be baptized. Quite likely surprised by this peremptory request, he asked how long Edith had been receiving instruction. When told, he was understandably skeptical, but she challenged him, "Prufen-Sie mich!" (test me!). The little girl who had pounded impatiently on the door, the young woman who had held her own in the disputations of the phenomenological circle was once more resisting obstacles, showing her stubbornness and *fortitudo*. Astounded by her profound understanding of the Catholic faith, the priest agreed, and Edith, after a brief period of further instruction, was baptized on January 1, 1922. In the preconciliar Catholic calendar, that day was the feast of the circumcision of Jesus, the first spilling of the Savior's blood. Joseph Malham remarks, "For Edith, who was to lose her life in the Shoah twenty years later, the date of her spiritual birthday was as portentous as her human birthday on the Day of Atonement."[17] She knew instinctively that her Christian life would be bound up with the work of redemptive suffering.

The first great challenge she faced after her conversion was to tell her pious Jewish mother, to whom she was tied by such powerful emotional bonds, that she had joined the religious community that for much of European history had been a persecutor of Jews. Though she loved her daughter intensely, Frau Stein could not accept this change, and despite Edith's prayer and constant attention to her, she never really reconciled herself to it. Edith's sisters reported that in her final illness, Frau Stein "constantly brooded, wondering why her youngest daughter had forsaken her." This resistance on the part of her mother was heartbreaking to Edith, and her perseverance in the faith, despite the pain it caused the woman she loved most in the world, was another telling sign of *fortitudo*.

A month after her baptism, Edith was confirmed by Ludwig Sebastian, the bishop of Speyer, and it was Sebastian's vicar general, Josef Schwind,

16. Maria Ruiz Scaperlanda, *Edith Stein: St. Teresa Benedicta of the Cross* (Huntington, IN: Our Sunday Visitor, 2001), 80.

17. Malham, *By Fire into Light*, 226.

who became Edith's spiritual director. From the time of her conversion under the influence of Teresa of Ávila, Edith desired to become a Carmelite, but Schwind rather firmly advised against this, convinced that, with her great intellectual gifts, she was called to more of an active, apostolic form of life. Through Schwind's intervention, she accepted a position in Speyer, teaching at St. Magdalena's, a teachers' training academy run by the Dominican sisters. Here Edith commenced to live an essentially religious life, taking a room adjacent to the nuns' quarters, praying the daily office in common with them, and assisting at Mass. Patricia Hempl comments, "In effect, she managed to mimic a monastic life years before her entrance into Carmel."[18]

At this point we begin to remark the transition from nature to grace, the effects of the breakthrough, the quality of the elevation. Edith's moral commitment—her love of family and friends, her fierce devotion to truth, her willingness to serve others as a wartime nurse, and her *fortitudo* in the face of obstacles interior and exterior—was, prior to her baptism, on clear display. She was, in the language of Aristotle and Aquinas, a person of rather impressive natural virtue. But now, grace would build on this foundation, or better, it would transform and transfigure it, raising it to a new pitch. To this point in her life, Edith had been relatively in control, but through the ministrations of Teresa of Ávila, Anna Reinach, the anonymous woman kneeling in the Frankfort cathedral, and many others, Jesus had gotten into her boat, and now he would be in control. Her love, passion, devotion, and courage would now appear in a new light and be oriented to a new *telos*.

This change is perhaps most immediately apparent in Edith's life of prayer. Despite her extremely hectic teaching schedule, she would spend hours in silent prayer, kneeling motionless before the Blessed Sacrament, sometimes passing an entire night in such devotion. So impressed were the Dominican sisters by her prayerfulness that they "allowed her to place a chair off to the side of the Altar, hidden from the community as well as the congregation, in the sanctuary of the church. There, tucked away behind a column, Edith could sit or kneel for hours either absorbed in the Mass or private prayer."[19] The presence of Jesus in the Eucharist would become the organizing center of her life, the beginning and end of all her activities.

In the years immediately following her conversion to Catholicism, Edith taught full time at St. Magdalena's, but she also commenced a career as a scholar and lecturer, traveling throughout the German-speaking world, addressing issues in phenomenology, Catholic theology, and the role of

18. Quoted in Scaperlanda, *Edith Stein*, 84.
19. Malham, *By Fire into Light*, 230.

women in church and society. During this period, she met Fr. Erich Przywara, a Jesuit writer who was already exercising a powerful influence in European theological circles. He encouraged her to work on two serious translation projects: the rendering into German of John Henry Newman's *Letters and Journals* and also of Thomas Aquinas's *Quaestiones disputatae de veritate*. The latter task especially would have a significant impact on Edith's thought. She knew that many scholastically trained philosophers had found Husserlian phenomenology attractive, but this was her first real immersion in the thought of the greatest of the scholastics. Poring over the Latin text of Aquinas, devoted to the very epistemological and psychological issues that Husserl found so compelling, she began to discern a way to bring together Thomism and phenomenology. What they principally shared in common was a deep devotion to the objectivity of truth: the Husserlian adage *Zu den Sachen selbst!* (To the things themselves!) was quite congruent with Thomas's stress on the knowability of reality outside of the mind. One of the most important differences between the two thinkers, she observed, was that for Thomas the quest for truth finally butts up against the unknowability of the Truth itself and thus becomes transfigured into a kind of attentive passivity under the influence of grace. This play between curiosity and docility at the epistemological level mirrors precisely, she found, the relation between nature and grace at the moral level.

Though her spiritual advisers continued adamantly to recommend that she stay active in the world of academe, Edith burned with a desire to enter the religious life. She was especially attracted to the Carmelite form, which had nurtured her spiritual hero Teresa of Ávila. So ardent became her interest in the contemplative life that she commented to a friend in 1932, "I notice that, actually, I have lost connection with it [the world] on all sides and am generally incompetent for this world."[20]

Simultaneous with Edith's growing dissatisfaction with the secular realm was the rise to power of National Socialism in Germany. Hitler became chancellor of the Reich in January 1933, and by April of that same year, Edith Stein was compelled to surrender her teaching position at the German Institute of Pedagogy in Munster, where she had gone to work after leaving St. Magdalena's. It became clear to her, despite encouraging words from her coworkers, that any prospects she had had for an academic career in Germany were now essentially finished. With Hitler in power, her friends' and spiritual advisers' objections to her embrace of the contemplative life were nugatory. Thus, Edith applied for admission at the Carmel of Cologne and was accepted there on June 19, 1933.

20. Edith Stein, *Self-Portrait in Letters*, quoted in Malham, *By Fire into Light*, 244.

Before she entered Carmel, however, she faced the terrible responsibility of telling her eighty-four-year-old mother of this latest development. Frau Stein, still deeply unreconciled to her daughter's decision to become a Catholic, reacted quite negatively to the news that her brilliant Edith would embrace a lifestyle that to her seemed mysterious and bizarre, running dramatically against the grain of human nature. Summoning once more her remarkable *fortitudo*, Edith managed to stay true to her conviction despite the pain that it caused her mother.

At the age of forty-two, twice the age of the usual postulant, Edith entered the Cologne Carmel. Any concerns that she or her superiors had about her adaptability to the rigorous discipline of life—rising between 4:30 and 5:00 a.m., hours spent in choir, daily Mass, ascetical practices, manual labor—were rather quickly dispelled. Undoubtedly due to her ten years of quasi-religious life, she took to the rhythms of Carmel very naturally, her greatest difficulty being the performance of certain domestic chores for which her scholar's life had not prepared her. The year of her postulancy passed swiftly, and on April 15, 1934, in accordance with Carmelite tradition, Edith donned the white silk dress of a bride and presented herself for formal reception into the community. Having declared her willingness to become the spouse of Jesus Christ, she exchanged her wedding dress for the coarse brown wool tunic and white veil of the Carmelite novice. In the course of the ceremony, she also adopted a new name, Teresia Benedicta a Cruce, literally Teresa Blessed by the Cross. The girl born on the Day of Atonement and baptized on the feast of the first shedding of Christ's blood was acknowledging with her new name her devotion to Teresa of Ávila but also her identification with the saving cross, the instrument of torture that saved the world. That her life would be transfigured and find its deepest purpose through a participation in the atoning death of Jesus was a conviction that seemed to be present from the very beginning of Edith's religious life.

Sr. Teresa's superiors realized that this novice had extraordinary intellectual gifts, and they encouraged her to exercise them. In the few hours a day that she had for intellectual work, and without access to libraries or journals, Edith wrote. That she produced under these conditions the lengthy philosophical treatise *Eternal and Finite Being* and the penetrating study of John of the Cross's mysticism *The Science of the Cross*, as well as numerous smaller studies and lives of saints, is little short of miraculous. Sadly, the same anti-Semitism that had prevented Edith from holding an academic position also prevented the publication of most of these texts during her lifetime.

Perhaps *The Science of the Cross* especially captures the graced transformation of Edith Stein's intellectual life. The carefully trained phenomenologist certainly appreciated John of the Cross's deep knowledge of Thomas

Aquinas's philosophy and his subtle psychological perceptiveness, so like Husserl's. But what she particularly cherished was the saint's presentation of a mode of knowledge that transcended even the highest attainments of natural forms of intellection, a type of knowing born of a participation in the cross, made possible by a gift of self that echoed however faintly the divine gift of self in the Paschal Mystery.

It is fair to observe that, however involved she became in her intellectual pursuits, Edith's deepest joy came from her immersion in the rhythms of the Carmelite liturgical life, the steady round of Masses, offices, and private prayer. The laywoman who could sit motionless for hours before the Blessed Sacrament became a religious intensely devoted to the mystical life. Early in her Carmelite career, Edith wrote, "All who enter Carmel must give themselves wholly to the Lord. Only one who values her little place in the choir before the tabernacle more highly than all the splendor of the world can live here, can then truly find a joy that no worldly splendor has to offer."[21] The Eucharist—Jesus's love unto death—was the unambiguous center of her existence, the light in which her life was becoming gradually transfigured.

In 1938, five years after her entry, Sr. Teresa Benedicta a Cruce made her final vows, becoming a full-fledged member of the community, privileged to wear the black veil symbolic of her total consecration. During that same year, she received the extraordinary news that Husserl, her beloved Master, had, just before his death, returned to God. Prevented by the anti-Semitic laws of the Reich from teaching or lecturing anywhere in Germany, and spurned even by his former disciple Heidegger, the aged Husserl had become a haunted, hunted man. With his wife, Husserl had fled to the Benedictine convent of Saint Lioba at the invitation of Sr. Adelgundis Jaegerschmid, a former student and a friend of Edith Stein. During Holy Week, as he lay near death, Husserl entered into a fierce spiritual struggle, which he recounted in great detail to Sr. Adelgundis. On April 27, 1938, he spoke with great passion and lucidity of an experience of God that he was having. "Saying that he was seeing something magnificent, he told her to write down what he had to say. When Sr. Adelgundis returned to his bedside with pencil and paper, the Master was dead."[22] Though her relationship to him had been ambiguous, Edith was deeply affected by the death of Husserl, seeing it as a definitive break with a key dimension of her former life.

At the end of that eventful year of 1938, the long-simmering Nazi hostility to Jews broke out into open violence. On November 9, Kristallnacht, gangs looted and destroyed Jewish businesses and homes throughout the

21. Quoted in Scaperlanda, *Edith Stein*, 121.
22. Malham, *By Fire into Light*, 265.

country, effectively disabusing most German Jews of any illusions they still guarded concerning the ultimate intentions of the Nazi leaders. Edith perceived immediately that her presence in the Cologne Carmel constituted a threat to all the sisters, since harboring non-Aryans was considered a serious offense. After much prayerful deliberation, it was decided that Edith should be transferred to a Carmelite community outside the Reich. And thus, with heavy heart, on December 31, 1938, Sr. Teresa Benedicta took leave of the Cologne community that had become her home and set out for the Carmel at Echt in Holland.

There, in a rural setting, she quickly adapted to a somewhat different pace and style of life, going so far as to learn Dutch and to master the field and orchard work that was necessary to that convent's survival. Her humility and kindness quickly made her a beloved member of the family. Soon after her arrival in Echt, on March 26, 1939, Edith made an extraordinary request of her prioress. She asked for permission to make a freewill offering of herself to the Sacred Heart of Jesus. In a formally composed statement, she pledged her life as an atonement for the sins of the world, in the hopes that "the Antichrist may perish, if possible without a new world war, and a new order may be established."[23] The woman born on the Jewish Day of Atonement, received into the church on the feast day of the first shedding of the Savior's blood, and given a name in religion designating the blessing of the cross, knew that her life was wound around the mystery of Christ's redemptive death. With her oblation, she was formally recognizing this connection and stating her desire that she might be mystically joined to Jesus's work of defeating evil through self-immolation in love. Under the influence of grace, her natural *fortitudo* was turning into the courage of the martyr. She was now pounding on the door that separated her from the crucified Jesus.

In another text from 1939, Edith wrote: "Therefore, the Savior today looks at us, solemnly probing us, and asks each one of us: Will you remain faithful to the Crucified? Consider carefully! The world is in flames, the battle between Christ and the Antichrist has broken out into the open. If you decide for Christ, it could cost you your life."[24] None of this constituted a morbid death wish: throughout this dangerous period of her life, Edith tried in numerous ways to protect herself and her sister, who had come to live with her. But she had signaled willingness to be used in this salvific way should God see fit. She did not have long to wait.

In 1940, the Nazi war machine overran Holland, and the same danger that threatened Edith's sisters in Cologne now loomed over them in Echt. In accord with National Socialist demands, Edith and her sister were,

23. Ibid., 268.
24. Scaperlanda, *Edith Stein*, 137.

despite their Catholic religious identity, registered as Jews and compelled to wear the yellow Star of David. They were also, like all Dutch Jews, subjected to harassment and arbitrary interrogations lasting sometimes for hours.

All over occupied Europe, Hitler was intensifying his persecution of the Catholic Church: arresting priests and religious, pilfering convents and monasteries, denouncing the hierarchy and Vatican leadership. So frightened were the sisters of the Cologne Carmel, for instance, that they destroyed all letters and documents linking them to Edith.

The Catholic Church in Holland was particularly brave in its resistance to these Nazi outrages. Many Dutch priests distinguished themselves by their willingness to shelter individual Jews and their families, and the Dutch hierarchy spoke out rather boldly against the brutal policies of the occupying power. In July 1942, the Catholic and Reformed churches of Holland telegrammed Nazi Reichkommisar Arthur Seyss-Inquart, informing him of their displeasure over the deportation of Dutch Jews and threatening to make their protest public unless action were taken. When the Catholic archbishop of Utrecht, Monsignor De Jong, received what he took to be an inadequate response, he went public, ordering that the Nazi policy be attacked from every Catholic pulpit in Holland on July 26, 1942. Stung, Seyss-Inquart struck back harshly. He commanded an immediate roundup of Christian Jews throughout the country, effectively sealing the fate of Sr. Teresa Benedicta a Cruce.

On Sunday August 2, 1942, just days after Seyss-Inquart's order, the Gestapo came for Edith and her sister. At five in the evening, while the sisters were at their meditation, loud knocking could be heard throughout the Carmel. Two officers said that they had orders to take Edith and Rosa Stein immediately and gave the women five minutes to gather their things. The Carmelites were stunned and disoriented by this invasion of their private world, but Edith remained calm. As they prepared to leave, Rosa was visibly shaken. Edith took her by the hand and, calling to mind their Jewish identity, said, "Come Rosa, we're going for our people." At this climactic moment of her life, Edith was, with the courage of a martyr, moving into the role of atoning victim, one who would, in imitation of the crucified Christ, conquer evil by refusing to fight on its terms.

The details of Edith's last days remain for the most part unclear, but there are several intriguing clues. It is certain that, along with other Catholics of Jewish origin, Edith and Rosa were transported to the Dutch concentration camp at Westerbork, which was memorably described in Etty Hillesum's letters and from which Anne Frank, two years later, was sent to her death.[25] Eyewitnesses recall the serenity and focus of the Carmelite

25. Ibid., 149.

nun amidst the confusion of that terrible place. Julius Marcan testified: "It was Edith Stein's complete calm and self-possession that marked her out from the rest of the prisoners There was a spirit of indescribable misery in the camp; the new prisoners especially suffered from extreme anxiety. Edith Stein moved among the women like an angel, comforting, helping, and consoling them."[26] In a letter to her sisters at Echt, written from West-erbork, Edith could say: "We are very calm and cheerful. . . . Now we have a chance to experience a little how to live purely from within." This was the fruit of the *fortitudo* and detachment cultivated over many years.

Sometime after August 6, Edith and Rosa were packed onto a transport train for a trip across Germany to points east. There are two fairly reliable eyewitness accounts of encounters with Sr. Teresa Benedicta on this final journey. On August 7, a young woman on the train platform at Schiffer-stadt, Germany, heard someone calling her name. She turned to see a face framed by the window of a dismal train car. Upon closer examination, she saw that the one who called to her was a nun, dressed in the distinc-tive habit of the Carmelites. Then she recognized her as Fraulein Stein, a professor she had had years before at the teacher's training institute in Speyer. The two women exchanged pleasantries and inquired after old friends until the train jerked into motion. As she was pulling away, Edith asked her young friend to remember her to the sisters at Speyer and to pass on a message to the mother superior in Echt: "Tell her we are heading toward the East." This was assuredly the conveyance of geographical infor-mation, but given Edith's intense religious imagination, it is not difficult to surmise that she was trying to communicate something more. In the biblical authors and the mystics of both the Jewish and Christian traditions, the East signifies paradise, the place of safety beyond the struggles of this world. It is intriguing to speculate whether Edith, so configured to the dynamics of the Paschal Mystery, was perhaps expressing her conviction that her passion would culminate in redemption.

There is yet another report, one that surfaced for the first time forty years after Edith's death. Johannes Wieners was a German soldier who in August 1942 was being transferred to the Eastern Front. On August 7, he and others in his unit were standing in the switching area of the railroad depot in Breslau, Edith's hometown. A freight train rumbled up next to them, and a guard pulled open a sliding door on one of the cars. The soldiers noticed, to their horror, that it was packed with people, herded together like cattle. The stench coming from within was unbearable.

Then a woman in a nun's habit appeared at the opening and said, "It's awful. We have nothing by way of containers for sanitation needs." Looking out over the town, she said, "This is my beloved hometown. I will never

26. Ibid., 150.

see it again." When Wieners looked at her inquisitively, she added, "We are riding to our death."

Profoundly shocked, he asked, "Do your companion prisoners believe that also?"

She responded, "It's better that they do not know it." When, many years later, Wieners saw a photo of Edith Stein accompanying an article about her, he was sure that she was the nun he had encountered in Breslau.[27]

Sometime shortly thereafter, perhaps on August 9, Edith and Rosa arrived at the concentration camp at Auschwitz. They were most likely taken directly from the train to the gas chamber, where they were put to death. Their bodies were subsequently burned.

At the time of her beatification and canonization, during the pontificate of John Paul II, there was a great deal of controversy in regard to the question whether Edith Stein died as a Christian martyr or as a Jewish victim. The question, I am quite sure, would have struck Edith herself as misguided. As she told her sister, she was going to her death "for our people," which is to say, in solidarity with her fellow Jews and in union with the crucified Jew whose death was for the salvation of all. The elevated *fortitudo* of Edith Stein was visible in her willingness to accept the full implications of that solidarity and that union.

27. Ibid., 153.

18

Thérèse of Lisieux

Elevated Prudence

I n the classical philosophical tradition, prudence is the *regina virtutum* (the queen of the virtues), that quality around which the other moral virtues cluster and find their order.[1] This is because prudence is the power according to which the ethical life as such unfolds. Thomas Aquinas tells us that *prudentia* is a sort of vision, a governing insight in regard to those things that should be done and sought: *recta ratio agibilium*. As such it is distinguishable from artistic knowledge, which is right reason in regard to things to be made, and speculative reason, which is contemplative insight into truth for its own sake. One of the marks of prudence is its orientation to particulars, to what Aquinas calls *singularia*, all of the elements, features, and contingencies that constitute a given moral situation. To be sure, a dimension of prudence is a firm grasp of the generalities by which the ethical life is governed, but its real distinguishing characteristic is a feel for the *hic et nunc* of the moral playing field. This is not unlike the sense that an experienced quarterback has for the flow of the football game, the shifting configuration of the defense that opposes him, the opportunities that can suddenly present themselves in the middle of a play.

1. See Josef Pieper, *The Four Cardinal Virtues* (Notre Dame, IN: Univ. of Notre Dame Press, 2003), 5–9.

In the breakthrough of grace, this natural virtue is transformed, elevated into supernatural prudence, which is to say, a moral sensibility radically in service of the love of God. The *ratio* of the supernaturally prudent person is rectified, ordered, by the radical desire to be like God, to will the good of the other as other. This is why Augustine can define elevated prudence as *amor bene discernens ea quibus adiuventur ad tendendum in Deum ab his quibus impediri potest* (the love that well discriminates between those things which foster the tending toward God and those which can impede it). A feel for the expression of divine love in concrete situations is infused or supernaturalized prudence.

I will take St. Thérèse of Lisieux as a model of this form of the moral life. What will become eminently clear in the sketch of her life that I offer is that many of her decisions and acts were anything but prudent in the accepted sense of the term. Just as Edith Stein's embrace of death on behalf of her people would probably have struck Aristotle as rash rather than courageous, so Thérèse's extravagant way of love will seem imprudent to the ordinary observer attuned to the finalities of the natural order. But hers is the virtue not of the "gentlewoman" but of the saint, and the very exaggerated quality of her ethical moves will help us to discern that difference.

Practically every commentator on Thérèse of Lisieux confesses to an initially negative reaction to *The Story of a Soul*, the saint's wildly popular spiritual autobiography. Ida Friederike Görres's account of her first assessment of Thérèse's book is typical: "How small everything is. How painfully little. It is as though we must stoop to enter into a world where everything is made to a bird-like measure, where everything is sweet, pale and fragile, like the lace in which the saint's mother dealt. What a shut-in faintly perfumed air seems to rise from it."[2] I must confess that when I first encountered *The Story of a Soul* in the context of a seminary course, I too found it off-putting, and my post-Freudian mind was only too eager to see in it ample evidence of neuroses and repressions.

But two phenomena tend to produce in even the most skeptical reader a desire to go back, to reconsider. First, some extremely sophisticated intellectuals have found Thérèse compelling: Popes Pius X, Pius XI, Pius XII, and John Paul II, Thomas Merton, Hans Urs von Balthasar, Dorothy Day, and Edith Stein, to name but a few. My thesis director in Paris, Michel Corbin, commented one day on the French custom of referring to Teresa of Ávila as *la grande Thérèse* and Thérèse of Lisieux as *la petite Thérèse*, and he mused, "Mais je crois bien que c'est Thérèse de Lisieux qui est vraiment la grande Thérèse." Second, there is the practically unprecedented

2. Ida Friederike Görres, *The Hidden Face: A Study of St. Thérèse of Lisieux* (San Francisco: Ignatius, 2003), 15.

phenomenon of Thérèse's postmortem popularity. Within a few years of her death, reports of favors and miracles granted through her intercession began to flood into the convent at Lisieux from all over the world. In *The Story of a Soul*, Thérèse had written that after her death she would send a *pluie de roses* (a shower of roses) on the earth, and this promise, it seemed, was being fulfilled. In 1925, just twenty-eight years after her death, a volume of three thousand closely printed pages reproducing excerpts from those letters was published, and that same year, supported by enormous popular acclaim, the nun who at her death was known to perhaps thirty people was canonized a saint and declared by the pope to be "the greatest saint of modern times." There is clearly something here, something beyond bourgeois religious sentimentality and Freudian repressions. So let us attend to *The Story of a Soul*.

Thérèse tells us that she endeavored to write down her spiritual memoir at the prompting of her sister, who was also her religious superior to whom she was bound in obedience. After praying that she say nothing displeasing to Christ, she took up the Gospel of Mark, and her eyes fell on these words: "Jesus, having gone up the mountain, called to him those whom he chose, and they came to him." This verse, she says, is the interpretive key to her life, for it describes the way Christ has worked in her soul: "he does not call those who are worthy, but those whom he pleases."[3] Hers will be a story of a divine love, graciously willing the good of the other, that awakens an imitative reaction in the one who is loved. It is not a narrative of economic exchange—rewards for worthiness—but of the loop of grace, unmerited love engendering disinterested love, the divine life propagating itself in what is other.

But there is more to it. She says that for a long time this purely gracious quality of the divine love bothered her, for it smacked of injustice: how could we explain how God gives more to some and less to others, if all reference to merit is removed? What solved the problem for her was a comparison with the variety of flowers: "I understood that if all the flowers wanted to be roses, nature would lose her springtime beauty, and the fields would no longer be decked with little wild flowers."[4] Aquinas said that God is an artist and his canvas the whole of creation and that the variety of created goods contributes to the beauty and complexity of the design that God is crafting. Thérèse will tell how, then, God the artist of creation worked in her case, cultivating one of his smaller flowers.

Then Thérèse uses a magnificent metaphor that shows that she grasped something about the divine-nondivine relationship that was also central to Aquinas: "Just as the sun shines simultaneously on the tall cedars and

---

3. Thérèse of Lisieux, *The Story of a Soul* (Washington, DC: ICS Publications, 1975), 13.
4. Ibid., 14.

on each little flower as though it were alone on the earth, so Our Lord is occupied particularly with each soul as though there were no others like it."[5] The noncompetitive divine reality, which does not become ingredient in the created world, is not "closer" to the greatest of his creatures than to the least and cannot be preoccupied with one at the expense of the other. Thus, Thérèse can honestly speak of herself, one of God's smallest flowers, as though she were the privileged object of God's affection and interest.

One notices in the pages of *The Story of a Soul*, amidst all of the girlish enthusiasms, a keen sense of order. Thérèse tells us that her life can be neatly divided into three periods: from her birth until the age of four, when her mother passed away; from the age of four until the age of thirteen, when she had a powerful "conversion" experience; and from the age of thirteen until the present, her time in the Carmelite convent of Lisieux. It will be useful for us to follow this same division. Thérèse was born on January 2, 1873, the youngest child of Louis Martin and Zélie Guérin, extremely pious and industrious members of the solid French middle class. Her mother was quite a successful purveyor of the delicate laces for which her native region of Alencon was internationally known, and her father was a watchmaker and jeweler. Both had, in their youth, sought the religious life—he among the Augustinians and she with the Sisters of Charity—but both had finally opted for secular careers. They married in 1858, when Louis was thirty-five and Zélie twenty-seven, and for the first ten months of their marriage they lived as brother and sister, until, at the prompting of a spiritual director and at Zélie's insistence, they commenced a sexual relationship. They eventually produced nine children, five of whom, all daughters, survived into adulthood. Though both parents were professionally tied to the world of fine things, they cultivated a home life that had an intensely religious, almost monastic flavor. Prayers, devotions, Mass, fasting, and abstinence according to the liturgical season were the structuring elements of their daily life.

By her own admission, Thérèse's childhood was idyllic. She was surrounded by an adoring family, all of whom doted on her. The youngest Martin's cherubic looks and pleasant, pious disposition only intensified the affection of her parents and sisters. With her father—whom she referred to as *le petit roi* and to whom she was *la petite reine*—Thérèse developed an especially intense rapport. Since he was nearly fifty when she was born, from Thérèse's perspective Louis was always a venerable and rather delicate old man, and there is no question that her strong sense of the fatherly love of God—evident throughout *The Story of a* Soul—was mediated to her by the unconditional affection of her *petit roi*.

5. Ibid.

Very early in her life, she had the intuition that she would become a religious. When someone told her that her sister Pauline was going to become a Carmelite, Thérèse thought, "I too will become a religious." This, she comments, "is one of my first memories and I haven't changed my resolution since then." It is certainly a mark of her elevated prudence that in regard to the religious life Thérèse would remain adamant, steadfast, clear, unambiguously committed to her last day. That she was called by God to serve him radically was the principal light by which she steered.

Supernatural prudence is a moral know-how informed by divine love, and divine love is, by nature, inexhaustible, all-embracing, and relentless. We discern a sign that Thérèse was in its grip in an anecdote from the opening section of her autobiography. "One day Léonie [one of her sisters] . . . came to us with a basket filled with dresses and pretty pieces for making others; her doll was resting on top. 'Here my little sister, *choose*; I'm giving you all this.' Céline stretched out her had and took a little ball of wool, which pleased her. After a moment's reflection, I stretched out mine saying: 'I choose all!'"[6] She comments that, surprisingly enough, no one in her family saw anything wrong with this. She herself sees it as a summation of her entire life: "Later on, when perfection was set before me, I understood that to become a saint one had to suffer much, seek out always the perfect thing to do and forget self. . . . Then as in the days of my childhood, I cried out: 'My God, *I choose all!* I don't want to be a saint by halves.'"[7] To govern one's life in accordance with the divine love is to be not moderate but necessarily excessive. Indeed, in the Christian moral tradition, charity is seen as the one virtue whose practice cannot be exaggerated, for it partakes most directly of the infinity of God's to-be. In *The Everlasting Man*, G. K. Chesterton notices that the great Christian saints are marked always by a quality of excess: "Francis of Assisi was a more shouting optimist than Walt Whitman . . . and St. Jerome, in denouncing all evil, could paint the world blacker than Schopenhauer."[8] Whatever form the saintly life takes, it can never be a halfway proposition, and it belongs to the heart of supernatural prudence to grasp this.

The idyll of her childhood came to an end with the death of her mother in 1877, when Thérèse was only four. One of the soberest passages in *The Story of a Soul* is Thérèse's account of her mother's reception of extreme unction. What she finds most remarkable was how unmoved she herself was, how emotionally distant from the scene, though her mother was

6. Ibid., 27.

7. Ibid.

8. Quoted in Robert Barron, *Bridging the Great Divide* (New York: Rowman and Littlefield, 2004), 6.

everything to her. This repression signaled the commencement of what she terms "the most painful" of the three stages of her life. In the months following her mother's passing, Thérèse became "retiring and sensitive to an excessive degree," scrupulous and self-regarding. She also began to develop a keen sense of the ephemerality of this world and a consequent longing for the permanence of heaven. While listening to sermons on Sunday mornings, Thérèse would gaze at her father's "handsome face" and take in his otherworldly air: "he seemed no longer held by earth, so much did his soul love to lose itself in the eternal truths."[9] Her spiritual feelings—both melancholy and blissful—came to full expression on Sunday, the beautiful sabbath day that seemed to pass far too quickly: "I longed for the everlasting repose of heaven, that never-ending Sunday of the Fatherland."[10] This deepening of perception and sentiment, occasioned by the loss of her mother, would in time become essential to Thérèse's mature religious prudence, but more immediately it would trigger terrible storms in her emotional life.

During this period, she experienced the terrifying vision that would haunt her and her family and that would later beguile innumerable biographers and commentators. While her father was away on a business trip, Thérèse was looking out her bedroom window on a particularly lovely day. To her surprise, she saw a man dressed like her father and of about his physical proportions, though far more stooped than M. Martin. She then noticed that his face was covered with something like an apron. Convinced that her father was home early from his trip and endeavoring to play a trick on her, she cried out to him, but the figure ignored her and continued to walk around the garden at a steady pace. He went toward a grove of trees, and Thérèse eagerly waited for him to emerge on the other side, but he had disappeared: "the prophetic vision had vanished."[11] Only many years later did the meaning of the scene became clear to Thérèse. In his old age, after four of his five daughters had entered religious life, M. Martin became psychologically imbalanced. He would sometimes speak incoherently and, to the horror of his children, would occasionally wander off to distant towns, leaving no indication as to his whereabouts. During these last sad years of his life, M. Martin would also, curiously, be known to cover his face with a cloth. His youngest daughter thus interpreted the vision as a sort of proleptic sign of her father's future suffering, and she furthermore linked it to the passion of Jesus: "just as the adorable Face of Jesus was veiled during his passion, so the face of His faithful servant had to be veiled in the days of his sufferings in order that it might shine

9. Thérèse, *Story of a Soul*, 42.
10. Ibid.
11. Ibid., 46.

in the heavenly Fatherland."[12] Now was all of this in fact a prophetic perception or simply a hallucination born of a young girl's anxiety and sense of loss? Perhaps it was both, for nothing prevents God from using a psychological disturbance to communicate some spiritual truth, but what matters is that Thérèse perceived the tight connection between the painfully self-emptying love of her father and the paradigmatically self-emptying love of Christ and that she used that link to bolster her sense of God's intimate providence in her life.

Her unsettled psyche would become even more shaken during what she termed "the saddest years" of her life, the five years spent at the Abbey school in Lisieux, the village to which the Martins had moved after Zélie's death. Academically gifted but socially inept, Thérèse had to endure the taunts and practical jokes of her relatively crude classmates. The incessant persecution she underwent helps to explain the insensitivity, even arrogance, of this remark: "It seemed hard to see myself among flowers of all kinds with roots frequently indelicate; and I had to find in the *common soil* the food necessary for sustenance." She hated the rough games that the other children played, but she found one friend with a quiet soul like her own, and with her she engaged in the unlikely "game" of hermit, in which each child would pretend to be a desert monk and outdo the other in silence and self-denial! One does not have to be an expert in child psychology to know that such behavior was bound to make her unpopular with her peers, and Thérèse internalized their critique, seeing herself for the first time in her life as something of a failure, "counted, weighed and found wanting."

The full effects of her mother's death would appear when her eldest sister, Pauline—whom Thérèse had claimed as a substitute mother—decided to enter the Carmelite convent. This second maternal loss proved to be too much, and not long after Pauline enter the Carmel, Thérèse fell victim to a frightening and mysterious malady, which she describes vividly in her autobiography. Toward the close of 1882, she began to experience severe headaches, but not so debilitating as to keep her from school. Around Easter of 1883, M. Martin went on a business trip with his older daughters, and Thérèse stayed at home with her late mother's brother. While they were talking about her mother, Thérèse began to cry so violently that her uncle became alarmed. Surprised that the emotional wound was still so tender, the uncle tried to divert her by talking about plans for an upcoming holiday, but it was too late. The fit of crying was succeeded by another round of severe headaches and then an attack of shivering, like fever chills. This physical assault went on the entire night. When her father returned, he found Thérèse *surexcité*, overstimulated,

12. Ibid., 47.

but he was convinced that she would soon enough be back to normal. In March, she felt well enough to attend the veil-taking of her sister Pauline, but the next morning, she fell again into a state so alarming that her family seriously feared that she had lost her reason. Here is Görres's description: "The child screamed and shrieked in extreme fear, contorted her face, rolled her eyes, saw monsters and nightmarish figures everywhere, sometimes failed to recognize members of the family, was shaken by convulsions, twisted her limbs, tried to throw herself out of bed and had to be forcibly restrained."[13] In a passage not included in the original published version of *Story of a Soul*, Thérèse remarked of her state of mind during this illness: "I was absolutely terrified by everything: my bed seemed to be surrounded by frightful precipices; some nails in the wall of the room took on the appearance of big charred fingers, making me cry out in fear. One day, while Papa was looking at me in silence, the hat in his hand was suddenly transformed into some indescribably dreadful shape, and I showed such great fear that poor Papa left the room, sobbing."[14]

Given these symptoms, it is not surprising that Thérèse herself would conclude, "I can't describe this strange sickness, but I'm now convinced it was the work of the devil."[15] Once again, it is easy enough to speculate that this was a psychotic episode prompted by a personal loss to a pampered and narcissistic child, but what matters is not so much the etiology of the struggle as Thérèse's reaction to and assessment of it. As I've argued throughout this book, God operates through secondary causes, and these can include emotional and psychological disturbances. She came in time to appreciate her illness as "a real martyrdom" for her soul, a testing, a trial, a cleansing, a putting to death. What was being purged in her? Perhaps it was precisely the narcissism, fussy self-absorption, and spiritual athleticism that had been inculcated in her by her family. Perhaps it was the childish overreliance on the approval of her peers and the need to be the center of attention.

In any case, what saved her was a manifestation of grace, of unmerited love. On Pentecost Sunday, May 13, 1883, Thérèse was, as usual, in bed, unable to function. While she muttered to herself, her sister Marie knelt by her bed and prayed to a statue of the Blessed Mother that stood on the table nearby. Thérèse joined her in prayer, and "all of a sudden, the Blessed Virgin appeared *beautiful* to me, so *beautiful* that never had I seen anything so attractive; her face was suffused with an ineffable benevolence and tenderness, but what penetrated to the very depths of my soul was

13. Görres, *Hidden Face*, 79.
14. Thérèse, *Story of a Soul*, 63.
15. Ibid., 62.

the *ravishing smile of the Virgin*."[16] At that moment, she tells us, all of her pain—physical and emotional—disappeared, and two tears of "unmixed joy" rolled down her face.

Was this a miracle or a hallucination, a supernatural phenomenon or a wish-fulfilling fantasy? Again, though we could debate those questions endlessly, they are perhaps not the central questions. What matters is that Thérèse took it to be a grace, a sign that she was loved by God despite her debility, and this realization rescued her from her fears. A person cannot live the divine life until she drops all her strategies of self-justification and allows herself to be drawn into the loop of grace. Supernatural prudence—concrete know-how in the arena of love—is impossible without this breakthrough. And this is why the smile of the Virgin is such a key moment in the spiritual development of St. Thérèse.

This sense of immersion in grace was intensified at Thérèse's First Communion the following spring. Introducing one of the most rapturous passages in *The Story of a Soul*, she tell us that "the smallest details of that heavenly day have left unspeakable memories in my soul."[17] At the heart of the experience was the feeling of being unconditionally loved by the divine reality. Regarding reception of the body of Christ for the first time, Thérèse exclaims, "Ah! How sweet was that first kiss of Jesus! It was a kiss of love; I felt that I was loved, and I said: 'I love you and I give myself to you forever!'" Then the nature of that love is made plain: "There were no demands made, no struggles, no sacrifices; for a long time now Jesus and poor little Thérèse looked at and understood each other. That day, it was no longer simply a look, it was a fusion; they were no longer two, Thérèse had vanished as a drop of water is lost in the immensity of the ocean."

When one enters into the dynamics of the divine life, all games of calculation, payment and return of payment, and economic considerations are necessarily set aside. The love that one receives awakens an answering love, but it is not a matter of strict justice, as though something were owed; it is rather a joyful participation, a desire to imitate what one loves. This is why the nonviolent language of "looking at"—found, by the way, in the Curé of Ars, Jacques Maritain, and a number of other spiritual writers—is so important. What this mutual regard effects is the coinherence that I have spoken of throughout the book, the radical one-in-the-otherness that Thérèse so evocatively refers to as "fusion."

Then comes the typically Christian consequence, the embrace of the cross: "The day after my Communion . . . I felt born within my heart a great desire to suffer, and at the same time the interior assurance that Jesus reserved a great number of crosses for me. . . . Suffering became my

16. Ibid., 66.
17. Ibid., 77.

attraction."[18] This has nothing to do with masochism and everything to do with coinherence. When we are connected to the divine life made available in Jesus, we become enamored of the cross, the instrument by which he effected a coinherence with the sinful human race, bearing and carrying away its sinfulness. We want to suffer, not because suffering is desirable in itself but because it is what he chose to endure out of love. Now we can understand that when Thérèse spoke earlier of the encounter with God in love that involved no "sacrifice," she did not mean that friendship with God is painless, cheap grace. Rather, it is a love—free of the complications and distortions of economic exchange—that makes one *want* to suffer on behalf of the other, that makes suffering, in this sense, attractive.

Thérèse concludes her reflection on First Communion thus: "Up until this time, I had suffered without *loving* suffering, but since this day I felt a real love for it."[19] As a child, she had "offered things up" to God and had endured trials and accepted mortifications, but these were all part of a game of the ego, a calculated attempt to win the approval of her family and of God. They were the strategies of the prodigal son's elder brother. But the "fusion" that took place at her First Communion burned those childish attitudes away.

But there was yet another decisive step in what Thérèse calls her "conversion." Like almost all the other events of her life, it was small, private, nothing to which a biographer would ordinarily call attention. But with her exquisite sensitivity to the subtle ways that grace insinuates itself into nature, she read it, quite properly, as spiritually momentous. It took place, appropriately enough, on Christmas Day, the memorial of the time when nature and grace met most definitively and dramatically. Thérèse tells us that prior to this event, she found herself in an ambiguous spiritual condition. On the one hand, the grace of her First Communion—the desire to suffer in love only because she was loved by God—was clearly operative; but on the other hand, she still felt the tug of her childish preoccupation with being praised and petted. She would typically perform simple acts of kindness for the benefit of her sister, but "if Céline was unfortunate enough not to seem happy or surprised because of these little services, I became unhappy and proved it by my tears."[20] What would enable her to love purely and simply, with the charity characteristic of the Trinity? "God would have to work a little miracle to make me grow up in an instant, and this miracle he performed on that unforgettable Christmas day."[21] As we've seen, the theological virtues—which elevate all of the

18. Ibid., 79.
19. Ibid.
20. Ibid., 97.
21. Ibid.

natural virtues—cannot be merited or attained through repetition or habituation; instead they must, as Thérèse rightly perceives, be received as
gifts, "little miracles."

The Martins had returned from Midnight Mass, and Thérèse, as was
her wont, hurried to look at her shoes, which, in accord with a family
Christmas tradition, would be filled with little presents. She tells us that
her father used to take particular delight in hearing his youngest daughter's
cries of happiness as she "drew each surprise from the *magic shoes*."[22] But
this time her father seemed annoyed at the ritual, and while Thérèse was
making her way upstairs and presumably out of earshot, he muttered to
no one in particular, "Well, fortunately this will be the last year!"

Both Thérèse and Céline heard the remark, and Céline, exquisitely
sensitive to her sister's feelings, said, "Oh, don't go downstairs; it would
cause you too much grief to look at your slippers right now!"

It was one of those quiet but decisive moments in a young person's
psychological development, when an illusion is shattered and a veil is
pulled back, when reality breaks through a carapace of self-protection
and self-delusion. The *petit roi* was not a flawless saint, and the *petite
reine* was not the center of the universe. One would suspect that this
cross remark of her father might have precipitated in Thérèse another
breakdown, comparable to the one that followed Pauline's entry into
Carmel, or at the very least a flood of self-pitying tears. "But Thérèse
was no longer the same; Jesus had changed her heart!"[23] Suppressing her
tears, she went rapidly back down the stairs, placed the shoes directly in
front of her father, and with unfeigned enthusiasm took each item out
and rejoiced over it. So contagious was her happiness that M. Martin
regained his customary good cheer and commenced laughing along with
his daughter.

When faced with the temptation to self-regard, she resolved to love,
to will not her own good but the good of her father. And this reversal
came not through habituation or moral achievement but as a sheer grace.
Like the apostles in the Gospel story, she had fished all night and caught
nothing, but then Jesus took the net himself and cast it into the sea. "I felt
charity enter into my soul, and the need to forget myself and to please
others; since then I've been happy!"[24] I cannot think of a more succinct
summary of the Christian way: the divine life, which can come only as a
gift, changes us in such a way that we want to live for the other, and this
conversion produces joy. Everything else in Christian ethics and dogmatics is commentary.

22. Ibid., 98.
23. Ibid.
24. Ibid., 99.

With the infusion of charity comes, as we have seen, the transformation of the natural virtues. In Thérèse's case, prudence was especially trans-figured and rendered prominent, so that she became adept at discerning the demand of love in the particular situation. We see this discernment immediately operative in Thérèse's desire to save sinners, to thirst for them with the intensity of Jesus himself: "I wanted to give my Beloved to drink and I felt myself consumed with a thirst for souls. . . . I burned with a desire to snatch them from the eternal flames."[25] Not long after her Christmas conversion, she heard of the notorious case of Henri Pranzini, a man convicted of multiple grisly murders and awaiting his execution in what appeared to be an attitude of complete impenitence. She made his conversion her special project; he became "her sinner." After offering in-numerable prayers, arranging for Masses, and drawing others into her circle of concern, she asked God for some sign that Pranzini had been brought to penitence. The morning after the execution, a copy of the newspaper *La Croix* came into her hands, and she read with astonishment that just before putting his head in the guillotine, Pranzini had "taken hold of the crucifix the priest was holding out to him and kissed the sacred wounds three times."[26] The ruthless killer had become Thérèse's "first child" in the order of grace. Her elevated prudence had told her what to do, even in what appeared to be a hopeless situation.

She also, very quickly, knew precisely what to do with the rest of her life. The desire for Carmel, which had been present to some degree ever since she was a small child, now became a burning conviction, a "divine call so strong that had I been forced to pass through flames, I would have done it out of love for Jesus." She felt, she tells us, the support of her mother from heaven, and Céline was, as usual, her great advocate, but she was afraid to tell her father of her vocation. She was, after all, barely fifteen. She broke the news to him on Pentecost Sunday 1887; after some hesitation, he became convinced that her desire was from God, and he accordingly gave his permission.

In the months that followed, Thérèse met obstacle after obstacle as key figures, both in her own family and in the church, expressed deep concern about the advisability of allowing a girl so young to make such a weighty decision. The section of *The Story of a Soul* in which this period of her life is narrated is actually quite funny, for we hear how this pampered and inexperienced teenager met with high ecclesiastics and bishops and, through a combination of intelligence, charm, stubbornness, and sheer moxie managed to outstare them and wear them down.

25. Ibid.
26. Ibid., 100.

When the bishop of Bayeux refused to circumvent the usual proce-
dures and allow her to enter Carmel early, Thérèse resolved to bring her
case to the highest court, to the pope himself. With her father and sister,
she joined a group of ultramontane French pilgrims on an Italian journey
that was far more sightseeing expedition than pilgrimage. Thérèse was
both fascinated and disgusted by the worldly ways of these purportedly
religious people, and she, with her exaggerated pieties, was undoubtedly
a source of amusement to them. They arrived, finally, in Rome, and on
November 20, 1887, after donning the traditional garb, Thérèse had her
papal audience. All of the pilgrims had been carefully instructed not to
address the pope, but Thérèse ignored this instruction. Kneeling before
Leo XIII, she blurted out, "Most Holy Father, I have a great favor to ask
you! Holy Father, in honor of your jubilee, permit me to enter Carmel at
the age of fifteen!"

When apprised of her situation, the pope responded, "Well, my child,
do what the Superiors tell you."

But Thérèse persisted: "Oh! Holy Father, if you say yes, everybody will
agree!"

Looking at her intently, he said, "Go . . . go . . . You will enter if God
wills it." At that point, still begging and weeping, she was carried off bodily
by two papal guards.

It probably would have appeared to any neutral observer that with
this bizarre performance Thérèse had spoiled any chance she might have
had to enter Carmel early. Nevertheless, just a month later, the bishop
of Bayeux granted permission for her to enter the cloister after Lent.
We will never be able to say with certainty precisely what it was that
convinced the various ecclesiastics to give in, but the sheer persistence
and singleness of purpose so plainly evident in Thérèse must have been
decisive factors.

So amidst much rejoicing and in the presence of the bishop, who kept
calling her "*his* little girl," Thérèse was formally received at the Lisieux
Carmel on April 9, 1888. For the remaining nine years of her short life,
she would remain cloistered within the walls of this small Carmelite
world and in the company of twenty or so sisters. But in this very restricted environment she would develop the distinctive spiritual path for
which she became famous, the "little way," which I will read as the fruit
of elevated prudence.

The best introduction to Thérèse's spiritual doctrine is a text that she
wrote at the behest of Sr. Marie of the Sacred Heart, a sort of memoir
of the retreat that she made in September 1896, just a year before her
death. What she offers is a "science of love," a way of knowing and acting
that is utterly conditioned by the love that Jesus has placed in her heart:
"Jesus deigned to show me the road that leads to this Divine Furnace,

and this road is the surrender of the little child who sleeps without fear in its Father's arms."[27]

Two Old Testament sources are particularly important for her: Proverbs 9, which includes "Whoever is a little one, let him come to me" (see v. 4); and Isaiah 40, where we find "[God] will feed his flock like a shepherd; he will gather the lambs in his arms, and carry them in his bosom" (v. 11). God, Thérèse concluded, is pleased to work with those who have become utterly docile to his direction, who have acknowledged their total dependence upon him, their readiness to receive gifts. As we have seen already in her account of her First Communion, any sense that God's love must be earned or that a relationship with him is a product of economic calculation is repugnant to a healthy spirituality: "Jesus does not demand great actions from us but simply surrender and gratitude."[28] Hans Urs von Balthasar comments that "her battle is to wipe out the hardcore of Pharisaism that persists in the midst of Christianity; that human will-to-power . . . that drives one to assert one's own greatness instead of acknowledging that God alone is great."[29]

When this attitude is in place, anything and everything is possible: *Gloria Dei homo vivens.* Thérèse writes that she had always longed to be a spouse of Christ, a good Carmelite, and a mother of souls, but that during her retreat she had begun to cultivate a desire for more: "And yet I feel within me other vocations. I feel the vocation of the warrior, the priest, the apostle, the doctor, the martyr. Finally, I feel the need and the desire of carrying out the most heroic deeds for You, O Jesus."[30] We notice that these mighty deeds and heroic vocations follow from the divine love and are not the condition for it. Filled with Jesus's love, Thérèse would know what to do in these various roles. If she were a priest, "with what love, O Jesus, I would carry you in my hands when, at my voice, you would come down from heaven"; if she were a martyr, "I would be scourged and crucified. I would die flayed like St. Bartholomew. I would be plunged into boiling oil like St. John; I would undergo all the tortures inflicted on the martyrs."[31]

But she is acutely aware, at the same time, that she is a very "little soul," confined to the narrow space of the Lisieux Carmel, and thus can never realize such lofty ambitions. The tension between the intensity of her desires and the truth of her situation becomes terrible: "Is there a soul more little, more powerless than mine? Nevertheless even because

27. Ibid., 188.

28. Ibid.

29. Hans Urs von Balthasar, *Two Sisters in the Spirit*, translated by Donald Nichols and Anne Englund Nash (San Francisco: Ignatius, 1992), 241.

30. Thérèse, *Story of a Soul*, 192.

31. Ibid., 193.

of my weakness, it has pleased you, O Lord, to grant my little childish desires and you desire, today, to grant other desires that are greater than the universe."[32] Like the prodigal son kneeling humbly at his father's feet, Thérèse intuits that her smallness is the condition for the possibility of her being filled, but it is not at all clear to her *how* this will happen.

During her retreat, she turned to the epistles of Paul to find a resolution of the tension. In 1 Corinthians, she read that not all can be apostles, prophets, doctors, and so on, but this did not satisfy her, for the desire that she felt was precisely to be all these things and more. But then she read to the end of the twelfth chapter of 1 Corinthians and found this passage: "Yet strive after the better gifts . . . and I will show you a still more excellent way." What follows in chapter 13, of course, is Paul's hymn to love, wherein it becomes clear that love is the form of every other virtue and accomplishment within the life of grace: "If I have faith to move the mountains, but have not love, I am nothing. . . . If I give away everything I own . . . but have not love, I gain nothing." Thérèse intuited that love is the energy that makes possible the preaching of the apostles, the endurance of the martyrs, the teaching of the doctors, the spiritual ascent of the mystic, and thus that it is love that she is secretly seeking when she desires to fulfill all of those roles. "Then, in the excess of my delirious joy, I cried out: O Jesus, my Love . . . my vocation at last I have found it . . . my vocation is love!"[33] She concluded that in the heart of the church she would *be love*—and the heart of the church could be as small as the Carmel at Lisieux.

Now she was in possession of a sure guide, a principle of spiritual measurement: "It [the insight into love] was rather the calm and serene peace of the navigator perceiving the beacon which must lead him to the port. . . . O luminous Beacon of love, I know how to reach you, I have found the secret of possessing your flame."[34] She had become a person of supernatural prudence, for she knew how to order all the moves of her life in the light of the highest possible good, the inner dynamics of the divine life. The breakthroughs that had occurred at her First Communion and on Christmas Day 1886 had now been fully appropriated: "the smallest act of pure love is of more value . . . than all other works together."[35] This means that she can be pleasing to God and valuable to the church in the humblest places and through the simplest acts.

This supernatural prudence—acquired through grace—gave Thérèse supreme confidence. Even when dealing with priests, the dignity of whose

32. Ibid.
33. Ibid., 194.
34. Ibid., 195.
35. Ibid., 197.

office she clearly recognized, Thérèse easily and naturally assumed the role of spiritual director. When others spoke of their spiritual guides, she could unabashedly say, "My spiritual director, Jesus, teaches . . ."[36] And supernatural prudence enabled her to live, even in narrow Carmelite confines, a life of heroic sanctity. All she had to do was to discern the path of love in whatever situation she found herself—and follow it.

A number of vividly related narratives in *Story of a Soul* exemplify this little path. Again, we will miss the point of these stories if we concentrate on the externals—which seem so homey and unimportant—and miss the quality of love that informs them. Thérèse tells us that there was a nun in the convent with whom she had what we would call a serious personality conflict; in her own words, "someone who managed to irritate me in everything she did." Knowing that love is not a matter of feeling but of works born of the will, she resolved to do for that sister what she would do for the person she loved the most. Thus, "each time I met her I prayed to God for her . . . and I took care to render her all the services possible, and when I was tempted to answer her back in a disagreeable manner, I was content with giving her my most friendly smile."[37]

So convincing was her manner that one day, during recreation, the troublesome nun asked her, "Would you tell me, Sister Thérèse of the Child Jesus, what attracts you so much towards me; everytime you look at me, I see you smile?"

Thérèse's public response to the other nun was "I am happy to see you," but her private response, shared with her readers, was "Ah! What attracted me was Jesus hidden in the depths of her soul."[38] As we have seen many times throughout this book, rootedness in the divine love connects us to everything else and everyone else in creation; to realize one's deepest ontological ground is to realize simultaneously a coinherence with even the most difficult or repugnant fellow creature. To act out of this awareness is to follow the little way.

During her novitiate, Thérèse was given the assignment of taking care of Sr. St. Pierre, a fussy and demanding elderly woman, "not easy to please." The younger sister's task was to escort the infirm sister from her stall at evening prayer to the refectory and then to help her prepare to eat. Here is Thérèse's humorous and psychologically penetrating account of her dealings with this difficult colleague: "I had to remove and carry her little bench in a certain way, above all I was not to hurry. . . . It was a question of following the poor invalid by holding her cincture; I did this with as much gentleness as possible. But if . . . she took a false step, immediately

36. Görres, *Hidden Face*, 339.
37. Thérèse, *Story of a Soul*, 223.
38. Ibid.

it appeared to her that I was holding her incorrectly." Then the old nun would protest: "Ah! My God! You are going too fast; I'm going to break something." When Thérèse would slow down, Sr. St. Pierre would say, "Well, come on! I don't feel your hand; I'm going to fall!" Adding insult to injury, she would then mutter, "Ah! I was right when I said you were too young to help me."

When they would arrive at the refectory, further difficulties arose. Thérèse had to get Sr. St. Pierre seated, but this had to be done skillfully "in order not to hurt her"; then she had to turn back the elderly nun's sleeves, again just so, lest the old lady be upset.

Night after night this ritual was repeated, and each time Thérèse resolved to conquer her feelings of annoyance and act in accord with the dictates of love. One winter night, in the midst of her routine, she indulged in a bit of fantasy: "I pictured a well-lighted drawing room, brilliantly gilded, filled with elegantly dressed young ladies conversing together and conferring upon each other all sorts of compliments and other worldly remarks." Then she surveyed her own surroundings, and all she took in were the drab colors of the cloister, the complaints of Sr. St. Pierre, the dimness and cold of the refectory. Her conclusion: "I would not have exchanged the ten minutes employed in carrying out my humble office of charity to enjoy a thousand years of worldly feasts."[39] The faculty that enabled Thérèse to make that extraordinary and counterintuitive assessment is supernatural prudence, a feel for the path of love.

I mentioned at the outset of this sketch that many readers of *Story of a Soul* are initially put off by Thérèse's cloying and sentimental style. However, even the most skeptical of her readers are usually converted by the account of her terrible struggle, at the end of her life, with unbelief. There is nothing childish or naive about this part of her story. Practically contemporaneous with the onset of the tuberculosis that would eventually kill her was the arrival in Thérèse's mind of the worst sort of doubts concerning the existence of heaven. She who had, throughout her life, enjoyed the easiest confidence in the spiritual realm now wondered, Hamlet-like, whether there was anything that followed the sleep of death. And this was no passing bout of intellectual scrupulosity; rather it lasted up until the moment of her death. In *The Story of a Soul*, she states the facts with a bluntness bordering on desperation: "This trial was to last not a few days or a few weeks, it was not be extinguished until the hour set by God Himself and the hour has not yet come."[40] What is most important to note is the highly paradoxical way in which Thérèse interprets this struggle. She reads it as a participation, granted to her by God, in the pain

39. Ibid., 248–49.
40. Ibid., 211–12.

experienced by her contemporaries who do not believe in God: "During those very joyful days of the Easter season, Jesus made me feel that there were really souls who have no faith and who, through the abuse of grace, lost this precious treasure, the source of the only real and pure joys. He permitted my soul to be invaded by the thickest darkness."[41]

On the cross, Jesus cried out, "My God, my God, why have you forsaken me?" Chesterton interpreted this as "the moment when God became an atheist," that is to say, when God entered so fully into the state of those abandoned by God that he felt their agony. There is something very similar in Thérèse's spiritual hermeneutic. Her wrestling with the possibility of atheism or agnosticism was not dumb suffering; rather, it was a gift given to her by God in order to facilitate her entry in love into the state of sinners. It was darkness to be sure, but a darkness that made possible a fuller coinherence. Strangely enough, even when she was "underground" in the murkiness of disbelief, her elevated prudence remained a sure guide. This is why Balthasar has it quite right when he maintains that her doubts—though real and painful—were not so much agnosticism as a *participation mystique* in the psychological and spiritual state of the modern unbeliever. It was her supernatural prudence that allowed her to turn even this dark passage in her life into a way of coinherence.

On April 3, Good Friday morning, 1896, Thérèse coughed up blood, the harbinger of tuberculosis. Though she appeared to be in fairly good health that summer and fall, the disease was progressing. By the spring of 1897, she was gravely ill and had to be relocated to the infirmary of the Carmel. Doctors who came to see her determined that the tuberculosis was widespread and that her illness was terminal.

During these last months of her life, Thérèse engaged in a series of extraordinary conversations with her sisters, wherein she continued to explicate her spiritual doctrine, in the midst of enormous struggles both physical and psychological. Sometimes she became exasperated with their fussing over her, but generally she remained kind and responsive during this terrible time. She was convinced that her final illness was a gift from Jesus, a final opportunity to love, the last step on the little way of elevated prudence.

41. Ibid., 211.

19

Katharine Drexel

Elevated Justice

For Thomas Aquinas, prudence is the "queen of the virtues," but justice is the heart and soul of the ethical life. Prudence is the practical/theoretical sense that allows one to apply general moral principles to concrete situations. Temperance and courage are those virtues that stave off obstacles—interior and exterior—which would keep one from being ethically upright. But *justice* denotes that virtue by which one actually performs what is morally praiseworthy. It is what prudence guides and what courage and temperance protect. Following the lead of Plato, Aquinas holds that justice is "giving to another his due," *suum cuique*.[1] In the soul, "it is the intentional habit whereby a person renders to the other his due with constant and perpetual will." Or to state it even more pithily, it is that virtue which "establishes order among things."

Now the formula "rendering to each his due" implies that something necessarily precedes justice, viz., the right that is the ground for claiming that anyone is due anything. To seek the nature and origin of right is to enter some delicate metaphysical territory, for it compels us to wrestle with the implications of a doctrine of creation. Taken in itself and as such, creation does not ground justice, since God is in no sense obliged to create.

---

1. Josef Pieper, *The Four Cardinal Virtues* (Notre Dame, IN: Univ. of Notre Dame Press, 2003), 44.

316

Nothing in the created world can claim a right vis-à-vis God, for finite existence is a pure gift. However, ex post facto, we can speak of creation as a source of right, inasmuch as God has placed in his human creatures a properly personal nature endowed with intellect, will, and freedom. It is on account of this personhood, this spiritual irreducibility, that "something *is* due to man in the fullest sense, *for that reason* he does inalienably have a *suum*, a 'right' which he can plead against everyone else."[2] Josef Pieper comments in this regard that the denial of an objective human nature is the necessary basis for all forms of totalitarianism.

Having determined this essential feature, we can further specify that justice is the sole cardinal virtue that is truly directed to the other: "it is proper to justice . . . to direct man in his relations with others," whereas "the other virtues perfect man only in those matters which befit him in relation to himself."[3] The classical authors, including Aquinas, subdivide justice into the three areas of "commutative justice," which governs the relations of individuals within a society to one another, "distributive justice," which speaks to the relations of the social whole to the many individuals, and "legal justice," which governs the relations between individuals and the social whole. The various dimensions of society respond to the "rights" inherent in each other, each rendering to the other its due.

Now what happens to the virtue of justice when it is transfigured by the love that is the divine life? It becomes radicalized, absolutized, elevated, perfected, turning into a total gift of self, a willingness to render to the other beyond what is merely his due. The woman whom I propose as an exemplification of elevated justice is St. Katharine Drexel, an heir to a multimillion-dollar fortune who was so impressed by the needs of the excluded "other" that she gave away the entirety of her wealth and the whole of her life on his behalf. By attending to the dynamics of her choices and moves, we will see supernaturalized justice on display.

Katharine Drexel was born in Philadelphia on November 26, 1858, to Francis Anthony Drexel, an internationally known banker, and Hannah Langstroth Drexel. Her mother died five weeks after Katharine's birth, leaving Francis with two young children to raise. A year and a half after Hannah's death, Francis Drexel married Emma Bouvier, whom Katharine would know and love as her mother. Katharine's paternal grandfather, Francis Martin Drexel, was by any measure an extraordinary figure.[4] A Tyrolean by birth and a painter by training, he had made his way to the New World and sought employment as a portrait painter in both North and

2. Ibid., 50.

3. Thomas Aquinas, *Summa theologiae*, IIa IIae, q. 57, art. 1.

4. Consuela Marie Duffy, *Katharine Drexel: A Biography* (Philadelphia: Peter Reilly, 1966), 17–19.

South America. When his clientele diminished, he established a brokerage firm in Louisville, Kentucky, and it prospered during the economic panic of 1837, due to frenzied trading in currencies. Flourishing financially, he moved to Philadelphia and founded the Drexel banking concern, which in rather short order became one of the most important in the nation. Katharine's father, Francis Anthony, received a thorough apprenticeship in the world of finance, working at his father's bank and keeping the books from the time he was a small child. He also, under his father's tutelage, developed into quite an accomplished organist. Eventually, when Francis Martin left to join the Gold Rush of 1849, his son became a senior partner in the firm. The common consensus of Katharine Drexel's biographers is that she inherited from her father and grandfather both a keen artistic sensitivity and a hard-nosed business sense.

Katharine's childhood was something of an idyll. Along with her siblings, she was given the finest private education available in nineteenth-century America, receiving tutoring from masters in a variety of languages, writing, mathematics, philosophy, and painting. She lived in a sumptuous mansion in Philadelphia, and during the vacation seasons she sojourned with her family in a lovely country estate. On several occasions during her youth, the Drexels made the grand tour of Europe, staying in the finest hotels and taking in the sights, especially those dear to Catholic pilgrims.

By all accounts, her father and her stepmother were unconditionally supportive of their children, providing them not only with every material advantage but also with emotional security and the example of a vibrant spiritual life. Along with their lessons in the secular disciplines, the Drexel children regularly heard tales of the saints. Katharine would maintain a lifelong interest in Francis of Assisi, and his devotion to poverty would strongly mark the order that she would eventually establish. Also, Mrs. Drexel had a beautiful chapel built in the Philadelphia residence, and she encouraged the children to avail themselves of it regularly. Thus Katharine cultivated from a very early age a discipline of prayer and developed a sense of comfort around the things of God. A practice of her father would burn itself into her memory: after returning from work and before sitting down to dinner, Mr. Drexel would typically spend a half hour in fervent prayer, communing with God.

One further spiritual lesson would perhaps most deeply sink into the consciousness of Katharine. Three afternoons a week, the doors of the Drexel house were opened to the poor and those in need of help. Mrs. Drexel drilled into her children the conviction—rooted in Thomas Aquinas, Ambrose, and Chrysostom—that their wealth had been entrusted to them by God and must therefore be used not simply for their benefit but for the common good. Inspired by this principle, the Drexel family gave away twenty thousand dollars a year, an enormous sum in the late nineteenth century.

In 1872, when she was fourteen, Katharine met a man who would exert a powerful influence on her spiritual development: Fr. James O'Connor. O'Connor was an Irish American priest who had held the position of rector of the major seminary in Pittsburgh and who was, by the early 1870's, parish priest of the region where the Drexels' summer house was situated. He became a friend to the whole family but especially to Katharine, and the letters that they exchanged until his death are perhaps the major source of information concerning her psychological and religious life. Katharine had by this time begun to cultivate a serious interest in becoming holy, striving, as she put it, to be perfect. With typical adolescent fervor, she set out a detailed program, resolving to say a variety of prayers daily, to overcome pride and vanity, not to eat between meals, to give money to the poor, and to receive Holy Communion frequently. In all of this, O'Connor was a moderate and helpful guide.

Katharine's formal education ended in 1878, when she was twenty, and in January 1879, she was officially presented to Philadelphia society. It is perhaps the greatest indicator of her growing spiritual interest that this event, which for someone of her time, gender, and class would normally have been judged as momentous, was greeted with a boredom bordering on indifference. In a letter to O'Connor, she recounted any number of her social engagements: "To this list of dissipations can be added dutiful evening calls on aunts and cousins, besides attending a little party where I made my debut." The understatement is, to say the least, remarkable. Jesus, who had been in Katharine Drexel's boat for some time already, was clearly beginning to take control of the vessel.

Soon after Katharine's debut, her stepmother developed cancer and entered into an extended period of declining health, during which Katharine nursed her with great devotion. She was powerfully impressed by her stepmother's total resignation to the will of God and her conviction that her suffering was ingredient in God's salvific plan for the world. This particular mode of coinherence would figure prominently in the spirituality of the order that Katharine would found. Mrs. Drexel died on January 29, 1883, and was deeply mourned by thousands of Philadelphians, but the reaction of her spiritually alert adopted daughter was especially intense. There is clear evidence that Katharine's sense of religious vocation, which had certainly been growing in her during the previous years, came to explicit consciousness in the wake of her stepmother's passing. The fleeting character of earthly goods and relationships awakened in her a deep desire for that which does not fade away.

Then, in February 1885, her father died suddenly after being stricken at work. Katharine herself frantically searched for a priest to administer the last rites, but he arrived too late. Francis Drexel's will gave rise to nationwide comment. His estate—worth the then staggering sum of $15.5 million—was divided among his three daughters and more than forty charitable institutions and organizations, including several that were non-Catholic. Katharine and her sisters inherited around four million dollars each.

The Drexel children were eager to see that the instructions in their father's will be assiduously followed, and they resolved that they themselves would follow his example of charitable giving. Confessing that she had had an interest since childhood in what were then called "American Indians," Katharine decided to focus her own giving on the Indian missions and schools of the Great Plains. Shortly after the death of Francis Drexel and no doubt inspired by the numerous newspaper accounts of his generous will, two priests presented themselves at the door of the Drexel mansion in Philadelphia and asked to speak to "the misses Drexel." Pressed by her sisters, Katharine went down stairs to speak to Bishop Martin Marty, O.S.B., vicar apostolic of Northern Minnesota, and Fr. Joseph Stephan, the director of the Bureau of Catholic Indian Missions. This interview would change her life. Deeply moved by their stories of the sufferings—both physical and spiritual—of the native peoples of the plains, Katharine determined to give a substantial portion of her inheritance to build schools, convents, hospitals, and churches so as to "hold the line of the Catholic Faith among the American Indians."[5] By 1907, the donations that the Drexel family had made to the Indian missions totaled $1.5 million, again a most substantial sum for that period. But more important, these early gifts tied Katharine by deep psychological and spiritual bonds to the work of Marty and Stephan. Another key link to the world of Native Americans was the appointment of Katharine's spiritual mentor, Fr. James O'Connor, as bishop of Omaha, a diocese encompassing much Indian territory.

These first connections to the work of missioners to Native Americans coincided with a period of great inner turmoil in Katharine. Following the death of her father, which had followed hard upon that of her stepmother, Katharine's health took a turn for the worse. Judging from contemporary descriptions of her malady, it was a problem far more psychological than physical, and she was encouraged, in accord with the accepted wisdom of the time, to go to Europe to "take the baths." Not many years before, another anxious young American, William James, had made the same journey for the same reason. So with her sisters she embarked on another grand tour of the Continent, visiting both spas and major religious sites. While she was away, Fr. Stephan sent her lengthy missives detailing how her funds were helping the work of the missions, and Bishop O'Connor

5. Duffy, *Katharine Drexel*, 89.

sent a communiqué in which he asked her to look for a European religious community that might be willing to provide priests to work with the Indians of the Omaha diocese.

All this time, Katharine was fretting mightily about the possibility of pursuing some form of the religious life. Her European sojourn culminated in a visit to Rome and an audience with the pope. Unwell, emotionally distraught at the death of her parents, concerned deeply about the work of the Indian missioners, and filled with both excitement and trepidation at the prospect of becoming a nun, Katharine found herself, in a scene eerily reminiscent of Thérèse of Lisieux, at the feet of Pope Leo XIII. Kneeling before the pontiff and convinced that he would never refuse such a pious request, Katharine pleaded for missionary priests for Bishop O'Connor's Indians. To her great surprise, Leo XII responded, "Why not, my child, yourself become a missionary?"

Flummoxed, all she could manage as a response was "Because, Holy Father, sisters can be had for the missions but no priests." But Leo's answer had cut to her soul. After the conversation, she was "sick all over, so sick that she could not get out of the Vatican quick enough."[6] Once outside—and here again the connection to Thérèse is remarkable—she "sobbed and sobbed, much to her sisters' dismay."[7] She did not understand what the pope meant, and she was exceedingly frightened and sick.

In order to understand more fully this reaction to Leo XIII's invitation, we must backtrack a bit and consider some details of Katharine's vocational quest. We have seen indications of it in her youthful spiritual resolutions and in her indifference to her debut, but there is a more complex story to tell. In letters written to Bishop O'Connor when she was still a teenager, Katharine had signaled an interest in the contemplative religious life, but her mentor consistently blocked that predilection, insisting that she should serve by example and charity "in the world." Just after her stepmother's death, when her desire for religious life intensified, O'Connor encouraged Katharine to write out, in the Ignatian mode, the pros and cons of becoming a nun. The ledger sheet is quite interesting. On the positive side, we find compelling invocations of the spiritual advantages of religious life: simplicity, clarity of purpose, unambiguous seeking of the highest good, etc. But on the negative side, equally compelling difficulties: "How could I bear separation from my family?" and "I hate community life. I should think it maddening to come in constant contact with many different old maidish dispositions," and perhaps most significant, "I should hate to owe submission to a woman whom I felt to be stupid."[8]

6. Ibid., 100.
7. Ibid., 101.
8. Ibid., 111.

O'Connor indicated his agreement that the negatives outweighed the positives, at least for her: "What most makes me hesitate to say that you have a vocation to religion is the fear that you might not have the strength of endure the sacrifices it calls for. From *your* home and *your* table to the cell and the refectory of a nun would be a very great change."[9] As a kind of compromise, O'Connor, in a letter written while the Drexel sisters were in Europe, proposed that Katharine remain in the world but take a vow of virginity for one year, renewable for another, becoming a sort of religious outside of convent walls. Katharine did so—making the vow before an icon of the Virgin Mary in the cathedral of St. Mark in Venice—but she still felt uneasy with what seemed a halfway measure.

A letter written by Katharine to Bishop O'Connor in January 1884 is both a fine example of spiritual writing and perhaps the most unambiguous indicator of the radical conversion that had occurred in the young woman. She tells her spiritual mentor that her heart is filled with sorrow, like that of a little girl who has just discovered that a beautiful doll is in fact stuffed with sawdust: "I too have made a horrifying discovery and my discovery like hers is true. I have ripped the doll open and the fact lies plainly and in all its glaring reality before me: *All, all, all* (there is no exception) is passing away and *will* pass away." She concludes: "The question *alone* important . . . is the state of my soul at the moment of death. Infinite misery or infinite happiness . . . This is ripping open the doll and discovering it to be made of sawdust." Her indifference to the glories of a society debut had hardened into hostility toward the ephemeral goods of the world, all those things to which Katharine Drexel's wealth had given her such ready access. This epiphany is analogous to Thérèse's Christmas conversion and Edith Stein's sudden awareness that *The Life* of Teresa of Ávila represents the truth. It was the moment when the merely natural fell away and the properly supernatural opened up, the moment when Jesus definitively took control of the boat.

Katharine's natural sense of moderation and self-control became a supernaturalized temperance, and her ordinary sense of fairness became elevated justice, a desire to render to the other even beyond what is his due. Since all here below is passing, she must give all to the demands of the eternal. The great irony, of course, is that this insight came to her just after an enormous sum of money—that which could buy her all of the goods of the ephemeral world—fell under her control. Having seen to the bottom the metaphysical status of the created world, she was now in a position to supernaturalize the natural, to use those funds for works of divine justice and love. The steady correspondence with O'Connor, culminating in that breakthrough perception, had turned over the soil

9. Ibid., 115.

of her soul and had readied her for the unexpected seed that Leo XIII would sow there. I would maintain that what Katharine experienced at the feet of the pope was a shock of recognition, a verification of what she had already begun to perceive—that her calling was to a life of neither worldly privilege nor contemplative withdrawal but rather active love in the context of religious life.

O'Connor was not utterly convinced, even after the powerful witness of the "sawdust" letter of 1884. He still felt that Katharine would do more good in the world, actively directing the distribution of her wealth to the Indian missions. In a letter of May 16, 1888, he wrote: "I take all the responsibility for having kept you out of the convent until now. The more I reflect on the matter, the more I am persuaded that you are where God wishes you to be at present."[10]

But in late 1888, almost two years after the audience with Leo XIII, Katharine's desire for religious life became so intense that it compelled her to stand against the wishes of the man whom she had revered as her spiritual father since her youth. In a communication of November 26, 1888, she wrote somewhat edgily to O'Connor:

> Are you afraid to give me to Jesus Christ? God knows how unworthy I am, and yet can he not supply my unworthiness if only he give me a vocation to the religious life? Then joyfully I shall run to him. I am afraid to receive your answer to this note. It appears to me, Reverend Father, that I am not obliged to submit my judgement to yours, as I have been doing for two years. . . . Will you, Reverend Father, please pardon the rudeness of this last remark?[11]

Perhaps it was just this declaration of independence that O'Connor was waiting for, because his capitulation to Katharine's wishes, after so long a resistance, was sudden and complete: "This letter of yours, and your bearing under the long and severe tests to which I subjected you, as well as your entire restoration to health, and the many spiritual dangers that surround you, make me withdraw all opposition to your entering religion."[12]

In response to O'Connor, Katharine then revealed the precise nature of the religious life that she was desiring: "I want a missionary order for Indians and Colored people." Once he heard of this resolution, O'Connor became increasingly persuaded that Katharine—with her ample resources both spiritual and financial—should found an order directed precisely to the good of Native Americans and African Americans. In a letter of February 16, 1889, the bishop of Omaha wrote: "The more I have thought of your case, the more convinced I become that God has called you to establish

10. Ibid., 128.
11. Ibid., 129.
12. Ibid., 130.

an order for the objects above mentioned. . . . The need for it is patent to everybody. All the help the established orders can give will be needed, but a strong order devoted to it exclusively is also needed."[13]

Initially, Katharine was horrified at the prospect of becoming a founder. She had determined to enter into the religious life, and she desired missionary work, but she felt distinctly unqualified to assume the spiritual and practical responsibility of shepherding a new religious community. Only after several months of cajoling from O'Connor and others did she relent.

In May 1889, she entered the novitiate of the Sisters of Mercy of Pittsburgh, intending not to enter their community but to learn the ways of religious life and the meaning of the vows of poverty, chastity, and obedience. Katharine thus found herself in the rather peculiar situation of being both novice and founder-in-training. There is something reminiscent of Edith Stein in the stories of the older and exceptional Katharine Drexel adjusting to the routines of novitiate life; by all accounts, she, like Edith, took to it well and with great humility, happily performing the most menial tasks. It appears as though her fears—shared by Bishop O'Connor—concerning her transition from aristocratic ease to the rigors of convent life were largely unfounded.

Katharine was formally "received" as a religious in November 1889, but very soon thereafter she faced a major crisis. Bishop O'Connor, her steady and indispensable spiritual counselor, passed away while on a trip through the South, and Katharine decided that, in his absence, she lacked the courage to go ahead with their plan. It was only when Archbishop Patrick John Ryan of Philadelphia intervened and assured her that he would give her all the practical support she needed that she agreed to continue.

In February 1891, almost two years after her entry into the convent, Katharine Drexel made her profession as the first Sister of the Blessed Sacrament for Indians and Colored People. We are well acquainted with her love for the marginalized, but why should the Blessed Sacrament play such a central role in her community? The Eucharist, devotion to which had been inculcated in her since she was a small child, provided the spiritual focus and energy of her order, for it is the embodiment of Jesus's love unto death, the act that reestablished justice between God and sinners. Accordingly, every particular act of justice in the life of the church must be, she felt, predicated upon and conditioned by the Eucharist. Here we see another clear connection to Edith Stein, whose elevated courage was the result of her long hours of silent eucharistic contemplation.

From the beginning, Mother Katharine managed to attract a number of young women eager to share her life. They gathered at a motherhouse

13. Ibid., 133.

established outside Philadelphia, and at the insistence of the archbishop they remained there in formation and training for three years before heading out on mission. One of the first outposts that they established was among the Pueblos of New Mexico; next they set up a school for African-American children along the James River in Virginia; then they went to work for the Navajos of Arizona, taking as their companion in mission the successor of Bishop Jean-Baptiste Lamy, the inspiration for Willa Cather's novel *Death Comes to the Archbishop*. Perhaps the most significant of Katharine Drexel's works was the founding of Xavier University in New Orleans as a center for advanced studies for black people, at a time and place when that sort of education for African Americans was unheard of.

For all these efforts of education, evangelization, health care, and practical assistance, the money from Mother Katharine's trust fund was essential. In the words of her biographer, "she despoiled herself voluntarily of her resources, to distribute them freely and magnanimously to the two races to whom she also dedicated her life."[14] What she had received as a gift she was giving as a gift, inserting herself in the loop of grace, supernaturally rendering to the other—in this case the largely ignored other—what was his due.

Poverty was absolutely essential to Mother Drexel. Much of her ministry as superior was to travel to the various outposts of her order to encourage and inspire her sisters. When traveling, she invariably chose the cheapest route and carried her lunch or supper with her. Her shoes, which wore out frequently, were mended and remended, lest she be compelled to spend money on herself. But once again, the most remarkable expression of her poverty was her willingness to give away her personal fortune. She donated funds not only to the works of her own community but to a plethora of other charities and institutions in Arizona, California, the Dakota Territory, Michigan, Minnesota, Montana, New Mexico, Oregon, the Washington Territory, Wyoming, Alabama, Arkansas, Delaware, Florida, Georgia, Illinois, Kansas, Kentucky, Louisiana, Maryland, Missouri, New Jersey, New York, North Carolina, Ohio, Oklahoma, Pennsylvania, South Carolina, South Dakota, Tennessee, Virginia, Washington, D.C., Wisconsin, and Idaho.[15]

In the early years of the twentieth century, Mother Drexel was especially preoccupied with the formulation and approval of a rule for her community. She took as her model the rule of the Sisters of Mercy, the community with which she was best acquainted, but she added special notes of utter reliance upon the providence of God, an insistence upon Franciscan-style

14. Ibid., 268.
15. Ibid., 270–71.

poverty, and of course devotion to the Blessed Sacrament and to the service of African and Native Americans. No less a personage than Mother Frances Xavier Cabrini urged her to go in person to Rome in order to assure acceptance of the document. Accordingly, in May 1907, Katharine sailed to Europe and, after some delay and bureaucratic wrangling throughout that summer, managed to secure the approval she sought.

For the next twenty-five years, Katharine ruled over her community, but she was hardly a prisoner of the motherhouse near Philadelphia. Rather, she ranged all over the country, personally visiting, monitoring, and overseeing her various establishments. The number of her journeys is staggering, especially when we consider the difficulty of traveling to remote areas in the early decades of the twentieth century. A trip undertaken in 1935, when she was seventy-seven, was fairly typical. After visiting her sisters at Xavier University in New Orleans, Mother Drexel went to Port Arthur, Texas, and then by night train to Gallup, New Mexico. From there, she journeyed to the West Coast and chartered a boat to San Francisco. After morning mass in San Francisco, she took a twenty-four-hour train trip to Portland, Oregon, where she changed trains and continued on to Seattle, Washington. At ten o'clock that night, she and her companions took a train to Wenatchee, the tiny town closest to St. Mary's Indian Mission at Omak, Washington, where her sisters were established. After a four hour auto trip from Wenatchee, she arrived at the mission. Despite the grueling grind of her travel, which would have exhausted a far younger woman, Mother Drexel, immediately upon arriving, went about her task of inspecting the mission and its environs.[16] The spending of herself accompanied the spending of her fortune.

Late in 1935, while on another trip, this time to St. Louis, Mother Drexel suffered a massive heart attack. Her doctor practically despaired of her life, telling her that her survival was possible only if she agreed to cut back severely on her workload. Finally willing to let go of her practical responsibilities, and perhaps lured by the prospect of the quiet, reflective life that she had desired as a young girl, Katharine acquiesced to her physician's request. With great detachment and serenity of spirit, she handed over the reins of the community to a general council, which in time elected Mother Mercedes as the second general of the congregation.

One of the great mysteries of Katharine Drexel's life is the way it ended: twenty years of quiet contemplation after so many years of frenetic activity. She spent the last two decades of her life either in her small room at the Mother House or on a mezzanine overlooking the chapel and tabernacle, where her practically exclusive preoccupation was prayer and adoration of the Blessed Sacrament. Even after a full day's contemplation, she would

16. Ibid., 344–46.

frequently spend an hour of meditation in the middle of the night, keeping vigil before the Eucharist. Yet even this quiet life had a missionary orientation, for her prayer was for the work of her community and for the needs of the people to whom she had dedicated her life. Her banker's daughter's sensibility still very much in place, she would carefully write out all the intentions for which she was praying and checked them off as the requests were granted.

After the Normandy invasion in June 1944, Mother Drexel made these notes during her "nocturnal adoration" of the Blessed Sacrament: "One hour placing every soldier, everyone bombed, into the Divine Love of the Sacred Heart. . . . While doing this, I said one hundred Hail Marys and ten Our Fathers on my indulgenced rosary." A few weeks later, she noted, "My soul is sorrowful at what is going on now in the bombed cities of Calais, of Normandy, and the suffering and anguish of France and Italy. . . . Jesus had to grieve over the sins of the whole world and it is sin which has wrought this world war."[17] We see here that her contemplative prayer was itself informed by elevated justice, the passion to render to the other what is his due and more than his due. When all she had left to give was time and prayer, she gave those away too.

Toward the end of her life, Katharine had some experiences that could perhaps be qualified as mystical. Her sisters would watch with amazement certain nights when, after all was quite still, she would fold her hands, fix her gaze on a definite spot, and carry on what appeared to be an intense conversation in a very low whisper. Even someone passing directly in front of her would neither break her concentration nor interrupt her speech.

One evening, a sister entered Katharine's room and found the founder gazing intently up toward the ceiling, a peaceful and joyful expression on her face. Turning to her sister, she said, "Did you see them?"

"See what?" asked her colleague, who saw nothing out of the ordinary.

"The children," Katharine replied. When asked about this vision the next morning, she said, "Oh all the children were there, all going past, so many of them. And the Pope was there too in all his regalia, and so many children. They were all there."[18]

Were these delusions or mystical visions? As with Thérèse's experience of the smiling statue of the Virgin, it is impossible finally to say, and perhaps it doesn't matter. What does matter is that they signal her deeply felt link through prayer to a world that transcends yet impinges on this one.

Mother Katharine Drexel died on March 3, 1955, as peacefully and calmly "as a child nestling in its mother's arms."

17. Ibid., 371.
18. Ibid., 376.

20

Mother Teresa of Calcutta

Elevated Temperance

Prudence is the virtue that oversees and governs the moral life, and justice is the heart and soul of ethical activity. Fortitude is the excellence that allows one to do the prudent thing in the face of external threats, most especially the prospect of death. The fourth and final cardinal virtue—temperance—is that which enables one to overcome obstacles to goodness coming from within the structure of one's own subjectivity. As such, it orders and renders peaceful the soul, producing what Aquinas calls *quies animi*, serenity of spirit. Josef Pieper comments that temperance is an attention to the self, but for the sake of selflessness, whereas intemperance is an inattentiveness to the self, conducing to self-destruction.[1]

Unlike the inner order of a plant or animal, human *ordo* is not simply a natural given but rather an achievement of intellect, will, and discipline: "the discipline of temperance defends one against all selfish perversion of the inner order through which alone the moral person exists and lives effectively."[2] The perversion in question has to do with excessive exercise of the drives for self-preservation: hunger, thirst, and sexual desire. Precisely because these are so strong and primal, they tend rather naturally toward

1. Josef Pieper, *The Four Cardinal Virtues* (Notre Dame, IN: Univ. of Notre Dame Press, 2003), 148.
2. Ibid., 150.

excess and distortion. Thomas Aquinas, borrowing from Aristotle, says that temperance concerns the ordering of the sense of touch, since all three of these elemental desires are related ultimately to the that most basic and perfect of the senses. Because we want so passionately to *touch*, to satisfy our longings for food, drink, and sexual pleasure, we will become quite easily twisted away from right moral action. Temperance is the *virtus* that monitors and limits this tendency.

The first dimension of temperance that Aquinas analyzes is chastity, the ordering of the sexual desire. Because the very words *chastity* and *temperance* have puritanical overtones, at least to our ears, it is most important to note that there is not a hint of Manichaeism in Thomas's approach to sex. He never tires of reminding us—over and against some fairly weighty intellectual authorities—that sex in itself is nothing but good. One of his more remarkable comments is that the sexual pleasure of Adam and Eve in paradise, prior to the fall, was greater than that which we heirs of original sin experience. Pieper reflects Thomas's view quite closely when he observes that "heresy and hyperasceticism are and always have been close neighbors."[3] Thus chastity is not a flight from sex but an ordering of sexual desire so as to place it in the higher context of self-forgetting love. An intriguing implication of chastity is a deepened appreciation for the beautiful, for it removes desire from preoccupation with the sexual. Pieper comments, "Unchaste lust has the tendency to relate the whole complex of the sensual world, and particularly of sensual beauty, to sexual pleasure exclusively."[4] The rightly ordered and disciplined self is thus far more capable of taking in the dense objectivity of the aesthetic.

Next, Aquinas examines the second major aspect of temperance, the ordering of the desire for food and drink. The basic purpose of abstinence and fasting is to free the soul for a readier contemplation of higher things and a more prompt exercise of moral virtue. Thomas Merton once observed that our desires for food and drink are something like little children in their persistence and tendency to dominate. Unless and until they are disciplined, they will skew the functions of the soul—including reason itself—according to their purposes.

Now what happens when this moral virtue is invaded and elevated by grace? Chastity becomes radicalized into what Aquinas calls "virginity," the willingness not only to order sexual desire but to eschew sexual relations altogether so as to realize a supernatural end. In Thomas's own language, "It [virginity] is made praiseworthy only by its end and purpose, to the extent that it aims to make him who practices it free for things divine." The love of God has so seized a person that she is willing to give up permanently

3. Ibid., 154.
4. Ibid., 166.

and definitively an activity that the naturally chaste person would only discipline, in order that she might be utterly available to God. And when ordinary abstinence is invaded by the divine life, it becomes the radical asceticism of the desert fathers, of St. Benedict, St. Francis, and Charles de Foucauld. Obviously, no one can sensibly abstain absolutely from food and drink as one might from sex, but one can press and push the natural disciplining of sensual desire into a radical form—once again, for the sake of loving and serving God more fully. In the strict sense, temperance is not in itself a realization of the good but rather the necessary prerequisite to that realization. This remains true in regard to elevated temperance. Neither celibacy nor radical asceticism is sought for its own sake. Were that the case, each would be at best a rather peculiar form of ascetical athleticism, a test of endurance. They are, in point of fact, *conditiones sine qua non* for the achievement of a love that seeks to imitate, however inadequately, the unlimited love of God.

The saint I have chosen to illumine this virtue of elevated temperance is Mother Teresa of Calcutta. I realize that this might strike my reader as a strange choice. In her utterly generous gift of self on behalf of the poor and the dying, Mother Teresa seems to be, even more than Katharine Drexel, the paragon of elevated justice. Let me observe first (and perhaps I haven't stressed this enough) that the virtues are mutually implicative and inter-dependent. In fact Thomas feels that it is next to impossible to have any one virtue in its integrity and not to have the others concomitantly. Thus it is not surprising that we should notice elevated justice, as well as courage and prudence, in someone marked by elevated temperance. Second, in her own accounts of her life and work, Mother Teresa put a constant emphasis on the utter necessity of asceticism and celibacy as conditions for the work that she and her sisters undertook. This protective and ordering virtue was, in a word, indispensable to the effecting of the justice that was the far more visible dimension of the life of Mother Teresa.

Agnes Gonxha Bojaxhiu was born on August 26, 1910, in Skopje, Serbia, the youngest child of Nikola and Dranafile Bojaxhiu. Agnes's father was a merchant and entrepreneur, trading in a variety of different goods and providing various services in Skopje, eventually becoming a prominent player in the town's civic life. Her mother was a dedicated housewife and mother whose very traditional views of a woman's role in the family would have a marked influence on her daughter. Nikola became involved in the political movement that eventually led to the independence of Albania from Serbia, and in the years just after World War I, he was active in bringing the province of Kosovo under the control of Albania.

In pursuit of this latter goal, one day he left with some friends to attend a political meeting in Belgrade. Though he departed in seemingly perfect health, he returned desperately ill from an internal hemorrhage, possibly the result of poisoning. Emergency surgery proved fruitless, and he died at the age of forty-five, leaving his wife and family in rather severe economic straits. In this regard, Mother Teresa's story comes quite close to Edith Stein's.

After an initial period of intense grief and psychological disorientation, Drana, Agnes's mother, gathered herself and stabilized her family both emotionally and financially. But she was well aware of the law of the gift. In a manner quite reminiscent of Katharine Drexel's mother, Drana insisted that their family table be open to the poor, both in her extended family and in the town. She also cared for an old woman who had been abandoned by her family and the six children of a destitute widow. Agnes often accompanied her on these missions of mercy, taking in the lesson that her goods, however meager, were meant to be shared.

When she was twelve, Agnes felt called to the religious life, though she had never, to that point in her life, so much as laid eyes on a nun. A key player in the shaping of her vocation was a young Croatian Jesuit priest, Fr. Jambrekovic, who had become her parish priest in 1925. He introduced the young people of the town to the Spiritual Exercises of St. Ignatius and their challenge to orient one's life radically toward the service of Jesus. When Agnes asked him to help her discern her call, he responded in the Ignatian spirit that joy is the compass by which one should steer one's life. Both of these themes, the totality of dedication and the primacy of joy in the spiritual life, would remain central to Agnes to her last day. But perhaps Fr. Jambrekovic's greatest impact on the future Mother Teresa came from his contagious enthusiasm for the missionary work undertaken by the Jesuit order throughout the world—especially in Bengal.

Inspired by his stories, Agnes applied at the age of eighteen to join the Loreto Sisters, the Irish branch of the Institute of the Blessed Virgin Mary, which had a strong missionary presence in India. After an initial interview, Agnes was recommended to the mother general of the order, who accepted her and sent her to begin a postulancy at Loreto Abbey in Rathfarnham, Ireland. There she commenced her study of English, the language in which she would operate, spiritually and practically, for the rest of her life, and there she endured her first of many culture shocks. But she had little time to adjust to her new environment, for she spent only six weeks in Ireland before setting sail for India. During her postulancy in Rathfarnham, Agnes took the name Sister Mary Teresa of the Child Jesus, devoting herself thereby to the recently canonized Thérèse of Lisieux. The spirituality of Thérèse—accepting one's littleness before God, taking every moment as an opportunity for great love, being happily subject to the divine providence—would come to radically mark Mother Teresa.

When she arrived in India, she was dazzled by its luxuriant natural beauty and shocked beyond words by its grinding poverty. Though she had associated with the poor in Skopje, nothing had prepared her for what she saw in India. We have this passage from the journal she kept at this time: "Many families live in the streets, along the city walls. . . . Day and night they live out in the open on mats they have made from large palm leaves. . . . They are virtually naked, wearing at best a ragged loincloth. . . . As we went along the street we chanced upon one family gathered around a dead relation, wrapped in worn red rags. . . . It was a horrifying scene."[5] The conviction that service to such poor would necessarily involve a radical simplifying of her own life, a willingness to join them in their destitution, began to form in Sister Teresa's mind.

After completing her novitiate in Darjeeling, Teresa made temporary vows and began teaching in the convent school there and working part time as an aide to the nursing staff at a small hospital. Here again she confronted the suffering face of India: "Many have come from a distance, walking for as much as three hours. What a state they are in! Their ears and feet are covered in sores. They have lumps and lesions on their backs. Many stay at home because they are too debilitated by tropical fever to come."[6]

Once a man arrived at the hospital with a bundle out of which protruded what appeared to be twigs. When Teresa looked more closely, she saw that they were the impossibly emaciated legs of a child, blind and on the point of death. The man told the young sister that if she didn't take the boy, he would throw him to the jackals. Teresa's journal takes up the story: "With much pity and love, I take the little one into my arms, and fold him in my apron. The child has found a second mother." And then the passage from the Scripture dawned upon her: "Whoever welcomes one such child in my name welcomes me" (Matt. 18:5). This is the key to the mature practical spirituality of Mother Teresa: in serving the suffering and the poorest of the poor, one moves into the mystical ontology assumed by Matthew 25, the coinherence of Christ and the least of his brothers and sisters.

From Darjeeling, Teresa was sent to Loreto Entaly, a school run by the Loreto Sisters in Calcutta. It was thus that she came to the city that would be her home and base for the rest of her life, a city that would, in many ways, define her and her ministry. At first, she was relatively isolated from the worst of Calcutta's poverty, teaching courses in geography and English behind the high walls of the boarding school, which served orphans and girls from broken homes. But in time she began to make her way to St. Teresa's primary school, some distance from Loreto Entaly, and there she came face to face with truly dire poverty. She taught outside, drawing

5. Kathryn Spink, *Mother Teresa: A Complete Authorized Biography* (San Francisco: HarperSanFrancisco, 1998), 13.

6. Ibid., 15.

figures and letters in the dirt, or inside a kind of stable, and the filthiness and destitution of the children filled her with anguish. But she discovered that her identification with these poorest of the poor, her willingness to live where they lived and do what they were compelled to do, brought great consolation to them: "Oh God," she wrote, "how easy it is to spread happiness in that place."[7]

On May 24, 1937, Sister Teresa took the formal religious vows of poverty, chastity, and obedience for life and thereby became, as was the Loreto custom, "Mother Teresa." Throughout the late 1930s and early 1940s, Mother Teresa worked at a furious pace, teaching, administering schools, visiting the sick, and making frequent forays into the poorest sections of Calcutta. Her frenetic activity led to a breakdown in her health, and her superiors decreed that she should spend three hours each afternoon resting in bed. When this did not prove sufficient, she was told to go on a kind of extended retreat, convalescing and praying at the hill station of Darjeeling where she had done her novitiate.

On September 10, 1946, while she was making her way on the dusty train to Darjeeling, Mother Teresa had an experience that would change her life. Though it is fair to say that Jesus had gotten into her boat many years before, when she accepted the call to religious life, on that train to Darjeeling he began to direct her life even more radically and completely. Though she would speak of it only sparingly, she specified that what she received during that train ride was "the call of God to be a Missionary of Charity." This was, she said, "the hidden treasure for me, for which I have sold all to purchase it. You remember in the Gospel, what the man did when he found the hidden treasure—he hid it. This is what I want to do for God."[8]

When she got to Darjeeling, she commenced her formal retreat, and during that extended time of reflection and prayer, she received even more inspirations in regard to this new vocation. She scribbled down her thoughts on tiny slips of white paper, and when she returned to Calcutta, she gave these to Fr. Celeste Van Exem, a Belgian Jesuit priest who had become, somewhat against his will, her spiritual director. What he read on those bits of paper was an outline of the order that Mother Teresa would found: a new congregation dedicated to working in poverty and a spirit of joy with the poorest of the poor, free of any connection to hospitals, schools, or other institutions.

In a series of talks that Mother Teresa herself would give upon her return from Darjeeling, another defining dimension of the spirituality of her new order would become clear: thirst. In the narrative of the woman at the well, as we have seen, Jesus expresses his thirst in the presence of

7. Ibid., 18.
8. Ibid., 22.

the Samaritan woman: "Give me a drink." Mother Teresa interpreted this, along Augustinian lines, as God's thirst for our faith and friendship. Accordingly, a principal work of her community would be to slake the thirst of Jesus for intimacy with human souls. Later in John's Gospel, Jesus says, "Let anyone who is thirsty come to me, and let the one who believes in me drink" (John 7:37). All human beings are thirsty, ultimately, for friendship with God, and thus Mother Teresa determined that a major work of her new order would be facilitating that relationship. The two motifs perfectly dovetail in the passage in chapter 25 of Matthew's Gospel, where Jesus explicitly identifies himself with those who suffer: "I was hungry and you gave me food, I was thirsty and you gave me something to drink" (v. 35). The human thirst for God becomes God's thirst for our love. This multivalent theological meditation on thirst would be expressed later in every house established by Mother Teresa's congregation, with an image of the crucified Jesus and, next to him, the words "I thirst."

Despite all of this spiritual inspiration, insight, and energy, Fr. Van Exem urged Mother Teresa to wait and to test her call. They would pray over the matter until January of the following year, and only if at that time both were convinced that this new congregation was congruent with God's will would they present the idea to Ferdinand Périer, the archbishop of Calcutta. When January came, both the young nun and the young priest were persuaded that God desired this undertaking, and they accordingly contacted Périer. The gruff archbishop, however, was not at all in agreement. There were, he argued, already a number of women's orders taking care of the poor; furthermore, it was highly irregular and more than a little spiritually dangerous for a nun to leave her congregation; and finally, it seemed impolitic during a time of intense Indian nationalism to found another order headed by a European. These were, to be sure, serious objections, but the archbishop's opposition was also a classic example of the kind of testing that is *de rigueur* in such situations: if she persevered despite all obstacles and pressures, her vocation might be from God.

For over a year, Mother Teresa and Fr. Van Exem exorted, cajoled, and demanded, and the archbishop remained adamant. When he fell seriously ill, Mother Teresa informed him that if he got better, she would take his recovery as a sign from God that she should move forward with her plan. He did recover but did not give in. Time and again, he impatiently rebuffed Van Exem when the Jesuit came to beg on Teresa's behalf. Secretly, however, the archbishop was intrigued by the idea and impressed by this prayerful, stubborn young nun. He thus consulted with experts in canon law to determine the feasibility of her proposal. In early 1948, convinced that her call was genuine, Périer gave permission for Mother Teresa to petition for permission to leave her Loreto community—but he insisted that she apply not for exclaustration, which would allow her to remain under vows, but for secularization, which would effectively and finally cut her off from Loreto. Once again he was testing her, seeing whether she would be able to trust totally in God's providence.

In her simple, unaffected style, Mother Teresa wrote the cardinal in charge of the Congregation for the Propagation of the Faith in Rome, explaining her mission and asking permission to leave her community to commence this work among the poor. In April 1948, a decree came from Rome, granting her a year to experiment with this new form of religious life, under the direction of Archbishop Périer. When Van Exem brought her the decree and explained it to her, Mother Teresa's immediate response was "Father, can I go to the slums now?"[9]

In preparation for leaving Loreto, Teresa bought three saris at a local bazaar: white garments, edged with blue stripes. They were the cheapest she could find, and the blue stripes appealed to her, for blue is the color of the Virgin Mary. In time, of course, these would provide the model for the distinctive habit of the Missionaries of Charity. Under cover of night, so as to avoid a tearful leave-taking, she slipped away from the Loreto convent by taxi, holding only five rupees in her pocket and trusting utterly in God's providence. She went first to the Holy Family Hospital in Patna, run by the Medical Mission Sisters, in order to acquire some basic medical know-how. After only a few weeks of instruction, she felt that she had sufficient training and was ready for her work. Returning to Calcutta, she began looking for suitable accommodations for herself and for those that would, she was convinced, eventually join her. Her first lodging was with the Little Sisters of the Poor, and from this small room she set out, on December 21, 1948, to work in the slum district of Motjhil.

Within a few weeks, she had established a school attended by dozens of children. Once more, she used the ground as a blackboard and sought to inculcate the rudiments of Bengali and English in her very young charges. When she had finished instructing the children for the day, she would take them with her on her rounds, visiting the sick and the destitute. Once she saw a woman lying on the street just outside a hospital that had refused her admittance. Mother Teresa petitioned on her behalf, but she was turned away, and the woman died on the open road. This experience convinced her to make a home for the dying, "a resting place," as she put it, "for people going to heaven."

These first several months of ministry in the slums were far from idyllic. Mother Teresa endured terrible bouts of loneliness, depression, and discouragement—and an accompanying desire to return to the relative stability and ease of Loreto. In her journal from this period, we find a powerful passage in which she recounts the struggle and the resolution:

9. Ibid., 31.

"Our Lord wants me to be a free nun covered with the poverty of the Cross. . . . The poverty of the poor must be so hard for them. While looking for a home, I walked and walked till my arms and legs ached. I thought how much they must ache in body and soul, looking for a home, food and health. Then the comfort of Loreto came to tempt me." The temptation was toward self-indulgence (*curvatus in se*), and the solution was a radicalized temperance conducing toward freedom.

As we have seen, courage holds off the threats to moral rectitude that come from without, and temperance battles those that come from within. Accordingly, both virtues are oriented toward freedom. The radical moral form that Mother Teresa chose required, she saw, an equally radical modality of temperance, the very destitution of the poor she served. Clothed in that "poverty of the Cross," she could be a "free nun."

In early 1949, with the help of Fr. Van Exem, Mother Teresa moved into a room on the second floor of a home in east Calcutta. The furnishings consisted of a bench, which served as a bookshelf, a cardboard box for a table, a single chair, and a green almirah which served as a small altar. When one of her former colleagues among the Little Sisters of the Poor came to inspect the place, she commented, "Well, you are sure to have Jesus with you. They cannot say that you left Loreto to become rich!"[10]

The third floor of the home was a single long room, and Mother Teresa immediately envisioned it as a dormitory for the girls who would, she was sure, in time come to join her. And they came soon enough. In March of 1949, Subhasini Das, a Bengali girl who had been one of Mother Teresa's pupils at the convent school of Entaly, moved into the sparsely furnished room, and she was joined in April by Magdalen Gomes, another former student whose fierce patriotic feelings Mother Teresa had managed to channel into a fierce love for the poor. In May of that same year a sixteen-year-old girl, the future Sister Margaret Mary, was taken on as a "boarder."

At this early stage, these four women did not constitute a religious order but simply—to use the formal canonical terminology—a group of "pious women living together." But Mother Teresa moved rapidly to form them in the rudiments of the religious life, for her goal was from the beginning to found a congregation. Thus, she brought them to a local parish for training in the Spiritual Exercises of Ignatius, which had had such an impact on her when she was very young, and she began to shape them, practically and theoretically, for work among the poorest of the poor.

All this time, Archbishop Périer was watching over the development of this group with a fatherly care, for he was technically Mother Teresa's religious superior. He urged her to formulate, with the help of Fr. Van Exem, a rule of life for her new community, and this she did, scribbling

10. Ibid., 38.

down her wishes in a little yellow notebook. Though they drew heavily from the rule of Loreto, which in turn was indebted to the constitutions of the Jesuits, Mother Teresa added special features dealing with poverty. For example, she carefully stipulated that "Missionaries of Charity" would own none of the buildings from which and in which they served the poor. Though this particular regulation was eventually deemed impractical, given the exigencies of both ecclesial and civil law, there remained in the rule much of the spirit of St. Francis, *il poverello*.

As the community increased in size, the sisters embodied this Franciscan love of poverty with a vengeance. Mother Teresa insisted that in order to understand those whom they served, they must live like them, and therefore all that the first Missionaries of Charity possessed was "their cotton saris, some coarse underwear, a pair of sandals, the crucifix they wore pinned to their left shoulder, a rosary, an umbrella to protect them against the monsoon rains, a metal bucket for washing, and a very thin palliasse to serve as a bed."[11] Since they were utterly dependent upon the generosity of others—much like the earliest Dominicans and Franciscans—the Missionaries of Charity often had trouble procuring even these simple staples. Once, they were short of shoes, and one of the sisters had to wear an old pair with red stiletto heels; another time, a sister was compelled to wear a habit made out of material that had been used to store wheat, so that through the thin fabric of her sari, across her behind, the words "not for resale" were clearly visible! One winter, they were short of shawls, and some of the sisters had to wear their bedclothes to attend Midnight Mass.

And there was a kind of poverty built into the very rhythm of their day. During the week the sisters rose at 4:40 a.m., and on Sundays at 4:15 a.m. They washed their faces with water drawn with empty milk tins out of a common tank; they brushed their teeth in ashes taken from the kitchen stove; and they scrubbed their bodies and their clothes with a small bar of soap, which had been divided into six. Between 5:15 and 6:45, they meditated, prayed, and attended Mass. Then they ate a very basic breakfast (though Mother Teresa stipulated that they drink plenty of water in order not to tire in the intense heat) and were on the streets doing their work by 7:45. Just after noon, they returned to the mother house for prayers and ate a meal consisting of five ladles of bulgur wheat and a few bits of meat, if meat was available. After housework, they rested, at Mother Teresa's insistence, for a half an hour, and then they did spiritual reading for an hour before returning to their pastoral work in the slums. At six, they gathered again at the mother house for dinner—usually a collation of rice and vegetables—and next engaged in whatever tasks of cleaning and sewing were necessary before recreation, evening prayer, and bed by ten o'clock.

11. Ibid., 44–45.

Mother Teresa called for a poverty that went beyond mere physical hardship and deprivation. One rather aristocratic newcomer to the order "found the toilet dirty one day and hid herself away in disgust. Mother Teresa happened to pass by without seeing the Sister. She immediately rolled up her sleeves and took out a broom and cleaned the toilet herself," manifesting to the reluctant novice the kind of spiritual simplicity called for by the community. Another time, a young member of the group won a gold medal for her medical studies, "and Mother Teresa directed her to surrender it to the student who had come in second."[12] The hoarding of honors would be just as detrimental to their work as the hoarding of food and drink. An essential aspect of the temperance and poverty of the Missionaries of Charity was an utter confidence in the efficacy of divine providence—and an accompanying abandonment of self-reliance and self-disposition. Once, when the sisters were completely without food for the evening meal, they resolved to pray. Suddenly, a knock came to the door and there stood a woman carrying some bags of rice—just enough, it turned out, to feed the community that night. She told the sisters that some inexplicable impulse had brought her to them.

A spirituality of detachment—which Mother Teresa had learned from the exercises of Ignatius—was inculcated at all times. The sisters were instructed to pray special prayers while they put on each article of clothing at the beginning of the day. While they donned their habit, they prayed that this distinctive garb would remind them of their separation from the world and its vanities: "Let the world be nothing to me and I nothing to the world."[13] While they girded their waist, they prayed for the purity of the Virgin Mary: "surrounded and protected by that absolute poverty which crowned all you did for Jesus." As they put on their sandals, they prayed that they might have the detachment to follow Jesus wherever he prompted them to go.

Further, they were compelled to be detached from their own will through a strict obedience. Despite her affability and kindness, Mother Teresa exhibited toward her sisters a toughness that outsiders sometimes found off-putting, or at the very least surprising. She consistently acted out of the conviction that obedience was "to be prompt, simple, blind, and cheerful," precisely because Jesus was obedient unto death.

Now all of this might strike us as a bit exaggerated, an asceticism bordering on puritanism. But we must recall the radicality of the love to which Mother Teresa was calling herself and her followers. To will the good of the poorest of the poor, the most destitute and alone, the most physically repulsive and spiritually hopeless, required, she discerned, a radicalized

12. Ibid., 49.
13. Ibid., 71.

temperance. Charity to an extreme degree necessitated a self-control and detachment that went far beyond the natural forms of those virtues. Because it is ordered most directly to God, love is in itself unlimited, and hence when love invades the soul, it causes the natural virtues to participate in its infinity. And so what we have already seen in regard to courage, prudence, and justice, we now see in regard to temperance: a natural virtue supernaturalized, a moderate ethical habit rendered immoderate.

For the first ten years of its existence—from 1949 to 1959—the Missionaries of Charity continued to grow, but its work was restricted, by canon law, to the confines of the diocese of Calcutta. When the period of probation was over, Mother Teresa was eager to extend her work throughout India, and almost immediately she received invitations to establish houses in Ranchi, Delhi, Jhansi, and Bombay. In 1965, almost twenty years after she had her first inspiration to establish an order to work among the poorest of the poor, Mother Teresa received word from Rome that the Missionaries of Charity had been formally named a society of pontifical right. For the public announcement of the decree in Calcutta, chairs and benches had to be borrowed so as to accommodate the visiting dignitaries; Mother Teresa squatted on the ground as she listened to the declaration. Following the formal establishment of the order, the Missionaries of Charity spread with amazing rapidity around the world. In late 1965, responding to an invitation from a local bishop, the community opened a house in Venezuela, where they worked among the millions of baptized Catholics who had fallen away from the practice of the faith and into extreme material poverty. In 1968, at the prompting of the pope himself, Mother Teresa set up a house in Rome, taking, she was proud to say, the poorest quarters ever occupied by the Missionaries of Charity. Later that same year, they opened houses in Tabora, Tanzania, and in Melbourne, Australia. By the end of the 1970s, there were Missionaries of Charity establishments on all six continents, and by the close of the 1990s, there were more than five hundred houses around the world. When she was asked how far her work would spread, Mother Teresa said, "If there are poor on the moon, we shall go there too."[14]

Although she could hardly supervise each convent personally, she determined, as far as was able, to monitor her followers' exercise of the virtue of poverty. Again and again, she insisted that fundraising on behalf of her work was against her wishes. "I don't want the work to become a business but to remain a work of love," she wrote her sisters. "I want you to have that complete confidence that God won't let us down."[15] When Terence Cardinal Cooke of New York offered to pay each of the Missionaries of

14. Ibid., 102.
15. Ibid., 93.

Charity in his archdiocese five hundred dollars a month, she retorted, "Do you think, Your Eminence, that God is going to become bankrupt in New York?"[16] And when, especially in Western countries, her sisters were offered gifts of labor-saving devices such as washing machines, she insisted that they accept nothing but a glass of water by way of hospitality, since that was all that the poor could offer.

For the remaining years of her life, Mother Teresa, though based in Calcutta, would travel widely, visiting her numerous establishments, in this regard calling to mind the lifestyle of Katharine Drexel, whose active career was coming to an end just as Mother Teresa's was beginning. Like Mother Drexel, she would try to travel in the simplest, least expensive way, sometimes sleeping in a luggage rack of a third-class train car. When she traveled by plane, her baggage would consist of a small paper package wrapped in string and marked "Mother Teresa." She accepted a number of prestigious prizes and honors during the 1970s, 1980s, and 1990s, including the Nobel Peace Prize in 1979 and the Presidential Medal of Freedom in 1985, using these occasions to raise the consciousness of the world concerning the plight of the poor and the responsibility of the wealthy nations. When she was invited by President Bill Clinton to speak at the National Prayer Breakfast in 1994, she dismayed her host by speaking vigorously against abortion, a mode of state-sanctioned abuse that, she argued, disproportionately affects the poor.

Throughout the 1990s Mother Teresa's health gradually deteriorated, and her travels became less frequent. In 1990, she tried to hand over direction of her order, but she was compelled by her community to take back the reins of authority. Finally, in early 1997, she insisted that her bad health precluded her continuing as superior, and a general chapter of the Missionaries of Charity elected as superior Sister Nirmala, a Hindu convert who had joined Mother Teresa in the early days and who had been head of the contemplative branch of the Missionaries of Charity. This transition seemed to please Mother Teresa, assuring her of a measure of institutional continuity in the community to which she had given her life. Throughout 1997, her condition steadily worsened, and she died on September 5 at the age of eighty-seven.

When it was displayed for public viewing, Mother Teresa's body was, of course, clothed in the habit of the Missionaries of Charity, but it was left shoeless, revealing her remarkably misshapen feet. For many people, those gnarled feet bore the most eloquent witness to the hard years that she spent on behalf of the poorest of the poor.

16. Ibid.

Conclusion

The Moment That Gives the Meaning

A friend of mine, an Irish priest, makes an annual retreat at Lough Dourg, sometimes known as St. Patrick's purgatory. Lough Dourg is a rocky, unpleasant little island located in the middle of a forlorn lake in northwest Ireland. Retreatants arrive by ferry and are told, immediately upon disembarking, to remove their shoes. They are to remain unshod for the duration of the weekend of spiritual exercises. They pray the rosary, they walk on their knees on punishing stone beds of rock, they attend services, and for the first day and night on the island, they don't sleep. My friend commented that the enforced sleeplessness is the most trying discipline. If a retreatant begins to nod off while at prayer, his fellows push him back into consciousness. At the end of two and a half days of constant prayer and spiritual exertion, the pilgrims put on their shoes and are ferried back to the mainland. My friend said that whatever happens to you on Lough Dourg, whatever spiritual insight or breakthrough occurs, "comes up through your feet."

Throughout these chapters, I have been insisting on the embodied, the iconic, the incarnational. We know God and ourselves, I have maintained, through a particular first-century Jew who walked the hills of Galilee—and through the saints who function as the living icons of Jesus up and down the centuries. Philosophy, ethics, and cultural forms do not position him; he positions them. To understand that reversal is to grasp the nettle of the Christian thing.

Late medieval Christianity, in its univocal conception of being and its proposition of God as a supreme being among beings, showed forgetfulness of the radicality of the incarnation. The God who becomes a creature without ceasing to be God or overwhelming the integrity of the creature he becomes is not a threat to the world and does not have to be presented over and against the world. But the occlusion of this view in decadent scholasticism is precisely, as we've seen, what gave rise to the protest movement of modernity. Much of the theologizing of the past several centuries has been a fruitless attempt to bridge this divide, to adjudicate this dispute.

What solves the problem, what indicates a way forward, is not an abstraction or a new philosophical conception but this Jesus, this incarnate Lord, crucified and risen from the dead. It is this Christ who rubs healing salve into sin-sick eyes; it is this Christ who, reflected iconically in his saints, provides the template for right living; it is this Christ who shows the face of God.

It is this Moment that gives the meaning.

Bibliography

Alison, James. *The Joy of Being Wrong: Original Sin through Easter Eyes.* New York: Crossroad, 1998.

Anselm of Canterbury. "Proslogion." In *L'oeuvre de S. Anselme de Cantorbery*, vol. 1, *Monologion/Proslogion*, edited by Michel Corbin. Paris: Editions du Cerf, 1986.

Augustinus, Aurelius. *De Trinitate.* In *Corpus Christianorum, Series Latina, Aurelii Augustini Opera.* Belgium: Turnholti Typographi Brepols Editores Pontificii, 1968.

Austin, J. L. *How to Do Things with Words.* Cambridge, MA: Harvard University Press, 1962.

Balthasar, Hans Urs von. *Explorations in Theology*, vol. 1, *The Word Made Flesh.* Translated by A. V. Littledale. San Francisco: Ignatius, 1989.

———. *The Glory of the Lord: A Theological Aesthetics*, vol. 1, *Seeing the Form;* vol. 5, *The Realm of Metaphysics in the Modern Age.* Translated by Erasmo Leiva-Merikakis. San Francisco: Ignatius, 1982.

———. *Mysterium Paschale.* Translated by Aidan Nichols. Edinburgh: T & T Clark, 1990.

———. *Two Sisters in the Spirit.* Translated by Donald Nichols and Anne Englund Nash. San Francisco: Ignatius, 1992.

Barnhart, Bruno. *The Good Wine: Reading John from the Center.* New York: Paulist, 1993.

Barron, Robert. *And Now I See: A Theology of Transformation.* New York: Crossroad, 1998.

———. *Bridging the Great Divide.* New York: Rowman and Littlefield, 2004.

———. *The Strangest Way: Walking the Christian Path.* Maryknoll, NY: Orbis, 2002.

———. *Thomas Aquinas: Spiritual Master.* New York: Crossroad, 1996.

Bonaventure. "Itinerarium mentis in Deum." In *Itinéraire de l'Esprit vers Dieu.* Paris: Vrin, 1990.

Burrell, David. *Aquinas: God and Action.* Notre Dame, IN: University of Notre Dame Press, 1979.

Calvin, John. *Institutes of the Christian Religion.* Grand Rapids: Eerdmans, 1998.

Caputo, John. *Against Ethics.* Bloomington: Indiana University Press, 1993.

Casey v. Planned Parenthood of Southeastern Pennsylvania. 112 U.S. Sup. Ct. 2791 at 2807. 1992.

Chesterton, G. K. *Orthodoxy.* In *G. K. Chesterton Collected Works*, vol. 1. San Francisco: Ignatius, 1986.

Corbin, Michel. *Le chemin de la théologie selon Thomas d'Aquin*. Paris: Beauchesne, 1974.

Crossan, John Dominic. *The Historical Jesus: The Life of a Mediterranean Jewish Peasant*. San Francisco: HarperSanFrancisco, 1991.

Descartes, René. *Discourse on the Method*. In *The Philosophical Works of Descartes*, vol. 1. Translated by Elizabeth Haldane. Cambridge: Cambridge University Press, 1979.

———. *Meditations on First Philosophy*. In *The Philosophical Works of Descartes*. vol. 1. Translated by Elizabeth Haldane. Cambridge: Cambridge University Press, 1979.

Duffy, Consuela Marie. *Katharine Drexel: A Biography*. Philadelphia: Peter Reilly, 1966.

Dungan, David Laird. *A History of the Synoptic Problem*. New York: Doubleday, 1999.

Dupré, Louis. *Passage to Modernity: An Essay in the Hermeneutics of Nature and Culture*. New Haven, CT: Yale University Press, 1993.

Eadmer, *Vita S. Anselm: Life of St. Anselm of Canterbury*. Edited by R. W. Southern. Oxford: Oxford University Press, 1972.

Eco, Umberto. *Art and Beauty in the Middle Ages*. New Haven, CT: Yale University Press, 1986.

Gerrish, Brian. *A Prince of the Church: Schleiermacher and the Beginnings of Modern Theology*. Philadelphia: Fortress, 1984.

Gilkey, Langdon. *Gilkey on Tillich*. New York: Crossroad, 1990.

Görres, Ida Friederike. *The Hidden Face: A Study of St. Thérèse of Lisieux*. San Francisco: Ignatius, 2003.

Gunton, Colin E. *The One, the Three, and the Many: God, Creation, and the Culture of Modernity*. Cambridge: Cambridge University Press, 2000.

Habermas, Jürgen. *Communication and the Evolution of Society*. Boston: Beacon, 1979.

———. *The Theory of Communicative Action*, vol. 1. Boston: Beacon, 1987.

Hadot, Pierre. *Philosophy as a Way of Life: Spiritual Exercises from Socrates to Foucault*. Oxford: Blackwell, 1995.

Haight, Roger. *Jesus: Symbol of God*. Maryknoll, NY: Orbis. 1999.

Hauerwas, Stanley. *Sanctify Them in the Truth: Holiness Exemplified*. Nashville: Abingdon, 1998.

Healy, Nicholas. *Thomas Aquinas: Theologian of the Christian Life*. Aldershot, UK: Ashgate, 2003.

Horner, Robyn. *Rethinking God as Gift: Marion, Derrida, and the Limits of Phenomenology*. New York: Fordham University Press, 2001.

James, William. *A Pluralistic Universe*. Lincoln: University of Nebraska Press, 1996.

Joyce, James. *A Portrait of the Artist as a Young Man*. In *The Portable James Joyce*. Edited by Harry Levin. New York: Penguin, 1987.

Kant, Immanuel. *Foundations of the Metaphysics of Morals*. Translated by Lewis White Beck. Indianapolis: Bobbs-Merrill, 1978.

———. *Religion within the Limits of Reason Alone*. Translated by Theodore M. Greene and Hoyt H. Hudson. New York: Harper and Row, 1960.

Kerr, Fergus. *After Aquinas: Versions of Thomism*. Oxford: Blackwell, 2002.

Küng, Hans. *On Being a Christian*. New York: Doubleday, 1976.

Lessing, G. E. "On the Proof of the Spirit and Power." In *Lessings Werke* 3, Schriften 2. Edited by K. Wolfel. Frankfurt: Insel, 1967.

Levinas, Emmanuel. *Basic Philosophical Writings*. Edited by Adriaan Peperzak. Bloomington: Indiana University Press, 1996.

Lonergan, Bernard. *Method in Theology*. Toronto: University of Toronto Press, 1990.

———. "Understanding and Being." In *The Collected Works of Bernard Lonergan*, vol. 5. Toronto: University of Toronto Press, 1990.

Luther, Martin. *On the Bondage of the Will*. In *Martin Luther: Selections from His Writings*, edited by John Dillenberger. New York: Doubleday, 1962.

Malham, Joseph M. *By Fire into Light: Four Catholic Martyrs of the Nazi Camps*. Louvain, Belgium: Peeters, 2002.

Marion, Jean-Luc. *God without Being*. Chicago: University of Chicago Press, 1991.

Marshall, Bruce. *Trinity and Truth*. Cambridge: Cambridge University Press, 2000.

Mauss, Marcel. *The Gift: The Form and Reason for Exchange in Archaic Societies.* Translated by W. D. Halls. London: Routledge, 1990.

McClendon, James William. *Ethics*, vol. 1 of *Systematic Theology.* Nashville: Abingdon, 1986.

McClendon, James William. *Doctrine*, vol. 2 of *Systematic Theology.* Nashville: Abingdon, 1994.

Meier, John P. *A Marginal Jew: Rethinking the Historical Jesus.* New York: Doubleday, 1991.

Milbank, John. *Theology and Social Theory.* Oxford: Blackwell, 1990.

———. *The Word Made Strange: Theology, Language, and Culture.* Oxford: Blackwell, 1997.

Neiman, Susan. *Evil in Modern Thought.* Princeton, NJ: Princeton University Press, 2002.

Newman, John Henry. *Apologia Pro Vita Sua.* New York: Doubleday, 1956.

———. *An Essay in Aid of a Grammar of Assent.* Notre Dame, IN: University of Notre Dame Press, 1979.

———. *An Essay on the Development of Christian Doctrine.* Westminster, MD: Christian Classics, 1968.

———. *The Idea of a University.* Notre Dame, IN: Notre Dame University Press, 1986.

Nietzsche, Friedrich. *Thus Spake Zarathustra.* In *The Portable Nietzsche.* Edited by Walter Kaufmann. New York: Penguin, 1976.

Nussbaum, Martha. *Upheavals of Thought: The Intelligence of Emotions.* Cambridge: Cambridge University Press, 2001.

O'Connell, Timothy. *Principles of a Catholic Morality.* New York: Harper and Row, 1990.

O'Connor, Flannery. "A Good Man Is Hard to Find." In *Collected Works.* New York: Library Classics, 1988.

Pieper, Josef. *The Four Cardinal Virtues.* Notre Dame, IN: University of Notre Dame Press, 2003.

Pinckaers, Servais. *The Sources of Christian Ethics.* Washington, DC: Catholic University Press, 1995.

Placher, William. *Narratives of a Vulnerable God.* Louisville, KY: Westminster John Knox, 1994.

———. *Unapologetic Theology: A Christian Voice in a Pluralistic Conversation.* Louisville, KY: Westminster John Knox, 1989.

Polkinghorne, John. *Faith, Science, and Understanding.* New Haven, CT: Yale University Press, 2000.

Putnam, Hilary. *Realism and Reason.* Cambridge: Cambridge University Press, 1983.

Rahner, Karl. *Hearers of the Word.* New York: Herder and Herder, 1969.

Ratzinger, Joseph. *Introduction to Christianity.* Translated by J. R. Foster. San Francisco: Ignatius, 1990.

Rousseau, Jean-Jacques. *The Social Contract.* New York: Hafner, 1947.

Sartre, Jean-Paul. *L'existentialisme est un humanisme.* Paris: Les Editions Nagel, 1970.

Scaperlanda, Maria Ruiz. *Edith Stein: St. Teresa Benedicta of the Cross.* Huntington, IN: Our Sunday Visitor, 2001.

Schillebeeckx, Edward. *Jesus: An Experiment in Christology.* New York: Seabury, 1979.

Schleiermacher, Friedrich. "Christmas Eve: Dialogue on the Incarnation." In *Friedrich Schleiermacher: Pioneer of Modern Theology.* Edited by Keith Clements. Minneapolis: Fortress, 1991.

———. "Glaubenslehre: First Doctrine—the Person of Christ." In *Friedrich Schleiermacher: Pioneer of Modern Theology.* Edited by Keith Clements. Minneapolis: Fortress, 1991.

———. "On Religion: Speeches to Its Cultured Despisers." In *Friedrich Schleiermacher: Pioneer of Modern Theology.* Edited by Keith Clements. Minneapolis: Fortress, 1991.

Sokolowski, Robert. *The God of Faith and Reason.* Washington, DC: Catholic University of America Press, 1995.

Southern, R. W. *Saint Anselm: A Portrait in a Landscape.* Cambridge: Cambridge University Press, 1990.

Spink, Kathryn. *Mother Teresa: A Complete Authorized Biography.* San Francisco: HarperSanFrancisco, 1998.

Spinoza, Baruch. *The Ethics*. Translated by R. H. M. Elwes. New York: Dover, 1955.

Stein, Edith. *Life in a Jewish Family, 1891–1916*. Translated by Josephine Koeppel. Washington, DC: ICS Publications, 1986.

Steiner, George. *After Babel: Aspects of Language and Translation*. Oxford: Oxford University Press, 1998.

Tanner, Norman P., ed. *Decrees of the Ecumenical Councils*, vol. 1. Washington, DC: Georgetown University Press, 1990.

Thérèse of Lisieux. *Story of a Soul*. Translated by John Clarke. Washington, DC: ICS Publications, 1975.

Thomas Aquinas. *De potentia. Quaestiones disputatae*, vol. 2. Torino: Marietti, 1965.

———. *In evangelium Ioannis*. Torino: Marietti, 1952.

———. *Summa contra gentiles*, bk. 1, *God*. Translated by Anton C. Pegis. Notre Dame, IN: University of Notre Dame Press, 1975.

———. *Summa theologiae*. Torino: Marietti, 1952.

Tillich, Paul. *Dogmatik: Marburger Vorlesung von 1925*. Edited by Werner Schussler. Dusseldorf: Patmos Verlag, 1986.

———. *Systematic Theology: Three Volumes in One*. Chicago: University of Chicago Press, 1967.

Tracy, David. *The Analogical Imagination*. New York: Crossroad, 1981.

Witherington III, Ben. *The Jesus Quest: The Third Search for the Jew of Nazareth*. Downers Grove, IL: InterVarsity Press, 1997.

Wittgenstein, Ludwig. *On Certainty*. Edited by G. E. M. Anscombe and G. H. von Wright. New York: Harper and Row, 1969.

Wright, N. T. *Jesus and the Victory of God*. Minneapolis: Fortress, 1996.

Index